W9-BNA-588

# Microsoft® SQL Server® 2012 T-SQL Fundamentals

Itzik Ben-Gan

Published with the authorization of Microsoft Corporation by:
O'Reilly Media, Inc.
1005 Gravenstein Highway North
Sebastopol, California 95472

Copyright © 2012 by Itzik Ben-Gan
All rights reserved. No part of the contents of this book may be reproduced or transmitted in any form or by any means without the written permission of the publisher.

ISBN: 978-0-735-65814-1

2 3 4 5 6 7 8 9 10 LSI 7 6 5 4 3 2

Printed and bound in the United States of America.

Microsoft Press books are available through booksellers and distributors worldwide. If you need support related to this book, email Microsoft Press Book Support at *mspinput@microsoft.com*. Please tell us what you think of this book at *http://www.microsoft.com/learning/booksurvey*.

Microsoft and the trademarks listed at *http://www.microsoft.com/about/legal/en/us/IntellectualProperty/Trademarks/EN-US.aspx* are trademarks of the Microsoft group of companies. All other marks are property of their respective owners.

The example companies, organizations, products, domain names, email addresses, logos, people, places, and events depicted herein are fictitious. No association with any real company, organization, product, domain name, email address, logo, person, place, or event is intended or should be inferred.

This book expresses the author's views and opinions. The information contained in this book is provided without any express, statutory, or implied warranties. Neither the author, O'Reilly Media, Inc., Microsoft Corporation, nor its resellers, or distributors will be held liable for any damages caused or alleged to be caused either directly or indirectly by this book.

**Acquisitions and Developmental Editor:** Russell Jones

**Production Editor:** Kristen Borg

**Editorial Production and Illustration:** Online Training Solutions, Inc.

**Technical Reviewer:** Gianluca Hotz and Herbert Albert

**Copyeditor:** Kathy Krause

**Indexer:** Allegro Technical Indexing

**Cover Design:** Twist Creative • Seattle

**Cover Composition:** Karen Montgomery

[2012-11-02]

*To Dato*

*To live in hearts we leave behind,*
    *Is not to die.*

        —THOMAS CAMPBELL

# Contents at a Glance

# Contents

---

**What do you think of this book? We want to hear from you!**

Microsoft is interested in hearing your feedback so we can continually improve our
books and learning resources for you. To participate in a brief online survey, please visit:

**microsoft.com/learning/booksurvey**

## Chapter 4  Subqueries     129

## Chapter 7   Beyond the Fundamentals of Querying   211

### What do you think of this book? We want to hear from you!

Microsoft is interested in hearing your feedback so we can continually improve our books and learning resources for you. To participate in a brief online survey, please visit:

**microsoft.com/learning/booksurvey**

## Chapter 8   Data Modification      247

## Chapter 9  Transactions and Concurrency                                     297

## Chapter 10  Programmable Objects         339

# Foreword

I'm very happy that Itzik has managed to find the time and energy to produce a book about T-SQL fundamentals. For many years, Itzik has been using his great Microsoft SQL Server teaching, mentoring, and consulting experience to write books on *advanced* programming subjects, leaving a significant gap not only for the novice and less experienced users but also for the many experts working with SQL Server in roles where T-SQL programming is not a high priority.

When it comes to T-SQL, Itzik is one of the most knowledgeable people in the world. In fact, we (members of the SQL Server development team), turn to Itzik for expert advice on most of the new language extensions we plan to implement. His feedback and consultations have become an important part of our SQL Server development process.

It is never an easy task for a person who is a subject matter expert to write an introductory book; however, Itzik has the advantage of having taught both introductory and advanced programming classes for many years. Such experience is a great asset when differentiating the fundamental T-SQL information from the more advanced topics. But in this book, Itzik is not simply avoiding anything considered *advanced*; he is not afraid to take on inherently complex subjects such as set theory, predicate logic, and the relational model, introducing them in simple terms, and providing just enough information for readers to understand their importance to the SQL language. The result is a book that rewards readers with an understanding of not only *what* and *how* T-SQL works, but also *why*.

In programming manuals and books, there is no better way to convey the subject under discussion than with a good example. This book includes many examples—and you can download them all from Itzik's website, *http://tsql.solidq.com*. T-SQL is a dialect of the official ISO and ANSI standards for the SQL language, but it has numerous extensions that can improve the expressiveness and brevity of your T-SQL code. Many of Itzik's examples show the T-SQL dialect solution and the equivalent ANSI SQL solution to the same exercise side by side. This is a great advantage for readers who are familiar with the ANSI version of SQL but who are new to T-SQL, as well as for programmers who need to write SQL code that can be deployed easily across several different database platforms.

Itzik's deep connection to the SQL Server team shows in his explanation of the Appliance, Box, Cloud (ABC) flavors of SQL Server in Chapter 1, "Background to T-SQL Querying and Programming." So far, I have seen the term "ABC" used only internally within the Microsoft SQL Server team, but I'm sure it is only a matter of time until the term spreads around. Itzik developed and tested the examples in the book against both the "B" (box) and "C" (cloud) flavors of SQL Server. And the Appendix points out where you can get started with the cloud version of SQL Server, known as Windows Azure SQL Database. Therefore, you can use this book as a starting point for your own cloud experiences. The Azure website shows how to start your free subscription to the Azure services, so you can then execute the examples in the book.

The cloud extension of SQL Server is an extremely important point that you should not miss. I consider it to be *so* important that I'm doing something here that never should be done in a Foreword—advertising another book (sorry, Itzik, I have to do this!). My own interest and belief in cloud computing skyrocketed after reading Nicholas G. Carr's *The Big Switch* (W.W. Norton and Company, 2009), and I want to share that experience. It is a great book that compares the advancement of cloud computing to electrification in the early 1900s. My certainty in the future of cloud computing was further cemented by watching James Hamilton's "Cloud Computing Economies of Scale" presentation at the MIX10 conference (the recording is available at *http://channel9.msdn.com/events/MIX/MIX10/EX01*).

Itzik mentions one more cloud-related change that you should be aware of. We were used to multi-year gaps between SQL Server releases, but that pattern is changing significantly with the cloud; you should instead be prepared for several smaller cloud releases (called Service Updates) deployed in the Microsoft Data Centers around the world every year. Therefore, Itzik wisely documents the discrepancies between SQL Server and Windows Azure SQL Database T-SQL on his *http://tsql.solidq.com* website rather than in the book, so he can easily keep the information up to date.

Enjoy the book—and even more—enjoy the new insights into T-SQL that this book will bring to you.

*Lubor Kollar, SQL Server development team, Microsoft*

# Introduction

This book walks you through your first steps in T-SQL (also known as Transact-SQL), which is the Microsoft SQL Server dialect of the ISO and ANSI standards for SQL. You'll learn the theory behind T-SQL querying and programming and how to develop T-SQL code to query and modify data, and you'll get an overview of programmable objects.

Although this book is intended for beginners, it is not merely a set of procedures for readers to follow. It goes beyond the syntactical elements of T SQL and explains the logic behind the language and its elements.

Occasionally, the book covers subjects that may be considered advanced for readers who are new to T-SQL; therefore, those sections are optional reading. If you already feel comfortable with the material discussed in the book up to that point, you might want to tackle the more advanced subjects; otherwise, feel free to skip those sections and re turn to them after you've gained more experience. The text will indicate when a section may be considered more advanced and is provided as optional reading.

Many aspects of SQL are unique to the language and are very different from other programming languages. This book helps you adopt the right state of mind and gain a true understanding of the language elements. You learn how to think in terms of sets and follow good SQL programming practices.

The book is not version-specific; it does, however, cover language elements that were introduced in recent versions of SQL Server, including SQL Server 2012. When I discuss language elements that were introduced recently, I specify the version in which they were added.

Besides being available in an on-premises flavor, SQL Server is also available as a cloud-based service called Windows Azure SQL Database (formerly called SQL Azure). The code samples in this book were tested against both on-premises SQL Server and SQL Database. The book's companion website (*http://tsql.solidq.com*) provides infor-mation about compatibility issues between the flavors—for example, features that are available in SQL Server 2012 but not yet in SQL Database.

To complement the learning experience, the book provides exercises that enable you to practice what you've learned. The book occasionally provides optional exercises that are more advanced. Those exercises are intended for readers who feel very comfortable with the material and want to challenge themselves with more difficult problems. The optional exercises for advanced readers are labeled as such.

# Who Should Read This Book

This book is intended for T-SQL developers, DBAs, BI practitioners, report writers, analysts, architects, and SQL Server power users who just started working with SQL Server and need to write queries and develop code using Transact-SQL.

## Assumptions

To get the most out of this book, you should have working experience with Windows and with applications based on Windows. You should also be familiar with basic concepts concerning relational database management systems.

# Who Should Not Read This Book

Not every book is aimed at every possible audience. This book covers fundamentals. It is mainly aimed at T-SQL practitioners with little or no experience. With that said, several readers of the previous edition of this book have mentioned that—even though they already had years of experience—they still found the book useful for filling gaps in their knowledge.

# Organization of This Book

This book starts with both a theoretical background to T-SQL querying and programming in Chapter 1, laying the foundations for the rest of the book, and also coverage of creating tables and defining data integrity. The book moves on to various aspects of querying and modifying data in Chapters 2 through 8, then to a discussion of concurrency and transactions in Chapter 9, and finally provides an overview of programmable objects in Chapter 10. The following section lists the chapter titles along with a short description:

- Chapter 1, "Background to T-SQL Querying and Programming," provides a theoretical background of SQL, set theory, and predicate logic; examines the relational model and more; describes SQL Server's architecture; and explains how to create tables and define data integrity.

- Chapter 2, "Single-Table Queries," covers various aspects of querying a single table by using the *SELECT* statement.

- Chapter 3, "Joins," covers querying multiple tables by using joins, including cross joins, inner joins, and outer joins.

- Chapter 4, "Subqueries," covers queries within queries, otherwise known as subqueries.

- Chapter 5, "Table Expressions," covers derived tables, common table expressions (CTEs), views, inline table-valued functions, and the *APPLY* operator.

- Chapter 6, "Set Operators," covers the set operators *UNION*, *INTERSECT*, and *EXCEPT*.

- Chapter 7, "Beyond the Fundamentals of Querying," covers window functions, pivoting, unpivoting, and working with grouping sets.

- Chapter 8, "Data Modification," covers inserting, updating, deleting, and merging data.

- Chapter 9, "Transactions and Concurrency," covers concurrency of user connections that work with the same data simultaneously; it covers concepts including transactions, locks, blocking, isolation levels, and deadlocks.

- Chapter 10, "Programmable Objects," provides an overview of the T-SQL programming capabilities in SQL Server.

- The book also provides an appendix, "Getting Started," to help you set up your environment, download the book's source code, install the *TSQL2012* sample database, start writing code against SQL Server, and learn how to get help by working with SQL Server Books Online.

## System Requirements

The Appendix, "Getting Started," explains which editions of SQL Server 2012 you can use to work with the code samples included with this book. Each edition of SQL Server might have different hardware and software requirements, and those requirements are well documented in SQL Server Books Online under "Hardware and Software Requirements for Installing SQL Server 2012." The Appendix also explains how to work with SQL Server Books Online.

If you're connecting to SQL Database, hardware and server software are handled by Microsoft, so those requirements are irrelevant in this case.

# Code Samples

This book features a companion website that makes available to you all the code used in the book, the errata, and additional resources.

*http://tsql.solidq.com*

Refer to the Appendix, "Getting Started," for details about the source code.

# Acknowledgments

Many people contributed to making this book a reality, whether directly or indirectly, and deserve thanks and recognition.

To Lilach, for giving reason to everything I do, and for not complaining about the endless hours I spend on SQL.

To my parents Mila and Gabi and to my siblings Mickey and Ina, thanks for the constant support. Thanks for accepting the fact that I'm away, which is now harder than ever. Mom, we're all counting on you to be well and are encouraged by your strength and determination. Dad, thanks for being so supportive.

To members of the Microsoft SQL Server development team; Lubor Kollar, Tobias Ternstrom, Umachandar Jayachandran (UC), and I'm sure many others. Thanks for the great effort, and thanks for all the time you spent meeting me and responding to my email messages, addressing my questions and requests for clarification. I think that SQL Server 2012 and SQL Database show great investment in T-SQL, and I hope this will continue.

To the editorial team at O'Reilly Media and Microsoft Press; to Ken Jones, thanks for all the Itzik hours you spent, and thanks for initiating the project. To Russell Jones, thanks for your efforts in taking over the project and running it from the O'Reilly side. Also thanks to Kristen Borg, Kathy Krause, and all others who worked on the book.

To Herbert Albert and Gianluca Hotz, thanks for your work as the technical editors of the book. Your edits were excellent and I'm sure they improved the book's quality and accuracy.

To SolidQ, my company for the last decade: it's gratifying to be part of such a great company that evolved to what it is today. The members of this company are much more than colleagues to me; they are partners, friends, and family. Thanks to Fernando G. Guerrero, Douglas McDowell, Herbert Albert, Dejan Sarka, Gianluca Hotz, Jeanne Reeves,

Glenn McCoin, Fritz Lechnitz, Eric Van Soldt, Joelle Budd, Jan Taylor, Marilyn Templeton, Berry Walker, Alberto Martin, Lorena Jimenez, Ron Talmage, Andy Kelly, Rushabh Mehta, Eladio Rincón, Erik Veerman, Jay Hackney, Richard Waymire, Carl Rabeler, Chris Randall, Johan Åhlén, Raoul Illyés, Peter Larsson, Peter Myers, Paul Turley, and so many others.

To members of the *SQL Server Pro* editorial team, Megan Keller, Lavon Peters, Michele Crockett, Mike Otey, and I'm sure many others; I've been writing for the magazine for more than a decade and am grateful for the opportunity to share my knowledge with the magazine's readers.

To SQL Server MVPs Alejandro Mesa, Erland Sommarskog, Aaron Bertrand, Tibor Karaszi, Paul White, and many others, and to the MVP lead, Simon Tien; this is a great program that I'm grateful and proud to be part of. The level of expertise of this group is amazing and I'm always excited when we all get to meet, both to share ideas and just to catch up at a personal level over beer. I believe that, in great part, Microsoft's inspiration to add new T-SQL capabilities in SQL Server is thanks to the efforts of SQL Server MVPs, and more generally the SQL Server community. It is great to see this synergy yielding such a meaningful and important outcome.

To Q2, Q3, and Q4, thanQ.

Finally, to my students: teaching SQL is what drives me. It's my passion. Thanks for allowing me to fulfill my calling, and for all the great questions that make me seek more knowledge.

# Errata & Book Support

We've made every effort to ensure the accuracy of this book and its companion content. Any errors that have been reported since this book was published are listed on our Microsoft Press site at oreilly.com:

> *http://go.microsoft.com/FWLink/?Linkid=248718*

If you find an error that is not already listed, you can report it to us through the same page.

If you need additional support, email Microsoft Press Book Support at *mspinput@microsoft.com*.

Please note that product support for Microsoft software is not offered through the addresses above.

## We Want to Hear from You

At Microsoft Press, your satisfaction is our top priority, and your feedback our most valuable asset. Please tell us what you think of this book at:

*http://www.microsoft.com/learning/booksurvey*

The survey is short, and we read every one of your comments and ideas. Thanks in advance for your input!

## Stay in Touch

Let's keep the conversation going! We're on Twitter: *http://twitter.com/MicrosoftPress*.

# CHAPTER 1

# Background to T-SQL Querying and Programming

You're about to embark on a journey to a land that is like no other—a land that has its own set of laws. If reading this book is your first step in learning Transact-SQL (T-SQL), you should feel like Alice—just before she started her adventures in Wonderland. For me, the journey has not ended; instead, it's an ongoing path filled with new discoveries. I envy you; some of the most exciting discoveries are still ahead of you!

I've been involved with T-SQL for many years: teaching, speaking, writing, and consulting about it. For me, T-SQL is more than just a language—it's a way of thinking. I've taught and written extensively on advanced topics, but until now, I have postponed writing about fundamentals. This is not because T-SQL fundamentals are simple or easy—in fact, just the opposite: The apparent simplicity of the language is misleading. I could explain the language syntax elements in a superficial manner and have you writing queries within minutes. But that approach would only hold you back in the long run and make it harder for you to understand the essence of the language.

Acting as your guide while you take your first steps in this realm is a big responsibility. I wanted to make sure that I spent enough time and effort exploring and understanding the language before writing about fundamentals. T-SQL is deep; learning the fundamentals the right way involves much more than just understanding the syntax elements and coding a query that returns the right output. You pretty much need to forget what you know about other programming languages and start thinking in terms of T-SQL.

## Theoretical Background

SQL stands for *Structured Query Language*. SQL is a standard language that was designed to query and manage data in relational database management systems (RDBMSs). An RDBMS is a database management system based on the relational model (a semantic model for representing data), which in turn is based on two mathematical branches: set theory and predicate logic. Many other programming languages and various aspects of computing evolved pretty much as a result of intuition. In contrast, to the degree that SQL is based on the relational model, it is based on a firm foundation—applied mathematics. T-SQL thus sits on wide and solid shoulders. Microsoft provides T-SQL as a dialect of, or extension to, SQL in Microsoft SQL Server data management software, its RDBMS.

This section provides a brief theoretical background about SQL, set theory and predicate logic, the relational model, and the data life cycle. Because this book is neither a mathematics book nor a design/data modeling book, the theoretical information provided here is informal and by no means complete. The goals are to give you a context for the T-SQL language and to deliver the key points that are integral to correctly understanding T-SQL later in the book.

> ## Language Independence
>
> The relational model is language-independent. That is, you can implement the relational model with languages other than SQL—for example, with C# in a class model. Today it is common to see RDBMSs that support languages other than a dialect of SQL, such as the CLR integration in SQL Server.
>
> Also, you should realize from the start that SQL deviates from the relational model in several ways. Some even say that a new language—one that more closely follows the relational model—should replace SQL. But to date, SQL is the industrial language used by all leading RDBMSs in practice.

**See Also**   *For details about the deviations of SQL from the relational model, as well as how to use SQL in a relational way, see this book on the topic:* SQL and Relational Theory: How to Write Accurate SQL Code, Second Edition *by C. J. Date (O'Reilly Media, 2011).*

# SQL

SQL is both an ANSI and ISO standard language based on the relational model, designed for querying and managing data in an RDBMS.

In the early 1970s, IBM developed a language called SEQUEL (short for Structured English QUEry Language) for their RDBMS product called System R. The name of the language was later changed from SEQUEL to SQL because of a trademark dispute. SQL first became an ANSI standard in 1986, and then an ISO standard in 1987. Since 1986, the American National Standards Institute (ANSI) and the International Organization for Standardization (ISO) have been releasing revisions for the SQL standard every few years. So far, the following standards have been released: SQL-86 (1986), SQL-89 (1989), SQL-92 (1992), SQL:1999 (1999), SQL:2003 (2003), SQL:2006 (2006), SQL:2008 (2008), and SQL:2011 (2011).

Interestingly, SQL resembles English and is also very logical. Unlike many programming languages, which use an imperative programming paradigm, SQL uses a declarative one. That is, SQL requires you to specify *what* you want to get and not *how* to get it, letting the RDBMS figure out the physical mechanics required to process your request.

SQL has several categories of statements, including Data Definition Language (DDL), Data Manipulation Language (DML), and Data Control Language (DCL). DDL deals with object definitions and includes statements such as *CREATE, ALTER,* and *DROP.* DML allows you to query and modify data and includes statements such as *SELECT, INSERT, UPDATE, DELETE, TRUNCATE,* and *MERGE.* It's a common misunderstanding that DML includes only data modification statements, but as I mentioned, it also includes *SELECT*. Another common misunderstanding is that *TRUNCATE* is a DDL statement, but in fact it is a DML statement. DCL deals with permissions and includes statements such as *GRANT* and *REVOKE*. This book focuses on DML.

T-SQL is based on standard SQL, but it also provides some nonstandard/proprietary extensions. When describing a language element for the first time, I'll typically mention whether it is standard.

## Set Theory

Set theory, which originated with the mathematician Georg Cantor, is one of the mathematical branches on which the relational model is based. Cantor's definition of a set follows:

> By a "set" we mean any collection M into a whole of definite, distinct objects m
> (which are called the "elements" of M) of our perception or of our thought.
> —Joseph W. Dauben and Georg Cantor (Princeton University Press, 1990)

Every word in the definition has a deep and crucial meaning. The definitions of a set and set membership are axioms that are not supported by proofs. Each element belongs to a universe, and either is or is not a member of the set.

Let's start with the word *whole* in Cantor's definition. A set should be considered a single entity. Your focus should be on the collection of objects as opposed to the individual objects that make up the collection. Later on, when you write T-SQL queries against tables in a database (such as a table of employees), you should think of the set of employees as a whole rather than the individual employees. This might sound trivial and simple enough, but apparently many programmers have difficulty adopting this way of thinking.

The word *distinct* means that every element of a set must be unique. Jumping ahead to tables in a database, you can enforce the uniqueness of rows in a table by defining key constraints. Without a key, you won't be able to uniquely identify rows, and therefore the table won't qualify as a set. Rather, the table would be a *multiset* or a *bag*.

The phrase *of our perception or of our thought* implies that the definition of a set is subjective. Consider a classroom: One person might perceive a set of people, whereas another might perceive a set of students and a set of teachers. Therefore, you have a substantial amount of freedom in defining sets. When you design a data model for your database, the design process should carefully consider the subjective needs of the application to determine adequate definitions for the entities involved.

As for the word *object*, the definition of a set is not restricted to physical objects such as cars or employees but rather is relevant to abstract objects as well, such as prime numbers or lines.

What Cantor's definition of a set leaves out is probably as important as what it includes. Notice that the definition doesn't mention any order among the set elements. The order in which set elements are listed is not important. The formal notation for listing set elements uses curly brackets: {a, b, c}. Because order has no relevance, you can express the same set as {b, a, c} or {b, c, a}. Jumping ahead to the set of attributes (called *columns* in SQL) that make up the header of a relation (called a *table* in SQL), an element is supposed to be identified by name—not by ordinal position.

Similarly, consider the set of tuples (called *rows* by SQL) that make up the body of the relation; an element is identified by its key values—not by position. Many programmers have a hard time adapting to the idea that, with respect to querying tables, there is no order among the rows. In other words, a query against a table can return table rows in *any order* unless you explicitly request that the data be sorted in a specific way, perhaps for presentation purposes.

## Predicate Logic

Predicate logic, whose roots reach back to ancient Greece, is another branch of mathematics on which the relational model is based. Dr. Edgar F. Codd, in creating the relational model, had the insight to connect predicate logic to both management and querying of data. Loosely speaking, a *predicate* is a property or an expression that either holds or doesn't hold—in other words, is either true or false. The relational model relies on predicates to maintain the logical integrity of the data and define its structure. One example of a predicate used to enforce integrity is a constraint defined in a table called *Employees* that allows only employees with a salary greater than zero to be stored in the table. The predicate is "salary greater than zero" (T-SQL expression: *salary > 0*).

You can also use predicates when filtering data to define subsets, and more. For example, if you need to query the *Employees* table and return only rows for employees from the sales department, you would use the predicate "department equals sales" in your query filter (T-SQL expression: *department = 'sales'*).

In set theory, you can use predicates to define sets. This is helpful because you can't always define a set by listing all its elements (for example, infinite sets), and sometimes for brevity it's more convenient to define a set based on a property. As an example of an infinite set defined with a predicate, the set of all prime numbers can be defined with the following predicate: "*x* is a positive integer greater than 1 that is divisible only by 1 and itself." For any specified value, the predicate is either true or not true. The set of all prime numbers is the set of all elements for which the predicate is true. As an example of a finite set defined with a predicate, the set *{0, 1, 2, 3, 4, 5, 6, 7, 8, 9}* can be defined as the set of all elements for which the following predicate holds true: "*x* is an integer greater than or equal to 0 and smaller than or equal to 9."

## The Relational Model

The relational model is a semantic model for data management and manipulation and is based on set theory and predicate logic. As mentioned earlier, it was created by Dr. Edgar F. Codd, and later explained and developed by Chris Date, Hugh Darwen, and others. The first version of the relational model was proposed by Codd in 1969 in an IBM research report called "Derivability, Redundancy, and Consistency of Relations Stored in Large Data Banks." A revised version was proposed by Codd in 1970 in a paper called "A Relational Model of Data for Large Shared Data Banks," published in the journal *Communications of the ACM*.

The goal of the relational model is to enable consistent representation of data with minimal or no redundancy and without sacrificing completeness, and to define data integrity (enforcement of data consistency) as part of the model. An RDBMS is supposed to implement the relational model and provide the means to store, manage, enforce the integrity of, and query data. The fact that the relational model is based on a strong mathematical foundation means that given a certain data model instance (from which a physical database will later be generated), you can tell with certainty when a design is flawed, rather than relying solely on intuition.

The relational model involves concepts such as propositions, predicates, relations, tuples, attributes, and more. For non-mathematicians, these concepts can be quite intimidating. The sections that follow cover some of the key aspects of the model in an informal, nonmathematical manner and explain how they relate to databases.

## Propositions, Predicates, and Relations

The common belief that the term *relational* stems from relationships between tables is incorrect. "Relational" actually pertains to the mathematical term *relation*. In set theory, a relation is a representation of a set. In the relational model, a relation is a set of related information, with the counterpart in SQL being a table—albeit not an exact counterpart. A key point in the relational model is that a single relation should represent a single set (for example, *Customers*). It is interesting to note that operations on relations (based on relational algebra) result in a relation (for example, a join between two relations).

> **Note** The relational model distinguishes between a *relation* and a *relation variable*, but to keep things simple, I won't get into this distinction; instead, I'll use the term *relation* for both cases. Also, a relation is made of a header and a body. The header consists of a set of attributes (called *columns* in SQL), where each element is identified by an attribute name and a type name. The body consists of a set of tuples (called *rows* in SQL), where each element is identified by a key. To keep things simple, I'll refer to a table as a set of rows.

When you design a data model for a database, you represent all data with relations (tables). You start by identifying propositions that you will need to represent in your database. A proposition is an assertion or a statement that must be true or false. For example, the statement, "Employee Itzik Ben-Gan was born on February 12, 1971, and works in the IT department" is a proposition. If this proposition is true, it will manifest itself as a row in a table of *Employees*. A false proposition simply won't manifest itself. This presumption is known as the *close world assumption (CWA)*.

The next step is to formalize the propositions. You do this by taking out the actual data (the body of the relation) and defining the structure (the heading of the relation)—for example, by creating predicates out of propositions. You can think of predicates as parameterized propositions. The heading of a relation comprises a set of attributes. Note the use of the term "set"; in the relational model, attributes are unordered and distinct. An attribute is identified by an attribute name and a type name. For example, the heading of an *Employees* relation might consist of the following attributes (expressed as pairs of attribute names and type names): *employeeid* integer, *firstname* character string, *lastname* character string, *birthdate* date, *departmentid* integer.

A type is one of the most fundamental building blocks for relations. A type constrains an attribute to a certain set of possible or valid values. For example, the type *INT* is the set of all integers in the range –2,147,483,648 to 2,147,483,647. A type is one of the simplest forms of a predicate in a database because it restricts the attribute values that are allowed. For example, the database would not accept a proposition where an employee birth date is February 31, 1971 (not to mention a birth date stated as something like "abc!"). Note that types are not restricted to base types such as integers or character strings; a type could also be an enumeration of possible values, such as an enumeration of possible job positions. A type can be complex. Probably the best way to think of a type is as a class—encapsulated data and the behavior supporting it. An example of a complex type would be a geometry type that supports polygons.

## Missing Values

One aspect of the relational model is the source of many passionate debates—whether predicates should be restricted to two-valued logic. That is, in two-valued predicate logic, a predicate is either true or false. If a predicate is not true, it must be false. Use of two-valued predicate logic follows a mathematical law called the law of excluded middle. However, some say that there's room for three-valued (or even four-valued) predicate logic, taking into account cases where values are missing. A predicate involving a missing value yields neither true nor false—it yields unknown. Take, for example, a mobile phone attribute of an *Employees* relation. Suppose that a certain employee's mobile phone number is missing. How do you represent this fact in the database? In a three-valued logic implementation, the mobile phone attribute should allow a special mark for a missing value. Then a predicate comparing the mobile phone attribute with some specific number will yield *unknown* for the case with the missing value. Three-valued predicate logic refers to the three possible logical values that can result from a predicate—*true*, *false*, and *unknown*.

Some people believe that three-valued predicate logic is non-relational, whereas others believe that it is relational. Codd actually advocated four-valued predicate logic, saying that there were two different cases of missing values: missing but applicable (A-Mark), and missing but inapplicable (I-Mark). An example of "missing but applicable" is when an employee has a mobile phone, but you don't know what the mobile phone number is. An example of missing but inapplicable is when an employee doesn't have a mobile phone at all. According to Codd, two special markers should be used to support these two cases of missing values. SQL implements three-valued predicate logic by supporting the *NULL* mark to signify the generic concept of a missing value. Support for *NULL* marks and three-valued predicate logic in SQL is the source of a great deal of confusion and complexity, though one can argue that missing values are part of reality. In addition, the alternative—using only two-valued predicate logic—is no less problematic.

## Constraints

One of the greatest benefits of the relational model is the ability to define data integrity as part of the model. Data integrity is achieved through rules called *constraints* that are defined in the data model and enforced by the RDBMS. The simplest methods of enforcing integrity are assigning an attribute type with its attendant "nullability" (whether it supports or doesn't support *NULL* marks). Constraints are also enforced through the model itself; for example, the relation *Orders(orderid, orderdate, duedate, shipdate)* allows three distinct dates per order, whereas the relations *Employees(empid)* and *EmployeeChildren(empid, childname)* allow zero to countable infinity children per employee.

Other examples of constraints include *candidate keys,* which provide entity integrity, and *foreign keys,* which provide referential integrity. A candidate key is a key defined on one or more attributes that prevents more than one occurrence of the same tuple (*row* in SQL) in a relation. A predicate based on a candidate key can uniquely identify a row (such as an employee). You can define multiple candidate keys in a relation. For example, in an *Employees* relation, you can define candidate keys on *employeeid*, on *SSN* (Social Security number), and others. Typically, you arbitrarily choose one of the candidate keys as the *primary key* (for example, *employeeid* in the *Employees* relation), and use that as the preferred way to identify a row. All other candidate keys are known as *alternate keys.*

Foreign keys are used to enforce referential integrity. A foreign key is defined on one or more attributes of a relation (known as the *referencing relation*) and references a candidate key in another (or possibly the same) relation. This constraint restricts the values in the referencing relation's foreign key attributes to the values that appear in the referenced relation's candidate key attributes. For example, suppose that the *Employees* relation has a foreign key defined on the attribute *departmentid*, which references the primary key attribute *departmentid* in the *Departments* relation. This means that the values in *Employees.departmentid* are restricted to the values that appear in *Departments.departmentid*.

## Normalization

The relational model also defines *normalization rules* (also known as *normal forms*). Normalization is a formal mathematical process to guarantee that each entity will be represented by a single relation. In a normalized database, you avoid anomalies during data modification and keep redundancy to a minimum without sacrificing completeness. If you follow Entity Relationship Modeling (ERM), and represent each entity and its attributes, you probably won't need normalization; instead, you will apply normalization only to reinforce and ensure that the model is correct. The following sections briefly cover the first three normal forms (1NF, 2NF, and 3NF) introduced by Codd.

**1NF** The first normal form says that the tuples (rows) in the relation (table) must be unique, and attributes should be atomic. This is a redundant definition of a relation; in other words, if a table truly represents a relation, it is already in first normal form.

You achieve unique rows by defining a unique key for the table.

You can only operate on attributes with operations that are defined as part of the attribute's type. Atomicity of attributes is subjective in the same way that the definition of a set is subjective. As an example, should an employee name in an *Employees* relation be expressed with one attribute (*fullname*), two (*firstname* and *lastname*), or three (*firstname, middlename,* and *lastname*)? The answer depends on the application. If the application needs to manipulate the parts of the employee's name separately (such as for search purposes), it makes sense to break them apart; otherwise, it doesn't.

In the same way that an attribute might not be atomic enough based on the needs of the application, an attribute might also be subatomic. For example, if an address attribute is considered atomic for a particular application, not including the city as part of the address would violate the first normal form.

This normal form is often misunderstood. Some people think that an attempt to mimic arrays violates the first normal form. An example would be defining a *YearlySales* relation with the following attributes: *salesperson*, *qty2010*, *qty2011*, and *qty2012*. However, in this example, you don't really violate the first normal form; you simply impose a constraint—restricting the data to three specific years: 2010, 2011, and 2012.

**2NF**  The second normal form involves two rules. One rule is that the data must meet the first normal form. The other rule addresses the relationship between non-key and candidate key attributes. For every candidate key, every non-key attribute has to be fully functionally dependent on the entire candidate key. In other words, a non-key attribute cannot be fully functionally dependent on part of a candidate key. To put it more informally, if you need to obtain any non-key attribute value, you need to provide the values of all attributes of a candidate key from the same tuple. You can find any value of any attribute of any tuple if you know all the attribute values of a candidate key.

As an example of violating the second normal form, suppose that you define a relation called *Orders* that represents information about orders and order lines (see Figure 1-1). The *Orders* relation contains the following attributes: *orderid*, *productid*, *orderdate*, *qty*, *customerid*, and *companyname*. The primary key is defined on *orderid* and *productid*.

| Orders | |
|---|---|
| PK | **orderid** |
| PK | **productid** |
| | orderdate |
| | qty |
| | customerid |
| | companyname |

**FIGURE 1-1** Data model before applying 2NF.

The second normal form is violated in Figure 1-1 because there are non-key attributes that depend on only part of a candidate key (the primary key, in this example). For example, you can find the *orderdate* of an order, as well as *customerid* and *companyname*, based on the *orderid* alone. To conform to the second normal form, you would need to split your original relation into two relations: *Orders* and *OrderDetails* (as shown in Figure 1-2). The *Orders* relation would include the attributes *orderid*, *orderdate*, *customerid*, and *companyname*, with the primary key defined on *orderid*. The *OrderDetails* relation would include the attributes *orderid*, *productid*, and *qty*, with the primary key defined on *orderid* and *productid*.

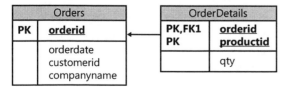

**FIGURE 1-2** Data model after applying 2NF and before 3NF.

**3NF**  The third normal form also has two rules. The data must meet the second normal form. Also, all non-key attributes must be dependent on candidate keys non-transitively. Informally this rule means that all non-key attributes must be mutually independent. In other words, one non-key attribute cannot be dependent on another non-key attribute.

The *Orders* and *OrderDetails* relations described previously now conform to the second normal form. Remember that the *Orders* relation at this point contains the attributes *orderid*, *orderdate*, *customerid*, and *companyname*, with the primary key defined on *orderid*. Both *customerid* and *companyname* depend on the whole primary key—*orderid*. For example, you need the entire primary key to find the *customerid* representing the customer who placed the order. Similarly, you need the whole primary key to find the company name of the customer who placed the order. However, *customerid* and *companyname* are also dependent on each other. To meet the third normal form, you need to add a *Customers* relation (shown in Figure 1-3) with the attributes *customerid* (as the primary key) and *companyname*. Then you can remove the *companyname* attribute from the *Orders* relation.

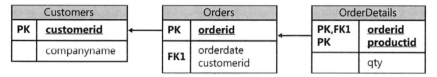

**FIGURE 1-3** Data model after applying 3NF.

Informally, 2NF and 3NF are commonly summarized with the sentence, "Every non-key attribute is dependent on the key, the whole key, and nothing but the key—so help me Codd."

There are higher normal forms beyond Codd's original first three normal forms that involve compound primary keys and temporal databases, but they are outside the scope of this book.

## The Data Life Cycle

Data is usually perceived as something static that is entered into a database and later queried. But in many environments, data is actually more similar to a product in an assembly line, moving from one environment to another and undergoing transformations along the way. This section describes the different environments in which data can reside and the characteristics of both the data and the environment at each stage of the data life cycle. Figure 1-4 illustrates the data life cycle.

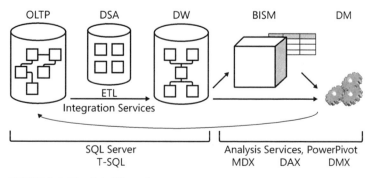

**FIGURE 1-4** The data life cycle.

Here's a quick description of what each acronym represents:

- OLTP: online transactional processing

- DSA: data staging area

- DW: data warehouse

- BISM: Business Intelligence Semantic Model

- DM: data mining

- ETL: extract, transform, and load

- MDX: Multidimensional Expressions

- DAX: Data Analysis Expressions

- DMX: Data Mining Extensions

## Online Transactional Processing

Data is entered initially into an online transactional processing (OLTP) system. The focus of an OLTP system is data entry and not reporting—transactions mainly insert, update, and delete data. The relational model is targeted primarily at OLTP systems, where a normalized model provides both good performance for data entry and data consistency. In a normalized environment, each table represents a single entity and keeps redundancy to a minimum. When you need to modify a fact, you need to modify it in only one place. This results in optimized performance for data modifications and little chance for error.

However, an OLTP environment is not suitable for reporting purposes because a normalized model usually involves many tables (one for each entity) with complex relationships. Even simple reports require joining many tables, resulting in complex and poorly performing queries.

You can implement an OLTP database in SQL Server and both manage it and query it with T-SQL.

## Data Warehouses

A *data warehouse* (DW) is an environment designed for data retrieval and reporting purposes. When it serves an entire organization, such an environment is called a data warehouse; when it serves only part of the organization (such as a specific department) or a subject matter area in the organization, it is called a *data mart*. The data model of a data warehouse is designed and optimized mainly to support data retrieval needs. The model has intentional redundancy, fewer tables, and simpler relationships, ultimately resulting in simpler and more efficient queries as compared to an OLTP environment.

The simplest data warehouse design is called a *star schema*. The star schema includes several dimension tables and a fact table. Each dimension table represents a subject by which you want to analyze the data. For example, in a system that deals with orders and sales, you will probably want to analyze data by customers, products, employees, time, and similar subjects. In a star schema, each dimension is implemented as a single table with redundant data. For example, a product dimension could be implemented as a single *ProductDim* table instead of three normalized tables: *Products*, *ProductSubCategories*, and *ProductCategories*. If you normalize a dimension table, which results in multiple tables representing that dimension, you get what's known as a *snowflake dimension*. A schema that contains snowflake dimensions is known as a *snowflake schema* (as opposed to a star schema).

The fact table holds the facts and measures such as quantity and value for each relevant combination of dimension keys. For example, for each relevant combination of customer, product, employee, and day, the fact table would have a row containing the quantity and value. Note that data in a data warehouse is typically preaggregated to a certain level of granularity (such as a day), unlike data in an OLTP environment, which is usually recorded at the transaction level.

Historically, early versions of SQL Server mainly targeted OLTP environments, but eventually SQL Server also started targeting data warehouse systems and data analysis needs. You can implement a data warehouse as a SQL Server database and manage and query it with T-SQL.

The process that pulls data from source systems (OLTP and others), manipulates it, and loads it into the data warehouse is called extract, transform, and load, or ETL. SQL Server provides a tool called Microsoft SQL Server Integration Services (SSIS) to handle ETL needs.

Often the ETL process will involve the use of a data staging area (DSA) between the OLTP and the DW. The DSA usually resides in a relational database such as a SQL Server database and is used as the data cleansing area. The DSA is not open to end users.

## The Business Intelligence Semantic Model

The Business Intelligence Semantic Model (BISM) is Microsoft's latest model for supporting the entire BI stack of applications. The idea is to provide rich, flexible, efficient, and scalable analytical and reporting capabilities. Its architecture includes three layers: the data model, business logic and queries, and data access.

The deployment of the model can be in an Analysis Services server or PowerPivot. Analysis Services is targeted at BI professionals and IT, whereas PowerPivot is targeted at business users. With Analysis Services, you can use either a multidimensional data model or a tabular (relational) one. With Power-Pivot, you use a tabular data model.

The business logic and queries use two languages: Multidimensional Expressions (MDX), based on multidimensional concepts, and Data Analysis Expressions (DAX), based on tabular concepts.

The data access layer can get its data from different sources: relational databases such as the DW, files, cloud services, line of business (LOB) applications, OData feeds, and others. The data access layer can either cache the data locally or just serve as a passthrough layer directly from the data sources. The cached mode can use one of two storage engines. One is a preaggregated form known as MOLAP that was originally designed to support the multidimensional model. Another is a newer engine called VertiPaq, which implements a columnstore concept, with very high levels of compression and a very fast processing engine, removing the need for preaggregations, indexing, and so on.

**See Also** *This section about BISM has a lot of concepts to digest—perhaps too many for a fundamentals book about T-SQL. If you are curious about BISM and would like a more detailed overview, you can find it in the following blog entry from the Analysis Services team:* http://blogs.msdn.com/b/analysisservices /archive/2011/05/16/analysis-services-vision-amp-roadmap-update.aspx.

### Data Mining

BISM provides the user with answers to all possible questions, but the user's task is to ask the right questions—to sift anomalies, trends, and other useful information from the sea of data. In the dynamic analysis process, the user navigates from one view of aggregates to another—again, slicing and dicing the data—to find useful information.

Data mining (DM) is the next step; instead of letting the user look for useful information in the sea of data, data mining models can do this for the user. That is, data mining algorithms comb the data and sift the useful information from it. Data mining has enormous business value for organizations, helping to identify trends, figure out which products are purchased together, predict customer choices based on specific parameters, and more.

Analysis Services supports data mining algorithms—including clustering, decision trees, and others—to address such needs. The language used to manage and query data mining models is Data Mining Extensions (DMX).

# SQL Server Architecture

This section will introduce you to the SQL Server architecture, the flavors of the product, the entities involved—SQL Server instances, databases, schemas, and database objects—and the purpose of each entity.

## The ABC Flavors of SQL Server

For many years, SQL Server was available only in one flavor—a box, or on-premises, flavor. More recently, Microsoft decided to offer multiple flavors to allow customers to choose the one that best suits their needs. At the date of this writing, Microsoft provides three main flavors of SQL Server that are internally referred to as the *ABC flavors*: A for Appliance, B for Box, and C for Cloud.

### Appliance

The idea behind the appliance flavor is to provide a complete solution including hardware, software, and services. The appliance is hosted locally at the customer site. There are several appliances available today, one of which is Parallel Data Warehouse (PDW). Microsoft partners with hardware vendors such as Dell and HP to provide the appliance offering. Experts from Microsoft and the hardware vendor handle the performance, security, and availability aspects for the customer.

This book's focus is T-SQL, so you are probably wondering which language is used to interact with the database engine. That depends on the appliance. For example, PDW doesn't use the same engine as the on-premises engine; it uses a specialized one. The specialized PDW engine uses its own flavor of SQL called *distributed SQL*, or DSQL. Microsoft's long-term goal is to align the language support in the different flavors of the product, but that has not yet been realized. This book focuses on T-SQL, which is supported by some of the appliances and the on-premises and cloud flavors.

## Box

The box flavor of SQL Server, formally referred to as *on-premises SQL Server*, is the traditional one, usually installed on the customer's premises. The customer is responsible for everything—getting the hardware; installing the software; and handling updates, high availability and disaster recovery (HADR), security, and everything else.

The customer can install multiple instances of the product in the same server (more on this in the next section) and can write queries that interact with multiple databases. It is also possible to switch the connection between databases, unless one of them is a contained database.

The querying language used is T-SQL. You can run all of the code samples and exercises in this book on an on-premises SQL Server implementation, if you want. See the Appendix for details about obtaining and installing an evaluation edition of SQL Server, as well as creating the sample database.

## Cloud

Microsoft supports two cloud flavors of SQL Server: private and public. The use of the term *cloud* for the private case could be a bit confusing, because it is hosted locally, but the private flavor uses virtualization technology. The engine is a box engine (hence the same T-SQL is used to query it), but it is limited by the virtualization technology's limitations, such as the number of supported CPUs and memory.

The public cloud flavor is called Windows Azure SQL Database (formerly called SQL Azure). It is hosted in Microsoft's data centers. Hardware, maintenance, HADR, and updates are all responsibilities of Microsoft. The customer is still responsible for index and query tuning, however.

> **Note** Subsequent references to "Windows Azure SQL Database" will use the shorter form "SQL Database."

Using SQL Database, the customer can have multiple databases in the cloud server (a conceptual server, of course) but can connect to only one database at a time. The customer cannot switch between databases and cannot write multi-database queries.

The SQL Database engine is a specialized engine, although Microsoft uses the same code base as in the on-premises version. So the T-SQL features exposed in SQL Database are basically the same as those exposed locally. Most of the T-SQL that you will learn in this book is applicable to both on-premises and cloud flavors of SQL Server, but there are some exceptions, such as on-premises SQL

Server T-SQL features that are not yet implemented or exposed in SQL Database. Books Online for SQL Database details those features in the Transact-SQL Reference section at *http://msdn.microsoft.com /en-us/library/windowsazure/ee336281.aspx*. You should also note that the update and deployment rate of new versions of SQL Database is faster than that of an on-premises SQL Server. Therefore, it's possible that some T-SQL features may be exposed in SQL Database before they show up in an on-premises SQL Server version.

As mentioned, most of the T-SQL discussed in this book is either already available—or will be available—in SQL Database. The section in the Appendix that covers the installation of the sample database for this book also describes how to install the sample database in SQL Database, in case you already have access to it.

## SQL Server Instances

A SQL Server instance, as illustrated in Figure 1-5, is an installation of a SQL Server database engine or service. You can install multiple instances of an on-premises SQL Server on the same computer. Each instance is completely independent of the others in terms of security, the data that it manages, and in all other respects. At the logical level, two different instances residing on the same computer have no more in common than two instances residing on two separate computers. Of course, same-computer instances do share the server's physical resources, such as CPU, memory, and disk.

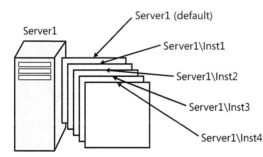

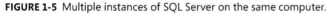

**FIGURE 1-5** Multiple instances of SQL Server on the same computer.

You can set up one of the multiple instances on a computer as the *default instance*, whereas all others must be *named instances*. You determine whether an instance is the default or a named one upon installation; you cannot change that decision later. To connect to a default instance, a client application needs to specify the computer's name or IP address. To connect to a named instance, the client needs to specify the computer's name or IP address, followed by a backslash (\), followed by the instance name (as provided upon installation). For example, suppose you have two instances of SQL Server installed on a computer called *Server1*. One of these instances was installed as the default instance, and the other was installed as a named instance called *Inst1*. To connect to the default instance, you need to specify only *Server1* as the server name. However, to connect to the named instance, you need to specify both the server and the instance name: *Server1\Inst1*.

There are various reasons why you might want to install multiple instances of SQL Server on the same computer, but I'll mention only a couple here. One reason is to save on support costs. For example, to be able to test the functionality of features in response to support calls or reproduce errors that users encounter in the production environment, the support department needs local installations of SQL Server that mimic the user's production environment in terms of version, edition, and service pack of SQL Server. If an organization has multiple user environments, the support department needs multiple installations of SQL Server. Rather than having multiple computers, each hosting a different installation of SQL Server that must be supported separately, the support department can have one computer with multiple installed instances. Of course, you can achieve a similar result by using multiple virtual machines.

As another example, consider people like me who teach and lecture about SQL Server. For us, it is very convenient to be able to install multiple instances of SQL Server on the same laptop. This way, we can perform demonstrations against different versions of the product, showing differences in behavior between versions, and so on.

As a final example, providers of database services sometimes need to guarantee their customers complete security separation of their data from other customers' data. At least in the past, the database provider could have a very powerful data center hosting multiple instances of SQL Server, rather than needing to maintain multiple less-powerful computers, each hosting a different instance. More recently, cloud solutions and advanced virtualization technologies make it possible to achieve similar goals.

## Databases

You can think of a database as a container of objects such as tables, views, stored procedures, and other objects. Each instance of SQL Server can contain multiple databases, as illustrated in Figure 1-6. When you install an on-premises flavor of SQL Server, the setup program creates several system databases that hold system data and serve internal purposes. After installation, you can create your own user databases that will hold application data.

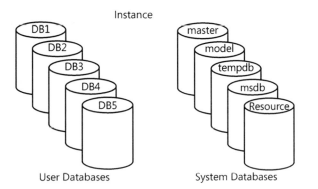

FIGURE 1-6 An example of multiple databases on a SQL Server instance.

The system databases that the setup program creates include *master*, *Resource*, *model*, *tempdb*, and *msdb*. A description of each follows.

- **master**  The *master* database holds instance-wide metadata information, server configuration, information about all databases in the instance, and initialization information.

- **Resource**  The *Resource* database is a hidden, read-only database that holds the definitions of all system objects. When you query system objects in a database, they appear to reside in the *sys schema* of the local database, but in actuality their definitions reside in the *Resource* database.

- **model**  The *model* database is used as a template for new databases. Every new database that you create is initially created as a copy of *model*. So if you want certain objects (such as data types) to appear in all new databases that you create, or certain database properties to be configured in a certain way in all new databases, you need to create those objects and configure those properties in the *model* database. Note that changes you apply to the *model* database will not affect existing databases—only new databases that you create in the future.

- **tempdb**  The *tempdb* database is where SQL Server stores temporary data such as work tables, sort space, row versioning information, and so on. SQL Server allows you to create temporary tables for your own use, and the physical location of those temporary tables is *tempdb*. Note that this database is destroyed and recreated as a copy of the *model* database every time you restart the instance of SQL Server.

- **msdb**  The *msdb* database is where a service called SQL Server Agent stores its data. SQL Server Agent is in charge of automation, which includes entities such as jobs, schedules, and alerts. The SQL Server Agent is also the service in charge of replication. The *msdb* database also holds information related to other SQL Server features such as Database Mail, Service Broker, backups, and more.

In an on-premises installation of SQL Server, you can connect directly to the system databases *master*, *model*, *tempdb*, and *msdb*. In SQL Database, you can connect directly only to the system database *master*. If you create temporary tables or declare table variables (more on this topic in Chapter 10, "Programmable Objects"), they are created in *tempdb*, but you cannot connect directly to *tempdb* and explicitly create user objects there.

You can create multiple user databases within an instance (up to 32767). A user database holds objects and data for an application.

You can define a property called *collation* at the database level that will determine language support, case sensitivity, and sort order for character data in that database. If you do not specify a collation for the database when you create it, the new database will use the default collation of the instance (chosen upon installation).

To run T-SQL code against a database, a client application needs to connect to a SQL Server instance and be in the context of, or use, the relevant database.

In terms of security, to be able to connect to a SQL Server instance, the database administrator (DBA) must create a *logon* for you. In an on-premises SQL Server instance, the logon can be tied to your Windows credentials, in which case it is called a *Windows authenticated logon*. With a Windows authenticated logon, you won't need to provide logon and password information when connecting to SQL Server because you already provided those when you logged on to Windows. With both on-premises SQL Server and SQL Database, the logon can be independent of your Windows credentials, in which case it is called a *SQL Server authenticated logon*. When connecting to SQL Server using a SQL Server authenticated logon, you will need to provide both a logon name and a password.

The DBA needs to map your logon to a *database user* in each database that you are supposed to have access to. The database user is the entity that is granted permissions to objects in the database.

SQL Server 2012 supports a feature called *contained databases* that breaks the connection between a database user and a server-level logon. The user is fully contained within the specific database and is not tied to a logon at the server level. When creating the user, the DBA also provides a password. When connecting to SQL Server, the user needs to specify the database he or she is connecting to, as well as the user name and password, and the user cannot subsequently switch to other user databases.

So far, I've mainly mentioned the logical aspects of databases. If you're using SQL Database, your only concern is that logical layer. You do not deal with the physical layout of the database data and log files, *tempdb*, and so on. But if you're using on-premises SQL Server, you are responsible for the physical layer as well. Figure 1-7 shows a diagram of the physical database layout.

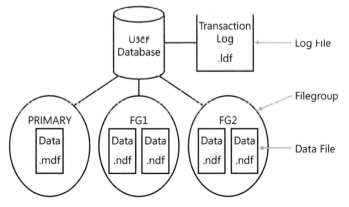

**FIGURE 1-7** Database layout.

The database is made up of data files and transaction log files. When you create a database, you can define various properties for each file, including the file name, location, initial size, maximum size, and an autogrowth increment. Each database must have at least one data file and at least one log file (the default in SQL Server). The data files hold object data, and the log files hold information that SQL Server needs to maintain transactions.

Although SQL Server can write to multiple data files in parallel, it can write to only one log file at a time, in a sequential manner. Therefore, unlike with data files, having multiple log files does not result in a performance benefit. You might need to add log files if the disk drive where the log resides runs out of space.

Data files are organized in logical groups called filegroups. A filegroup is the target for creating an object, such as a table or an index. The object data will be spread across the files that belong to the target filegroup. Filegroups are your way of controlling the physical locations of your objects. A database must have at least one filegroup called *PRIMARY*, and can optionally have other user filegroups as well. The *PRIMARY* filegroup contains the primary data file (which has an .mdf extension) for the database, and the database's system catalog. You can optionally add secondary data files (which have an .ndf extension) to *PRIMARY*. User filegroups contain only secondary data files. You can decide which filegroup is marked as the default filegroup. Objects are created in the default filegroup when the object creation statement does not explicitly specify a different target filegroup.

---

### File Extensions .mdf, .ldf, and .ndf

The database file extensions .mdf and .ldf are quite straightforward. The extension .mdf stands for Master Data File (not to be confused with the *master* database), and .ldf stands for Log Data File. According to one anecdote, when discussing the extension for the secondary data files, one of the developers suggested, humorously, using .ndf to represent "Not Master Data File," and the idea was accepted.

---

## Schemas and Objects

When I said earlier that a database is a container of objects, I simplified things a bit. As illustrated in Figure 1-8, a database contains schemas, and schemas contain objects. You can think of a schema as a container of objects such as tables, views, stored procedures, and others.

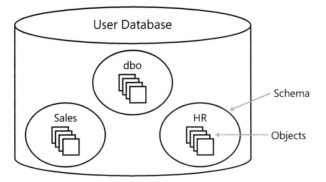

**FIGURE 1-8** A database, schemas, and database objects.

You can control permissions at the schema level. For example, you can grant a user SELECT permissions on a schema, allowing the user to query data from all objects in that schema. So security is one of the considerations for determining how to arrange objects in schemas.

The schema is also a namespace—it is used as a prefix to the object name. For example, suppose you have a table named *Orders* in a schema named *Sales*. The schema-qualified object name (also known as the *two-part object name*) is *Sales.Orders*. If you omit the schema name when referring to an object, SQL Server will apply a process to resolve the schema name, such as checking whether the object exists in the user's default schema, and if it doesn't, checking whether it exists in the *dbo* schema. Microsoft recommends that when you refer to objects in your code you always use the two-part object names. There are some relatively insignificant extra costs involved in resolving the object name when you don't specify it explicitly. But as insignificant as this extra cost might be, why pay it? Also, if multiple objects with the same name exist in different schemas, you might end up getting a different object than the one you wanted.

# Creating Tables and Defining Data Integrity

This section describes the fundamentals of creating tables and defining data integrity using T-SQL. Feel free to run the included code samples in your environment.

**More Info** If you don't know yet how to run code against SQL Server, the Appendix will help you get started.

As mentioned earlier, DML rather than DDL is the focus of this book. Still, it is important that you understand how to create tables and define data integrity. I will not go into the explicit details here, but I will provide a brief description of the essentials.

Before you look at the code for creating a table, remember that tables reside within schemas, and schemas reside within databases. The examples use the book's sample database, *TSQL2012*, and a schema called *dbo*.

**More Info** See the Appendix for details on creating the sample database.

The examples here use a schema named *dbo* that is created automatically in every database and is also used as the default schema for users who are not explicitly associated with a different schema.

# Creating Tables

The following code creates a table named *Employees* in the *dbo* schema in the *TSQL2012* database.

```
USE TSQL2012;

IF OBJECT_ID('dbo.Employees', 'U') IS NOT NULL
  DROP TABLE dbo.Employees;

CREATE TABLE dbo.Employees
(
  empid     INT         NOT NULL,
  firstname VARCHAR(30) NOT NULL,
  lastname  VARCHAR(30) NOT NULL,
  hiredate  DATE        NOT NULL,
  mgrid     INT         NULL,
  ssn       VARCHAR(20) NOT NULL,
  salary    MONEY       NOT NULL
);
```

The *USE* statement sets the current database context to that of *TSQL2012*. It is important to incorporate the *USE* statement in scripts that create objects to ensure that SQL Server creates the objects in the specified database. In an on-premises SQL Server implementation, the *USE* statement can actually change the database context from one to another. In SQL Database, you cannot switch between different databases, but the *USE* statement will not fail as long as you are already connected to the target database. So even in SQL Database, I recommend having the *USE* statement to ensure that you are connected to the right database when creating your objects.

The *IF* statement invokes the *OBJECT_ID* function to check whether the *Employees* table already exists in the current database. The *OBJECT_ID* function accepts an object name and type as inputs. The type *'U'* represents a user table. This function returns the internal object ID if an object with the specified input name and type exists, and *NULL* otherwise. If the function returns a *NULL*, you know that the object doesn't exist. In our case, the code drops the table if it already exists, and then creates a new one. Of course, you could have chosen a different treatment, such as simply not creating the object if it already exists.

The *CREATE TABLE* statement is in charge of defining what I referred to earlier as the header of the relation. Here you specify the name of the table and, in parentheses, the definition of its attributes (columns).

Notice the use of the two-part name *dbo.Employees* for the table name, as recommended earlier. If you omit the schema name, SQL Server will assume the default schema associated with the database user running the code.

For each attribute, you specify the attribute name, data type, and whether the value can be *NULL* (this is called *nullability*).

In the *Employees* table, the attributes *empid* (employee ID) and *mgrid* (manager ID) are each defined with the *INT* (four-byte integer) data type; the *firstname*, *lastname*, and *ssn* (Social Security number) are defined as *VARCHAR* (variable-length character string with the specified maximum supported number of characters); and *hiredate* is defined as *DATE* and *salary* is defined as *MONEY*.

If you don't explicitly specify whether a column allows or disallows *NULL* marks, SQL Server will have to rely on defaults. Standard SQL dictates that when a column's nullability is not specified, the assumption should be *NULL* (allowing *NULL* marks), but SQL Server has settings that can change that behavior. I strongly recommend that you be explicit and not rely on defaults. Also, I strongly recommend defining a column as *NOT NULL* unless you have a compelling reason to support *NULL* marks. If a column is not supposed to allow *NULL* marks and you don't enforce this with a *NOT NULL* constraint, you can rest assured that *NULL* marks will occur. In the *Employees* table, all columns are defined as *NOT NULL* except for the *mgrid* column. A *NULL* in the *mgrid* attribute would represent the fact that the employee has no manager, as in the case of the CEO of the organization.

## Coding Style

You should be aware of a few general notes regarding coding style, the use of white spaces (space, tab, new line, and so on), and semicolons. I'm not aware of any formal coding styles. My advice is that you use a style that you and your fellow developers feel comfortable with. What ultimately matters most is the consistency, readability, and maintainability of your code. I have tried to reflect these aspects in my code throughout the book.

T-SQL lets you use white spaces quite freely in your code. You can take advantage of whitespace to facilitate readability. For example, I could have written the code in the previous section as a single line. However, the code wouldn't have been as readable as when it is broken into multiple lines that use indentation.

The practice of using a semicolon to terminate statements is standard and in fact is a requirement in several other database platforms. SQL Server requires the semicolon only in particular cases—but in cases where a semicolon is not required, using one doesn't cause problems. I strongly recommend that you adopt the practice of terminating all statements with a semicolon. Not only will doing this improve the readability of your code, but in some cases it can save you some grief. (When a semicolon is required and is *not* specified, the error message SQL Server produces is not always very clear.)

**Note** The SQL Server documentation indicates that not terminating T-SQL statements with a semicolon is a deprecated feature. This means that the long-term goal is to enforce use of the semicolon in a future version of the product. That's one more reason to get into the habit of terminating all of your statements, even where it's currently not required.

# Defining Data Integrity

As mentioned earlier, one of the great benefits of the relational model is that data integrity is an integral part of it. Data integrity enforced as part of the model—namely, as part of the table definitions—is considered *declarative data integrity*. Data integrity enforced with code—such as with stored procedures or triggers—is considered *procedural data integrity*.

Data type and nullability choices for attributes and even the data model itself are examples of declarative data integrity constraints. In this section, I will describe other examples of declarative constraints: primary key, unique, foreign key, check, and default constraints. You can define such constraints when creating a table as part of the *CREATE TABLE* statement, or you can define them for already-created tables by using an *ALTER TABLE* statement. All types of constraints except for default constraints can be defined as *composite constraints*—that is, based on more than one attribute.

## Primary Key Constraints

A primary key constraint enforces uniqueness of rows and also disallows *NULL* marks in the constraint attributes. Each unique set of values in the constraint attributes can appear only once in the table—in other words, only in one row. An attempt to define a primary key constraint on a column that allows *NULL* marks will be rejected by the RDBMS. Each table can have only one primary key.

Here's an example of defining a primary key constraint on the *empid* attribute in the *Employees* table that you created earlier.

```
ALTER TABLE dbo.Employees
  ADD CONSTRAINT PK_Employees
  PRIMARY KEY(empid);
```

With this primary key in place, you can be assured that all *empid* values will be unique and known. An attempt to insert or update a row such that the constraint would be violated will be rejected by the RDBMS and result in an error.

To enforce the uniqueness of the logical primary key constraint, SQL Server will create a unique index behind the scenes. A unique index is a physical mechanism used by SQL Server to enforce uniqueness. Indexes (not necessarily unique ones) are also used to speed up queries by avoiding unnecessary full table scans (similar to indexes in books).

## Unique Constraints

A unique constraint enforces the uniqueness of rows, allowing you to implement the concept of alternate keys from the relational model in your database. Unlike with primary keys, you can define multiple unique constraints within the same table. Also, a unique constraint is not restricted to columns defined as *NOT NULL*. According to standard SQL, a column with a unique constraint is supposed to allow multiple *NULL* marks (as if two *NULL* marks were different from each other). However, SQL Server's implementation rejects duplicate *NULL* marks (as if two *NULL* marks were equal to each other).

The following code defines a unique constraint on the *ssn* column in the *Employees* table.

```
ALTER TABLE dbo.Employees
  ADD CONSTRAINT UNQ_Employees_ssn
  UNIQUE(ssn);
```

As with a primary key constraint, SQL Server will create a unique index behind the scenes as the physical mechanism to enforce the logical unique constraint.

## Foreign Key Constraints

A foreign key enforces referential integrity. This constraint is defined on one or more attributes in what's called the *referencing* table and points to candidate key (primary key or unique constraint) attributes in what's called the *referenced* table. Note that the referencing and referenced tables can be one and the same. The foreign key's purpose is to restrict the values allowed in the foreign key columns to those that exist in the referenced columns.

The following code creates a table called *Orders* with a primary key defined on the *orderid* column.

```
IF OBJECT_ID('dbo.Orders', 'U') IS NOT NULL
  DROP TABLE dbo.Orders;

CREATE TABLE dbo.Orders
(
  orderid   INT           NOT NULL,
  empid     INT           NOT NULL,
  custid    VARCHAR(10)   NOT NULL,
  orderts   DATETIME2     NOT NULL,
  qty       INT           NOT NULL,
  CONSTRAINT PK_Orders
    PRIMARY KEY(orderid)
);
```

Suppose you want to enforce an integrity rule that restricts the values supported by the *empid* column in the *Orders* table to the values that exist in the *empid* column in the *Employees* table. You can achieve this by defining a foreign key constraint on the *empid* column in the *Orders* table pointing to the *empid* column in the *Employees* table, like the following.

```
ALTER TABLE dbo.Orders
  ADD CONSTRAINT FK_Orders_Employees
  FOREIGN KEY(empid)
  REFERENCES dbo.Employees(empid);
```

Similarly, if you want to restrict the values supported by the *mgrid* column in the *Employees* table to the values that exist in the *empid* column of the same table, you can do so by adding the following foreign key.

```
ALTER TABLE dbo.Employees
  ADD CONSTRAINT FK_Employees_Employees
  FOREIGN KEY(mgrid)
  REFERENCES dbo.Employees(empid);
```

Note that NULL marks are allowed in the foreign key columns (*mgrid* in the last example) even if there are no NULL marks in the referenced candidate key columns.

The preceding two examples are basic definitions of foreign keys that enforce a referential action called *no action*. No action means that attempts to delete rows from the referenced table or update the referenced candidate key attributes will be rejected if related rows exist in the referencing table. For example, if you try to delete an employee row from the *Employees* table when there are related orders in the *Orders* table, the RDBMS will reject such an attempt and produce an error.

You can define the foreign key with actions that will compensate for such attempts (to delete rows from the referenced table or update the referenced candidate key attributes when related rows exist in the referencing table). You can define the options *ON DELETE* and *ON UPDATE* with actions such as *CASCADE*, *SET DEFAULT*, and *SET NULL* as part of the foreign key definition. *CASCADE* means that the operation (delete or update) will be cascaded to related rows. For example, *ON DELETE CASCADE* means that when you delete a row from the referenced table, the RDBMS will delete the related rows from the referencing table. *SET DEFAULT* and *SET NULL* mean that the compensating action will set the foreign key attributes of the related rows to the column's default value or *NULL*, respectively. Note that regardless of which action you chose, the referencing table will only have orphaned rows in the case of the exception with *NULL* marks that I mentioned earlier.

## Check Constraints

A check constraint allows you to define a predicate that a row must meet to be entered into the table or to be modified. For example, the following check constraint ensures that the salary column in the *Employees* table will support only positive values.

```
ALTER TABLE dbo.Employees
  ADD CONSTRAINT CHK_Employees_salary
  CHECK(salary > 0.00);
```

An attempt to insert or update a row with a nonpositive salary value will be rejected by the RDBMS. Note that a check constraint rejects an attempt to insert or update a row when the predicate evaluates to *FALSE*. The modification will be accepted when the predicate evaluates to either *TRUE* or *UNKNOWN*. For example, salary –1000 will be rejected, whereas salaries 50000 and *NULL* will both be accepted.

When adding check and foreign key constraints, you can specify an option called *WITH NOCHECK* that tells the RDBMS that you want it to bypass constraint checking for existing data. This is considered a bad practice because you cannot be sure that your data is consistent. You can also disable or enable existing check and foreign key constraints.

## Default Constraints

A default constraint is associated with a particular attribute. It is an expression that is used as the default value when an explicit value is not specified for the attribute when you insert a row. For example, the following code defines a default constraint for the *orderts* attribute (representing the order's time stamp):

```
ALTER TABLE dbo.Orders
  ADD CONSTRAINT DFT_Orders_orderts
  DEFAULT(SYSDATETIME()) FOR orderts;
```

The default expression invokes the *SYSDATETIME* function, which returns the current date and time value. After this default expression is defined, whenever you insert a row in the *Orders* table and do not explicitly specify a value in the *orderts* attribute, SQL Server will set the attribute value to *SYSDATETIME*.

When you're done, run the following code for cleanup.

```
DROP TABLE dbo.Orders, dbo.Employees;
```

# Conclusion

This chapter provided a brief background to T-SQL querying and programming. It presented a theoretical background, explaining the strong foundations that T-SQL is based on. It gave an overview of the SQL Server architecture and concluded with sections that demonstrated how to use T-SQL to create tables and define data integrity. I hope that by now you see that there's something special about SQL, and that it's not just a language that can be learned as an afterthought. This chapter equipped you with fundamental concepts—the actual journey is just about to begin.

# CHAPTER 2

# Single-Table Queries

This chapter introduces you to the fundamentals of the *SELECT* statement, focusing for now on queries against a single table. The chapter starts by describing logical query processing—namely, the series of logical phases involved in producing the correct result set of a particular *SELECT* query. The chapter then covers other aspects of single-table queries, including predicates and operators, *CASE* expressions, *NULL* marks, all-at-once operations, manipulating character data and date and time data, and querying metadata. Many of the code samples and exercises in this book use a sample database called *TSQL2012*. You can find the instructions for downloading and installing this sample database in the Appendix, "Getting Started."

## Elements of the *SELECT* Statement

The purpose of a *SELECT* statement is to query tables, apply some logical manipulation, and return a result. In this section, I talk about the phases involved in logical query processing. I describe the logical order in which the different query clauses are processed, and what happens in each phase.

Note that by "logical query processing," I'm referring to the conceptual way in which standard SQL defines how a query should be processed and the final result achieved. Don't be alarmed if some logical processing phases that I describe here seem inefficient. The Microsoft SQL Server engine doesn't have to follow logical query processing to the letter; rather, it is free to physically process a query differently by rearranging processing phases, as long as the final result would be the same as that dictated by logical query processing. SQL Server can—and in fact, often does—make many shortcuts in the physical processing of a query.

To describe logical query processing and the various *SELECT* query clauses, I use the query in Listing 2-1 as an example.

**LISTING 2-1** Sample Query

```
USE TSQL2012;

SELECT empid, YEAR(orderdate) AS orderyear, COUNT(*) AS numorders
FROM Sales.Orders
WHERE custid = 71
GROUP BY empid, YEAR(orderdate)
HAVING COUNT(*) > 1
ORDER BY empid, orderyear;
```

This query filters orders that were placed by customer 71; groups those orders by employee and order year; and filters only groups of employees and years that have more than one order. For the remaining groups, the query presents the employee ID, order year, and count of orders, sorted by the employee ID and order year. For now, don't worry about understanding how this query does what it does; I'll explain the query clauses one at a time, and gradually build this query.

The code starts with a *USE* statement that ensures that the database context of your session is the *TSQL2012* sample database. If your session is already in the context of the database you need to query, the *USE* statement is not required.

Before getting into the details of each phase of the *SELECT* statement, notice the order in which the query clauses are logically processed. In most programming languages, the lines of code are processed in the order that they are written. In SQL, things are different. Even though the *SELECT* clause appears first in the query, it is logically processed almost last. The clauses are logically processed in the following order:

1. *FROM*

2. *WHERE*

3. *GROUP BY*

4. *HAVING*

5. *SELECT*

6. *ORDER BY*

So even though syntactically the sample query in Listing 2-1 starts with a *SELECT* clause, logically its clauses are processed in the following order.

```
FROM Sales.Orders
WHERE custid = 71
GROUP BY empid, YEAR(orderdate)
HAVING COUNT(*) > 1
SELECT empid, YEAR(orderdate) AS orderyear, COUNT(*) AS numorders
ORDER BY empid, orderyear
```

Or, to present it in a more readable manner, here's what the statement does:

1. Queries the rows *from* the *Sales.Orders* table

2. Filters only orders *where* the customer ID is equal to 71

3. *Groups* the orders *by* employee ID and order year

4. Filters only groups (employee ID and order year) *having* more than one order

5. *Selects* (returns) for each group the employee ID, order year, and number of orders

6. *Orders* (sorts) the rows in the output *by* employee ID and order year

You cannot write the query in correct logical order. You have to start with the *SELECT* clause as shown in Listing 2-1. There's reason behind this discrepancy between the keyed-in order and the logical processing order of the clauses. The designers of SQL envisioned a declarative language with which you provide your request in an English-like manner. Consider an instruction made by one human to another in English, such as, "Bring me the car keys from the top-left drawer in the kitchen." Notice that you start the instruction with the object and then indicate the location where the object resides. But if you were to express the same instruction to a robot, or a computer program, you would have had to start with the location, before indicating what can be obtained from that location. Your instruction would have probably been something like, "Go to the kitchen; open the top-left drawer; grab the car keys; bring them to me." The keyed-in order of the query clauses is similar to English— it starts with the *SELECT* clause. Logical query processing order is similar to how you would provide instructions to a robot—with the *FROM* clause processed first.

Now that you understand the order in which the query clauses are logically processed, the next sections explain the details of each phase.

When discussing logical query processing, I refer to query *clauses* and query *phases*, (the *WHERE* clause and the *WHERE* phase, for example). A query clause is a syntactical component of a query, so when discussing the syntax of a query element I usually use the term *clause*—for example, "In the *WHERE* clause, you specify a predicate." When discussing the logical manipulation taking place as part of logical query processing, I usually use the term *phase*—for example, "The *WHERE* phase returns rows for which the predicate evaluates to *TRUE*."

Recall my recommendation from the previous chapter regarding the use of a semicolon to terminate statements. At the moment, SQL Server doesn't require you to terminate all statements with a semicolon. This is a requirement only in particular cases where the meaning of the code might otherwise be ambiguous. However, I recommend that you terminate all statements with a semicolon because it is standard, it improves the code readability, and it is likely that SQL Server will require this in more—if not all—cases in the future. Currently, when a semicolon is not required, adding one doesn't interfere. Therefore, I recommend that you make it a practice to terminate all statements with a semicolon.

## The *FROM* Clause

The *FROM* clause is the very first query clause that is logically processed. In this clause, you specify the names of the tables that you want to query and table operators that operate on those tables. This chapter doesn't get into table operators; I describe those in Chapters 3, 5, and 7. For now, you can just consider the *FROM* clause to be simply where you specify the name of the table you want to query. The sample query in Listing 2-1 queries the *Orders* table in the *Sales* schema, finding 830 rows.

```
FROM Sales.Orders
```

Recall the recommendation I gave in the previous chapter to always schema-qualify object names in your code. When you don't specify the schema name explicitly, SQL Server must resolve it implicitly based on its implicit name resolution rules. This creates some minor cost and can result in SQL Server choosing a different object than the one you intended. By being explicit, your code is safer in the sense that you ensure that you get the object that you intended to get. Plus, you don't pay any unnecessary penalties.

To return all rows from a table with no special manipulation, all you need is a query with a *FROM* clause in which you specify the table you want to query, and a *SELECT* clause in which you specify the attributes you want to return. For example, the following statement queries all rows from the *Orders* table in the *Sales* schema, selecting the attributes *orderid*, *custid*, *empid*, *orderdate*, and *freight*.

```
SELECT orderid, custid, empid, orderdate, freight
FROM Sales.Orders;
```

The output of this statement is shown here in abbreviated form.

```
orderid      custid       empid        orderdate                      freight
-----------  -----------  -----------  -----------------------------  -------------
10248        85           5            2006-07-04 00:00:00.000        32.38
10249        79           6            2006-07-05 00:00:00.000        11.61
10250        34           4            2006-07-08 00:00:00.000        65.83
10251        84           3            2006-07-08 00:00:00.000        41.34
10252        76           4            2006-07-09 00:00:00.000        51.30
10253        34           3            2006-07-10 00:00:00.000        58.17
10254        14           5            2006-07-11 00:00:00.000        22.98
10255        68           9            2006-07-12 00:00:00.000        148.33
10256        88           3            2006-07-15 00:00:00.000        13.97
10257        35           4            2006-07-16 00:00:00.000        81.91
...

(830 row(s) affected)
```

Although it might seem that the output of the query is returned in a particular order, this is not guaranteed. I'll elaborate on this point later in this chapter, in the sections "The *SELECT* Clause" and "The *ORDER BY* Clause."

## Delimiting Identifier Names

As long as the identifiers in your query comply with rules for the format of regular identifiers, you don't need to delimit the identifier names used for schemas, tables, and columns. The rules for the format of regular identifiers can be found in SQL Server Books Online at the following URL: *http://msdn.microsoft.com/en-us/library/ms175874*. If an identifier is irregular—for example, if it has embedded spaces or special characters, starts with a digit, or is a reserved keyword—you have to delimit it. You can delimit identifiers in SQL Server in a couple of ways. The standard SQL form is to use double quotes—for example, *"Order Details"*. The form specific to SQL Server is to use square brackets—for example, *[Order Details]*, but SQL Server also supports the standard form.

With identifiers that do comply with the rules for the format of regular identifiers, delimiting is optional. For example, a table called *OrderDetails* residing in the *Sales* schema can be referred to as *Sales.OrderDetails* or *"Sales"."OrderDetails"* or *[Sales].[OrderDetails]*. My personal preference is not to use delimiters when they are not required, because they tend to clutter the code. Also, when you're in charge of assigning identifiers, I recommend always using regular ones, for example, *OrderDetails* instead of *Order Details*.

## The *WHERE* Clause

In the *WHERE* clause, you specify a predicate or logical expression to filter the rows returned by the *FROM* phase. Only rows for which the logical expression evaluates to *TRUE* are returned by the *WHERE* phase to the subsequent logical query processing phase. In the sample query in Listing 2-1, the *WHERE* phase filters only orders placed by customer 71.

```
FROM Sales.Orders
WHERE custid = 71
```

Out of the 830 rows returned by the *FROM* phase, the *WHERE* phase filters only the 31 rows where the customer ID is equal to 71. To see which rows you get back after applying the filter *custid = 71*, run the following query.

```
SELECT orderid, empid, orderdate, freight
FROM Sales.Orders
WHERE custid = 71;
```

This query generates the following output.

```
orderid      empid       orderdate                   freight
-----------  ----------  --------------------------  ------------
10324        9           2006-10-08 00:00:00.000     214.27
10393        1           2006-12-25 00:00:00.000     126.56
10398        2           2006-12-30 00:00:00.000     89.16
10440        4           2007-02-10 00:00:00.000     86.53
10452        8           2007-02-20 00:00:00.000     140.26
10510        6           2007-04-18 00:00:00.000     367.63
10555        6           2007-06-02 00:00:00.000     252.49
10603        8           2007-07-18 00:00:00.000     48.77
10607        5           2007-07-22 00:00:00.000     200.24
10612        1           2007-07-28 00:00:00.000     544.08
10627        8           2007-08-11 00:00:00.000     107.46
10657        2           2007-09-04 00:00:00.000     352.69
10678        7           2007-09-23 00:00:00.000     388.98
10700        3           2007-10-10 00:00:00.000     65.10
10711        5           2007-10-21 00:00:00.000     52.41
10713        1           2007-10-22 00:00:00.000     167.05
10714        5           2007-10-22 00:00:00.000     24.49
10722        8           2007-10-29 00:00:00.000     74.58
10748        3           2007-11-20 00:00:00.000     232.55
10757        6           2007-11-27 00:00:00.000     8.19
10815        2           2008-01-05 00:00:00.000     14.62
10847        4           2008-01-22 00:00:00.000     487.57
10882        4           2008-02-11 00:00:00.000     23.10
10894        1           2008-02-18 00:00:00.000     116.13
10941        7           2008-03-11 00:00:00.000     400.81
10983        2           2008-03-27 00:00:00.000     657.54
10984        1           2008-03-30 00:00:00.000     211.22
11002        4           2008-04-06 00:00:00.000     141.16
11030        7           2008-04-17 00:00:00.000     830.75
11031        6           2008-04-17 00:00:00.000     227.22
11064        1           2008-05-01 00:00:00.000     30.09

(31 row(s) affected)
```

The *WHERE* clause has significance when it comes to query performance. Based on what you have in the filter expression, SQL Server evaluates the use of indexes to access the required data. By using indexes, SQL Server can sometimes get the required data with much less work compared to applying full table scans. Query filters also reduce the network traffic created by returning all possible rows to the caller and filtering on the client side.

Earlier, I mentioned that only rows for which the logical expression evaluates to *TRUE* are returned by the *WHERE* phase. Always keep in mind that T-SQL uses three-valued predicate logic, where logical expressions can evaluate to *TRUE*, *FALSE*, or *UNKNOWN*. With three-valued logic, saying "returns *TRUE*" is not the same as saying "does not return *FALSE*." The *WHERE* phase returns rows for which the logical expression evaluates to *TRUE*, and doesn't return rows for which the logical expression evaluates to *FALSE* or *UNKNOWN*. I elaborate on this point later in this chapter in the section "*NULL* Marks."

## The *GROUP BY* Clause

The *GROUP BY* phase allows you to arrange the rows returned by the previous logical query processing phase in groups. The groups are determined by the elements you specify in the *GROUP BY* clause. For example, the *GROUP BY* clause in the query in Listing 2-1 has the elements *empid* and *YEAR(orderdate)*.

```
FROM Sales.Orders
WHERE custid = 71
GROUP BY empid, YEAR(orderdate)
```

This means that the *GROUP BY* phase produces a group for each unique combination of employee ID and order year values that appears in the data returned by the *WHERE* phase. The expression *YEAR(orderdate)* invokes the *YEAR* function to return only the year part from the *orderdate* column.

The *WHERE* phase returned 31 rows, within which there are 16 unique combinations of employee ID and order year values, as shown here.

```
empid       YEAR(orderdate)
----------- ----------------
1           2006
1           2007
1           2008
2           2006
2           2007
2           2008
3           2007
4           2007
4           2008
5           2007
6           2007
6           2008
7           2007
7           2008
8           2007
9           2006
```

Thus the *GROUP BY* phase creates 16 groups, and associates each of the 31 rows returned from the *WHERE* phase with the relevant group.

If the query involves grouping, all phases subsequent to the *GROUP BY* phase—including *HAVING*, *SELECT*, and *ORDER BY*—must operate on groups as opposed to operating on individual rows. Each group is ultimately represented by a single row in the final result of the query. This implies that all expressions that you specify in clauses that are processed in phases subsequent to the *GROUP BY* phase are required to guarantee returning a scalar (single value) per group.

Expressions based on elements that participate in the *GROUP BY* list meet the requirement because by definition each group has only one unique occurrence of each *GROUP BY* element. For example, in the group for employee ID 8 and order year 2007, there's only one unique employee ID value and only one unique order year value. Therefore, you're allowed to refer to the expressions *empid* and *YEAR(orderdate)* in clauses that are processed in phases subsequent to the *GROUP BY* phase, such as the *SELECT* clause. The following query, for example, returns 16 rows for the 16 groups of employee ID and order year values.

```
SELECT empid, YEAR(orderdate) AS orderyear
FROM Sales.Orders
WHERE custid = 71
GROUP BY empid, YEAR(orderdate);
```

This query returns the following output.

```
empid         orderyear
-----------   -----------
1             2006
1             2007
1             2008
2             2006
2             2007
2             2008
3             2007
4             2007
4             2008
5             2007
6             2007
6             2008
7             2007
7             2008
8             2007
9             2006

(16 row(s) affected)
```

Elements that do not participate in the GROUP BY list are allowed only as inputs to an aggregate function such as COUNT, SUM, AVG, MIN, or MAX. For example, the following query returns the total freight and number of orders per each employee and order year.

```
SELECT
  empid,
  YEAR(orderdate) AS orderyear,
  SUM(freight) AS totalfreight,
  COUNT(*) AS numorders
FROM Sales.Orders
WHERE custid = 71
GROUP BY empid, YEAR(orderdate);
```

This query generates the following output.

```
empid       orderyear   totalfreight          numorders
----------- ----------- --------------------- -----------
1           2006        126.56                1
2           2006        89.16                 1
9           2006        214.27                1
1           2007        711.13                2
2           2007        352.69                1
3           2007        297.65                2
4           2007        86.53                 1
5           2007        277.14                3
6           2007        628.31                3
7           2007        388.98                1
8           2007        371.07                4
1           2008        357.44                3
2           2008        672.16                2
4           2008        651.83                3
6           2008        227.22                1
7           2008        1231.56               2
```

```
(16 row(s) affected)
```

The expression SUM(freight) returns the sum of all freight values in each group, and the function COUNT(*) returns the count of rows in each group—which in this case means number of orders. If you try to refer to an attribute that does not participate in the GROUP BY list (such as freight) and not as an input to an aggregate function in any clause that is processed after the GROUP BY clause, you get an error—in such a case, there's no guarantee that the expression will return a single value per group. For example, the following query will fail.

```
SELECT empid, YEAR(orderdate) AS orderyear, freight
FROM Sales.Orders
WHERE custid = 71
GROUP BY empid, YEAR(orderdate);
```

SQL Server produces the following error.

```
Msg 8120, Level 16, State 1, Line 1
Column 'Sales.Orders.freight' is invalid in the select list because it is not contained in
either an aggregate function or the GROUP BY clause.
```

Note that all aggregate functions ignore *NULL* marks with one exception—*COUNT(\*)*. For example, consider a group of five rows with the values *30, 10, NULL, 10, 10* in a column called *qty*. The expression *COUNT(\*)* would return 5 because there are five rows in the group, whereas *COUNT(qty)* would return 4 because there are four known values. If you want to handle only distinct occurrences of known values, specify the *DISTINCT* keyword in the parentheses of the aggregate function. For example, the expression *COUNT(DISTINCT qty)* would return 2, because there are two distinct known values. The *DISTINCT* keyword can be used with other functions as well. For example, although the expression *SUM(qty)* would return 60, the expression *SUM(DISTINCT qty)* would return 40. The expression *AVG(qty)* would return 15, whereas the expression *AVG(DISTINCT qty)* would return 20. As an example of using the *DISTINCT* option with an aggregate function in a complete query, the following code returns the number of distinct (different) customers handled by each employee in each order year.

```
SELECT
  empid,
  YEAR(orderdate) AS orderyear,
  COUNT(DISTINCT custid) AS numcusts
FROM Sales.Orders
GROUP BY empid, YEAR(orderdate);
```

This query generates the following output.

| empid | orderyear | numcusts |
| --- | --- | --- |
| 1 | 2006 | 22 |
| 2 | 2006 | 15 |
| 3 | 2006 | 16 |
| 4 | 2006 | 26 |
| 5 | 2006 | 10 |
| 6 | 2006 | 15 |
| 7 | 2006 | 11 |
| 8 | 2006 | 19 |
| 9 | 2006 | 5 |
| 1 | 2007 | 40 |
| 2 | 2007 | 35 |
| 3 | 2007 | 46 |
| 4 | 2007 | 57 |
| 5 | 2007 | 13 |
| 6 | 2007 | 24 |
| 7 | 2007 | 30 |
| 8 | 2007 | 36 |
| 9 | 2007 | 16 |
| 1 | 2008 | 32 |
| 2 | 2008 | 34 |
| 3 | 2008 | 30 |
| 4 | 2008 | 33 |
| 5 | 2008 | 11 |
| 6 | 2008 | 17 |
| 7 | 2008 | 21 |
| 8 | 2008 | 23 |
| 9 | 2008 | 16 |

(27 row(s) affected)

# The *HAVING* Clause

With the *HAVING* clause, you can specify a predicate to filter groups as opposed to filtering individual rows, which happens in the *WHERE* phase. Only groups for which the logical expression in the *HAVING* clause evaluates to *TRUE* are returned by the *HAVING* phase to the next logical query processing phase. Groups for which the logical expression evaluates to *FALSE* or *UNKNOWN* are filtered out.

Because the *HAVING* clause is processed after the rows have been grouped, you can refer to aggregate functions in the logical expression. For example, in the query from Listing 2-1, the *HAVING* clause has the logical expression *COUNT(\*) > 1*, meaning that the *HAVING* phase filters only groups (employee and order year) with more than one row. The following fragment of the Listing 2-1 query shows the steps that have been processed so far.

```
FROM Sales.Orders
WHERE custid = 71
GROUP BY empid, YEAR(orderdate)
HAVING COUNT(*) > 1
```

Recall that the *GROUP BY* phase created 16 groups of employee ID and order year. Seven of those groups have only one row, so after the *HAVING* clause is processed, nine groups remain. Run the following query to return those nine groups.

```
SELECT empid, YEAR(orderdate) AS orderyear
FROM Sales.Orders
WHERE custid = 71
GROUP BY empid, YEAR(orderdate)
HAVING COUNT(*) > 1;
```

This query returns the following output.

```
empid       orderyear
----------- -----------
1           2007
3           2007
5           2007
6           2007
8           2007
1           2008
2           2008
4           2008
7           2008

(9 row(s) affected)
```

# The *SELECT* Clause

The *SELECT* clause is where you specify the attributes (columns) that you want to return in the result table of the query. You can base the expressions in the *SELECT* list on attributes from the queried tables, with or without further manipulation. For example, the *SELECT* list in Listing 2-1 has the following expressions: *empid*, *YEAR(orderdate)*, and *COUNT(\*)*. If an expression refers to an attribute with no manipulation, such as *empid*, the name of the target attribute is the same as the name of the source attribute. You can optionally assign your own name to the target attribute by using the *AS* clause—for example, *empid AS employee_id*. Expressions that do apply manipulation, such as *YEAR(orderdate)*, or that are not based on a source attribute, such as a call for the function *CURRENT_TIMESTAMP*, don't have a name in the result of the query if you don't alias them. T-SQL allows a query to return result columns with no names in certain cases, but the relational model doesn't. I strongly recommend that you alias such expressions as *YEAR(orderdate) AS orderyear* so that all result attributes have names. In this respect, the result table returned from the query would be considered relational.

In addition to the *AS* clause, T-SQL supports a couple of other forms with which you can alias expressions, but to me, the *AS* clause seems the most readable and intuitive form, and therefore I recommend using it. I will cover the other forms for the sake of completeness and also in order to describe an elusive bug related to one of them. Besides the form *<expression> AS <alias>*, T-SQL also supports the forms *<alias> = <expression>* ("alias equals expression"), and *<expression> <alias>* ("expression space alias"). An example of the former is *orderyear = YEAR(orderdate)*, and an example of the latter is *YEAR(orderdate) orderyear*. I find the latter form, in which you specify the expression followed by a space and the alias, particularly unclear, and I strongly recommend that you avoid using it.

It is interesting to note that if by mistake you don't specify a comma between two column names in the *SELECT* list, your code won't fail. Instead, SQL Server will assume that the second name is an alias for the first column name. As an example, suppose that you wanted to write a query that selects the *orderid* and *orderdate* columns from the *Sales.Orders* table, and by mistake you didn't specify the comma between the column names, as follows.

```
SELECT orderid orderdate
FROM Sales.Orders;
```

This query is considered syntactically valid, as if you intended to alias the *orderid* column as *orderdate*. In the output, you will get only one column holding the order IDs, with the alias *orderdate*.

```
orderdate
-----------
10248
10249
10250
10251
10252
...

(830 row(s) affected)
```

It can be hard to detect such a bug, so the best you can do is to be alert when writing code.

With the addition of the *SELECT* phase, the following query clauses from the query in Listing 2-1 have been processed so far.

```
SELECT empid, YEAR(orderdate) AS orderyear, COUNT(*) AS numorders
FROM Sales.Orders
WHERE custid = 71
GROUP BY empid, YEAR(orderdate)
HAVING COUNT(*) > 1
```

The *SELECT* clause produces the result table of the query. In the case of the query in Listing 2-1, the heading of the result table has the attributes *empid*, *orderyear*, and *numorders*, and the body has nine rows (one for each group). Run the following query to return those nine rows.

```
SELECT empid, YEAR(orderdate) AS orderyear, COUNT(*) AS numorders
FROM Sales.Orders
WHERE custid = 71
GROUP BY empid, YEAR(orderdate)
HAVING COUNT(*) > 1;
```

This query generates the following output.

```
empid       orderyear   numorders
----------- ----------- -----------
1           2007        2
3           2007        2
5           2007        3
6           2007        3
8           2007        4
1           2008        3
2           2008        2
4           2008        3
7           2008        2
```

```
(9 row(s) affected)
```

Remember that the *SELECT* clause is processed after the *FROM, WHERE, GROUP BY,* and *HAVING* clauses. This means that aliases assigned to expressions in the *SELECT* clause do not exist as far as clauses that are processed before the *SELECT* clause are concerned. A very typical mistake made by programmers who are not familiar with the correct logical processing order of query clauses is to refer to expression aliases in clauses that are processed prior to the *SELECT* clause. Here's an example of such an invalid attempt in the *WHERE* clause.

```
SELECT orderid, YEAR(orderdate) AS orderyear
FROM Sales.Orders
WHERE orderyear > 2006;
```

On the surface, this query might seem valid, but if you consider the fact that the column aliases are created in the *SELECT* phase—which is processed after the *WHERE* phase—you can see that the reference to the *orderyear* alias in the *WHERE* clause is invalid. And in fact, SQL Server produces the following error.

```
Msg 207, Level 16, State 1, Line 3
Invalid column name 'orderyear'.
```

One way around this problem is to repeat the expression *YEAR(orderdate)* in both the *WHERE* and the *SELECT* clauses.

```
SELECT orderid, YEAR(orderdate) AS orderyear
FROM Sales.Orders
WHERE YEAR(orderdate) > 2006;
```

It's interesting to note that SQL Server is capable of identifying the repeated use of the same expression—*YEAR(orderdate)*—in the query. The expression only needs to be evaluated or calculated once.

The following query is another example of an invalid reference to a column alias. The query attempts to refer to a column alias in the *HAVING* clause, which is also processed before the *SELECT* clause.

```
SELECT empid, YEAR(orderdate) AS orderyear, COUNT(*) AS numorders
FROM Sales.Orders
WHERE custid = 71
GROUP BY empid, YEAR(orderdate)
HAVING numorders > 1;
```

This query fails with an error saying that the column name *numorders* is invalid. You would also need to repeat the expression *COUNT(\*)* in both clauses.

```
SELECT empid, YEAR(orderdate) AS orderyear, COUNT(*) AS numorders
FROM Sales.Orders
WHERE custid = 71
GROUP BY empid, YEAR(orderdate)
HAVING COUNT(*) > 1;
```

In the relational model, operations on relations are based on relational algebra and result in a relation (a set). In SQL, things are a bit different in the sense that a *SELECT* query is not guaranteed to return a true set—namely, unique rows with no guaranteed order. To begin with, SQL doesn't require a table to qualify as a set. Without a key, uniqueness of rows is not guaranteed, in which case the table isn't a set; it's a multiset or a bag. But even if the tables you query have keys and qualify as sets, a *SELECT* query against the tables can still return a result with duplicate rows. The term "result set" is often used to describe the output of a *SELECT* query, but a result set doesn't necessarily qualify as a set in the mathematical sense. For example, even though the *Orders* table is a set because uniqueness is enforced with a key, a query against the *Orders* table returns duplicate rows, as shown in Listing 2-2.

**LISTING 2-2** Query Returning Duplicate Rows

```
SELECT empid, YEAR(orderdate) AS orderyear
FROM Sales.Orders
WHERE custid = 71;
```

This query generates the following output.

```
empid        orderyear
-----------  -----------
9            2006
1            2006
2            2006
4            2007
8            2007
6            2007
6            2007
8            2007
5            2007
1            2007
8            2007
2            2007
7            2007
3            2007
5            2007
1            2007
5            2007
8            2007
3            2007
6            2007
2            2008
4            2008
4            2008
1            2008
7            2008
2            2008
1            2008
4            2008
7            2008
6            2008
1            2008

(31 row(s) affected)
```

SQL provides the means to guarantee uniqueness in the result of a *SELECT* statement in the form of a *DISTINCT* clause that removes duplicate rows, as shown in Listing 2-3.

**LISTING 2-3** Query with a *DISTINCT* Clause

```
SELECT DISTINCT empid, YEAR(orderdate) AS orderyear
FROM Sales.Orders
WHERE custid = 71;
```

This query generates the following output.

```
empid         orderyear
-----------   -----------
1             2006
1             2007
1             2008
2             2006
2             2007
2             2008
3             2007
4             2007
4             2008
5             2007
6             2007
6             2008
7             2007
7             2008
8             2007
9             2006

(16 row(s) affected)
```

Of the 31 rows in the multiset returned by the query in Listing 2-2, 16 rows are in the set returned by the query in Listing 2-3 after removal of duplicates.

SQL supports the use of an asterisk (*) in the *SELECT* list to request all attributes from the queried tables instead of listing them explicitly, as in the following example.

```
SELECT *
FROM Sales.Shippers;
```

Such use of an asterisk is a bad programming practice in most cases, with very few exceptions. It is recommended that you explicitly specify the list of attributes that you need even if you need all of the attributes from the queried table. There are many reasons for this recommendation. Unlike the relational model, SQL keeps ordinal positions for columns based on the order in which the columns were specified in the *CREATE TABLE* statement. By specifying *SELECT **, you're guaranteed to get the columns back in order based on their ordinal positions. Client applications can refer to columns in the result by their ordinal positions (a bad practice in its own right) instead of by name. Any schema changes applied to the table—such as adding or removing columns, rearranging their order, and so on—might result in failures in the client application, or even worse, in logical bugs that will go un-noticed. By explicitly specifying the attributes that you need, you always get the right ones, as long as the columns exist in the table. If a column referenced by the query was dropped from the table, you get an error and can fix your code accordingly.

Some people wonder whether there's any performance difference between specifying an asterisk and explicitly listing column names. Some extra work may be required in resolving column names when the asterisk is used, but it is usually so negligible compared to other costs involved in the query that it is unlikely to be noticed. If there is any performance difference, as minor as it may be, it is most probably in the favor of explicitly listing column names. Because that's the recommended practice anyway, it's a win-win situation.

Within the *SELECT* clause, you are still not allowed to refer to a column alias that was created in the same *SELECT* clause, regardless of whether the expression that assigns the alias appears to the left or right of the expression that attempts to refer to it. For example, the following attempt is invalid.

```
SELECT orderid,
  YEAR(orderdate) AS orderyear,
  orderyear + 1 AS nextyear
FROM Sales.Orders;
```

I'll explain the reason for this restriction later in this chapter, in the section, "All-at-Once Operations." As explained earlier in this section, one of the ways around this problem is to repeat the expression.

```
SELECT orderid,
  YEAR(orderdate) AS orderyear,
  YEAR(orderdate) + 1 AS nextyear
FROM Sales.Orders;
```

## The *ORDER BY* Clause

The *ORDER BY* clause allows you to sort the rows in the output for presentation purposes. In terms of logical query processing, *ORDER BY* is the very last clause to be processed. The sample query shown in Listing 2-4 sorts the rows in the output by employee ID and order year.

**LISTING 2-4** Query Demonstrating the *ORDER BY* Clause

```
SELECT empid, YEAR(orderdate) AS orderyear, COUNT(*) AS numorders
FROM Sales.Orders
WHERE custid = 71
GROUP BY empid, YEAR(orderdate)
HAVING COUNT(*) > 1
ORDER BY empid, orderyear;
```

This query generates the following output.

```
empid       orderyear   numorders
----------- ----------- -----------
1           2007        2
1           2008        3
2           2008        2
3           2007        2
4           2008        3
5           2007        3
6           2007        3
7           2008        2
8           2007        4

(9 row(s) affected)
```

This time, presentation ordering in the output is guaranteed—unlike with queries that don't have a presentation *ORDER BY* clause.

One of the most important points to understand about SQL is that a table has no guaranteed order, because a table is supposed to represent a set (or multiset, if it has duplicates), and a set has no order. This means that when you query a table without specifying an *ORDER BY* clause, the query returns a table result, and SQL Server is free to return the rows in the output in any order. The only way for you to guarantee that the rows in the result are sorted is to explicitly specify an *ORDER BY* clause. However, if you do specify an *ORDER BY* clause, the result cannot qualify as a table, because the order of the rows in the result is guaranteed. A query with an *ORDER BY* clause results in what standard SQL calls a cursor—a nonrelational result with order guaranteed among rows. You're probably wondering why it matters whether a query returns a table result or a cursor. Some language elements and operations in SQL expect to work with table results of queries and not with cursors; examples include table expressions and set operators, which I cover in detail in Chapter 5, "Table Expressions," and in Chapter 6, "Set Operators."

Notice that the *ORDER BY* clause refers to the column alias *orderyear*, which was created in the *SELECT* phase. The *ORDER BY* phase is in fact the only phase in which you can refer to column aliases created in the *SELECT* phase, because it is the only phase that is processed after the *SELECT* phase. Note that if you define a column alias that is the same as an underlying column name, as in *1 - col1 AS col1*, and refer to that alias in the *ORDER BY* clause, the new column is the one that is considered for ordering.

When you want to sort by an expression in ascending order, you either specify *ASC* right after the expression, as in *orderyear ASC*, or don't specify anything after the expression, because *ASC* is the default. If you want to sort in descending order, you need to specify *DESC* after the expression, as in *orderyear DESC*.

T-SQL allows you to specify ordinal positions of columns in the *ORDER BY* clause, based on the order in which the columns appear in the *SELECT* list. For example, in the query in Listing 2-4, instead of using:

```
ORDER BY empid, orderyear
```

you could use:

```
ORDER BY 1, 2
```

However, this is considered bad programming practice for a couple of reasons. First, in the relational model, attributes don't have ordinal positions and need to be referred to by name. Second, when you make revisions to the *SELECT* clause, you might forget to make the corresponding revisions in the *ORDER BY* clause. When you use column names, your code is safe from this type of mistake.

T-SQL allows you to specify elements in the *ORDER BY* clause that do not appear in the *SELECT* clause, meaning that you can sort by something that you don't necessarily want to return in the output. For example, the following query sorts the employee rows by hire date without returning the *hiredate* attribute.

```
SELECT empid, firstname, lastname, country
FROM HR.Employees
ORDER BY hiredate;
```

However, when *DISTINCT* is specified, you are restricted in the *ORDER BY* list only to elements that appear in the *SELECT* list. The reasoning behind this restriction is that when *DISTINCT* is specified, a single result row might represent multiple source rows; therefore, it might not be clear which of the multiple possible values in the *ORDER BY* expression should be used. Consider the following invalid query.

```
SELECT DISTINCT country
FROM HR.Employees
ORDER BY empid;
```

There are nine employees in the *Employees* table—five from the United States and four from the United Kingdom. If you omit the invalid *ORDER BY* clause from this query, you get two rows back—one for each distinct country. Because each country appears in multiple rows in the source table, and each such row has a different employee ID, the meaning of *ORDER BY empid* is not really defined.

# The *TOP* and *OFFSET-FETCH* Filters

Earlier in this chapter, I covered filters that are based on the predicates *WHERE* and *HAVING*. In this section, I cover filters that are based on number of rows and ordering. I'll start with a filter called *TOP* that has been supported in SQL Server for quite some time—since version 7.0. Then I'll introduce a new filter called *OFFSET-FETCH* that was introduced in SQL Server 2012.

## The *TOP* Filter

The *TOP* option is a proprietary T-SQL feature that allows you to limit the number or percentage of rows that your query returns. It relies on two elements as part of its specification; one is the number or percent of rows to return, and the other is the ordering. For example, to return from the *Orders* table the five most recent orders, you would specify *TOP (5)* in the *SELECT* clause and *orderdate DESC* in the *ORDER BY* clause, as shown in Listing 2-5.

**LISTING 2-5** Query Demonstrating the *TOP* Option

```
SELECT TOP (5) orderid, orderdate, custid, empid
FROM Sales.Orders
ORDER BY orderdate DESC;
```

This query returns the following output.

```
orderid     orderdate                     custid      empid
----------- ----------------------------- ----------- -----------
11077       2008-05-06 00:00:00.000       65          1
11076       2008-05-06 00:00:00.000       9           4
11075       2008-05-06 00:00:00.000       68          8
11074       2008-05-06 00:00:00.000       73          7
11073       2008-05-05 00:00:00.000       58          2

(5 row(s) affected)
```

Remember that the *ORDER BY* clause is evaluated after the *SELECT* clause, which includes the *DISTINCT* option. The same is true with *TOP*, which relies on *ORDER BY* to give it its filtering-related meaning. This means that if *DISTINCT* is specified in the *SELECT* clause, the *TOP* filter is evaluated after duplicate rows have been removed.

It's also important to note that when *TOP* is specified, the *ORDER BY* clause serves a dual purpose in the query. One purpose is to define presentation ordering for the rows in the query result. Another purpose is to define which rows to filter for *TOP*. For example, the query in Listing 2-5 returns the five rows with the highest *orderdate* values and presents the rows in the output in *orderdate DESC* ordering.

If you're confused about whether a *TOP* query returns a table result or a cursor, you have every reason to be. Normally, a query with an *ORDER BY* clause returns a cursor—not a relational result. But what if you need to filter rows with *TOP* based on some ordering, but still return a relational result? Also, what if you need to filter rows with *TOP* based on one order, but present the output rows in another order? To achieve this, you have to use a table expression, but I'll save the discussion of table expressions for Chapter 5, "Table Expressions." All I want to say for now is that if the design of the *TOP* option seems confusing, there's a good reason. In other words, it's not you—it's the feature's design.

You can use the *TOP* option with the *PERCENT* keyword, in which case SQL Server calculates the number of rows to return based on a percentage of the number of qualifying rows, rounded up. For example, the following query requests the top 1 percent of the most recent orders.

```
SELECT TOP (1) PERCENT orderid, orderdate, custid, empid
FROM Sales.Orders
ORDER BY orderdate DESC;
```

This query generates the following output.

```
orderid     orderdate                     custid      empid
----------- ----------------------------- ----------- -----------
11074       2008-05-06 00:00:00.000       73          7
11075       2008-05-06 00:00:00.000       68          8
11076       2008-05-06 00:00:00.000       9           4
11077       2008-05-06 00:00:00.000       65          1
11070       2008-05-05 00:00:00.000       44          2
11071       2008-05-05 00:00:00.000       46          1
11072       2008-05-05 00:00:00.000       20          4
11073       2008-05-05 00:00:00.000       58          2
11067       2008-05-04 00:00:00.000       17          1

(9 row(s) affected)
```

The query returns nine rows because the *Orders* table has 830 rows, and 1 percent of 830, rounded up, is 9.

In the query in Listing 2-5, you might have noticed that the *ORDER BY* list is not unique because no primary key or unique constraint is defined on the *orderdate* column. Multiple rows can have the same order date. In a case in which no tiebreaker is specified, ordering among rows with the same order date is undefined. This fact makes the query nondeterministic—more than one result can be considered correct. In case of ties, SQL Server determines order of rows based on whichever row it physically happens to access first. Note that you are even allowed to use *TOP* in a query without an *ORDER BY* clause, and then the ordering is completely undefined—SQL Server returns whichever *n* rows it happens to physically access first, where *n* is the number of requested rows.

Notice in the output for the query in Listing 2-5 that the minimum order date in the rows returned is May 5, 2008, and one row in the output has that date. Other rows in the table might have the same order date, and with the existing non-unique *ORDER BY* list, there is no guarantee which of those will be returned.

If you want the query to be deterministic, you need to make the *ORDER BY* list unique; in other words, add a tiebreaker. For example, you can add *orderid DESC* to the *ORDER BY* list as shown in Listing 2-6 so that, in case of ties, the row with the greater order ID will be preferred.

**LISTING 2-6** Query Demonstrating *TOP* with Unique *ORDER BY* List

```
SELECT TOP (5) orderid, orderdate, custid, empid
FROM Sales.Orders
ORDER BY orderdate DESC, orderid DESC;
```

This query returns the following output.

```
orderid     orderdate                        custid       empid
----------- -------------------------------- ----------- -----------
11077       2008-05-06 00:00:00.000          65           1
11076       2008-05-06 00:00:00.000          9            4
11075       2008-05-06 00:00:00.000          68           8
11074       2008-05-06 00:00:00.000          73           7
11073       2008-05-05 00:00:00.000          58           2

(5 row(s) affected)
```

If you examine the results of the queries from Listing 2-5 and Listing 2-6, you'll notice that they seem to be the same. The important difference is that the result shown in the query output for Listing 2-5 is one of several possible valid results for this query, whereas the result shown in the query output for Listing 2-6 is the only possible valid result.

Instead of adding a tiebreaker to the *ORDER BY* list, you can request to return all ties. For example, besides the five rows that you get back from the query in Listing 2-5, you can ask to return all other rows from the table that have the same sort value (order date, in this case) as the last one found (May 5, 2008, in this case). You achieve this by adding the *WITH TIES* option, as shown in the following query.

```
SELECT TOP (5) WITH TIES orderid, orderdate, custid, empid
FROM Sales.Orders
ORDER BY orderdate DESC;
```

This query returns the following output.

```
orderid     orderdate                 custid      empid
----------- ------------------------- ----------- -----------
11077       2008-05-06 00:00:00.000   65          1
11076       2008-05-06 00:00:00.000   9           4
11075       2008-05-06 00:00:00.000   68          8
11074       2008-05-06 00:00:00.000   73          7
11073       2008-05-05 00:00:00.000   58          2
11072       2008-05-05 00:00:00.000   20          4
11071       2008-05-05 00:00:00.000   46          1
11070       2008-05-05 00:00:00.000   44          2
```

```
(8 row(s) affected)
```

Notice that the output has eight rows, even though you specified *TOP (5)*. SQL Server first returned the *TOP (5)* rows based on *orderdate DESC* ordering, and also all other rows from the table that had the same *orderdate* value as in the last of the five rows that was accessed.

## The OFFSET-FETCH Filter

The *TOP* option is a very practical type of filter, but it has two shortcomings—it's not standard, and it doesn't support skipping capabilities. Standard SQL defines a *TOP*-like filter called *OFFSET-FETCH* that does support skipping capabilities, and this makes it very useful for ad-hoc paging purposes. SQL Server 2012 introduces support for the *OFFSET-FETCH* filter.

The *OFFSET-FETCH* filter in SQL Server 2012 is considered part of the *ORDER BY* clause, which normally serves a presentation ordering purpose. By using the *OFFSET* clause, you can indicate how many rows to skip, and by using the *FETCH* clause, you can indicate how many rows to filter after the skipped rows. As an example, consider the following query.

```
SELECT orderid, orderdate, custid, empid
FROM Sales.Orders
ORDER BY orderdate, orderid
OFFSET 50 ROWS FETCH NEXT 25 ROWS ONLY;
```

The query orders the rows from the *Orders* table based on *orderdate*, *orderid* ordering (from least to most recent, with *orderid* as the tiebreaker). Based on this ordering, the *OFFSET* clause skips the first 50 rows, and the *FETCH* clause filters the next 25 rows only.

Note that a query that uses *OFFSET-FETCH* must have an *ORDER BY* clause. Also, the *FETCH* clause isn't supported without an *OFFSET* clause. If you do not want to skip any rows but do want to filter with *FETCH*, you must indicate that by using *OFFSET 0 ROWS*. However, *OFFSET* without *FETCH* is allowed. In such a case, the query skips the indicated number of rows and returns all remaining rows in the result.

There are interesting language aspects to note about the syntax for *OFFSET-FETCH*. The singular and plural forms *ROW* and *ROWS* are interchangeable. The idea is to allow you to phrase the filter in an intuitive English-like manner. For example, suppose you wanted to fetch only one row; though it would be syntactically valid, it would nevertheless look strange if you specified *FETCH 1 ROWS*. Therefore, you're allowed to use the form *FETCH 1 ROW*. The same applies to the *OFFSET* clause. Also, if you're not skipping any rows (*OFFSET 0 ROWS*), you may find the term "first" more suitable than "next." Hence, the forms *FIRST* and *NEXT* are interchangeable.

As you can see, the *OFFSET-FETCH* clause is more flexible than *TOP* in the sense that it supports skipping capabilities. However, *OFFSET-FETCH* doesn't support the *PERCENT* and *WITH TIES* options that *TOP* does. Because *OFFSET-FETCH* is standard and *TOP* isn't, I recommend using *OFFSET-FETCH* as your default choice, unless you need the capabilities that *TOP* supports and *OFFSET-FETCH* doesn't.

## A Quick Look at Window Functions

A window function is a function that, for each row in the underlying query, operates on a window (set) of rows and computes a scalar (single) result value. The window of rows is defined by using an *OVER* clause. Window functions are very profound and allow you to address a wide variety of needs. There are several categories of window functions that SQL Server supports, and each category supports several different functions. However, at this point in the book, it could be premature to get into too much detail. So for now, I'll provide just a glimpse of the concept, and demonstrate it by using the *ROW_NUMBER* window function. Later in the book, in Chapter 7, "Beyond the Fundamentals of Querying," I provide more details.

As mentioned, a window function operates on a set of rows exposed to it by a clause called *OVER*. For each row in the underlying query, the *OVER* clause exposes to the function a subset of the rows from the underlying query's result set. The *OVER* clause can restrict the rows in the window by using the *PARTITION BY* subclause, and it can define ordering for the calculation (if relevant) by using the *ORDER BY* subclause (not to be confused with the query's presentation *ORDER BY* clause).

Consider the following query as an example.

```
SELECT orderid, custid, val,
  ROW_NUMBER() OVER(PARTITION BY custid
                    ORDER BY val) AS rownum
FROM Sales.OrderValues
ORDER BY custid, val;
```

This query generates the following output.

```
orderid       custid        val             rownum
-----------   -----------   -------------   -------
10702         1             330.00          1
10952         1             471.20          2
10643         1             814.50          3
10835         1             845.80          4
10692         1             878.00          5
11011         1             933.50          6
10308         2             88.80           1
10759         2             320.00          2
10625         2             479.75          3
10926         2             514.40          4
10682         3             375.50          1
...

(830 row(s) affected)
```

The *ROW_NUMBER* function assigns unique, sequential, incrementing integers to the rows in the result within the respective partition, based on the indicated ordering. The *OVER* clause in the example function partitions the window by the *custid* attribute, hence the row numbers are unique to each customer. The *OVER* clause also defines ordering in the window by the *val* attribute, so the sequential row numbers are incremented within the partition based on *val*.

Note that the *ROW_NUMBER* function must produce unique values within each partition. This means that even when the ordering value doesn't increase, the row number still must increase. Therefore, if the *ROW_NUMBER* function's *ORDER BY* list is non-unique, as in the preceding example, the query is nondeterministic. That is, more than one correct result is possible. If you want to make a row number calculation deterministic, you must add elements to the *ORDER BY* list to make it unique. For example, you can add the *orderid* attribute as a tiebreaker to the *ORDER BY* list to make the row number calculation deterministic.

As mentioned, the *ORDER BY* specified in the *OVER* clause should not be confused with presentation and does not change the nature of the result from being relational. If you do not specify a presentation *ORDER BY* in the query, as explained earlier, you don't have any guarantees in terms of the order of the rows in the output. If you need to guarantee presentation ordering, you have to add a presentation *ORDER BY* clause, as I did in the last query.

Note that expressions in the *SELECT* list are evaluated before the *DISTINCT* clause (if one exists). This applies to expressions based on window functions that appear in the *SELECT* list. I explain the significance of this in Chapter 7.

To put it all together, the following list presents the logical order in which all clauses discussed so far are processed:

- *FROM*
- *WHERE*
- *GROUP BY*
- *HAVING*
- *SELECT*
  - Expressions
  - *DISTINCT*
- *ORDER BY*
  - *TOP / OFFSET-FETCH*

# Predicates and Operators

T-SQL has language elements in which predicates can be specified—for example, query filters such as *WHERE* and *HAVING*, *CHECK* constraints, and others. Remember that predicates are logical expressions that evaluate to *TRUE*, *FALSE*, or *UNKNOWN*. You can combine predicates by using logical operators such as *AND* and *OR*. You can also involve other types of operators, such as comparison operators, in your expressions.

Examples of predicates supported by T-SQL include *IN*, *BETWEEN*, and *LIKE*. The *IN* predicate allows you to check whether a value, or scalar expression, is equal to at least one of the elements in a set. For example, the following query returns orders in which the order ID is equal to 10248, 10249, or 10250.

```
SELECT orderid, empid, orderdate
FROM Sales.Orders
WHERE orderid IN(10248, 10249, 10250);
```

The *BETWEEN* predicate allows you to check whether a value is in a specified range, inclusive of the two specified boundary values. For example, the following query returns all orders in the inclusive range 10300 through 10310.

```
SELECT orderid, empid, orderdate
FROM Sales.Orders
WHERE orderid BETWEEN 10300 AND 10310;
```

The *LIKE* predicate allows you to check whether a character string value meets a specified pattern. For example, the following query returns employees whose last names start with D.

```
SELECT empid, firstname, lastname
FROM HR.Employees
WHERE lastname LIKE N'D%';
```

Later in this chapter, I'll elaborate on pattern matching and the *LIKE* predicate.

Notice the use of the letter *N* to prefix the string *'D%'*; it stands for *National* and is used to denote that a character string is of a Unicode data type (*NCHAR* or *NVARCHAR*), as opposed to a regular character data type (*CHAR* or *VARCHAR*). Because the data type of the *lastname* attribute is *NVARCHAR(40)*, the letter *N* is used to prefix the string. Later in this chapter, in the section "Working with Character Data," I elaborate on the treatment of character strings.

T-SQL supports the following comparison operators: =, >, <, >=, <=, <>, !=, !>, !<, of which the last three are not standard. Because the nonstandard operators have standard alternatives (such as <> instead of !=), I recommend that you avoid the use of the nonstandard operators. For example, the following query returns all orders placed on or after January 1, 2008.

```
SELECT orderid, empid, orderdate
FROM Sales.Orders
WHERE orderdate >= '20080101';
```

If you need to combine logical expressions, you can use the logical operators *OR* and *AND*. If you want to negate an expression, you can use the *NOT* operator. For example, the following query returns orders that were placed on or after January 1, 2008, and that were handled by one of the employees whose ID is 1, 3, or 5.

```
SELECT orderid, empid, orderdate
FROM Sales.Orders
WHERE orderdate >= '20080101'
  AND empid IN(1, 3, 5);
```

T-SQL supports the four obvious arithmetic operators: +, −, *, and /, and also the % operator (modulo), which returns the remainder of integer division. For example, the following query calculates the net value as a result of arithmetic manipulation of the *quantity*, *unitprice*, and *discount* attributes.

```
SELECT orderid, productid, qty, unitprice, discount,
  qty * unitprice * (1 - discount) AS val
FROM Sales.OrderDetails;
```

Note that the data type of a scalar expression involving two operands is determined in T-SQL by the higher of the two in terms of data type precedence. If both operands are of the same data type, the result of the expression is of the same data type as well. For example, a division between two integers (*INT*) yields an integer. The expression 5/2 returns the integer 2 and not the numeric 2.5. This is not a problem when you are dealing with constants, because you can always specify the values as numeric ones with a decimal point. But when you are dealing with, say, two integer columns, as in *col1/col2*, you need to cast the operands to the appropriate type if you want the calculation to be a numeric one: *CAST(col1 AS NUMERIC(12, 2))/CAST(col2 AS NUMERIC(12, 2))*. The data type *NUMERIC(12, 2)* has a precision of 12 and a scale of 2, meaning that it has 12 digits in total, 2 of which are after the decimal point.

If the two operands are of different types, the one with the lower precedence is promoted to the one that is higher. For example, in the expression 5/2.0, the first operand is *INT* and the second is *NUMERIC*. Because *NUMERIC* is considered higher than *INT*, the *INT* operand 5 is implicitly converted to the *NUMERIC* 5.0 before the arithmetic operation, and you get the result 2.5.

You can find the precedence order among types in SQL Server Books Online under "Data Type Precedence."

When multiple operators appear in the same expression, SQL Server evaluates them based on operator precedence rules. The following list describes the precedence among operators, from highest to lowest:

1.  ( ) (Parentheses)

2.  * (Multiplication), / (Division), % (Modulo)

3.  + (Positive), – (Negative), + (Addition), + (Concatenation), – (Subtraction)

4.  =, >, <, >=, <=, <>, !=, !>, !< (Comparison operators)

5.  *NOT*

6.  *AND*

7.  *BETWEEN, IN, LIKE, OR*

8.  = (Assignment)

For example, in the following query, *AND* has precedence over *OR*.

```
SELECT orderid, custid, empid, orderdate
FROM Sales.Orders
WHERE
        custid = 1
  AND empid IN(1, 3, 5)
  OR  custid = 85
  AND empid IN(2, 4, 6);
```

The query returns orders that were either "placed by customer 1 and handled by employees 1, 3, or 5" or "placed by customer 85 and handled by employees 2, 4, or 6."

Parentheses have the highest precedence, so they give you full control. For the sake of other people who need to review or maintain your code and for readability purposes, it's a good practice to use parentheses even when they are not required. The same is true for indentation. For example, the following query is the logical equivalent of the previous query, only its logic is much clearer.

```
SELECT orderid, custid, empid, orderdate
FROM Sales.Orders
WHERE
      (custid = 1
        AND empid IN(1, 3, 5))
   OR
      (custid = 85
        AND empid IN(2, 4, 6));
```

Using parentheses to force precedence with logical operators is similar to using parentheses with arithmetic operators. For example, without parentheses in the following expression, multiplication precedes addition.

```
SELECT 10 + 2 * 3;
```

Therefore, this expression returns 16. You can use parentheses to force the addition to be calculated first.

```
SELECT (10 + 2) * 3;
```

This time, the expression returns 36.

# *CASE* Expressions

A *CASE* expression is a scalar expression that returns a value based on conditional logic. Note that *CASE* is an expression and not a statement; that is, it doesn't let you control flow of activity or do something based on conditional logic. Instead, the value it returns is based on conditional logic. Because *CASE* is a scalar expression, it is allowed wherever scalar expressions are allowed, such as in the *SELECT*, *WHERE*, *HAVING*, and *ORDER BY* clauses and in *CHECK* constraints.

The two forms of *CASE* expression are *simple* and *searched*. The simple form allows you to compare one value or scalar expression with a list of possible values and return a value for the first match. If no value in the list is equal to the tested value, the *CASE* expression returns the value that appears in the *ELSE* clause (if one exists). If a *CASE* expression doesn't have an *ELSE* clause, it defaults to *ELSE NULL*.

For example, the following query against the *Production.Products* table uses a *CASE* expression In the *SELECT* clause to produce the description of the *categoryid* column value.

```
SELECT productid, productname, categoryid,
  CASE categoryid
    WHEN 1 THEN 'Beverages'
    WHEN 2 THEN 'Condiments'
    WHEN 3 THEN 'Confections'
    WHEN 4 THEN 'Dairy Products'
    WHEN 5 THEN 'Grains/Cereals'
    WHEN 6 THEN 'Meat/Poultry'
    WHEN 7 THEN 'Produce'
    WHEN 8 THEN 'Seafood'
    ELSE 'Unknown Category'
  END AS categoryname
FROM Production.Products;
```

This query produces the following output, shown in abbreviated form.

```
productid    productname          categoryid   categoryname
-----------  -------------------  -----------  ----------------
1            Product HHYDP        1            Beverages
2            Product RECZE        1            Beverages
3            Product IMEHJ        2            Condiments
4            Product KSBRM        2            Condiments
5            Product EPEIM        2            Condiments
6            Product VAIIV        2            Condiments
7            Product HMLNI        7            Produce
8            Product WVJFP        2            Condiments
9            Product AOZBW        6            Meat/Poultry
10           Product YHXGE        8            Seafood
...
```

(77 row(s) affected)

The preceding query is a simple example of using the *CASE* expression. Unless the set of categories is very small and static, your best design choice is probably to maintain (for example) the product categories in a table, and join that table with the *Products* table when you need to get the category descriptions. In fact, the *TSQL2012* database has just such a *Categories* table.

The simple *CASE* form has a single test value or expression right after the *CASE* keyword that is compared with a list of possible values in the *WHEN* clauses. The searched *CASE* form is more flexible because it allows you to specify predicates, or logical expressions, in the *WHEN* clauses rather than restricting you to equality comparisons. The searched *CASE* expression returns the value in the *THEN* clause that is associated with the first *WHEN* logical expression that evaluates to *TRUE*. If none of the *WHEN* expressions evaluates to *TRUE*, the *CASE* expression returns the value that appears in the *ELSE* clause (or *NULL* if an *ELSE* clause is not specified). For example, the following query produces a value category description based on whether the value is less than 1,000.00, between 1,000.00 and 3,000.00, or greater than 3,000.00.

```
SELECT orderid, custid, val,
  CASE
    WHEN val < 1000.00                      THEN 'Less than 1000'
    WHEN val BETWEEN 1000.00 AND 3000.00 THEN 'Between 1000 and 3000'
    WHEN val > 3000.00                      THEN 'More than 3000'
    ELSE 'Unknown'
  END AS valuecategory
FROM Sales.OrderValues;
```

This query generates the following output.

```
orderid      custid       val       valuecategory
-----------  -----------  --------  ----------------------
10248        85           440.00    Less than 1000
10249        79           1863.40   Between 1000 and 3000
10250        34           1552.60   Between 1000 and 3000
10251        84           654.06    Less than 1000
10252        76           3597.90   More than 3000
10253        34           1444.80   Between 1000 and 3000
10254        14           556.62    Less than 1000
```

```
10255      68       2490.50  Between 1000 and 3000
10256      88       517.80   Less than 1000
10257      35       1119.90  Between 1000 and 3000
. . .
```

```
(830 row(s) affected)
```

You can see that every simple *CASE* expression can be converted to the searched *CASE* form, but the reverse is not necessarily true.

T-SQL supports some functions that you can consider as abbreviations of the *CASE* expression: *ISNULL, COALESCE, IIF*, and *CHOOSE*. Note that of the four, only *COALESCE* is standard. Also, *IIF* and *CHOOSE* are available only in SQL Server 2012.

The *ISNULL* function accepts two arguments as input and returns the first that is not *NULL*, or *NULL* if both are *NULL*. For example *ISNULL(col1, '')* returns the *col1* value if it isn't *NULL*, and an empty string if it is *NULL*. The *COALESCE* function is similar, only it supports two or more arguments and returns the first that isn't *NULL*, or *NULL* if all are *NULL*. As mentioned earlier, when there's a choice, it is generally recommended that you use standard features, hence it is recommended that you use the *COALESCE* function and not *ISNULL*.

The nonstandard *IIF* and *CHOOSE* functions were added in SQL Server 2012 to support easier migrations from Microsoft Access. The function *IIF(<logical_expression>, <expr1>, <expr2>)* returns *expr1* if *logical_expression* is *TRUE* and *expr2* otherwise. For example, the expression *IIF(col1 <> 0, col2/col1, NULL)* returns the result of *col2/col1* if *col1* is not zero, otherwise it returns a *NULL*. The function *CHOOSE(<index>, <expr1>, <expr2>, ..., <exprn>)* returns the expression from the list in the specified index. For example, the expression *CHOOSE(3, col1, col2, col3)* returns the value of *col3*. Of course, actual expressions that use the *CHOOSE* function tend to be more dynamic—for example, relying on user input.

So far, I've just used a few examples to familiarize you with the *CASE* expression and functions that can be considered abbreviations of the *CASE* expression. Even though it might not be apparent at this point from these examples, the *CASE* expression is an extremely powerful and useful language element.

# *NULL* Marks

As explained in Chapter 1, "Background to T-SQL Querying and Programming," SQL supports the *NULL* mark to represent missing values and uses three-valued logic, meaning that predicates can evaluate to *TRUE*, *FALSE*, or *UNKNOWN*. T-SQL follows the standard in this respect. Treatment of *NULL* marks and *UNKNOWN* in SQL can be very confusing because intuitively people are more accustomed to thinking in terms of two-valued logic (*TRUE* and *FALSE*). To add to the confusion, different language elements in SQL treat *NULL* marks and *UNKNOWN* differently.

Let's start with three-valued predicate logic. A logical expression involving only existing or present values evaluates to either *TRUE* or *FALSE*, but when the logical expression involves a missing value, it evaluates to *UNKNOWN*. For example, consider the predicate *salary > 0*. When *salary* is equal to 1,000, the expression evaluates to *TRUE*. When *salary* is equal to –1,000, the expression evaluates to *FALSE*. When *salary* is *NULL*, the expression evaluates to *UNKNOWN*.

SQL treats *TRUE* and *FALSE* in an intuitive and probably expected manner. For example, if the predicate *salary > 0* appears in a query filter (such as in a *WHERE* or *HAVING* clause), rows or groups for which the expression evaluates to *TRUE* are returned, whereas those for which the expression evaluates to *FALSE* are filtered out. Similarly, if the predicate *salary > 0* appears in a *CHECK* constraint in a table, *INSERT* or *UPDATE* statements for which the expression evaluates to *TRUE* for all rows are accepted, whereas those for which the expression evaluates to *FALSE* for any row are rejected.

SQL has different treatments for *UNKNOWN* in different language elements (and for some people, not necessarily the expected treatments). The correct definition of the treatment SQL has for query filters is "accept *TRUE*," meaning that both *FALSE* and *UNKNOWN* are filtered out. Conversely, the definition of the treatment SQL has for *CHECK* constraints is "reject FALSE," meaning that both *TRUE* and *UNKNOWN* are accepted. If SQL used two-valued predicate logic, there wouldn't be a difference between the definitions "accept *TRUE*" and "reject *FALSE*." But with three-valued predicate logic, "accept *TRUE*" rejects *UNKNOWN* (it accepts only *TRUE*, hence it rejects both *FALSE* and *UNKNOWN*), whereas "reject *FALSE*" accepts it (it rejects only *FALSE*, hence it accepts both *TRUE* and *UNKNOWN*). With the predicate *salary > 0* from the previous example, a *NULL* salary would cause the expression to evaluate to *UNKNOWN*. If this predicate appears in a query's *WHERE* clause, a row with a *NULL* salary will be filtered out. If this predicate appears in a *CHECK* constraint in a table, a row with a *NULL* salary will be accepted.

One of the tricky aspects of *UNKNOWN* is that when you negate it, you still get *UNKNOWN*. For example, given the predicate *NOT (salary > 0)*, when salary is *NULL*, *salary > 0* evaluates to *UNKNOWN*, and *NOT UNKNOWN* remains *UNKNOWN*.

What some people find surprising is that an expression comparing two *NULL* marks (*NULL = NULL*) evaluates to *UNKNOWN*. The reasoning for this from SQL's perspective is that a *NULL* represents a missing or unknown value, and you can't really tell whether one unknown value is equal to another. Therefore, SQL provides you with the predicates *IS NULL* and *IS NOT NULL*, which you should use instead of *= NULL* and *<> NULL*.

To make things a bit more tangible, I'll demonstrate the aforementioned aspects of the three-valued predicate logic. The *Sales.Customers* table has three attributes called *country*, *region*, and *city*, where the customer's location information is stored. All locations have existing countries and cities. Some have existing regions (such as *country*: USA, *region*: WA, *city*: Seattle), yet for some the *region* element is missing and inapplicable (such as *country*: UK, *region*: NULL, *city*: London). Consider the following query, which attempts to return all customers where the region is equal to WA.

```
SELECT custid, country, region, city
FROM Sales.Customers
WHERE region = N'WA';
```

This query generates the following output.

```
custid       country          region           city
-----------  ---------------  ---------------  ---------------
43           USA              WA               Walla Walla
82           USA              WA               Kirkland
89           USA              WA               Seattle
```

Out of the 91 rows in the *Customers* table, the query returns the three rows where the *region* attribute is equal to WA. The query returns neither rows in which the value in the *region* attribute is present and different than WA (the predicate evaluates to *FALSE*) nor those where the *region* attribute is *NULL* (the predicate evaluates to *UNKNOWN*).

The following query attempts to return all customers for whom the region is different than WA.

```
SELECT custid, country, region, city
FROM Sales.Customers
WHERE region <> N'WA';
```

This query generates the following output:

```
custid        country           region           city
-----------   ---------------   ---------------   ---------------
10            Canada            BC                Tsawassen
15            Brazil            SP                Sao Paulo
21            Brazil            SP                Sao Paulo
31            Brazil            SP                Campinas
32            USA               OR                Eugene
33            Venezuela         DF                Caracas
34            Brazil            RJ                Rio de Janeiro
35            Venezuela         Táchira           San Cristóbal
36            USA               OR                Elgin
37            Ireland           Co. Cork          Cork
38            UK                Isle of Wight     Cowes
42            Canada            BC                Vancouver
45            USA               CA                San Francisco
46            Venezuela         Lara              Barquisimeto
47            Venezuela         Nueva Esparta     I. de Margarita
48            USA               OR                Portland
51            Canada            Québec            Montréal
55            USA               AK                Anchorage
61            Brazil            RJ                Rio de Janeiro
62            Brazil            SP                Sao Paulo
65            USA               NM                Albuquerque
67            Brazil            RJ                Rio de Janeiro
71            USA               ID                Boise
75            USA               WY                Lander
77            USA               OR                Portland
78            USA               MT                Butte
81            Brazil            SP                Sao Paulo
88            Brazil            SP                Resende

(28 row(s) affected)
```

If you expected to get 88 rows back (91 rows in the table minus 3 returned by the previous query), you might find the fact that this query returned only 28 rows surprising. But remember, a query filter "accepts *TRUE*," meaning that it rejects both rows for which the logical expression evaluates to *FALSE* and those for which it evaluates to *UNKNOWN*. So this query returned rows in which a value was present in the *region* attribute and that value was different than WA. It returned neither rows in which the *region* attribute was equal to WA nor rows in which *region* was *NULL*. You will get the same output if you use the predicate *NOT (region = N'WA')* because in the rows where *region* is *NULL* and the expression *region = N'WA'* evaluates to *UNKNOWN*, *NOT (region = N'WA')* evaluates to *UNKNOWN* also.

If you want to return all rows for which *region* is *NULL*, do not use the predicate *region = NULL*, because the expression evaluates to *UNKNOWN* in all rows—both those in which the value is present and those in which the value is missing (is *NULL*). The following query returns an empty set.

```
SELECT custid, country, region, city
FROM Sales.Customers
WHERE region = NULL;
```

```
custid      country         region          city
----------- --------------- --------------- ---------------
```

(0 row(s) affected)

Instead, you should use the *IS NULL* predicate.

```
SELECT custid, country, region, city
FROM Sales.Customers
WHERE region IS NULL;
```

This query generates the following output, shown in abbreviated form.

```
custid      country         region          city
----------- --------------- --------------- ---------------
1           Germany         NULL            Berlin
2           Mexico          NULL            México D.F.
3           Mexico          NULL            México D.F.
4           UK              NULL            London
5           Sweden          NULL            Luleå
6           Germany         NULL            Mannheim
7           France          NULL            Strasbourg
8           Spain           NULL            Madrid
9           France          NULL            Marseille
11          UK              NULL            London
...
```

(60 row(s) affected)

If you want to return all rows for which the *region* attribute is not WA, including those in which the value is present and different than WA, along with those in which the value is missing, you need to include an explicit test for *NULL* marks, like this.

```
SELECT custid, country, region, city
FROM Sales.Customers
WHERE region <> N'WA'
   OR region IS NULL;
```

This query generates the following output, shown in abbreviated form.

```
custid      country         region          city
----------- --------------- --------------- ---------------
1           Germany         NULL            Berlin
2           Mexico          NULL            México D.F.
3           Mexico          NULL            México D.F.
4           UK              NULL            London
```

| 5  | Sweden  | NULL | Luleå      |
|----|---------|------|------------|
| 6  | Germany | NULL | Mannheim   |
| 7  | France  | NULL | Strasbourg |
| 8  | Spain   | NULL | Madrid     |
| 9  | France  | NULL | Marseille  |
| 10 | Canada  | BC   | Tsawassen  |
| ...|         |      |            |

(88 row(s) affected)

SQL also treats *NULL* marks inconsistently in different language elements for comparison and sorting purposes. Some elements treat two *NULL* marks as equal to each other and others treat them as different.

For example, for grouping and sorting purposes, two *NULL* marks are considered equal. That is, the *GROUP BY* clause arranges all *NULL* marks in one group just like present values, and the *ORDER BY* clause sorts all *NULL* marks together. Standard SQL leaves it to the product implementation as to whether *NULL* marks sort before present values or after. T-SQL sorts *NULL* marks before present values.

As mentioned earlier, query filters "accept *TRUE*." An expression comparing two *NULL* marks yields *UNKNOWN*; therefore, such a row is filtered out.

For the purposes of enforcing a *UNIQUE* constraint, standard SQL treats *NULL* marks as different from each other (allowing multiple *NULL* marks). Conversely, in T-SQL, a *UNIQUE* constraint considers two *NULL* marks as equal (allowing only one *NULL* if the constraint is defined on a single column).

Keeping in mind the inconsistent treatment SQL has for *UNKNOWN* and *NULL* marks and the potential for logical errors, you should explicitly think of *NULL* marks and three-valued logic in every query that you write. If the default treatment is not what you want, you must intervene explicitly; otherwise, just ensure that the default behavior is in fact what you want.

# All-at-Once Operations

SQL supports a concept called *all-at-once operations*, which means that all expressions that appear in the same logical query processing phase are evaluated logically at the same point in time.

This concept explains why, for example, you cannot refer to column aliases assigned in the *SELECT* clause within the same *SELECT* clause, even if it seems intuitively that you should be able to. Consider the following query.

```
SELECT
  orderid,
  YEAR(orderdate) AS orderyear,
  orderyear + 1 AS nextyear
FROM Sales.Orders;
```

The reference to the column alias *orderyear* in the third expression in the *SELECT* list is invalid, even though the referencing expression appears "after" the one in which the alias is assigned. The reason is that logically there is no order of evaluation of the expressions in the *SELECT* list—the list is a set of expressions. At the logical level, all expressions in the *SELECT* list are evaluated at the same point in time. Therefore, this query generates the following error.

```
Msg 207, Level 16, State 1, Line 4
Invalid column name 'orderyear'.
```

Here's another example of the relevance of all-at-once operations: Suppose you have a table called *T1* with two integer columns called *col1* and *col2*, and you want to return all rows for which *col2/col1* is greater than 2. Because there may be rows in the table for which *col1* is equal to zero, you need to ensure that the division doesn't take place in those cases—otherwise, the query fails because of a divide-by-zero error. So you write a query using the following format.

```
SELECT col1, col2
FROM dbo.T1
WHERE col1 <> 0 AND col2/col1 > 2;
```

You might very well assume that SQL Server evaluates the expressions from left to right, and that if the expression *col1 <> 0* evaluates to *FALSE*, SQL Server will short-circuit; that is, it doesn't bother to evaluate the expression *10/col1 > 2* because at this point it is known that the whole expression is *FALSE*. So you might think that this query never produces a divide-by-zero error.

SQL Server does support short circuits, but because of the all-at-once operations concept in standard SQL, SQL Server is free to process the expressions in the *WHERE* clause in any order. SQL Server usually makes decisions like this based on cost estimations, meaning that typically the expression that is cheaper to evaluate is evaluated first. You can see that if SQL Server decides to process the expression *10/col1 > 2* first, this query might fail because of a divide-by-zero error.

You have several ways to avoid a failure here. For example, the order in which the *WHEN* clauses of a *CASE* expression are evaluated is guaranteed. So you could revise the query as follows.

```
SELECT col1, col2
FROM dbo.T1
WHERE
  CASE
    WHEN col1 = 0 THEN 'no' -- or 'yes' if row should be returned
    WHEN col2/col1 > 2 THEN 'yes'
    ELSE 'no'
  END = 'yes';
```

In rows where *col1* is equal to zero, the first *WHEN* clause evaluates to *TRUE* and the *CASE* expression returns the string *'no'* (replace *'no'* with *'yes'* if you want to return the row when *col1* is equal to zero). Only if the first *CASE* expression does not evaluate to *TRUE*—meaning that *col1* is not 0—does the second *WHEN* clause check whether the expression *col2/col1 > 2* evaluates to *TRUE*. If it does, the *CASE* expression returns the string *'yes.'* In all other cases, the *CASE* expression returns the string *'no.'* The predicate in the *WHERE* clause returns *TRUE* only when the result of the *CASE* expression is equal to the string *'yes'*. This means that there will never be an attempt here to divide by zero.

This workaround turned out to be quite convoluted. In this particular case, you can use a mathematical workaround that avoids division altogether.

```
SELECT col1, col2
FROM dbo.T1
WHERE (col1 > 0 AND col2 > 2*col1) OR (col1 < 0 AND col2 < 2*col1);
```

I included this example to explain the unique and important concept of all-at-once operations and to elaborate on the fact that SQL Server guarantees the processing order of the *WHEN* clauses in a *CASE* expression.

# Working with Character Data

In this section, I cover query manipulation of character data, including data types, collation, operators and functions, and pattern matching.

## Data Types

SQL Server supports two kinds of character data types—regular and Unicode. Regular data types include *CHAR* and *VARCHAR*, and Unicode data types include *NCHAR* and *NVARCHAR*. Regular characters use one byte of storage for each character, whereas Unicode data requires two bytes per character, and in cases in which a surrogate pair is needed, four bytes are required. If you choose a regular character type for a column, you are restricted to only one language in addition to English. The language support for the column is determined by the column's effective collation, which I'll describe shortly. With Unicode data types, multiple languages are supported. So if you store character data in multiple languages, make sure that you use Unicode character types and not regular ones.

The two kinds of character data types also differ in the way in which literals are expressed. When expressing a regular character literal, you simply use single quotes: *'This is a regular character string literal'*. When expressing a Unicode character literal, you need to specify the character *N* (for *National*) as a prefix: *N'This is a Unicode character string literal'*.

Any data type without the *VAR* element (*CHAR*, *NCHAR*) in its name has a fixed length, which means that SQL Server preserves space in the row based on the column's defined size and not on the actual number of characters in the character string. For example, when a column is defined as *CHAR(25)*, SQL Server preserves space for 25 characters in the row regardless of the length of the stored character string. Because no expansion of the row is required when the strings are expanded, fixed-length data types are more suited for write-focused systems. But because storage consumption is not optimal with fixed-length strings, you pay more when reading data.

A data type with the *VAR* element (*VARCHAR*, *NVARCHAR*) in its name has a variable length, which means that SQL Server uses as much storage space in the row as required to store the characters that appear in the character string, plus two extra bytes for offset data. For example, when a column is defined as *VARCHAR(25)*, the maximum number of characters supported is 25, but in practice, the actual number of characters in the string determines the amount of storage. Because storage consumption for these data types is less than that for fixed-length types, read operations are faster. However, updates might result in row expansion, which might result in data movement outside the current page. Therefore, updates of data having variable-length data types are less efficient than updates of data having fixed-length data types.

> **Note** If compression is used, the storage requirements change. For details about compression, see "Data Compression" in SQL Server Books Online at *http://msdn.microsoft.com /en-us/library/cc280449.aspx*.

You can also define the variable-length data types with the *MAX* specifier instead of a maximum number of characters. When the column is defined with the *MAX* specifier, any value with a size up to a certain threshold (8,000 bytes by default) can be stored inline in the row (as long as it can fit in the row). Any value with a size above the threshold is stored external to the row as a large object (LOB).

Later in this chapter, in the "Querying Metadata" section, I explain how you can obtain metadata information about objects in the database, including the data types of columns.

## Collation

Collation is a property of character data that encapsulates several aspects, including language support, sort order, case sensitivity, accent sensitivity, and more. To get the set of supported collations and their descriptions, you can query the table function *fn_helpcollations* as follows.

```
SELECT name, description
FROM sys.fn_helpcollations();
```

For example, the following list explains the collation *Latin1_General_CI_AS*:

- **Latin1_General**   Code page 1252 is used. (This supports English and German characters, as well as characters used by most Western European countries.)

- **Dictionary sorting**   Sorting and comparison of character data are based on dictionary order (A and a < B and b).

  You can tell that dictionary order is used because that's the default when no other ordering is defined explicitly. More specifically, the element *BIN* doesn't explicitly appear in the collation name. If the element *BIN* appeared, it would mean that sorting and comparison of character data was based on the binary representation of characters (A < B < a < b).

- **CI**   The data is case insensitive (a = A).

- **AS**   The data is accent sensitive (à <> ä).

In an on-premises SQL Server implementation, collation can be defined at four different levels: instance, database, column, and expression. The lowest effective level is the one that should be used. In Windows Azure SQL Database, collation can be indicated at the database, column, and expression levels.

The collation of the instance is chosen as part of the setup program. It determines the collations of all system databases and is used as the default for user databases.

When you create a user database, you can specify a collation for the database by using the *COLLATE* clause. If you don't, the instance's collation is assumed by default.

The database collation determines the collation of the metadata of objects in the database and is used as the default for user table columns. I want to emphasize the importance of the fact that the database collation determines the collation of the metadata, including object and column names. For example, if the database collation is case insensitive, you can't create two tables called *T1* and *t1* within the same schema, but if the database collation is case sensitive, you can.

You can explicitly specify a collation for a column as part of its definition by using the *COLLATE* clause. If you don't, the database collation is assumed by default.

You can convert the collation of an expression by using the *COLLATE* clause. For example, in a case-insensitive environment, the following query uses a case-insensitive comparison.

```
SELECT empid, firstname, lastname
FROM HR.Employees
WHERE lastname = N'davis';
```

The following query returns the row for Sara Davis, even though the casing doesn't match, because the effective casing is insensitive.

```
empid       firstname  lastname
----------- ---------- --------------------
1           Sara       Davis
```

If you want to make the filter case sensitive even though the column's collation is case insensitive, you can convert the collation of the expression.

```
SELECT empid, firstname, lastname
FROM HR.Employees
WHERE lastname COLLATE Latin1_General_CS_AS = N'davis';
```

This time the query returns an empty set because no match is found when a case-sensitive comparison is used.

## Quoted Identifiers

In standard SQL, single quotes are used to delimit literal character strings (for example, *'literal'*) and double quotes are used to delimit irregular identifiers such as table or column names that include a space or start with a digit (for example, *"Irregular Identifier"*). In SQL Server, there's a setting called *QUOTED_IDENTIFIER* that controls the meaning of double quotes. You can apply this setting either at the database level by using the *ALTER DATABASE* command or at the session level by using the *SET* command. When the setting is turned on, the behavior is according to standard SQL, meaning that double quotes are used to delimit identifiers. When the setting is turned off, the behavior is nonstandard, and double quotes are used to delimit literal character strings. It is strongly recommended that you follow best practices and use standard behavior (with the setting on). Most database interfaces, including OLEDB and ODBC, turn this setting on by default.

> **Tip** As an alternative to using double quotes to delimit identifiers, SQL Server also supports square brackets (for example, *[Irregular Identifier]*).

Regarding single quotes that are used to delimit literal character strings, if you want to incorporate a single quote character as part of the string, you need to specify two single quotes. For example, to express the literal *abc'de*, specify **'abc''de'**.

## Operators and Functions

This section covers string concatenation and functions that operate on character strings. For string concatenation, T-SQL provides the + operator and the *CONCAT* function. For other operations on character strings, T-SQL provides several functions, including *SUBSTRING, LEFT, RIGHT, LEN, DATALENGTH, CHARINDEX, PATINDEX, REPLACE, REPLICATE, STUFF, UPPER, LOWER, RTRIM, LTRIM*, and *FORMAT*. In the following sections, I describe these commonly used operators and functions.

### String Concatenation (Plus Sign [+] Operator and *CONCAT* Function)

T-SQL provides the plus sign (+) operator and the *CONCAT* function (in SQL Server 2012) to concatenate strings. For example, the following query against the *Employees* table produces the *fullname* result column by concatenating *firstname*, a space, and *lastname*.

```
SELECT empid, firstname + N' ' + lastname AS fullname
FROM HR.Employees;
```

This query produces the following output.

```
empid       fullname
----------- -------------------------------
1           Sara Davis
2           Don Funk
3           Judy Lew
4           Yael Peled
5           Sven Buck
6           Paul Suurs
7           Russell King
8           Maria Cameron
9           Zoya Dolgopyatova
```

Standard SQL dictates that a concatenation with a *NULL* should yield a *NULL*. This is the default behavior of SQL Server. For example, consider the query against the *Customers* table shown in Listing 2-7.

**LISTING 2-7** Query Demonstrating String Concatenation

```
SELECT custid, country, region, city,
   country + N',' + region + N',' + city AS location
FROM Sales.Customers;
```

Some of the rows in the *Customers* table have a *NULL* in the region column. For those, SQL Server returns by default a *NULL* in the location result column.

```
custid      country         region city             location
----------- --------------- ------ ---------------- --------------------
1           Germany         NULL   Berlin           NULL
2           Mexico          NULL   México D.F.      NULL
3           Mexico          NULL   México D.F.      NULL
4           UK              NULL   London           NULL
5           Sweden          NULL   Luleå            NULL
6           Germany         NULL   Mannheim         NULL
7           France          NULL   Strasbourg       NULL
8           Spain           NULL   Madrid           NULL
9           France          NULL   Marseille        NULL
10          Canada          BC     Tsawassen        Canada,BC,Tsawassen
11          UK              NULL   London           NULL
12          Argentina       NULL   Buenos Aires     NULL
13          Mexico          NULL   México D.F.      NULL
14          Switzerland     NULL   Bern             NULL
15          Brazil          SP     Sao Paulo        Brazil,SP,Sao Paulo
16          UK              NULL   London           NULL
17          Germany         NULL   Aachen           NULL
18          France          NULL   Nantes           NULL
19          UK              NULL   London           NULL
20          Austria         NULL   Graz             NULL
...

(91 row(s) affected)
```

To treat a *NULL* as an empty string—or more accurately, to substitute a *NULL* with an empty string—you can use the *COALESCE* function. This function accepts a list of input values and returns the first that is not *NULL*. Here's how you can revise the query from Listing 2-7 to programmatically substitute *NULL* marks with empty strings.

```
SELECT custid, country, region, city,
  country + COALESCE( N',' + region, N'') + N',' + city AS location
FROM Sales.Customers;
```

SQL Server 2012 introduces a new function called *CONCAT* that accepts a list of inputs for concatenation and automatically substitutes NULL marks with empty strings. For example, the expression *CONCAT('a', NULL, 'b')* returns the string 'ab'.

Here's how to use the *CONCAT* function to concatenate the customer's location elements, replacing *NULL* marks with empty strings.

```
SELECT custid, country, region, city,
  CONCAT(country, N',' + region, N',' + city) AS location
FROM Sales.Customers;
```

## The *SUBSTRING* Function

The *SUBSTRING* function extracts a substring from a string.

### Syntax

SUBSTRING(*string*, *start*, *length*)

This function operates on the input *string* and extracts a substring starting at position *start* that is *length* characters long. For example, the following code returns the output 'abc'.

```
SELECT SUBSTRING('abcde', 1, 3);
```

If the value of the third argument exceeds the end of the input string, the function returns everything until the end without raising an error. This can be convenient when you want to return everything from a certain point until the end of the string—you can simply specify the maximum length of the data type or a value representing the full length of the input string.

## The *LEFT* and *RIGHT* Functions

The *LEFT* and *RIGHT* functions are abbreviations of the *SUBSTRING* function, returning a requested number of characters from the left or right end of the input string.

**Syntax**

LEFT(*string*, *n*), RIGHT(*string*, *n*)

The first argument, *string*, is the string the function operates on. The second argument, *n*, is the number of characters to extract from the left or right end of the string. For example, the following code returns the output 'cde'.

```
SELECT RIGHT('abcde', 3);
```

## The *LEN* and *DATALENGTH* Functions

The *LEN* function returns the number of characters in the input string.

**Syntax**

LEN(*string*)

Note that this function returns the number of characters in the input string and not necessarily the number of bytes. With regular characters, both numbers are the same because each character requires one byte of storage. With Unicode characters, each character requires two bytes of storage (in most cases, at least); therefore, the number of characters is half the number of bytes. To get the number of bytes, use the *DATALENGTH* function instead of *LEN*. For example, the following code returns 5.

```
SELECT LEN(N'abcde');
```

The following code returns 10.

```
SELECT DATALENGTH(N'abcde');
```

Another difference between *LEN* and *DATALENGTH* is that the former excludes trailing blanks but the latter doesn't.

## The *CHARINDEX* Function

The *CHARINDEX* function returns the position of the first occurrence of a substring within a string.

**Syntax**

CHARINDEX(*substring*, *string*[, *start_pos*])

This function returns the position of the first argument, *substring*, within the second argument, *string*. You can optionally specify a third argument, *start_pos*, to tell the function the position from which to start looking. If you don't specify the third argument, the function starts looking from the first character. If the substring is not found, the function returns 0. For example, the following code returns the first position of a space in *'Itzik Ben-Gan'*, so it returns the output 6.

```
SELECT CHARINDEX(' ','Itzik Ben-Gan');
```

## The *PATINDEX* Function

The *PATINDEX* function returns the position of the first occurrence of a pattern within a string.

### Syntax

PATINDEX(*pattern, string*)

The argument *pattern* uses similar patterns to those used by the *LIKE* predicate in T-SQL. I'll explain patterns and the *LIKE* predicate later in this chapter, in "The *LIKE* Predicate." Even though I haven't explained yet how patterns are expressed in T-SQL, I include the following example here to show how to find the position of the first occurrence of a digit within a string.

```
SELECT PATINDEX('%[0-9]%', 'abcd123efgh');
```

This code returns the output 5.

## The *REPLACE* Function

The *REPLACE* function replaces all occurrences of a substring with another.

### Syntax

REPLACE(*string, substring1, substring2*)

The function replaces all occurrences of *substring1* in *string* with *substring2*. For example, the following code substitutes all occurrences of a dash in the input string with a colon.

```
SELECT REPLACE('1-a 2-b', '-', ':');
```

This code returns the output: '1:a 2:b'.

You can use the *REPLACE* function to count the number of occurrences of a character within a string. To do this, you replace all occurrences of the character with an empty string (zero characters) and calculate the original length of the string minus the new length. For example, the following query returns, for each employee, the number of times the character *e* appears in the *lastname* attribute.

```
SELECT empid, lastname,
  LEN(lastname) - LEN(REPLACE(lastname, 'e', '')) AS numoccur
FROM HR.Employees;
```

This query generates the following output.

```
empid        lastname              numoccur
-----------  --------------------  -----------
5            Buck                  0
8            Cameron               1
1            Davis                 0
9            Dolgopyatova          0
2            Funk                  0
7            King                  0
3            Lew                   1
4            Peled                 2
6            Suurs                 0
```

## The *REPLICATE* Function

The *REPLICATE* function replicates a string a requested number of times.

**Syntax**

REPLICATE(*string*, *n*)

For example, the following code replicates the string 'abc' three times, returning the string 'abcabcabc'.

```
SELECT REPLICATE('abc', 3);
```

The next example demonstrates the use of the *REPLICATE* function, along with the *RIGHT* function and string concatenation. The following query against the *Production.Suppliers* table generates a 10-digit string representation of the supplier ID integer with leading zeros.

```
SELECT supplierid,
  RIGHT(REPLICATE('0', 9) + CAST(supplierid AS VARCHAR(10)), 10) AS strsupplierid
FROM Production.Suppliers;
```

The expression producing the result column *strsupplierid* replicates the character *0* nine times (producing the string '000000000') and concatenates the string representation of the supplier ID to form the result. The string representation of the supplier ID integer is produced by the *CAST* function, which is used to convert the data type of the input value. Finally, the expression extracts the 10 rightmost characters of the result string, returning the 10-digit string representation of the supplier ID with leading zeros. Here's the output of this query, shown in abbreviated form.

```
supplierid  strsupplierid
----------  -------------
29          0000000029
28          0000000028
4           0000000004
21          0000000021
2           0000000002
22          0000000022
14          0000000014
11          0000000011
25          0000000025
7           0000000007
...

(29 row(s) affected)
```

Note that SQL Server 2012 introduces a new function called *FORMAT* that allows you to achieve such formatting needs much more easily. I'll describe it later in this section.

## The *STUFF* Function

The *STUFF* function allows you to remove a substring from a string and insert a new substring instead.

### Syntax

STUFF(*string, pos, delete_length, insertstring*)

This function operates on the input parameter *string*. It deletes as many characters as the number specified in the *delete_length* parameter, starting at the character position specified in the *pos* input parameter. The function inserts the string specified in the *insertstring* parameter in position *pos*. For example, the following code operates on the string ' xyz', removes one character from the second character, and inserts the substring 'abc' instead.

```
SELECT STUFF('xyz', 2, 1, 'abc');
```

The output of this code is 'xabcz'.

If you just want to insert a string and not delete anything, you can specify a length of 0 as the third argument.

## The *UPPER* and *LOWER* Functions

The *UPPER* and *LOWER* functions return the input string with all uppercase or lowercase characters, respectively.

### Syntax

UPPER(*string*), LOWER(*string*)

For example, the following code returns 'ITZIK BEN-GAN'.

```
SELECT UPPER('Itzik Ben-Gan');
```

The following code returns 'itzik ben-gan'.

```
SELECT LOWER('Itzik Ben-Gan');
```

## The *RTRIM* and *LTRIM* Functions

The *RTRIM* and *LTRIM* functions return the input string with leading or trailing spaces removed.

### Syntax

RTRIM(*string*), LTRIM(*string*)

If you want to remove both leading and trailing spaces, use the result of one function as the input to the other. For example, the following code removes both leading and trailing spaces from the input string, returning 'abc'.

```
SELECT RTRIM(LTRIM('   abc   '));
```

## The *FORMAT* Function

The *FORMAT* function allows you to format an input value as a character string based on a Microsoft .NET format string and an optional culture.

### Syntax

FORMAT(*input* , *format_string*, *culture*)

There are numerous possibilities for formatting inputs using both standard and custom format strings. The MSDN article at *http://go.microsoft.com/fwlink/?LinkId=211776* provides more information. But just as a simple example, recall the convoluted expression used earlier to format a number as a 10-digit string with leading zeros. By using *FORMAT*, you can achieve the same task with either the custom form string '0000000000' or the standard one, 'd10'. As an example, the following code returns '0000001759'.

```
SELECT FORMAT(1759, '000000000');
```

# The *LIKE* Predicate

T-SQL provides a predicate called *LIKE* that allows you to check whether a character string matches a specified pattern. Similar patterns are used by the *PATINDEX* function described earlier. The following section describes the wildcards supported in the patterns and demonstrates their use.

## The % (Percent) Wildcard

The percent sign represents a string of any size, including an empty string. For example, the following query returns employees where the last name starts with *D*.

```
SELECT empid, lastname
FROM HR.Employees
WHERE lastname LIKE N'D%';
```

This query returns the following output.

```
empid       lastname
----------- --------------------
1           Davis
9           Dolgopyatova
```

Note that often you can use functions such as *SUBSTRING* and *LEFT* instead of the *LIKE* predicate to represent the same meaning. But the *LIKE* predicate tends to get optimized better—especially when the pattern starts with a known prefix.

## The _ (Underscore) Wildcard

An underscore represents a single character. For example, the following query returns employees where the second character in the last name is *e*.

```
SELECT empid, lastname
FROM HR.Employees
WHERE lastname LIKE N'_e%';
```

This query returns the following output.

```
empid       lastname
----------- --------------------
3           Lew
4           Peled
```

## The [<*List of Characters*>] Wildcard

Square brackets with a list of characters (such as *[ABC]*) represent a single character that must be one of the characters specified in the list. For example, the following query returns employees where the first character in the last name is *A*, *B*, or *C*.

```
SELECT empid, lastname
FROM HR.Employees
WHERE lastname LIKE N'[ABC]%';
```

This query returns the following output.

```
empid       lastname
----------- --------------------
5           Buck
8           Cameron
```

## The [<*Character*>-<*Character*>] Wildcard

Square brackets with a character range (such as *[A-E]*) represent a single character that must be within the specified range. For example, the following query returns employees where the first character in the last name is a letter in the range *A* through *E*.

```
SELECT empid, lastname
FROM HR.Employees
WHERE lastname LIKE N'[A-E]%';
```

This query returns the following output.

```
empid       lastname
----------- --------------------
5           Buck
8           Cameron
1           Davis
9           Dolgopyatova
```

### The [^<*Character List or Range*>] Wildcard

Square brackets with a caret sign (^) followed by a character list or range (such as *[^A-E]*) represent a single character that is not in the specified character list or range. For example, the following query returns employees where the first character in the last name is not a letter in the range *A* through *E*.

```
SELECT empid, lastname
FROM HR.Employees
WHERE lastname LIKE N'[^A-E]%';
```

This query returns the following output.

```
empid       lastname
----------- --------------------
2           Funk
7           King
3           Lew
4           Peled
6           Suurs
```

### The *ESCAPE* Character

If you want to search for a character that is also used as a wildcard, (such as %, _, [, or ]), you can use an escape character. Specify a character that you know for sure doesn't appear in the data as the escape character in front of the character you are looking for, and specify the keyword *ESCAPE* followed by the escape character right after the pattern. For example, to check whether a column called *col1* contains an underscore, use *col1 LIKE '%!_%' ESCAPE '!'*.

For the wildcards %, _, and [ you can use square brackets instead of an escape character. For example, instead of *col1 LIKE '%!_%' ESCAPE '!'* you can use *col1 LIKE '%[_]%'*.

# Working with Date and Time Data

Working with date and time data in SQL Server is not trivial. You will face several challenges in this area, such as expressing literals in a language-neutral manner and working with date and time separately.

In this section, I first introduce the date and time data types supported by SQL Server; then I explain the recommended way to work with those types; and finally I cover date-related and time-related functions.

## Date and Time Data Types

Prior to SQL Server 2008, SQL Server supported two date and time data types called *DATETIME* and *SMALLDATETIME*. Both types include date and time components that are inseparable. The two data types differ in their storage requirements, their supported date range, and their accuracy. SQL Server 2008 introduced separate *DATE* and *TIME* data types, as well as *DATETIME2*, which has a bigger date range and better accuracy than *DATETIME*; and *DATETIMEOFFSET*, which also has a time zone offset component. Table 2-1 lists details about date and time data types, including storage requirements, supported date range, accuracy, and recommended entry format.

**TABLE 2-1** Date and Time Data Types

| Data Type | Storage (bytes) | Date Range | Accuracy | Recommended Entry Format and Example |
|---|---|---|---|---|
| *DATETIME* | 8 | January 1, 1753, through December 31, 9999 | 3 1/3 milliseconds | 'YYYYMMDD hh:mm:ss.nnn' '20090212 12:30:15.123' |
| *SMALLDATETIME* | 4 | January 1, 1900, through June 6, 2079 | 1 minute | ''YYYYMMDD hh:mm' '20090212 12:30' |
| *DATE* | 3 | January 1, 0001, through December 31, 9999 | 1 day | 'YYYY-MM-DD' '2009-02-12' |
| *TIME* | 3 to 5 | N/A | 100 nanoseconds | 'hh:mm:ss.nnnnnnn' '12:30:15.1234567' |
| *DATETIME2* | 6 to 8 | January 1, 0001, through December 31, 9999 | 100 nanoseconds | 'YYYY-MM-DD hh:mm:ss.nnnnnnn' '2009-02-12 12:30:15.1234567' |
| *DATETIMEOFFSET* | 8 to 10 | January 1, 0001, through December 31, 9999 | 100 nanoseconds | 'YYYY-MM-DD hh:mm:ss.nnnnnnn [+\|-] hh:mm' '2009-02-12 12:30:15.1234567 +02:00' |

The storage requirements for the last three data types in Table 2-1 (*TIME*, *DATETIME2*, and *DATETIMEOFFSET*) depend on the precision you choose. You specify the precision as an integer in the range 0 to 7 representing the fractional-second precision. For example, *TIME(0)* means 0 fractional-second precision—in other words, one-second precision. *TIME(3)* means one-millisecond precision, and *TIME(7)* means 100-nanosecond accuracy. If you don't specify a fractional-second precision, SQL Server assumes 7 by default with all three aforementioned types.

# Literals

When you need to specify a literal (constant) of a date and time data type, you should consider several things. First, though it might sound a bit strange, SQL Server doesn't provide the means to express a date and time literal; instead, it allows you to specify a literal of a different type that can be converted—explicitly or implicitly—to a date and time data type. It is a best practice to use character strings to express date and time values, as shown in the following example.

```
SELECT orderid, custid, empid, orderdate
FROM Sales.Orders
WHERE orderdate = '20070212';
```

SQL Server recognizes the literal '20070212' as a character string literal and not as a date and time literal, but because the expression involves operands of two different types, one operand needs to be implicitly converted to the other's type. Normally, implicit conversion between types is based on what's called *data type precedence*. SQL Server defines precedence among data types and will usually implicitly convert the operand that has a lower data type precedence to the one that has higher precedence.

In this example, the character string literal is converted to the column's data type (*DATETIME*) because character strings are considered lower in terms of data type precedence with respect to date and time data types. Implicit conversion rules are not always that simple, and in fact different rules are applied with filters and in other expressions, but for the purposes of this discussion, I'll keep things simple. For the complete description of data type precedence, see "Data Type Precedence" in SQL Server Books Online.

The point I'm trying to make is that in the preceding example, implicit conversion takes place behind the scenes. This query is logically equivalent to the following one, which explicitly converts the character string to a *DATETIME* data type.

```
SELECT orderid, custid, empid, orderdate
FROM Sales.Orders
WHERE orderdate = CAST('20070212' AS DATETIME);
```

It is important to note that some character string formats of date and time literals are language dependent, meaning that when you convert them to a date and time data type, SQL Server might interpret the value differently based on the language setting in effect in the session. Each logon defined by the database administrator has a default language associated with it, and unless it is changed explicitly, that language becomes the effective language in the session. You can overwrite the default language in your session by using the *SET LANGUAGE* command, but this is generally not recommended because some aspects of the code might rely on the user's default language.

The effective language in the session sets several language-related settings behind the scenes, among them one called *DATEFORMAT*, which determines how SQL Server interprets the literals you enter when they are converted from a character string type to a date and time type. The *DATEFORMAT* setting is expressed as a combination of the characters *d*, *m*, and *y* For example, the *us_english* language setting sets the *DATEFORMAT* to *mdy*, whereas the *British* language setting sets the *DATEFORMAT* to *dmy*. You can override the *DATEFORMAT* setting in your session by using the *SET DATEFORMAT* command, but as mentioned earlier, changing language-related settings is generally not recommended.

Consider, for example, the literal '02/12/2007'. SQL Server can interpret the date as either February 12, 2007 or December 2, 2007 when you convert this literal to one of the following types: *DATETIME*, *DATE*, *DATETIME2*, or *DATETIMEOFFSET*. The effective *LANGUAGE/DATEFORMAT* setting is the determining factor. To demonstrate different interpretations of the same character string literal, run the following code.

```
SET LANGUAGE British;
SELECT CAST('02/12/2007' AS DATETIME);

SET LANGUAGE us_english;
SELECT CAST('02/12/2007' AS DATETIME);
```

Notice in the output that the literal was interpreted differently in the two different language environments.

```
Changed language setting to British.

----------------------
2007-12-02 00:00:00.000

Changed language setting to us_english.

----------------------
2007-02-12 00:00:00.000
```

Note that the *LANGUAGE/DATEFORMAT* setting only affects the way the values you enter are interpreted; these settings have no impact on the format used in the output for presentation purposes, which is determined by the database interface used by the client tool (such as ODBC) and not by the *LANGUAGE/DATEFORMAT* setting. For example, OLEDB and ODBC present *DATETIME* values in the format ' *YYYY-MM-DD hh:mm:ss.nnn*'.

Because the code you write might end up being used by international users with different language settings for their logons, understanding that some formats of literals are language dependent is crucial. It is strongly recommended that you phrase your literals in a language-neutral manner. Language-neutral formats are always interpreted by SQL Server the same way and are not affected by language-related settings. Table 2-2 provides literal formats that are considered neutral for each of the date and time types.

**TABLE 2-2** Language-Neutral Date and Time Data Type Formats

| Data Type | Accuracy | Recommended Entry Format and Example |
|---|---|---|
| *DATETIME* | 'YYYYMMDD hh:mm:ss.nnn'<br>'YYYY-MM-DDThh:mm:ss.nnn'<br>'YYYYMMDD' | '20090212 12:30:15.123'<br>'2009-02-12T12:30:15.123'<br>'20090212' |
| *SMALLDATETIME* | 'YYYYMMDD hh:mm'<br>'YYYY-MM-DDThh:mm'<br>'YYYYMMDD' | '20090212 12:30'<br>'2009-02-12T12:30'<br>'20090212' |
| *DATE* | 'YYYYMMDD'<br>'YYYY-MM-DD' | '20090212'<br>'2009-02-12' |
| *DATETIME2* | 'YYYYMMDD hh:mm:ss.nnnnnnn'<br>'YYYY-MM-DD hh:mm:ss.nnnnnnn'<br>'YYYY-MM-DDThh:mm:ss.nnnnnnn'<br>'YYYYMMDD'<br>'YYYY-MM-DD' | '20090212 12:30:15.1234567'<br>'2009-02-12 12:30:15.1234567'<br>'2009-02-12T12:30:15.1234567'<br>'20090212'<br>'2009-02-12' |
| *DATETIMEOFFSET* | 'YYYYMMDD hh:mm:ss.nnnnnnn [+|-]hh:mm'<br>'YYYY-MM-DD hh:mm:ss.nnnnnnn [+|-]hh:mm'<br>'YYYYMMDD'<br>'YYYY-MM-DD' | '20090212 12:30:15.1234567 +02:00'<br>'2009-02-12 12:30:15.1234567 +02:00'<br>'20090212'<br>'2009-02-12' |
| *TIME* | 'hh:mm:ss.nnnnnnn' | '12:30:15.1234567' |

Note a couple of things about Table 2-2. With all types that include both date and time components, if you don't specify a time part in your literal, SQL Server assumes midnight. If you don't specify a time-zone offset, SQL Server assumes 00:00. It is also important to note that the formats 'YYYY-MM-DD' and 'YYYY-MM-DD hh:mm...' are language dependent when converted to *DATETIME* or *SMALLDATETIME*, and language neutral when converted to *DATE*, *DATETIME2* and *DATETIMEOFFSET*.

For example, notice in the following code that the language setting has no impact on how a literal expressed with the format 'YYYYMMDD' is interpreted when it is converted to *DATETIME*.

```
SET LANGUAGE British;
SELECT CAST('20070212' AS DATETIME);

SET LANGUAGE us_english;
SELECT CAST('20070212' AS DATETIME);
```

The output shows that the literal was interpreted in both cases as February 12, 2007.

```
Changed language setting to British.


-----------------------
2007-02-12 00:00:00.000

Changed language setting to us_english.


-----------------------
2007-02-12 00:00:00.000
```

I probably can't emphasize enough that using language-neutral formats such as 'YYYYMMDD' is a best practice, because such formats are interpreted the same way regardless of the *LANGUAGE/DATEFORMAT* settings.

If you insist on using a language-dependent format to express literals, there are two options available to you. One is by using the *CONVERT* function to explicitly convert the character string literal to the requested data type, in the third argument specifying a number representing the style you used. SQL Server Books Online has a table with all of the style numbers and the formats they represent, in "The *CAST* and *CONVERT* Functions." For example, if you want to specify the literal '02/12/2007' with the format *mm/dd/yyyy*, use style number 101, as shown here.

```
SELECT CONVERT(DATETIME, '02/12/2007', 101);
```

The literal is interpreted as February 12, 2007 regardless of the language setting that is in effect.

If you want to use the format *dd/mm/yyyy*, use style number 103.

```
SELECT CONVERT(DATETIME, '02/12/2007', 103);
```

This time, the literal is interpreted as December 2, 2007.

Another option is to use the *PARSE* function, which is available in SQL Server 2012. This function allows you to parse a value as a requested type and indicate the culture. For example, the following is the equivalent of using *CONVERT* with style 101 (US English).

```
SELECT PARSE('02/12/2007' AS DATETIME USING 'en-US');
```

The following is the equivalent to using *CONVERT* with style 103 (British English):

```
SELECT PARSE('02/12/2007' AS DATETIME USING 'en-GB');
```

## Working with Date and Time Separately

SQL Server 2008 introduced separate *DATE* and *TIME* data types, but in previous versions there is no separation between the two components. If you want to work only with dates or only with times in versions of SQL Server prior to SQL Server 2008, you can use either *DATETIME* or *SMALLDATETIME*, which contain both components. You can also use types such as integers or character strings on which you implement the date and time logic, but I won't discuss this option here. If you want to use the *DATETIME* or *SMALLDATETIME* type, when you want to work only with dates, you store the date with a value of midnight (all zeros in the time parts). When you want to work only with times, you store the time with the base date January 1, 1900.

For example, the *orderdate* column in the *Sales.Orders* table is of a *DATETIME* data type, but because only the date component is actually relevant, all values were stored at midnight. When you need to filter only orders from a certain date, you don't have to use a range filter. Instead, you can use the equality operator like this.

```
SELECT orderid, custid, empid, orderdate
FROM Sales.Orders
WHERE orderdate = '20070212';
```

When the character string literal is converted to *DATETIME*, SQL Server assumes midnight as the time component if time is not specified. Because all values in the *orderdate* column were stored with midnight in the time component, all orders placed on the requested date will be returned. Note that you can use a *CHECK* constraint to ensure that only midnight is used as the time part.

If the time component is stored with non-midnight values, you can use a range filter like this.

```
SELECT orderid, custid, empid, orderdate
FROM Sales.Orders
WHERE orderdate >= '20070212'
  AND orderdate < '20070213';
```

If you want to work only with times in versions prior to SQL Server 2008, you can store all values with the base date of January 1, 1900. When SQL Server converts a character string literal that contains only a time component to *DATETIME* or *SMALLDATETIME*, SQL Server assumes that the date is the base date. For example, run the following code.

```
SELECT CAST('12:30:15.123' AS DATETIME);
```

You get the following output.

```
------------------------
1900-01-01 12:30:15.123
```

Suppose you have a table with a column called *tm* of a *DATETIME* data type and you store all values by using the base date. Again, this could be enforced with a *CHECK* constraint. To return all rows for which the time value is 12:30:15.123, you use the filter *WHERE tm = '12:30:15.123'*. Because you did not specify a date component, SQL Server assumes that the date is the base date when it implicitly converts the character string to a *DATETIME* data type.

If you want to work only with dates or only with times, but the input values you get include both date and time components, you need to apply some manipulation on the input values to "zero" the irrelevant part. That is, set the time component to midnight if you want to work only with dates, and set the date component to the base date if you want to work only with times. I'll explain how you can achieve this shortly, in the "Date and Time Functions" section.

## Filtering Date Ranges

When you need to filter a range of dates, such as a whole year or a whole month, it seems natural to use functions such as *YEAR* and *MONTH*. For example, the following query returns all orders placed in the year 2007.

```
SELECT orderid, custid, empid, orderdate
FROM Sales.Orders
WHERE YEAR(orderdate) = 2007;
```

However, you should be aware that in most cases, when you apply manipulation on the filtered column, SQL Server cannot use an index in an efficient manner. This is probably hard to understand without some background about indexes and performance, which are outside the scope of this book, but for now, just keep this general point in mind: To have the potential to use an index efficiently, you need to revise the predicate so that there is no manipulation on the filtered column, like this.

```
SELECT orderid, custid, empid, orderdate
FROM Sales.Orders
WHERE orderdate >= '20070101' AND orderdate < '20080101';
```

Similarly, instead of using functions to filter orders placed in a particular month, like this:

```
SELECT orderid, custid, empid, orderdate
FROM Sales.Orders
WHERE YEAR(orderdate) = 2007 AND MONTH(orderdate) = 2;
```

use a range filter, like the following.

```
SELECT orderid, custid, empid, orderdate
FROM Sales.Orders
WHERE orderdate >= '20070201' AND orderdate < '20070301';
```

# Date and Time Functions

In this section, I describe functions that operate on date and time data types, including *GETDATE, CURRENT_TIMESTAMP, GETUTCDATE, SYSDATETIME, SYSUTCDATETIME, SYSDATETIMEOFFSET, CAST, CONVERT, SWITCHOFFSET, TODATETIMEOFFSET, DATEADD, DATEDIFF, DATEPART, YEAR, MONTH, DAY, DATENAME*, various *FROMPARTS* functions, and *EOMONTH*.

The functions *SYSDATETIME, SYSUTCDATETIME, SYSDATETIMEOFFSET, SWITCHOFFSET*, and *TODATETIMEOFFSET* were introduced in SQL Server 2008. Existing functions were enhanced to support the newer types and parts. The various *FROMPARTS* functions and the *EOMONTH* function were introduced in SQL Server 2012.

## Current Date and Time

The following *niladic* (parameterless) functions return the current date and time values in the system where the SQL Server instance resides: *GETDATE, CURRENT_TIMESTAMP, GETUTCDATE, SYSDATETIME, SYSUTCDATETIME*, and *SYSDATETIMEOFFSET*. Table 2-3 provides the description of these functions.

**TABLE 2-3** Functions Returning Current Date and Time

| Function | Return Type | Description |
|---|---|---|
| *GETDATE* | *DATETIME* | Current date and time |
| *CURRENT_TIMESTAMP* | *DATETIME* | Same as *GETDATE* but ANSI SQL–compliant |
| *GETUTCDATE* | *DATETIME* | Current date and time in UTC |
| *SYSDATETIME* | *DATETIME2* | Current date and time |
| *SYSUTCDATETIME* | *DATETIME2* | Current date and time in UTC |
| *SYSDATETIMEOFFSET* | *DATETIMEOFFSET* | Current date time including time zone |

Note that you need to specify empty parentheses with all functions that should be specified without parameters, except the ANSI function *CURRENT_TIMESTAMP*. Also, because *CURRENT_TIMESTAMP* and *GETDATE* return the same thing but only the former is standard, it is recommended that you use the former. This is a practice that I try to follow in general—when I have several options that do the same thing with no functional or performance difference, and one is standard but others aren't, my preference is to use the standard option.

The following code demonstrates using the current date and time functions.

```
SELECT
    GETDATE()              AS [GETDATE],
    CURRENT_TIMESTAMP      AS [CURRENT_TIMESTAMP],
    GETUTCDATE()           AS [GETUTCDATE],
    SYSDATETIME()          AS [SYSDATETIME],
    SYSUTCDATETIME()       AS [SYSUTCDATETIME],
    SYSDATETIMEOFFSET()    AS [SYSDATETIMEOFFSET];
```

As you probably noticed, none of the functions return only the current system date or only the current system time. However, you can get those easily by converting *CURRENT_TIMESTAMP* or *SYSDATETIME* to *DATE* or *TIME* like this.

```
SELECT
  CAST(SYSDATETIME() AS DATE) AS [current_date],
  CAST(SYSDATETIME() AS TIME) AS [current_time];
```

## The *CAST, CONVERT,* and *PARSE* Functions and Their *TRY_* Counterparts

The *CAST, CONVERT* and *PARSE* functions are used to convert an input value to some target type. If the conversion succeeds, the functions return the converted value; otherwise, they cause the query to fail. The three functions have counterparts called *TRY_CAST, TRY_CONVERT,* and *TRY_PARSE,* respectively. Each version with the prefix TRY_ accepts the same input as its counterpart, and does the same thing; the difference is that if the input isn't convertible to the target type, the function returns a *NULL* instead of failing the query.

The functions *TRY_CAST, TRY_CONVERT, PARSE,* and *TRY_PARSE* were added in SQL Server 2012.

### Syntax

CAST(*value* AS *datatype*)

TRY_CAST(*value* AS *datatype*)

CONVERT (*datatype, value* [, *style_number*])

TRY_CONVERT (*datatype, value* [, *style_number*])

PARSE (*value* AS *datatype* [USING *culture*])

TRY_PARSE (*value* AS *datatype* [USING *culture*])

All three base functions convert the input *value* to the specified target *datatype*. In some cases, *CONVERT* has a third argument with which you can specify the style of the conversion. For example, when you are converting from a character string to one of the date and time data types (or the other way around), the style number indicates the format of the string. For example, style 101 indicates 'MM/DD/YYYY', and style 103 indicates 'DD/MM/YYYY'. You can find the full list of style numbers and their meanings in SQL Server Books Online under "*CAST* and *CONVERT.*" Similarly, where applicable, the *PARSE* function supports indication of a culture—for example, *'en-US'* for U.S. English and *'en-GB'* for British English.

As mentioned earlier, when you are converting from a character string to one of the date and time data types, some of the string formats are language dependent. I recommend either using one of the language-neutral formats or using the *CONVERT/PARSE* functions and explicitly specifying the style number or culture. This way, your code is interpreted the same way regardless of the language of the logon running it.

Note that *CAST* is ANSI and *CONVERT* and *PARSE* aren't, so unless you need to use the style number or culture, it is recommended that you use the *CAST* function; this way, your code is as standard as possible.

Following are a few examples of using the *CAST*, *CONVERT*, and *PARSE* functions with date and time data types. The following code converts the character string literal '20090212' to a *DATE* data type.

```
SELECT CAST('20090212' AS DATE);
```

The following code converts the current system date and time value to a *DATE* data type, practically extracting only the current system date.

```
SELECT CAST(SYSDATETIME() AS DATE);
```

The following code converts the current system date and time value to a *TIME* data type, practically extracting only the current system time.

```
SELECT CAST(SYSDATETIME() AS TIME);
```

As suggested earlier, if you need to work with the *DATETIME* or *SMALLDATETIME* types (for example, to be compatible with systems using versions earlier than SQL Server 2008) and want to represent only a date or only a time, you can "zero" the irrelevant part. In other words, to work only with dates, you set the time to midnight. To work only with time, you set the date to the base date January 1, 1900.

The following code converts the current date and time value to *CHAR(8)* by using style 112 ('YYYYMMDD').

```
SELECT CONVERT(CHAR(8), CURRENT_TIMESTAMP, 112);
```

For example, if the current date is February 12, 2009, this code returns '20090212'. Remember that this style is language neutral, so when the code is converted back to *DATETIME*, you get the current date at midnight.

```
SELECT CAST(CONVERT(CHAR(8), CURRENT_TIMESTAMP, 112) AS DATETIME);
```

Similarly, to zero the date portion to the base date, you can first convert the current date and time value to *CHAR(12)* by using style 114 ('hh:mm:ss.nnn').

```
SELECT CONVERT(CHAR(12), CURRENT_TIMESTAMP, 114);
```

When the code is converted back to *DATETIME*, you get the current time on the base date.

```
SELECT CAST(CONVERT(CHAR(12), CURRENT_TIMESTAMP, 114) AS DATETIME);
```

As for using the *PARSE* function, here are a couple of examples that I also demonstrated previously in this chapter.

```
SELECT PARSE('02/12/2007' AS DATETIME USING 'en-US');
SELECT PARSE('02/12/2007' AS DATETIME USING 'en-GB');
```

The first parses the input string by using a U.S. English culture, and the second by using a British English culture.

## The *SWITCHOFFSET* Function

The *SWITCHOFFSET* function adjusts an input *DATETIMEOFFSET* value to a specified time zone.

### Syntax

SWITCHOFFSET(*datetimeoffset_value, time_zone*)

For example, the following code adjusts the current system *datetimeoffset* value to time zone -05:00.

```
SELECT SWITCHOFFSET(SYSDATETIMEOFFSET(), '-05:00');
```

So if the current system *datetimeoffset* value is February 12, 2009 10:00:00.0000000 -08:00, this code returns the value February 12, 2009 13:00:00.0000000 -05:00.

The following code adjusts the current *datetimeoffset* value to UTC.

```
SELECT SWITCHOFFSET(SYSDATETIMEOFFSET(), '+00:00');
```

Assuming the aforementioned current *datetimeoffset* value, this code returns the value February 12, 2009 18:00:00.0000000 +00:00.

## The *TODATETIMEOFFSET* Function

The *TODATETIMEOFFSET* function sets the time zone offset of an input date and time value.

### Syntax

TODATETIMEOFFSET(*date_and_time_value, time_zone*)

This function is different from *SWITCHOFFSET* in that its first input will usually be a date and time type that is not offset aware. This function simply merges the input date and time value with the specified time zone offset to create a new *datetimeoffset* value.

You will typically use this function when migrating non-offset-aware data to offset-aware data. Imagine that you have a table holding local date and time values in an attribute called *dt* of a *DATETIME* data type and the offset in an attribute called *theoffset*. You then decide to merge the two to one offset-aware attribute called *dto*. You alter the table and add the new attribute. Then you update it to the result of the expression *TODATETIMEOFFSET(dt, theoffset)*. Then you can drop the two existing attributes *dt* and *theoffset*.

## The *DATEADD* Function

The *DATEADD* function allows you to add a specified number of units of a specified date part to an input date and time value.

**Syntax**

DATEADD(*part, n, dt_val*)

Valid values for the *part* input include *year, quarter, month, dayofyear, day, week, weekday, hour, minute, second, millisecond, microsecond,* and *nanosecond*. You can also specify the part in abbreviated form, such as *yy* instead of *year*. Refer to SQL Server Books Online for details.

The return type for a date and time input is the same type as the input's type. If this function is given a string literal as input, the output is *DATETIME*.

For example, the following code adds one year to February 12, 2009.

```
SELECT DATEADD(year, 1, '20090212');
```

This code returns the following output.

```
-----------------------
2010-02-12 00:00:00.000
```

## The *DATEDIFF* Function

The *DATEDIFF* function returns the difference between two date and time values in terms of a specified date part.

**Syntax**

DATEDIFF(*part, dt_val1, dt_val2*)

For example, the following code returns the difference in terms of days between two values.

```
SELECT DATEDIFF(day, '20080212', '20090212');
```

This code returns the output 366.

Ready for a bit more sophisticated use of the *DATEADD* and *DATEDIFF* functions? You can use the following code in versions prior to SQL Server 2008 to set the time component of the current system date and time value to midnight.

```
SELECT
  DATEADD(
    day,
    DATEDIFF(day, '20010101', CURRENT_TIMESTAMP), '20010101');
```

This is achieved by first using the *DATEDIFF* function to calculate the difference in terms of whole days between an anchor date at midnight ('20010101' in this case) and the current date and time (call that difference *diff*). Then, the *DATEADD* function is used to add *diff* days to the anchor. You get the current system date at midnight.

Interestingly, if you use this expression with a month part instead of a day, and make sure to use an anchor that is the first day of a month (as in this example), you get the first day of the current month.

```
SELECT
  DATEADD(
    month,
    DATEDIFF(month, '20010101', CURRENT_TIMESTAMP), '20010101');
```

Similarly, by using a year part and an anchor that is the first day of a year, you get back the first day of the current year.

If you want the last day of the month or year, simply use an anchor that is the last day of a month or year. For example, the following expression returns the last day of the current month.

```
SELECT
  DATEADD(
    month,
    DATEDIFF(month, '19991231', CURRENT_TIMESTAMP), '19991231');
```

Note that in SQL Server 2012 there's a simpler way to get the last day of the month: by using a new function called *EOMONTH*. I'll describe it shortly.

## The *DATEPART* Function

The *DATEPART* function returns an integer representing a requested part of a date and time value.

### Syntax

DATEPART(*part, dt_val*)

Valid values for the *part* argument include *year, quarter, month, dayofyear, day, week, weekday, hour, minute, second, millisecond, microsecond, nanosecond, TZoffset*, and *ISO_WEEK*. The last four parts are available in SQL Server 2008 and SQL Server 2012. As I mentioned earlier, you can use abbreviations for the date and time parts, such as *yy* instead of *year*, *mm* instead of *month*, *dd* instead of *day*, and so on.

For example, the following code returns the month part of the input value.

```
SELECT DATEPART(month, '20090212');
```

This code returns the integer 2.

## The *YEAR, MONTH*, and *DAY* Functions

The *YEAR, MONTH*, and *DAY* functions are abbreviations for the *DATEPART* function returning the integer representation of the year, month, and day parts of an input date and time value.

### Syntax

YEAR(*dt_val*)

MONTH(*dt_val*)

DAY(*dt_val*)

For example, the following code extracts the day, month, and year parts of an input value.

```
SELECT
  DAY('20090212') AS theday,
  MONTH('20090212') AS themonth,
  YEAR('20090212') AS theyear;
```

This code returns the following output.

```
theday      themonth    theyear
----------- ----------- -----------
12          2           2009
```

## The *DATENAME* Function

The *DATENAME* function returns a character string representing a part of a date and time value.

### Syntax

DATENAME(*dt_val*, *part*)

This function is similar to *DATEPART* and in fact has the same options for the *part* input. However, when relevant, it returns the name of the requested part rather than the number. For example, the following code returns the month name of the given input value.

```
SELECT DATENAME(month, '20090212');
```

Recall that *DATEPART* returned the integer 2 for this input. *DATENAME* returns the name of the month, which is language dependent. If your session's language is one of the English languages (such as U.S. English or British English), you get back the value 'February'. If your session's language is Italian, you get back the value 'febbraio'. If a part is requested that has no name, but only a numeric value (such as *year*), the *DATENAME* function returns its numeric value as a character string. For example, the following code returns '2009'.

```
SELECT DATENAME(year, '20090212');
```

## The *ISDATE* Function

The *ISDATE* function accepts a character string as input and returns 1 if it is convertible to a date and time data type and 0 if it isn't.

### Syntax

ISDATE(*string*)

For example, the following code returns 1.

```
SELECT ISDATE('20090212');
```

And the following code returns 0.

```
SELECT ISDATE('20090230');
```

## The *FROMPARTS* Functions

The *FROMPARTS* functions were introduced in SQL Server 2012. They accept integer inputs representing parts of a date and time value and construct a value of the requested type from those parts.

**Syntax**

DATEFROMPARTS (*year, month, day*)

DATETIME2FROMPARTS (*year, month, day, hour, minute, seconds, fractions, precision*)

DATETIMEFROMPARTS (*year, month, day, hour, minute, seconds, milliseconds*)

DATETIMEOFFSETFROMPARTS (*year, month, day, hour, minute, seconds, fractions, hour_offset, minute_offset, precision*)

SMALLDATETIMEFROMPARTS (*year, month, day, hour, minute*)

TIMEFROMPARTS (*hour, minute, seconds, fractions, precision*)

These functions make it easier for applications to construct date and time values from the different components, and they also simply migrate from other environments that already support similar functions. The following code demonstrates the use of these functions.

```
SELECT
  DATEFROMPARTS(2012, 02, 12),
  DATETIME2FROMPARTS(2012, 02, 12, 13, 30, 5, 1, 7),
  DATETIMEFROMPARTS(2012, 02, 12, 13, 30, 5, 997),
  DATETIMEOFFSETFROMPARTS(2012, 02, 12, 13, 30, 5, 1, -8, 0, 7),
  SMALLDATETIMEFROMPARTS(2012, 02, 12, 13, 30),
  TIMEFROMPARTS(13, 30, 5, 1, 7),
```

## The *EOMONTH* Function

The *EOMONTH* function was introduced in SQL Server 2012. It accepts an input date and time value and returns the respective end-of-month date, at midnight, as a *DATE* data type. The function also supports an optional second argument indicating how many months to add.

**Syntax**

EOMONTH(*input* [, *months_to_add*])

For example, the following code returns the end of the current month.

```
SELECT EOMONTH(SYSDATETIME());
```

The following query returns orders placed on the last day of the month.

```
SELECT orderid, orderdate, custid, empid
FROM Sales.Orders
WHERE orderdate = EOMONTH(orderdate);
```

# Querying Metadata

SQL Server provides tools for getting information about the metadata of objects, such as information about tables in a database and columns in a table. Those tools include catalog views, information schema views, and system stored procedures and functions. This area is documented well in SQL Server Books Online in the "Querying the SQL Server System Catalog" section, so I won't cover it in great detail here. I'll just give a couple of examples of each metadata tool to give you a sense of what's available and get you started.

## Catalog Views

Catalog views provide very detailed information about objects in the database, including information that is specific to SQL Server. For example, if you want to list the tables in a database along with their schema names, you can query the *sys.tables* view as follows.

```
USE TSQL2012;

SELECT SCHEMA_NAME(schema_id) AS table_schema_name, name AS table_name
FROM sys.tables;
```

The *SCHEMA_NAME* function is used to convert the schema ID integer to its name. This query returns the following output.

```
table_schema_name  table_name
------------------ --------------
HR                 Employees
Production         Suppliers
Production         Categories
Production         Products
Sales              Customers
Sales              Shippers
Sales              Orders
Sales              OrderDetails
Stats              Tests
Stats              Scores
dbo                Nums
```

To get information about columns in a table, you can query the *sys.columns* table. For example, the following code returns information about columns in the *Sales.Orders* table including column names, data types (with the system type ID translated to a name by using the *TYPE_NAME* function), maximum length, collation name, and nullability.

```
SELECT
  name AS column_name,
  TYPE_NAME(system_type_id) AS column_type,
  max_length,
  collation_name,
  is_nullable
FROM sys.columns
WHERE object_id = OBJECT_ID(N'Sales.Orders');
```

This query returns the following output.

| column_name | column_type | max_length | collation_name | is_nullable |
|---|---|---|---|---|
| orderid | int | 4 | NULL | 0 |
| custid | int | 4 | NULL | 1 |
| empid | int | 4 | NULL | 0 |
| orderdate | datetime | 8 | NULL | 0 |
| requireddate | datetime | 8 | NULL | 0 |
| shippeddate | datetime | 8 | NULL | 1 |
| shipperid | int | 4 | NULL | 0 |
| freight | money | 8 | NULL | 0 |
| shipname | nvarchar | 80 | Latin1_General_CI_AI | 0 |
| shipaddress | nvarchar | 120 | Latin1_General_CI_AI | 0 |
| shipcity | nvarchar | 30 | Latin1_General_CI_AI | 0 |
| shipregion | nvarchar | 30 | Latin1_General_CI_AI | 1 |
| shippostalcode | nvarchar | 20 | Latin1_General_CI_AI | 1 |
| shipcountry | nvarchar | 30 | Latin1_General_CI_AI | 0 |

## Information Schema Views

An information schema view is a set of views that resides in a schema called *INFORMATION_SCHEMA* and provides metadata information in a standard manner. That is, the views are defined in the SQL standard, so naturally they don't cover aspects specific to SQL Server.

For example, the following query against the *INFORMATION_SCHEMA.TABLES* view lists the user tables in the current database along with their schema names.

```
SELECT TABLE_SCHEMA, TABLE_NAME
FROM INFORMATION_SCHEMA.TABLES
WHERE TABLE_TYPE = N'BASE TABLE';
```

The following query against the *INFORMATION_SCHEMA.COLUMNS* view provides most of the available information about columns in the *Sales.Orders* table.

```
SELECT
  COLUMN_NAME, DATA_TYPE, CHARACTER_MAXIMUM_LENGTH,
  COLLATION_NAME, IS_NULLABLE
FROM INFORMATION_SCHEMA.COLUMNS
WHERE TABLE_SCHEMA = N'Sales'
  AND TABLE_NAME = N'Orders';
```

## System Stored Procedures and Functions

System stored procedures and functions internally query the system catalog and give you back more "digested" metadata information. Again, you can find the full list of objects and their detailed descriptions in SQL Server Books Online, but here are a few examples. The *sp_tables* stored procedure returns a list of objects (such as tables and views) that can be queried in the current database.

```
EXEC sys.sp_tables;
```

The *sp_help* procedure accepts an object name as input and returns multiple result sets with general information about the object, and also information about columns, indexes, constraints, and more. For example, the following code returns detailed information about the *Orders* table.

```
EXEC sys.sp_help
  @objname = N'Sales.Orders';
```

The *sp_columns* procedure returns information about columns in an object. For example, the following code returns information about columns in the *Orders* table.

```
EXEC sys.sp_columns
  @table_name = N'Orders',
  @table_owner = N'Sales';
```

The *sp_helpconstraint* procedure returns information about constraints in an object. For example, the following code returns information about constraints in the *Orders* table.

```
EXEC sys.sp_helpconstraint
  @objname = N'Sales.Orders';
```

One set of functions returns information about properties of entities such as the SQL Server instance, database, object, column, and so on. The *SERVERPROPERTY* function returns the requested property of the current instance. For example, the following code returns the product level (such as RTM, SP1, SP2, and so on) of the current instance.

```
SELECT
  SERVERPROPERTY('ProductLevel');
```

The *DATABASEPROPERTYEX* function returns the requested property of the specified database name. For example, the following code returns the collation of the TSQL2012 database.

```
SELECT
  DATABASEPROPERTYEX(N'TSQL2012', 'Collation');
```

The *OBJECTPROPERTY* function returns the requested property of the specified object name. For example, the output of the following code indicates whether the *Orders* table has a primary key.

```
SELECT
  OBJECTPROPERTY(OBJECT_ID(N'Sales.Orders'), 'TableHasPrimaryKey');
```

Notice the nesting of the function *OBJECT_ID* within *OBJECTPROPERTY*. The *OBJECTPROPERTY* function expects an object ID and not a name, so the *OBJECT_ID* function is used to return the ID of the *Orders* table.

The *COLUMNPROPERTY* function returns the requested property of a specified column. For example, the output of the following code indicates whether the *shipcountry* column in the *Orders* table is nullable.

```
SELECT
  COLUMNPROPERTY(OBJECT_ID(N'Sales.Orders'), N'shipcountry', 'AllowsNull');
```

# Conclusion

This chapter introduced you to the *SELECT* statement, logical query processing, and various other aspects of single-table queries. I covered quite a few subjects here, including many new and unique concepts. If you're new to T-SQL, you might feel overwhelmed at this point. But remember, this chapter introduces some of the most important points about SQL that might be hard to digest at the beginning. If some of the concepts weren't completely clear, you might want to revisit sections from this chapter later on, after you've had a chance to sleep on it.

For an opportunity to practice what you've learned and absorb the material better, I recommend going over the chapter exercises.

# Exercises

This section provides exercises to help you familiarize yourself with the subjects discussed in Chapter 2. Solutions to the exercises appear in the section that follows.

You can find instructions for downloading and installing the *TSQL2012* sample database in the Appendix.

## 1

Write a query against the *Sales.Orders* table that returns orders placed in June 2007.

- Tables involved: *TSQL2012* database and the *Sales.Orders* table

- Desired output (abbreviated):

```
orderid      orderdate               custid    empid
-----------  ----------------------  ------    -----------
10555        2007-06-02 00:00:00.000 71        6
10556        2007-06-03 00:00:00.000 73        2
10557        2007-06-03 00:00:00.000 44        9
10558        2007-06-04 00:00:00.000 4         1
10559        2007-06-05 00:00:00.000 7         6
10560        2007-06-06 00:00:00.000 25        8
10561        2007-06-06 00:00:00.000 24        2
10562        2007-06-09 00:00:00.000 66        1
10563        2007-06-10 00:00:00.000 67        2
10564        2007-06-10 00:00:00.000 65        4
...

(30 row(s) affected)
```

## 2

Write a query against the *Sales.Orders* table that returns orders placed on the last day of the month.

- Tables involved: *TSQL2012* database and the *Sales.Orders* table

- Desired output (abbreviated):

```
orderid     orderdate               custid      empid
----------- ----------------------- ----------- -----------
10269       2006-07-31 00:00:00.000 89          5
10317       2006-09-30 00:00:00.000 48          6
10343       2006-10-31 00:00:00.000 44          4
10399       2006-12-31 00:00:00.000 83          8
10432       2007-01-31 00:00:00.000 75          3
10460       2007-02-28 00:00:00.000 24          8
10461       2007-02-28 00:00:00.000 46          1
10490       2007-03-31 00:00:00.000 35          7
10491       2007-03-31 00:00:00.000 28          8
10522       2007-04-30 00:00:00.000 44          4
...

(26 row(s) affected)
```

## 3

Write a query against the *HR.Employees* table that returns employees with last name containing the letter *a* twice or more.

- Tables involved: *TSQL2012* database and the *HR.Employees* table

- Desired output:

```
empid       firstname  lastname
----------- ---------- --------------------
9           Zoya       Dolgopyatova

(1 row(s) affected)
```

## 4

Write a query against the *Sales.OrderDetails* table that returns orders with total value (quantity * unit-price) greater than 10,000, sorted by total value.

- Tables involved: *TSQL2012* database and the *Sales.OrderDetails* table

- Desired output:

```
orderid     totalvalue
----------- ---------------------
10865       17250.00
11030       16321.90
10981       15810.00
10372       12281.20
```

```
10424     11493.20
10817     11490.70
10889     11380.00
10417     11283.20
10897     10835.24
10353     10741.60
10515     10588.50
10479     10495.60
10540     10191.70
10691     10164.80

(14 row(s) affected)
```

## 5

Write a query against the *Sales.Orders* table that returns the three shipped-to countries with the highest average freight in 2007.

- Tables involved: *TSQL2012* database and the *Sales.Orders* table

- Desired output:

```
shipcountry      avgfreight
---------------  ---------------------
Austria          178.3642
Switzerland      117.1775
Sweden           105.16

(3 row(s) affected)
```

## 6

Write a query against the *Sales.Orders* table that calculates row numbers for orders based on order date ordering (using the order ID as the tiebreaker) for each customer separately.

- Tables involved: *TSQL2012* database and the *Sales.Orders* table

- Desired output (abbreviated):

```
custid       orderdate                 orderid      rownum
-----------  ------------------------  -----------  ---------------------
1            2007-08-25 00:00:00.000   10643        1
1            2007-10-03 00:00:00.000   10692        2
1            2007-10-13 00:00:00.000   10702        3
1            2008-01-15 00:00:00.000   10835        4
1            2008-03-16 00:00:00.000   10952        5
1            2008-04-09 00:00:00.000   11011        6
2            2006-09-18 00:00:00.000   10308        1
2            2007-08-08 00:00:00.000   10625        2
2            2007-11-28 00:00:00.000   10759        3
2            2008-03-04 00:00:00.000   10926        4
...

(830 row(s) affected)
```

# 7

Using the *HR.Employees* table, figure out the *SELECT* statement that returns for each employee the gender based on the title of courtesy. For 'Ms. ' and 'Mrs.' return 'Female'; for 'Mr. ' return 'Male'; and in all other cases (for example, 'Dr. ') return 'Unknown'.

- Tables involved: *TSQL2012* database and the *HR.Employees* table

- Desired output:

```
empid        firstname   lastname              titleofcourtesy            gender
----------   ----------  --------------------  -------------------------  -------
1            Sara        Davis                 Ms.                        Female
2            Don         Funk                  Dr.                        Unknown
3            Judy        Lew                   Ms.                        Female
4            Yael        Peled                 Mrs.                       Female
5            Sven        Buck                  Mr.                        Male
6            Paul        Suurs                 Mr.                        Male
7            Russell     King                  Mr.                        Male
8            Maria       Cameron               Ms.                        Female
9            Zoya        Dolgopyatova          Ms.                        Female

(9 row(s) affected)
```

# 8

Write a query against the *Sales.Customers* table that returns for each customer the customer ID and region. Sort the rows in the output by region, having *NULL* marks sort last (after non-*NULL* values). Note that the default sort behavior for *NULL* marks in T-SQL is to sort first (before non-*NULL* values).

- Tables involved: *TSQL2012* database and the *Sales.Customers* table

- Desired output (abbreviated):

```
custid        region
----------   ----------------
55            AK
10            BC
42            BC
45            CA
37            Co. Cork
33            DF
71            ID
38            Isle of Wight
46            Lara
78            MT
...
1             NULL
2             NULL
3             NULL
4             NULL
5             NULL
6             NULL
7             NULL
```

```
8          NULL
9          NULL
11         NULL
...

(91 row(s) affected)
```

# Solutions

This section provides the solutions to the exercises for this chapter, accompanied by explanations where needed.

## 1

You might have considered using the *YEAR* and *MONTH* functions in the *WHERE* clause of your solution query, like this.

```
USE TSQL2012;

SELECT orderid, orderdate, custid, empid
FROM Sales.Orders
WHERE YEAR(orderdate) = 2007 AND MONTH(orderdate) = 6;
```

This solution is valid and returns the correct result. However, I explained that if you apply manipulation on the filtered column, in most cases SQL Server can't use an index efficiently if such manipulation exists on that column. Therefore, I advise using a range filter instead.

```
SELECT orderid, orderdate, custid, empid
FROM Sales.Orders
WHERE orderdate >= '20070601'
  AND orderdate < '20070701';
```

## 2

In SQL Server 2012 you can use the *EOMONTH* function to address this task, like this.

```
SELECT orderid, orderdate, custid, empid
FROM Sales.Orders
WHERE orderdate = EOMONTH(orderdate);
```

Prior to SQL Server 2012 the solution is more complex. As part of the discussion about date and time functions, I provided the following expression format to calculate the last day of the month corresponding to a specified date.

```
DATEADD(month, DATEDIFF(month, '19991231', date_val), '19991231')
```

This expression first calculates the difference in terms of whole months between an anchor last day of some month (December 31, 1999 in this case) and the specified date. Call this difference *diff*. By adding *diff* months to the anchor date, you get the last day of the specified date's month. Here's the full solution query, returning only orders for which the order date is equal to the last day of the month.

```
SELECT orderid, orderdate, custid, empid
FROM Sales.Orders
WHERE orderdate = DATEADD(month, DATEDIFF(month, '19991231', orderdate), '19991231');
```

## 3

This exercise involves using pattern matching with the *LIKE* predicate. Remember that the percent sign (%) represents a character string of any size, including an empty string. Therefore, you can use the pattern *'%a%a%'* to express at least two occurrences of the character *a* anywhere in the string. Here's the full solution query.

```
SELECT empid, firstname, lastname
FROM HR.Employees
WHERE lastname LIKE '%a%a%';
```

## 4

This exercise is quite tricky, and if you managed to solve it correctly, you should be proud of yourself. A subtle requirement in the request might be overlooked or interpreted incorrectly. Observe that the request said "return orders with *total value* greater than 10,000" and not "return orders with *value* greater than 10,000." In other words, the individual order detail row shouldn't meet the requirement. Instead, the group of all order details within the order should meet the requirement. This means that the query shouldn't have a filter in the *WHERE* clause like this.

```
WHERE quantity * unitprice > 10000
```

Rather, the query should group the data by order ID and have a filter in the *HAVING* clause like this.

```
HAVING SUM(quantity*unitprice) > 10000
```

Here's the complete solution query.

```
SELECT orderid, SUM(qty*unitprice) AS totalvalue
FROM Sales.OrderDetails
GROUP BY orderid
HAVING SUM(qty*unitprice) > 10000
ORDER BY totalvalue DESC;
```

# 5

Because the request involves activity in the year 2007, the query should have a *WHERE* clause with the appropriate date range filter (*orderdate >= '20070101' AND orderdate < '20080101'*). Because the request involves average freight values per shipping country and the table can have multiple rows per country, the query should group the rows by country, and calculate the average freight. To get the three countries with the highest average freights, the query should specify *TOP (3)*, based on logical order of average freight descending. Here's the complete solution query.

```
SELECT TOP (3) shipcountry, AVG(freight) AS avgfreight
FROM Sales.Orders
WHERE orderdate >= '20070101' AND orderdate < '20080101'
GROUP BY shipcountry
ORDER BY avgfreight DESC;
```

Remember that in SQL Server 2012 you can use the standard *OFFSET-FETCH* option instead of the proprietary *TOP* option. Here's the revised solution using *OFFSET-FETCH*.

```
SELECT shipcountry, AVG(freight) AS avgfreight
FROM Sales.Orders
WHERE orderdate >= '20070101' AND orderdate < '20080101'
GROUP BY shipcountry
ORDER BY avgfreight DESC
OFFSET 0 ROWS FETCH FIRST 3 ROWS ONLY;
```

# 6

Because the exercise requests that the row number calculation be done for each customer separately, the expression should have *PARTITION BY custid*. In addition, the request was to use logical ordering by *orderdate*, with *orderid* as a tiebreaker. Therefore, the *OVER* clause should have *ORDER BY orderdate, orderid*. Here's the complete solution query.

```
SELECT custid, orderdate, orderid,
  ROW_NUMBER() OVER(PARTITION BY custid ORDER BY orderdate, orderid) AS rownum
FROM Sales.Orders
ORDER BY custid, rownum;
```

# 7

You can handle the conditional logic required by this exercise by using a *CASE* expression. Using the simple *CASE* expression form, you specify the *titleofcourtesy* attribute right after the *CASE* keyword; list each possible title of courtesy in a separate *WHEN* clause followed by the *THEN* clause and the gender; and in the *ELSE* clause, specify *'Unknown'*.

```
SELECT empid, firstname, lastname, titleofcourtesy,
  CASE titleofcourtesy
    WHEN 'Ms.'  THEN 'Female'
    WHEN 'Mrs.' THEN 'Female'
    WHEN 'Mr.'  THEN 'Male'
    ELSE             'Unknown'
  END AS gender
FROM HR.Employees;
```

You can also use the searched *CASE* form with two predicates—one to handle all cases where the gender is female and one for all cases where the gender is male—and an *ELSE* clause with *'Unknown'*.

```
SELECT empid, firstname, lastname, titleofcourtesy,
  CASE
    WHEN titleofcourtesy IN('Ms.', 'Mrs.') THEN 'Female'
    WHEN titleofcourtesy = 'Mr.'           THEN 'Male'
    ELSE                                        'Unknown'
  END AS gender
FROM HR.Employees;
```

# 8

By default, SQL Server sorts *NULL* marks before non-*NULL* values. To get *NULL* marks to sort last, you can use a *CASE* expression that returns 1 when the *region* column is *NULL* and 0 when it is not *NULL*. Non-*NULL* marks get 0 back from the expression; therefore, they sort before *NULL* marks (which get 1). This *CASE* expression is used as the first sort column. The *region* column should be specified as the second sort column. This way, non-*NULL* marks sort correctly among themselves. Here's the complete solution query.

```
SELECT custid, region
FROM Sales.Customers
ORDER BY
  CASE WHEN region IS NULL THEN 1 ELSE 0 END, region;
```

# CHAPTER 3

# Joins

The *FROM* clause of a query is the first clause to be logically processed, and within the *FROM* clause, table operators operate on input tables. Microsoft SQL Server supports four table operators—*JOIN*, *APPLY*, *PIVOT*, and *UNPIVOT*. The *JOIN* table operator is standard, whereas *APPLY*, *PIVOT*, and *UNPIVOT* are T-SQL extensions to the standard. Each table operator acts on tables provided to it as input, applies a set of logical query processing phases, and returns a table result. This chapter focuses on the *JOIN* table operator. The *APPLY* operator will be covered in Chapter 5, "Table Expressions," and the *PIVOT* and *UNPIVOT* operators will be covered in Chapter 7, "Beyond the Fundamentals of Querying."

A *JOIN* table operator operates on two input tables. The three fundamental types of joins are cross joins, inner joins, and outer joins. These three types of joins differ in how they apply their logical query processing phases; each type applies a different set of phases. A cross join applies only one phase—Cartesian Product. An inner join applies two phases—Cartesian Product and Filter. An outer join applies three phases—Cartesian Product, Filter, and Add Outer Rows. This chapter explains each of the join types and the phases involved in detail.

*Logical query processing* describes a generic series of logical steps that for any specified query produces the correct result, whereas *physical query processing* is the way the query is processed by the RDBMS engine in practice. Some phases of logical query processing of joins might sound inefficient, but the inefficient phases will be optimized by the physical implementation. It's important to stress the term logical in logical query processing. The steps in the process apply operations to the input tables based on relational algebra. The database engine does not have to follow logical query processing phases literally, as long as it can guarantee that the result that it produces is the same as that dictated by logical query processing. The SQL Server relational engine often applies many shortcuts for optimization purposes when it knows that it can still produce the correct result. Even though this book's focus is on understanding the logical aspects of querying, I want to stress this point to avoid any misunderstanding and confusion.

## Cross Joins

Logically, a cross join is the simplest type of join. A cross join implements only one logical query processing phase—a Cartesian Product. This phase operates on the two tables provided as inputs to the join and produces a Cartesian product of the two. That is, each row from one input is matched with all rows from the other. So if you have m rows in one table and n rows in the other, you get m×n rows in the result.

SQL Server supports two standard syntaxes for cross joins—the ANSI SQL-92 and ANSI SQL-89 syntaxes. I recommend that you use the ANSI-SQL 92 syntax for reasons that I'll describe shortly. Therefore, ANSI-SQL 92 syntax is the main syntax that I use throughout the book. For the sake of completeness, I describe both syntaxes in this section.

## ANSI SQL-92 Syntax

The following query applies a cross join between the *Customers* and *Employees* tables (using the ANSI SQL-92 syntax) in the *TSQL2012* database, and returns the *custid* and *empid* attributes in the result set.

```
USE TSQL2012;

SELECT C.custid, E.empid
FROM Sales.Customers AS C
  CROSS JOIN HR.Employees AS E;
```

Because there are 91 rows in the *Customers* table and 9 rows in the *Employees* table, this query produces a result set with 819 rows, as shown here in abbreviated form.

```
custid        empid
-----------   -----------
1             1
1             2
1             3
1             4
1             5
1             6
1             7
1             8
1             9
2             1
2             2
2             3
2             4
2             5
2             6
2             7
2             8
2             9
. . .

(819 row(s) affected)
```

When you use the ANSI SQL-92 syntax, you specify the CROSS JOIN keywords between the two tables involved in the join.

Notice that in the *FROM* clause of the preceding query, I assigned the aliases *C* and *E* to the *Customers* and *Employees* tables, respectively. The result set produced by the cross join is a virtual table with attributes that originate from both sides of the join. Because I assigned aliases to the source tables, the names of the columns in the virtual table are prefixed by the table aliases (for example, *C.custid, E.empid*). If you do not assign aliases to the tables in the *FROM* clause, the names of the columns in the virtual table are prefixed by the full source table names (for example, *Customers.custid*,

*Employees.empid*). The purpose of the prefixes is to facilitate the identification of columns in an unambiguous manner when the same column name appears in both tables. The aliases of the tables are assigned for brevity. Note that you are required to use column prefixes only when referring to ambiguous column names (column names that appear in more than one table); in unambiguous cases, column prefixes are optional. However, some people find it a good practice to always use column prefixes for the sake of clarity. Also note that if you assign an alias to a table, it is invalid to use the full table name as a column prefix; in ambiguous cases you have to use the table alias as a prefix.

## ANSI SQL-89 Syntax

SQL Server also supports an older syntax for cross joins that was introduced in ANSI SQL-89. In this syntax you simply specify a comma between the table names, like this.

```
SELECT C.custid, E.empid
FROM Sales.Customers AS C, HR.Employees AS E;
```

There is no logical or performance difference between the two syntaxes. Both syntaxes are integral parts of the latest SQL standard (ANSI SQL:2011 at the time of this writing), and both are fully supported by the latest version of SQL Server (Microsoft SQL Server 2012 at the time of this writing). I am not aware of any plans to deprecate the older syntax, and I don't see any reason to do so while it's an integral part of the standard. However, I recommend using the ANSI SQL-92 syntax for reasons that will become clear after inner joins are explained.

## Self Cross Joins

You can join multiple instances of the same table. This capability is known as a self join and is supported with all fundamental join types (cross joins, inner joins, and outer joins). For example, the following query performs a self cross join between two instances of the *Employees* table.

```
SELECT
  E1.empid, E1.firstname, E1.lastname,
  E2.empid, E2.firstname, E2.lastname
FROM HR.Employees AS E1
  CROSS JOIN HR.Employees AS E2;
```

This query produces all possible combinations of pairs of employees. Because the *Employees* table has 9 rows, this query returns 81 rows, shown here in abbreviated form.

| empid | firstname | lastname | empid | firstname | lastname |
| ------ | ---------- | ---------------- | ------ | ---------- | --------- |
| 1 | Sara | Davis | 1 | Sara | Davis |
| 2 | Don | Funk | 1 | Sara | Davis |
| 3 | Judy | Lew | 1 | Sara | Davis |
| 4 | Yael | Peled | 1 | Sara | Davis |
| 5 | Sven | Buck | 1 | Sara | Davis |
| 6 | Paul | Suurs | 1 | Sara | Davis |
| 7 | Russell | King | 1 | Sara | Davis |
| 8 | Maria | Cameron | 1 | Sara | Davis |
| 9 | Zoya | Dolgopyatova | 1 | Sara | Davis |

| 1 | Sara | Davis | 2 | Don | Funk |
|---|---|---|---|---|---|
| 2 | Don | Funk | 2 | Don | Funk |
| 3 | Judy | Lew | 2 | Don | Funk |
| 4 | Yael | Peled | 2 | Don | Funk |
| 5 | Sven | Buck | 2 | Don | Funk |
| 6 | Paul | Suurs | 2 | Don | Funk |
| 7 | Russell | King | 2 | Don | Funk |
| 8 | Maria | Cameron | 2 | Don | Funk |
| 9 | Zoya | Dolgopyatova | 2 | Don | Funk |

. . .

```
(81 row(s) affected)
```

In a self join, aliasing tables is not optional. Without table aliases, all column names in the result of the join would be ambiguous.

## Producing Tables of Numbers

One situation in which cross joins can be very handy is when they are used to produce a result set with a sequence of integers (1, 2, 3, and so on). Such a sequence of numbers is an extremely powerful tool that I use for many purposes. By using cross joins, you can produce the sequence of integers in a very efficient manner.

You can start by creating a table called *Digits* with a column called *digit*, and populate the table with 10 rows with the digits 0 through 9. Run the following code to create the *Digits* table in the *TSQL2012* database (for test purposes) and populate it with the 10 digits.

```
USE TSQL2012;
IF OBJECT_ID('dbo.Digits', 'U') IS NOT NULL DROP TABLE dbo.Digits;
CREATE TABLE dbo.Digits(digit INT NOT NULL PRIMARY KEY);

INSERT INTO dbo.Digits(digit)
  VALUES (0),(1),(2),(3),(4),(5),(6),(7),(8),(9);

SELECT digit FROM dbo.Digits;
```

This code also uses an *INSERT* statement to populate the *Digits* table. If you're not familiar with the syntax of the *INSERT* statement, see Chapter 8, "Data Modification," for details.

The contents of the *Digits* table are shown here.

```
digit
-----------
0
1
2
3
4
5
6
7
8
9
```

Suppose you need to write a query that produces a sequence of integers in the range 1 through 1,000. You can cross three instances of the *Digits* table, each representing a different power of 10 (1, 10, 100). By crossing three instances of the same table, each instance with 10 rows, you get a result set with 1,000 rows. To produce the actual number, multiply the digit from each instance by the power of 10 it represents, sum the results, and add 1. Here's the complete query.

```
SELECT D3.digit * 100 + D2.digit * 10 + D1.digit + 1 AS n
FROM        dbo.Digits AS D1
  CROSS JOIN dbo.Digits AS D2
  CROSS JOIN dbo.Digits AS D3
ORDER BY n;
```

This query returns the following output, shown here in abbreviated form.

```
n
-----------
1
2
3
4
5
6
7
8
9
10
...
998
999
1000

(1000 row(s) affected)
```

This was just an example producing a sequence of 1,000 integers. If you need more numbers, you can add more instances of the *Digits* table to the query. For example, if you need to produce a sequence of 1,000,000 rows, you would need to join six instances.

# Inner Joins

An inner join applies two logical query processing phases—it applies a Cartesian product between the two input tables as in a cross join, and then it filters rows based on a predicate that you specify. Like cross joins, inner joins have two standard syntaxes: ANSI SQL-92 and ANSI SQL-89.

## ANSI SQL-92 Syntax

Using the ANSI SQL-92 syntax, you specify the INNER JOIN keywords between the table names. The INNER keyword is optional, because an inner join is the default, so you can specify the JOIN keyword alone. You specify the predicate that is used to filter rows in a designated clause called *ON*. This predicate is also known as the join condition.

For example, the following query performs an inner join between the *Employees* and *Orders* tables in the *TSQL2012* database, matching employees and orders based on the predicate *E.empid = O.empid*.

```
USE TSQL2012;

SELECT E.empid, E.firstname, E.lastname, O.orderid
FROM HR.Employees AS E
  JOIN Sales.Orders AS O
    ON E.empid = O.empid;
```

This query produces the following result set, shown here in abbreviated form.

```
empid       firstname  lastname              orderid
----------- ---------- -------------------- -----------
1           Sara       Davis                 10258
1           Sara       Davis                 10270
1           Sara       Davis                 10275
1           Sara       Davis                 10285
1           Sara       Davis                 10292
...
2           Don        Funk                  10265
2           Don        Funk                  10277
2           Don        Funk                  10280
2           Don        Funk                  10295
2           Don        Funk                  10300
...

(830 row(s) affected)
```

For most people, the easiest way to think of such an inner join is to think of it as matching each employee row to all order rows that have the same employee ID as the employee's employee ID. This is a simplified way to think of the join. The more formal way to think of the join based on relational algebra is that first the join performs a Cartesian product of the two tables (9 employee rows × 830 order rows = 7,470 rows), and then filters rows based on the predicate *E.empid = O.empid*, eventually returning 830 rows. As mentioned earlier, that's just the logical way that the join is processed; in practice, physical processing of the query by the database engine can be different.

Recall the discussion from previous chapters about the three-valued predicate logic used by SQL. As with the *WHERE* and *HAVING* clauses, the *ON* clause also returns only rows for which the predicate returns *TRUE*, and does not return rows for which the predicate evaluates to *FALSE* or *UNKNOWN*.

In the *TSQL2012* database, all employees have related orders, so all employees show up in the output. However, had there been employees with no related orders, they would have been filtered out by the filter phase.

## ANSI SQL-89 Syntax

Similar to cross joins, inner joins can be expressed by using the ANSI SQL-89 syntax. You specify a comma between the table names just as in a cross join, and specify the join condition in the query's *WHERE* clause, like this.

```
SELECT E.empid, E.firstname, E.lastname, O.orderid
FROM HR.Employees AS E, Sales.Orders AS O
WHERE E.empid = O.empid;
```

Note that the ANSI SQL-89 syntax has no *ON* clause.

Again, both syntaxes are standard, fully supported by SQL Server, and interpreted in the same way by the engine, so you shouldn't expect any performance difference between the two. But one syntax is safer, as explained in the next section.

## Inner Join Safety

I strongly recommend that you stick to the ANSI SQL-92 join syntax because it is safer in several ways. Suppose you intend to write an inner join query, and by mistake you forget to specify the join condition. With the ANSI SQL-92 syntax, the query becomes invalid, and the parser generates an error. For example, try to run the following code.

```
SELECT E.empid, E.firstname, E.lastname, O.orderid
FROM HR.Employees AS E
  JOIN Sales.Orders AS O;
```

You get the following error:

```
Msg 102, Level 15, State 1, Line 3
Incorrect syntax near ';'.
```

Even though it might not be immediately obvious that the error involves a missing join condition, you will figure it out eventually and fix the query. However, if you forget to specify the join condition when you are using the ANSI SQL-89 syntax, you get a valid query that performs a cross join.

```
SELECT E.empid, E.firstname, E.lastname, O.orderid
FROM HR.Employees AS E, Sales.Orders AS O;
```

Because the query doesn't fail, the logical error might go unnoticed for a while, and users of your application might end up relying on incorrect results. It is unlikely that a programmer would forget to specify the join condition with such short and simple queries; however, most production queries are much more complicated and have multiple tables, filters, and other query elements. In those cases, the likelihood of forgetting to specify a join condition increases.

If I've convinced you that it is important to use the ANSI SQL-92 syntax for inner joins, you might wonder whether the recommendation holds for cross joins. Because no join condition is involved, you might think that both syntaxes are just as good for cross joins. However, I recommend staying with the ANSI SQL-92 syntax with cross joins for a couple of reasons—one being consistency. Also, suppose you do use the ANSI SQL-89 syntax. Even if you intended to write a cross join, when other developers need to review or maintain your code, how will they know whether you intended to write a cross join or intended to write an inner join and forgot to specify the join condition?

## More Join Examples

This section covers a few join examples that are known by specific names: composite joins, non-equi joins, and multi-join queries.

## Composite Joins

A *composite join* is simply a join based on a predicate that involves more than one attribute from each side. A composite join is commonly required when you need to join two tables based on a primary key–foreign key relationship and the relationship is composite; that is, based on more than one attribute. For example, suppose you have a foreign key defined on *dbo.Table2*, columns *col1*, *col2*, referencing *dbo.Table1*, columns *col1*, *col2*, and you need to write a query that joins the two based on a primary key–foreign key relationship. The *FROM* clause of the query would look like this.

```
FROM dbo.Table1 AS T1
  JOIN dbo.Table2 AS T2
    ON T1.col1 = T2.col1
    AND T1.col2 = T2.col2
```

For a more tangible example, suppose that you need to audit updates to column values against the *OrderDetails* table in the *TSQL2012* database. You create a custom auditing table called *OrderDetailsAudit*.

```
USE TSQL2012;
IF OBJECT_ID('Sales.OrderDetailsAudit', 'U') IS NOT NULL
  DROP TABLE Sales.OrderDetailsAudit;
CREATE TABLE Sales.OrderDetailsAudit
(
  lsn        INT NOT NULL IDENTITY,
  orderid    INT NOT NULL,
  productid  INT NOT NULL,
  dt         DATETIME NOT NULL,
  loginname  sysname NOT NULL,
  columnname sysname NOT NULL,
  oldval     SQL_VARIANT,
  newval     SQL_VARIANT,
  CONSTRAINT PK_OrderDetailsAudit PRIMARY KEY(lsn),
  CONSTRAINT FK_OrderDetailsAudit_OrderDetails
    FOREIGN KEY(orderid, productid)
    REFERENCES Sales.OrderDetails(orderid, productid)
);
```

Each audit row stores a log serial number (*lsn*), the key of the modified row (*orderid*, *productid*), the name of the modified column (*columnname*), the old value (*oldval*), the new value (*newval*), when the change took place (*dt*), and who made the change (*loginname*). The table has a foreign key defined on the attributes *orderid*, *productid*, referencing the primary key of the *OrderDetails* table, which is defined on the attributes *orderid*, *productid*. Assume that you already have in place in the *OrderDetailsAudit* table a process that logs, or audits, all changes taking place in column values in the *OrderDetails* table.

You need to write a query against the *OrderDetails* and *OrderDetailsAudit* tables that returns information about all value changes that took place in the column *qty*. In each result row, you need to return the current value from the *OrderDetails* table and the values before and after the change from the *OrderDetailsAudit* table. You need to join the two tables based on a primary key–foreign key relationship, like this.

```
SELECT OD.orderid, OD.productid, OD.qty,
  ODA.dt, ODA.loginname, ODA.oldval, ODA.newval
FROM Sales.OrderDetails AS OD
  JOIN Sales.OrderDetailsAudit AS ODA
    ON OD.orderid = ODA.orderid
    AND OD.productid = ODA.productid
WHERE ODA.columnname = N'qty';
```

Because the relationship is based on multiple attributes, the join condition is composite.

## Non-Equi Joins

When a join condition involves only an equality operator, the join is said to be an *equi join*. When a join condition involves any operator besides equality, the join is said to be a *non-equi join*.

> **Note** Standard SQL supports a concept called *natural join*, which represents an inner join based on a match between columns with the same name in both sides. For example, *T1 NATURAL JOIN T2* joins the rows between *T1* and *T2* based on a match between the columns with the same names in both sides. T-SQL doesn't have an implementation of a natural join, as of SQL Server 2012. A join that has an explicit join predicate that is based on a binary operator (equality or inequality) is known as a *theta join*. So both equi-joins and non-equi joins are types of theta joins.

As an example of a non-equi join, the following query joins two instances of the *Employees* table to produce unique pairs of employees.

```
SELECT
  E1.empid, E1.firstname, E1.lastname,
  E2.empid, E2.firstname, E2.lastname
FROM HR.Employees AS E1
  JOIN HR.Employees AS E2
    ON E1.empid < E2.empid;
```

Notice the predicate specified in the *ON* clause. The purpose of the query is to produce unique pairs of employees. Had a cross join been used, the result would have included self pairs (for example, 1 with 1) and also mirrored pairs (for example, 1 with 2 and also 2 with 1). Using an inner join with a join condition that says that the key in the left side must be smaller than the key in the right side eliminates the two inapplicable cases. Self pairs are eliminated because both sides are equal. With mirrored pairs, only one of the two cases qualifies because, of the two cases, only one will have a left key that is smaller than the right key. In this example, of the 81 possible pairs of employees that a cross join would have returned, this query returns the 36 unique pairs shown here.

```
empid firstname  lastname           empid  firstname  lastname
----- ---------- ----------------   ------ ---------- -----------------
1     Sara       Davis              2      Don        Funk
1     Sara       Davis              3      Judy       Lew
2     Don        Funk               3      Judy       Lew
1     Sara       Davis              4      Yael       Peled
2     Don        Funk               4      Yael       Peled
3     Judy       Lew                4      Yael       Peled
1     Sara       Davis              5      Sven       Buck
2     Don        Funk               5      Sven       Buck
3     Judy       Lew                5      Sven       Buck
4     Yael       Peled              5      Sven       Buck
1     Sara       Davis              6      Paul       Suurs
2     Don        Funk               6      Paul       Suurs
3     Judy       Lew                6      Paul       Suurs
4     Yael       Peled              6      Paul       Suurs
5     Sven       Buck               6      Paul       Suurs
1     Sara       Davis              7      Russell    King
2     Don        Funk               7      Russell    King
3     Judy       Lew                7      Russell    King
4     Yael       Peled              7      Russell    King
5     Sven       Buck               7      Russell    King
6     Paul       Suurs              7      Russell    King
1     Sara       Davis              8      Maria      Cameron
2     Don        Funk               8      Maria      Cameron
3     Judy       Lew                8      Maria      Cameron
4     Yael       Peled              8      Maria      Cameron
5     Sven       Buck               8      Maria      Cameron
6     Paul       Suurs              8      Maria      Cameron
7     Russell    King               8      Maria      Cameron
1     Sara       Davis              9      Zoya       Dolgopyatova
2     Don        Funk               9      Zoya       Dolgopyatova
3     Judy       Lew                9      Zoya       Dolgopyatova
4     Yael       Peled              9      Zoya       Dolgopyatova
5     Sven       Buck               9      Zoya       Dolgopyatova
6     Paul       Suurs              9      Zoya       Dolgopyatova
7     Russell    King               9      Zoya       Dolgopyatova
8     Maria      Cameron            9      Zoya       Dolgopyatova

(36 row(s) affected)
```

If it is still not clear to you what this query does, try to process it one step at a time with a smaller set of employees. For example, suppose that the *Employees* table contained only employees 1, 2, and 3. First, produce the Cartesian product of two instances of the table.

```
E1.empid       E2.empid
-------------  -------------
1              1
1              2
1              3
2              1
2              2
2              3
3              1
3              2
3              3
```

Next, filter the rows based on the predicate *E1.empid* < *E2.empid*, and you are left with only three rows.

```
E1.empid       E2.empid
-------------  -------------
1              2
1              3
2              3
```

## Multi-Join Queries

A join table operator operates only on two tables, but a single query can have multiple joins. In general, when more than one table operator appears in the *FROM* clause, the table operators are logically processed from left to right. That is, the result table of the first table operator is treated as the left input to the second table operator; the result of the second table operator is treated as the left input to the third table operator; and so on. So if there are multiple joins in the *FROM* clause, the first join operates on two base tables, but all other joins get the result of the preceding join as their left input. With cross joins and inner joins, the database engine can (and often does) internally rearrange join ordering for optimization purposes because it won't have an impact on the correctness of the result of the query.

As an example, the following query joins the *Customers* and *Orders* tables to match customers with their orders, and then it joins the result of the first join with the *OrderDetails* table to match orders with their order lines.

```
SELECT
  C.custid, C.companyname, O.orderid,
  OD.productid, OD.qty
FROM Sales.Customers AS C
  JOIN Sales.Orders AS O
    ON C.custid = O.custid
  JOIN Sales.OrderDetails AS OD
    ON O.orderid = OD.orderid;
```

This query returns the following output, shown here in abbreviated form.

```
custid      companyname         orderid      productid    qty
----------- ------------------- ------------ ------------ ------
85          Customer ENQZT      10248        11           12
85          Customer ENQZT      10248        42           10
85          Customer ENQZT      10248        72           5
79          Customer FAPSM      10249        14           9
79          Customer FAPSM      10249        51           40
34          Customer IBVRG      10250        41           10
34          Customer IBVRG      10250        51           35
34          Customer IBVRG      10250        65           15
84          Customer NRCSK      10251        22           6
84          Customer NRCSK      10251        57           15
...

(2155 row(s) affected)
```

# Outer Joins

Compared to the other types of joins, outer joins are usually harder for people to grasp. First I will describe the fundamentals of outer joins. If by the end of the "Fundamentals of Outer Joins" section, you feel very comfortable with the material and are ready for more advanced content, you can read an optional section describing aspects of outer joins that are beyond the fundamentals. Otherwise, feel free to skip that part and return to it when you feel comfortable with the material.

## Fundamentals of Outer Joins

Outer joins were introduced in ANSI SQL-92 and, unlike inner joins and cross joins, have only one standard syntax—the one in which the JOIN keyword is specified between the table names, and the join condition is specified in the ON clause. Outer joins apply the two logical processing phases that inner joins apply (Cartesian product and the ON filter), plus a third phase called Adding Outer Rows that is unique to this type of join.

In an outer join, you mark a table as a "preserved" table by using the keywords LEFT OUTER JOIN, RIGHT OUTER JOIN, or FULL OUTER JOIN between the table names. The OUTER keyword is optional. The LEFT keyword means that the rows of the left table are preserved; the RIGHT keyword means that the rows in the right table are preserved; and the FULL keyword means that the rows in both the left and right tables are preserved. The third logical query processing phase of an outer join identifies the rows from the preserved table that did not find matches in the other table based on the ON predicate. This phase adds those rows to the result table produced by the first two phases of the join, and uses *NULL* marks as placeholders for the attributes from the nonpreserved side of the join in those outer rows.

A good way to understand outer joins is through an example. The following query joins the *Customers* and *Orders* tables based on a match between the customer's customer ID and the order's customer ID, to return customers and their orders. The join type is a left outer join; therefore, the query also returns customers who did not place any orders.

```
SELECT C.custid, C.companyname, O.orderid
FROM Sales.Customers AS C
  LEFT OUTER JOIN Sales.Orders AS O
    ON C.custid = O.custid;
```

This query returns the following output, shown here in abbreviated form.

```
custid       companyname       orderid
-----------  ----------------  -----------
1            Customer NRZBB    10643
1            Customer NRZBB    10692
1            Customer NRZBB    10702
1            Customer NRZBB    10835
1            Customer NRZBB    10952
...
21           Customer KIDPX    10414
21           Customer KIDPX    10512
21           Customer KIDPX    10581
21           Customer KIDPX    10650
21           Customer KIDPX    10725
22           Customer DTDMN    NULL
23           Customer WVFAF    10408
23           Customer WVFAF    10480
23           Customer WVFAF    10634
23           Customer WVFAF    10763
23           Customer WVFAF    10780
...
56           Customer QNIVZ    10684
56           Customer QNIVZ    10766
56           Customer QNIVZ    10833
56           Customer QNIVZ    10999
56           Customer QNIVZ    11020
57           Customer WVAXS    NULL
58           Customer AHXHT    10322
58           Customer AHXHT    10354
58           Customer AHXHT    10474
58           Customer AHXHT    10502
58           Customer AHXHT    10995
...
91           Customer CCFIZ    10792
91           Customer CCFIZ    10870
91           Customer CCFIZ    10906
91           Customer CCFIZ    10998
91           Customer CCFIZ    11044

(832 row(s) affected)
```

Two customers in the *Customers* table did not place any orders. Their IDs are 22 and 57. Observe that in the output of the query, both customers are returned with *NULL* marks in the attributes from the *Orders* table. Logically, the rows for these two customers were filtered out by the second phase of the join (the filter based on the *ON* predicate), but the third phase added those as outer rows. Had the join been an inner join, these two rows would not have been returned. These two rows are added to preserve all the rows of the left table.

It might help to think of the result of an outer join as having two kinds of rows with respect to the preserved side—inner rows and outer rows. Inner rows are rows that have matches in the other side based on the *ON* predicate, and outer rows are rows that don't. An inner join returns only inner rows, whereas an outer join returns both inner and outer rows.

A common question about outer joins that is the source of a lot of confusion is whether to specify a predicate in the *ON* or *WHERE* clause of a query. You can see that with respect to rows from the preserved side of an outer join, the filter based on the *ON* predicate is not final. In other words, the *ON* predicate does not determine whether a row will show up in the output, only whether it will be matched with rows from the other side. So when you need to express a predicate that is not final— meaning a predicate that determines which rows to match from the nonpreserved side—specify the predicate in the *ON* clause. When you need a filter to be applied after outer rows are produced, and you want the filter to be final, specify the predicate in the *WHERE* clause. The *WHERE* clause is processed after the *FROM* clause—specifically, after all table operators have been processed and (in the case of outer joins) after all outer rows have been produced. Also, the *WHERE* clause is final with respect to rows that it filters out, unlike the *ON* clause.

Suppose that you need to return only customers who did not place any orders or, more technically speaking, you need to return only outer rows. You can use the previous query as your basis, adding a *WHERE* clause that filters only outer rows. Remember that outer rows are identified by the *NULL* marks in the attributes from the nonpreserved side of the join. So you can filter only the rows in which one of the attributes in the nonpreserved side of the join is *NULL*, like this.

```
SELECT C.custid, C.companyname
FROM Sales.Customers AS C
  LEFT OUTER JOIN Sales.Orders AS O
    ON C.custid = O.custid
WHERE O.orderid IS NULL;
```

This query returns only two rows, with the customers 22 and 57.

```
custid       companyname
-----------  ---------------
22           Customer DTDMN
57           Customer WVAXS

(2 row(s) affected)
```

Notice a couple of important things about this query. Recall the discussions about *NULL* marks earlier in the book: When looking for a *NULL*, you should use the operator *IS NULL* and not an equality operator, because when an equality operator compares something with a *NULL*, it always returns *UNKNOWN*—even when it is comparing two *NULL* marks. Also, the choice of which attribute from the nonpreserved side of the join to filter is important. You should choose an attribute that can only have a *NULL* when the row is an outer row and not otherwise (for example, not a *NULL* originating from the base table). For this purpose, three cases are safe to consider—a primary key column, a join column, and a column defined as *NOT NULL*. A primary key column cannot be *NULL*; therefore, a *NULL* in such a column can only mean that the row is an outer row. If a row has a *NULL* in the join column, that row is filtered out by the second phase of the join, so a *NULL* in such a column can only mean that it's an outer row. And obviously, a *NULL* in a column that is defined as *NOT NULL* can only mean that the row is an outer row.

To practice what you've learned and get a better grasp of outer joins, make sure that you perform the exercises for this chapter.

# Beyond the Fundamentals of Outer Joins

This section covers more advanced aspects of outer joins and is provided as optional reading for when you feel very comfortable with the fundamentals of outer joins.

## Including Missing Values

You can use outer joins to identify and include missing values when querying data. For example, suppose that you need to query all orders from the *Orders* table in the *TSQL2012* database. You need to ensure that you get at least one row in the output for each date in the range January 1, 2006 through December 31, 2008. You don't want to do anything special with dates within the range that have orders, but you do want the output to include the dates with no orders, with *NULL* marks as placeholders in the attributes of the order.

To solve the problem, you can first write a query that returns a sequence of all dates in the requested date range. You can then perform a left outer join between that set and the *Orders* table. This way, the result also includes the missing order dates.

To produce a sequence of dates in a given range, I usually use an auxiliary table of numbers. I create a table called *dbo.Nums* with a column called *n*, and populate it with a sequence of integers (1, 2, 3, and so on). I find that an auxiliary table of numbers is an extremely powerful general-purpose tool that I end up using to solve many problems. You need to create it only once in the database and populate it with as many numbers as you might need. The *TSQL2012* sample database already has such an auxiliary table.

As the first step in the solution, you need to produce a sequence of all dates in the requested range. You can achieve this by querying the *Nums* table and filtering as many numbers as the number of days in the requested date range. You can use the DATEDIFF function to calculate that number. By adding n – 1 days to the starting point of the date range (January 1, 2006) you get the actual date in the sequence. Here's the solution query.

```
SELECT DATEADD(day, n-1, '20060101') AS orderdate
FROM dbo.Nums
WHERE n <= DATEDIFF(day, '20060101', '20081231') + 1
ORDER BY orderdate;
```

This query returns a sequence of all dates in the range January 1, 2006 through December 31, 2008, as shown here in abbreviated form.

```
orderdate
----------------------
2006-01-01 00:00:00.000
2006-01-02 00:00:00.000
2006-01-03 00:00:00.000
2006-01-04 00:00:00.000
2006-01-05 00:00:00.000
...
2008-12-27 00:00:00.000
2008-12-28 00:00:00.000
2008-12-29 00:00:00.000
2008-12-30 00:00:00.000
2008-12-31 00:00:00.000

(1096 row(s) affected)
```

The next step is to extend the previous query, adding a left outer join between *Nums* and the *Orders* tables. The join condition compares the order date produced from the *Nums* table and the *orderdate* from the *Orders* table by using the expression *DATEADD(day, Nums.n − 1, '20060101')* like this.

```
SELECT DATEADD(day, Nums.n - 1, '20060101') AS orderdate,
  O.orderid, O.custid, O.empid
FROM dbo.Nums
  LEFT OUTER JOIN Sales.Orders AS O
    ON DATEADD(day, Nums.n - 1, '20060101') = O.orderdate
WHERE Nums.n <= DATEDIFF(day, '20060101', '20081231') + 1
ORDER BY orderdate;
```

This query produces the following output, shown here in abbreviated form.

```
orderdate                orderid      custid       empid
------------------------ -----------  -----------  -----------
2006-01-01 00:00:00.000  NULL         NULL         NULL
2006-01-02 00:00:00.000  NULL         NULL         NULL
2006-01-03 00:00:00.000  NULL         NULL         NULL
2006-01-04 00:00:00.000  NULL         NULL         NULL
2006-01-05 00:00:00.000  NULL         NULL         NULL
...
2006-06-29 00:00:00.000  NULL         NULL         NULL
2006-06-30 00:00:00.000  NULL         NULL         NULL
2006-07-01 00:00:00.000  NULL         NULL         NULL
2006-07-02 00:00:00.000  NULL         NULL         NULL
2006-07-03 00:00:00.000  NULL         NULL         NULL
2006-07-04 00:00:00.000  10248        85           5
2006-07-05 00:00:00.000  10249        79           6
2006-07-06 00:00:00.000  NULL         NULL         NULL
2006-07-07 00:00:00.000  NULL         NULL         NULL
2006-07-08 00:00:00.000  10250        34           4
2006-07-08 00:00:00.000  10251        84           3
2006-07-09 00:00:00.000  10252        76           4
2006-07-10 00:00:00.000  10253        34           3
```

```
2006-07-11 00:00:00.000     10254       14          5
2006-07-12 00:00:00.000     10255       68          9
2006-07-13 00:00:00.000     NULL        NULL        NULL
2006-07-14 00:00:00.000     NULL        NULL        NULL
2006-07-15 00:00:00.000     10256       88          3
2006-07-16 00:00:00.000     10257       35          4
...
2008-12-27 00:00:00.000     NULL        NULL        NULL
2008-12-28 00:00:00.000     NULL        NULL        NULL
2008-12-29 00:00:00.000     NULL        NULL        NULL
2008-12-30 00:00:00.000     NULL        NULL        NULL
2008-12-31 00:00:00.000     NULL        NULL        NULL

(1446 row(s) affected)
```

Order dates that do not appear in the *Orders* table appear in the output of the query with *NULL* marks in the order attributes.

## Filtering Attributes from the Nonpreserved Side of an Outer Join

When you need to review code involving outer joins to look for logical bugs, one of the things you should examine is the *WHERE* clause. If the predicate in the *WHERE* clause refers to an attribute from the nonpreserved side of the join using an expression in the form *<attribute> <operator> <value>*, it's usually an indication of a bug. This is because attributes from the nonpreserved side of the join are *NULL* marks in outer rows, and an expression in the form *NULL <operator> <value>* yields *UNKNOWN* (unless it's the *IS NULL* operator explicitly looking for *NULL* marks). Recall that a *WHERE* clause filters *UNKNOWN* out. Such a predicate in the *WHERE* clause causes all outer rows to be filtered out, effectively nullifying the outer join. In other words, it's as if the join type logically becomes an inner join. So the programmer either made a mistake in the choice of the join type or made a mistake in the predicate. If this is not clear yet, the following example might help. Consider the following query.

```
SELECT C.custid, C.companyname, O.orderid, O.orderdate
FROM Sales.Customers AS C
  LEFT OUTER JOIN Sales.Orders AS O
    ON C.custid = O.custid
WHERE O.orderdate >= '20070101';
```

The query performs a left outer join between the *Customers* and *Orders* tables. Prior to applying the *WHERE* filter, the join operator returns inner rows for customers who placed orders and outer rows for customers who didn't place orders, with *NULL* marks in the order attributes. The predicate *O.orderdate >= '20070101'* in the *WHERE* clause evaluates to *UNKNOWN* for all outer rows because those have a *NULL* in the *O.orderdate* attribute. All outer rows are eliminated by the *WHERE* filter, as you can see in the output of the query, shown here in abbreviated form.

```
custid       companyname        orderid     orderdate
-----------  -----------------  ----------  -----------------------
19           Customer RFNQC     10400       2007-01-01 00:00:00.000
65           Customer NYUHS     10401       2007-01-01 00:00:00.000
20           Customer THHDP     10402       2007-01-02 00:00:00.000
20           Customer THHDP     10403       2007-01-03 00:00:00.000
49           Customer CQRAA     10404       2007-01-03 00:00:00.000
...
```

```
58          Customer AHXHT      11073       2008-05-05 00:00:00.000
73          Customer JMIKW      11074       2008-05-06 00:00:00.000
68          Customer CCKOT      11075       2008-05-06 00:00:00.000
9           Customer RTXGC      11076       2008-05-06 00:00:00.000
65          Customer NYUHS      11077       2008-05-06 00:00:00.000
```

```
(678 row(s) affected)
```

This means that the use of an outer join here was futile. The programmer either made a mistake in using an outer join or made a mistake in the *WHERE* predicate.

## Using Outer Joins in a Multi-Join Query

Recall the discussion about all-at-once operations in Chapter 2, "Single-Table Queries." The concept describes the fact that all expressions that appear in the same logical query processing phase are logically evaluated at the same point in time. However, this concept is not applicable to the processing of table operators in the *FROM* phase. Table operators are logically evaluated from left to right. Rearranging the order in which outer joins are processed might result in different output, so you cannot rearrange them at will.

Some interesting logical bugs have to do with the logical order in which outer joins are processed. For example, a common logical bug involving outer joins could be considered a variation of the bug in the previous section. Suppose that you write a multi-join query with an outer join between two tables, followed by an inner join with a third table. If the predicate in the inner join's *ON* clause compares an attribute from the nonpreserved side of the outer join and an attribute from the third table, all outer rows are filtered out. Remember that outer rows have *NULL* marks in the attributes from the nonpreserved side of the join, and comparing a *NULL* with anything yields *UNKNOWN*. *UNKNOWN* is filtered out by the *ON* filter. In other words, such a predicate would nullify the outer join, and logically it would be as if you specified an inner join. For example, consider the following query.

```
SELECT C.custid, O.orderid, OD.productid, OD.qty
FROM Sales.Customers AS C
  LEFT OUTER JOIN Sales.Orders AS O
    ON C.custid = O.custid
  JOIN Sales.OrderDetails AS OD
    ON O.orderid = OD.orderid;
```

The first join is an outer join returning customers and their orders and also customers who did not place any orders. The outer rows representing customers with no orders have *NULL* marks in the order attributes. The second join matches order lines from the *OrderDetails* table with rows from the result of the first join, based on the predicate *O.orderid = OD.orderid*; however, in the rows representing customers with no orders, the *O.orderid* attribute is *NULL*. Therefore, the predicate evaluates to *UNKNOWN*, and those rows are filtered out. The output shown here in abbreviated form doesn't contain the customers 22 and 57, the two customers who did not place orders.

| custid | orderid | productid | qty |
| --- | --- | --- | --- |
| 85 | 10248 | 11 | 12 |
| 85 | 10248 | 42 | 10 |
| 85 | 10248 | 72 | 5 |
| 79 | 10249 | 14 | 9 |
| 79 | 10249 | 51 | 40 |
| ... | | | |
| 65 | 11077 | 64 | 2 |
| 65 | 11077 | 66 | 1 |
| 65 | 11077 | 73 | 2 |
| 65 | 11077 | 75 | 4 |
| 65 | 11077 | 77 | 2 |

(2155 row(s) affected)

Generally speaking, outer rows are dropped whenever any kind of outer join (left, right, or full) is followed by a subsequent inner join or right outer join. That's assuming, of course, that the join condition compares the *NULL* marks from the left side with something from the right side.

There are several ways to get around the problem if you want to return customers with no orders in the output. One option is to use a left outer join in the second join as well.

```
SELECT C.custid, O.orderid, OD.productid, OD.qty
FROM Sales.Customers AS C
  LEFT OUTER JOIN Sales.Orders AS O
    ON C.custid = O.custid
  LEFT OUTER JOIN Sales.OrderDetails AS OD
    ON O.orderid = OD.orderid;
```

This way, the outer rows produced by the first join aren't filtered out, as you can see in the output shown here in abbreviated form.

| custid | orderid | productid | qty |
| --- | --- | --- | --- |
| 85 | 10248 | 11 | 12 |
| 85 | 10248 | 42 | 10 |
| 85 | 10248 | 72 | 5 |
| 79 | 10249 | 14 | 9 |
| 79 | 10249 | 51 | 40 |
| ... | | | |
| 65 | 11077 | 64 | 2 |
| 65 | 11077 | 66 | 1 |
| 65 | 11077 | 73 | 2 |
| 65 | 11077 | 75 | 4 |
| 65 | 11077 | 77 | 2 |
| 22 | NULL | NULL | NULL |
| 57 | NULL | NULL | NULL |

(2157 row(s) affected)

A second option is to first join *Orders* and *OrderDetails* by using an inner join, and then join to the *Customers* table by using a right outer join.

```
SELECT C.custid, O.orderid, OD.productid, OD.qty
FROM Sales.Orders AS O
  JOIN Sales.OrderDetails AS OD
    ON O.orderid = OD.orderid
  RIGHT OUTER JOIN Sales.Customers AS C
    ON O.custid = C.custid;
```

This way, the outer rows are produced by the last join and are not filtered out.

A third option is to use parentheses to turn the inner join between *Orders* and *OrderDetails* into an independent logical phase. This way, you can apply a left outer join between the *Customers* table and the result of the inner join between *Orders* and *OrderDetails*. The query would look like this.

```
SELECT C.custid, O.orderid, OD.productid, OD.qty
FROM Sales.Customers AS C
  LEFT OUTER JOIN
      (Sales.Orders AS O
          JOIN Sales.OrderDetails AS OD
            ON O.orderid = OD.orderid)
    ON C.custid = O.custid;
```

## Using the *COUNT* Aggregate with Outer Joins

Another common logical bug involves using *COUNT* with outer joins. When you group the result of an outer join and use the COUNT(*) aggregate, the aggregate takes into consideration both inner rows and outer rows, because it counts rows regardless of their contents. Usually, you're not supposed to take outer rows into consideration for the purposes of counting. For example, the following query is supposed to return the count of orders for each customer.

```
SELECT C.custid, COUNT(*) AS numorders
FROM Sales.Customers AS C
  LEFT OUTER JOIN Sales.Orders AS O
    ON C.custid = O.custid
GROUP BY C.custid;
```

However, the COUNT(*) aggregate counts rows regardless of their meaning or contents, and customers who did not place orders—such as customers 22 and 57—each have an outer row in the result of the join. As you can see in the output of the query, shown here in abbreviated form, both 22 and 57 show up with a count of 1, whereas the number of orders they placed is actually 0.

```
custid       numorders
-----------  -----------
1            6
2            4
3            7
4            13
5            18
...
22           1
...
57           1
...
87           15
88           9
89           14
90           7
91           7
```

(91 row(s) affected)

The COUNT(*) aggregate function cannot detect whether a row really represents an order. To fix the problem, you should use *COUNT(<column>)* instead of COUNT(*), and provide a column from the nonpreserved side of the join. This way, the COUNT() aggregate ignores outer rows because they have a *NULL* in that column. Remember to use a column that can only be *NULL*, in case the row is an outer row—for example, the primary key column *orderid*.

```
SELECT C.custid, COUNT(O.orderid) AS numorders
FROM Sales.Customers AS C
  LEFT OUTER JOIN Sales.Orders AS O
    ON C.custid = O.custid
GROUP BY C.custid;
```

Notice in the output shown here in abbreviated form that the customers 22 and 57 now show up with a count of 0.

```
custid       numorders
-----------  -----------
1            6
2            4
3            7
4            13
5            18
...
22           0
...
57           0
...
87           15
88           9
89           14
90           7
91           7
```

(91 row(s) affected)

# Conclusion

This chapter covered the *JOIN* table operator. It described the logical query processing phases involved in the three fundamental types of joins—cross joins, inner joins, and outer joins. The chapter also covered further join examples, including composite joins, non-equi joins, and multi-join queries. The chapter concluded with an optional reading section covering more advanced aspects of outer joins. To practice what you've learned, go over the exercises for this chapter.

# Exercises

This section provides exercises to help you familiarize yourself with the subjects discussed in this chapter. All exercises involve querying objects in the *TSQL2012* database.

## 1-1

Write a query that generates five copies of each employee row.

- Tables involved: *HR.Employees* and *dbo.Nums*

- Desired output:

```
empid       firstname  lastname              n
----------- ---------- -------------------- -----------
1           Sara       Davis                1
2           Don        Funk                 1
3           Judy       Lew                  1
4           Yael       Peled                1
5           Sven       Buck                 1
6           Paul       Suurs                1
7           Russell    King                 1
8           Maria      Cameron              1
9           Zoya       Dolgopyatova         1
1           Sara       Davis                2
2           Don        Funk                 2
3           Judy       Lew                  2
4           Yael       Peled                2
5           Sven       Buck                 2
6           Paul       Suurs                2
7           Russell    King                 2
8           Maria      Cameron              2
9           Zoya       Dolgopyatova         2
1           Sara       Davis                3
2           Don        Funk                 3
3           Judy       Lew                  3
4           Yael       Peled                3
5           Sven       Buck                 3
6           Paul       Suurs                3
7           Russell    King                 3
8           Maria      Cameron              3
9           Zoya       Dolgopyatova         3
```

```
1       Sara        Davis           4
2       Don         Funk            4
3       Judy        Lew             4
4       Yael        Peled           4
5       Sven        Buck            4
6       Paul        Suurs           4
7       Russell     King            4
8       Maria       Cameron         4
9       Zoya        Dolgopyatova     4
1       Sara        Davis           5
2       Don         Funk            5
3       Judy        Lew             5
4       Yael        Peled           5
5       Sven        Buck            5
6       Paul        Suurs           5
7       Russell     King            5
8       Maria       Cameron         5
9       Zoya        Dolgopyatova     5

(45 row(s) affected)
```

# 1-2 (Optional, Advanced)

Write a query that returns a row for each employee and day in the range June 12, 2009 through June 16, 2009.

- Tables involved: *HR.Employees* and *dbo.Nums*

- Desired output:

```
empid       dt
----------  -----------------------
1           2009-06-12 00:00:00.000
1           2009-06-13 00:00:00.000
1           2009-06-14 00:00:00.000
1           2009-06-15 00:00:00.000
1           2009-06-16 00:00:00.000
2           2009-06-12 00:00:00.000
2           2009-06-13 00:00:00.000
2           2009-06-14 00:00:00.000
2           2009-06-15 00:00:00.000
2           2009-06-16 00:00:00.000
3           2009-06-12 00:00:00.000
3           2009-06-13 00:00:00.000
3           2009-06-14 00:00:00.000
3           2009-06-15 00:00:00.000
3           2009-06-16 00:00:00.000
4           2009-06-12 00:00:00.000
4           2009-06-13 00:00:00.000
4           2009-06-14 00:00:00.000
4           2009-06-15 00:00:00.000
4           2009-06-16 00:00:00.000
5           2009-06-12 00:00:00.000
5           2009-06-13 00:00:00.000
5           2009-06-14 00:00:00.000
```

```
5              2009-06-15 00:00:00.000
5              2009-06-16 00:00:00.000
6              2009-06-12 00:00:00.000
6              2009-06-13 00:00:00.000
6              2009-06-14 00:00:00.000
6              2009-06-15 00:00:00.000
6              2009-06-16 00:00:00.000
7              2009-06-12 00:00:00.000
7              2009-06-13 00:00:00.000
7              2009-06-14 00:00:00.000
7              2009-06-15 00:00:00.000
7              2009-06-16 00:00:00.000
8              2009-06-12 00:00:00.000
8              2009-06-13 00:00:00.000
8              2009-06-14 00:00:00.000
8              2009-06-15 00:00:00.000
8              2009-06-16 00:00:00.000
9              2009-06-12 00:00:00.000
9              2009-06-13 00:00:00.000
9              2009-06-14 00:00:00.000
9              2009-06-15 00:00:00.000
9              2009-06-16 00:00:00.000

(45 row(s) affected)
```

## 2

Return United States customers, and for each customer return the total number of orders and total quantities.

- Tables involved: *Sales.Customers*, *Sales.Orders*, and *Sales.OrderDetails*

- Desired output:

```
custid      numorders   totalqty
----------- ----------- -----------
32          11          345
36          5           122
43          2           20
45          4           181
48          8           134
55          10          603
65          18          1383
71          31          4958
75          9           327
77          4           46
78          3           59
82          3           89
89          14          1063

(13 row(s) affected)
```

## 3

Return customers and their orders, including customers who placed no orders.

- Tables involved: *Sales.Customers* and *Sales.Orders*

- Desired output (abbreviated):

```
custid       companyname      orderid      orderdate
-----------  ---------------- -----------  ------------------------
85           Customer ENQZT   10248        2006-07-04 00:00:00.000
79           Customer FAPSM   10249        2006-07-05 00:00:00.000
34           Customer IBVRG   10250        2006-07-08 00:00:00.000
84           Customer NRCSK   10251        2006-07-08 00:00:00.000
...
73           Customer JMIKW   11074        2008-05-06 00:00:00.000
68           Customer CCKOT   11075        2008-05-06 00:00:00.000
9            Customer RTXGC   11076        2008-05-06 00:00:00.000
65           Customer NYUHS   11077        2008-05-06 00:00:00.000
22           Customer DTDMN   NULL         NULL
57           Customer WVAXS   NULL         NULL

(832 row(s) affected)
```

## 4

Return customers who placed no orders.

- Tables involved: *Sales.Customers* and *Sales.Orders*

- Desired output:

```
custid       companyname
-----------  ----------------
22           Customer DTDMN
57           Customer WVAXS

(2 row(s) affected)
```

## 5

Return customers with orders placed on February 12, 2007, along with their orders.

- Tables involved: *Sales.Customers* and *Sales.Orders*

- Desired output:

```
custid       companyname      orderid      orderdate
-----------  ---------------- -----------  ------------------------
66           Customer LHANT   10443        2007-02-12 00:00:00.000
5            Customer HGVLZ   10444        2007-02-12 00:00:00.000

(2 row(s) affected)
```

# 6 (Optional, Advanced)

Return customers with orders placed on February 12, 2007, along with their orders. Also return customers who didn't place orders on February 12, 2007.

- Tables involved: *Sales.Customers* and *Sales.Orders*

- Desired output (abbreviated):

```
custid       companyname          orderid       orderdate
-----------  -------------------  -----------   -----------------------
72           Customer AHPOP       NULL          NULL
58           Customer AHXHT       NULL          NULL
25           Customer AZJED       NULL          NULL
18           Customer BSVAR       NULL          NULL
91           Customer CCFIZ       NULL          NULL
...
33           Customer FVXPQ       NULL          NULL
53           Customer GCJSG       NULL          NULL
39           Customer GLLAG       NULL          NULL
16           Customer GYBBY       NULL          NULL
4            Customer HFBZG       NULL          NULL
5            Customer HGVLZ       10444         2007-02-12 00:00:00.000
42           Customer IAIJK       NULL          NULL
34           Customer IBVRG       NULL          NULL
63           Customer IRRVL       NULL          NULL
73           Customer JMIKW       NULL          NULL
15           Customer JUWXK       NULL          NULL
...
21           Customer KIDPX       NULL          NULL
30           Customer KSLQF       NULL          NULL
55           Customer KZQZT       NULL          NULL
71           Customer LCOUJ       NULL          NULL
77           Customer LCYBZ       NULL          NULL
66           Customer LHANT       10443         2007-02-12 00:00:00.000
38           Customer LJUCA       NULL          NULL
59           Customer LOLJO       NULL          NULL
36           Customer LVJSO       NULL          NULL
64           Customer LWGMD       NULL          NULL
29           Customer MDLWA       NULL          NULL
...

(91 row(s) affected)
```

## 7 (Optional, Advanced)

Return all customers, and for each return a Yes/No value depending on whether the customer placed an order on February 12, 2007.

- Tables involved: *Sales.Customers* and *Sales.Orders*

- Desired output (abbreviated):

```
custid       companyname         HasOrderOn20070212
-----------  ------------------  ------------------
1            Customer NRZBB      No
2            Customer MLTDN      No
3            Customer KBUDE      No
4            Customer HFBZG      No
5            Customer HGVLZ      Yes
6            Customer XHXJV      No
7            Customer QXVLA      No
8            Customer QUHWH      No
9            Customer RTXGC      No
10           Customer EEALV      No
...

(91 row(s) affected)
```

# Solutions

This section provides solutions to the exercises for this chapter.

## 1-1

Producing multiple copies of rows can be achieved with a fundamental technique that utilizes a cross join. If you need to produce five copies of each employee row, you need to perform a cross join between the *Employees* table and a table that has five rows; alternatively, you can perform a cross join between *Employees* and a table that has more than five rows, but filter only five from that table in the *WHERE* clause. The *Nums* table is very convenient for this purpose. Simply cross *Employees* and *Nums*, and filter from *Nums* as many rows as the number of requested copies (five, in this case). Here's the solution query.

```
SELECT E.empid, E.firstname, E.lastname, N.n
FROM HR.Employees AS E
  CROSS JOIN dbo.Nums AS N
WHERE N.n <= 5
ORDER BY n, empid;
```

## 1-2

This exercise is an extension of the previous exercise. Instead of being asked to produce a predetermined constant number of copies of each employee row, you are asked to produce a copy for each day in a certain date range. So here you need to calculate the number of days in the requested date range by using the DATEDIFF function, and refer to the result of that expression in the query's *WHERE* clause instead of referring to a constant. To produce the dates, simply add n − 1 days to the date that starts the requested range. Here's the solution query.

```
SELECT E.empid,
  DATEADD(day, D.n - 1, '20090612') AS dt
FROM HR.Employees AS E
  CROSS JOIN dbo.Nums AS D
WHERE D.n <= DATEDIFF(day, '20090612', '20090616') + 1
ORDER BY empid, dt;
```

The DATEDIFF function returns *4* because there is a four-day difference between June 12, 2009 and June 16, 2009. Add 1 to the result, and you get 5 for the five days in the range. So the *WHERE* clause filters five rows from *Nums* where n is less than or equal to 5. By adding n − 1 days to June 12, 2009, you get all dates in the range June 12, 2009 and June 16, 2009.

## 2

This exercise requires you to write a query that joins three tables: *Customers*, *Orders*, and *OrderDetails*. The query should use the *WHERE* clause to filter only rows where the customer's country is the United States. Because you are asked to return aggregates per customer, the query should group the rows by customer ID. You need to resolve a tricky issue here to return the right number of orders for each customer. Because of the join between *Orders* and *OrderDetails*, you don't get only one row per order—you get one row per order line. So if you use the COUNT(*) function in the *SELECT* list, you get back the number of order lines for each customer and not the number of orders. To resolve this issue, you need to take each order into consideration only once. You can do this by using *COUNT(DISTINCT O.orderid)* instead of COUNT(*). The total quantities don't create any special issues because the quantity is associated with the order line and not the order. Here's the solution query.

```
SELECT C.custid, COUNT(DISTINCT O.orderid) AS numorders, SUM(OD.qty) AS totalqty
FROM Sales.Customers AS C
  JOIN Sales.Orders AS O
    ON O.custid = C.custid
  JOIN Sales.OrderDetails AS OD
    ON OD.orderid = O.orderid
WHERE C.country = N'USA'
GROUP BY C.custid;
```

# 3

To get both customers who placed orders and customers who didn't place orders in the result, you need to use an outer join, like this.

```
SELECT C.custid, C.companyname, O.orderid, O.orderdate
FROM Sales.Customers AS C
  LEFT OUTER JOIN Sales.Orders AS O
    ON O.custid = C.custid;
```

This query returns 832 rows (including the customers 22 and 57, who didn't place orders). An inner join between the tables would return only 830 rows, without those customers.

# 4

This exercise is an extension of the previous one. To return only customers who didn't place orders, you need to add a *WHERE* clause to the query that filters only outer rows; namely, rows that represent customers with no orders. Outer rows have *NULL* marks in the attributes from the nonpreserved side of the join (*Orders*). But to make sure that the *NULL* is a placeholder for an outer row and not a *NULL* that originated from the table, it is recommended that you refer to an attribute that is the primary key, or the join column, or one defined as not allowing *NULL* marks. Here's the solution query, which refers to the primary key of the *Orders* table in the *WHERE* clause.

```
SELECT C.custid, C.companyname
FROM Sales.Customers AS C
  LEFT OUTER JOIN Sales.Orders AS O
    ON O.custid = C.custid
WHERE O.orderid IS NULL;
```

This query returns only two rows, for customers 22 and 57, who didn't place orders.

# 5

This exercise involves writing a query that performs an inner join between *Customers* and *Orders* and filters only rows in which the order date is February 12, 2007.

```
SELECT C.custid, C.companyname, O.orderid, O.orderdate
FROM Sales.Customers AS C
  JOIN Sales.Orders AS O
    ON O.custid = C.custid
WHERE O.orderdate = '20070212';
```

The *WHERE* clause filtered out customers who didn't place orders on February 12, 2007, but that was the request.

# 6

This exercise builds on the previous one. The trick here is to realize two things. First, you need an outer join because you are supposed to return customers who do not meet a certain criteria. Second, the filter on the order date must appear in the *ON* clause and not the *WHERE* clause. Remember that the *WHERE* filter is applied after outer rows are added and is final. Your goal is to match orders to customers only if the order was placed by the customer on February 12, 2007. You still want to get customers who didn't place orders on that date in the output; in other words, the filter on the order date should only determine matches and not be considered final in regard to the customer rows. Hence, the *ON* clause should match customers and orders based on both an equality between the customer's customer ID and the order's customer ID, and on the order date being February 12, 2007. Here's the solution query.

```
SELECT C.custid, C.companyname, O.orderid, O.orderdate
FROM Sales.Customers AS C
  LEFT OUTER JOIN Sales.Orders AS O
    ON O.custid = C.custid
    AND O.orderdate = '20070212';
```

# 7

This exercise is an extension of the previous exercise. Here, instead of returning matching orders, you just need to return a Yes/No value indicating whether there is a matching order. Remember that in an outer join, a nonmatch is identified as an outer row with *NULL* marks in the attributes of the non-preserved side. So you can use a simple *CASE* expression that checks whether the current row is not an outer one, in which case it returns *Yes*; otherwise, it returns *No*. Because technically you can have more than one match per customer, you should add a *DISTINCT* clause to the *SELECT* list. This way, you get only one row back for each customer. Here's the solution query.

```
SELECT DISTINCT C.custid, C.companyname,
  CASE WHEN O.orderid IS NOT NULL THEN 'Yes' ELSE 'No' END AS [HasOrderOn20070212]
FROM Sales.Customers AS C
  LEFT OUTER JOIN Sales.Orders AS O
    ON O.custid = C.custid
    AND O.orderdate = '20070212';
```

# CHAPTER 4

# Subqueries

SQL supports writing queries within queries, or *nesting* queries. The outermost query is a query whose result set is returned to the caller and is known as the *outer query*. The inner query is a query whose result is used by the outer query and is known as a *subquery*. The inner query acts in place of an expression that is based on constants or variables and is evaluated at run time. Unlike the results of expressions that use constants, the result of a subquery can change, because of changes in the queried tables. When you use subqueries, you avoid the need for separate steps in your solutions that store intermediate query results in variables.

A subquery can be either self-contained or correlated. A self-contained subquery has no dependency on the outer query that it belongs to, whereas a correlated subquery does. A subquery can be single-valued, multivalued, or table-valued. That is, a subquery can return a single value (a scalar value), multiple values, or a whole table result.

This chapter focuses on subqueries that return a single value (scalar subqueries) and subqueries that return multiple values (multivalued subqueries). I'll cover subqueries that return whole tables (table subqueries) later in the book in Chapter 5, "Table Expressions."

Both self-contained and correlated subqueries can return a scalar or multiple values. I'll first describe self-contained subqueries and demonstrate both scalar and multivalued examples, and explicitly identify those as scalar or multivalued subqueries. Then I'll describe correlated subqueries, but I won't explicitly identify them as scalar or multivalued, assuming that you will already understand the difference.

Again, exercises at the end of the chapter can help you practice what you've learned.

## Self-Contained Subqueries

Every subquery has an outer query that it belongs to. Self-contained subqueries are subqueries that are independent of the outer query that they belong to. Self-contained subqueries are very convenient to debug, because you can always highlight the subquery code, run it, and ensure that it does what it's supposed to do. Logically, it's as if the subquery code is evaluated only once before the outer query is evaluated, and then the outer query uses the result of the subquery. The following sections take a look at some concrete examples of self-contained subqueries.

# Self-Contained Scalar Subquery Examples

A scalar subquery is a subquery that returns a single value—regardless of whether it is self-contained. Such a subquery can appear anywhere in the outer query where a single-valued expression can appear (such as *WHERE* or *SELECT*).

For example, suppose that you need to query the *Orders* table in the *TSQL2012* database and return information about the order that has the maximum order ID in the table. You could accomplish the task by using a variable. The code could retrieve the maximum order ID from the *Orders* table and store the result in a variable. Then the code could query the *Orders* table and filter the order where the order ID is equal to the value stored in the variable. The following code demonstrates this technique.

```
USE TSQL2012;

DECLARE @maxid AS INT = (SELECT MAX(orderid)
                        FROM Sales.Orders);

SELECT orderid, orderdate, empid, custid
FROM Sales.Orders
WHERE orderid = @maxid;
```

This query returns the following output.

```
orderid      orderdate                    empid        custid
------------ ---------------------------- ------------ -----------
11077        2008-05-06 00:00:00.000      1            65
```

You can substitute the technique that uses a variable with an embedded subquery. You achieve this by substituting the reference to the variable with a scalar self-contained subquery that returns the maximum order ID. This way, your solution has a single query instead of the two-step process.

```
SELECT orderid, orderdate, empid, custid
FROM Sales.Orders
WHERE orderid = (SELECT MAX(O.orderid)
                 FROM Sales.Orders AS O);
```

For a scalar subquery to be valid, it must return no more than one value. If a scalar subquery can return more than one value, it might fail at run time. The following query happens to run without failure.

```
SELECT orderid
FROM Sales.Orders
WHERE empid =
  (SELECT E.empid
   FROM HR.Employees AS E
   WHERE E.lastname LIKE N'B%');
```

The purpose of this query is to return the order IDs of orders placed by any employee whose last name starts with the letter *B*. The subquery returns employee IDs of all employees whose last names start with the letter *B*, and the outer query returns order IDs of orders where the employee ID is equal to the result of the subquery. Because an equality operator expects single-valued expressions from both sides, the subquery is considered scalar. Because the subquery can potentially return more than one value, the choices of using an equality operator and a scalar subquery here are wrong. If the subquery returns more than one value, the query fails.

This query happens to run without failure because currently the *Employees* table contains only one employee whose last name starts with *B* (Sven Buck with employee ID 5). This query returns the following output, shown here in abbreviated form.

```
orderid
-----------
10248
10254
10269
10297
10320
...
10874
10899
10922
10954
11043

(42 row(s) affected)
```

Of course, if the subquery returns more than one value, the query fails. For example, try running the query with employees whose last names start with *D*.

```
SELECT orderid
FROM Sales.Orders
WHERE empid =
  (SELECT E.empid
   FROM HR.Employees AS E
   WHERE E.lastname LIKE N'D%');
```

Apparently, two employees have a last name starting with *D* (Sara Davis and Zoya Dolgopyatova). Therefore, the query fails at run time with the following error.

```
Msg 512, Level 16, State 1, Line 1
Subquery returned more than 1 value. This is not permitted when the subquery follows =, !=, <,
<= , >, >= or when the subquery is used as an expression.
```

If a scalar subquery returns no value, it returns a *NULL*. Recall that a comparison with a *NULL* yields *UNKNOWN* and that query filters do not return a row for which the filter expression evaluates to *UNKNOWN*. For example, the *Employees* table currently has no employees whose last names start with *A*; therefore, the following query returns an empty set.

```
SELECT orderid
FROM Sales.Orders
WHERE empid =
  (SELECT E.empid
   FROM HR.Employees AS E
   WHERE E.lastname LIKE N'A%');
```

# Self-Contained Multivalued Subquery Examples

A multivalued subquery is a subquery that returns multiple values as a single column, regardless of whether the subquery is self-contained. Some predicates, such as the *IN* predicate, operate on a multivalued subquery.

> **Note** There are other predicates that operate on a multivalued subquery; those are *SOME*, *ANY*, and *ALL*. They are very rarely used and therefore not covered in this book.

The form of the *IN* predicate is:

<scalar_expression> IN (<multivalued subquery>)

The predicate evaluates to *TRUE* if *scalar_expression* is equal to any of the values returned by the subquery. Recall the last request discussed in the previous section—returning order IDs of orders that were handled by employees with a last name starting with a certain letter. Because more than one employee can have a last name starting with the same letter, this request should be handled with the *IN* predicate and a multivalued subquery, and not with an equality operator and a scalar subquery. For example, the following query returns order IDs of orders placed by employees with a last name starting with *D*.

```
SELECT orderid
FROM Sales.Orders
WHERE empid IN
  (SELECT E.empid
   FROM HR.Employees AS E
   WHERE E.lastname LIKE N'D%');
```

Because it uses the *IN* predicate, this query is valid with any number of values returned—none, one, or more. This query returns the following output, shown here in abbreviated form.

```
orderid
-----------
10258
10270
10275
10285
10292
...
10978
11016
11017
11022
11058

(166 row(s) affected)
```

You might wonder why you wouldn't implement this task by using a join instead of subqueries, like this.

```
SELECT O.orderid
FROM HR.Employees AS E
  JOIN Sales.Orders AS O
    ON E.empid = O.empid
WHERE E.lastname LIKE N'D%';
```

Similarly, you are likely to stumble into many other querying problems that you can solve with either subqueries or joins. In my experience, there's no reliable rule of thumb that says that a subquery is better than a join. In some cases, the database engine interprets both types of queries the same way. Sometimes joins perform better than subqueries, and sometimes the opposite is true. My approach is to first write the solution query for the specified task in an intuitive form, and if performance is not satisfactory, one of my tuning approaches is to try query revisions. Such query revisions might include using joins instead of subqueries or using subqueries instead of joins.

As another example of using multivalued subqueries, suppose that you need to write a query that returns orders placed by customers from the United States. You can write a query against the *Orders* table that returns orders where the customer ID is in the set of customer IDs of customers from the United States. You can implement the last part in a self-contained, multivalued subquery. Here's the complete solution query.

```
SELECT custid, orderid, orderdate, empid
FROM Sales.Orders
WHERE custid IN
  (SELECT C.custid
   FROM Sales.Customers AS C
   WHERE C.country = N'USA');
```

This query returns the following output, shown here in abbreviated form.

```
custid       orderid      orderdate                    empid
-----------  -----------  ---------------------------  -----------
65           10262        2006-07-22 00:00:00.000      8
89           10269        2006-07-31 00:00:00.000      5
75           10271        2006-08-01 00:00:00.000      6
65           10272        2006-08-02 00:00:00.000      6
65           10294        2006-08-30 00:00:00.000      4
...
32           11040        2008-04-22 00:00:00.000      4
32           11061        2008-04-30 00:00:00.000      4
71           11064        2008-05-01 00:00:00.000      1
89           11066        2008-05-01 00:00:00.000      7
65           11077        2008-05-06 00:00:00.000      1

(122 row(s) affected)
```

As with any other predicate, you can negate the *IN* predicate with the *NOT* logical operator. For example, the following query returns customers who did not place any orders.

```
SELECT custid, companyname
FROM Sales.Customers
WHERE custid NOT IN
  (SELECT O.custid
   FROM Sales.Orders AS O);
```

Note that best practice is to qualify the subquery to exclude *NULL* marks. Here, to keep the example simple, I didn't exclude *NULL* marks, but later in the chapter, in the "*NULL* Trouble" section, I explain this recommendation.

The self-contained, multivalued subquery returns all customer IDs that appear in the *Orders* table. Naturally, only IDs of customers who did place orders appear in the *Orders* table. The outer query returns customers from the *Customers* table where the customer ID is not in the set of values returned by the subquery—in other words, customers who did not place orders. This query returns the following output.

```
custid      companyname
----------- ----------------
22          Customer DTDMN
57          Customer WVAXS
```

You might wonder whether specifying a *DISTINCT* clause in the subquery can help performance, because the same customer ID can occur more than once in the *Orders* table. The database engine is smart enough to consider removing duplicates without you asking it to do so explicitly, so this isn't something you need to worry about.

The last example in this section demonstrates the use of multiple self-contained subqueries in the same query—both single-valued and multivalued. Before I describe the task at hand, run the following code to create a table called *dbo.Orders* in the *TSQL2012* database (for test purposes), and populate it with order IDs from the *Sales.Orders* table that have even-numbered order IDs.

```
USE TSQL2012;
IF OBJECT_ID('dbo.Orders', 'U') IS NOT NULL DROP TABLE dbo.Orders;
CREATE TABLE dbo.Orders(orderid INT NOT NULL CONSTRAINT PK_Orders PRIMARY KEY);

INSERT INTO dbo.Orders(orderid)
  SELECT orderid
  FROM Sales.Orders
  WHERE orderid % 2 = 0;
```

I describe the *INSERT* statement in more detail in Chapter 8, "Data Modification," so don't worry if you're not familiar with it yet.

The task at hand is to return all individual order IDs that are missing between the minimum and maximum in the table. It can be quite complicated to solve this problem with a query without any helper tables. You might find the *Nums* table introduced in Chapter 3, "Joins," very useful here. Remember that the *Nums* table contains a sequence of integers, starting with 1, with no gaps. To return all missing order IDs from the *Orders* table, query the *Nums* table and filter only numbers that are between the minimum and maximum in the *dbo.Orders* table and that do not appear in the set of order IDs in the *Orders* table. You can use scalar self-contained subqueries to return the minimum and maximum order IDs and a multivalued self-contained subquery to return the set of all existing order IDs. Here's the complete solution query.

```
SELECT n
FROM dbo.Nums
WHERE n BETWEEN (SELECT MIN(O.orderid) FROM dbo.Orders AS O)
           AND (SELECT MAX(O.orderid) FROM dbo.Orders AS O)
  AND n NOT IN (SELECT O.orderid FROM dbo.Orders AS O);
```

Because the code that populated the *dbo.Orders* table filtered only even-numbered order IDs, this query returns all odd-numbered values between the minimum and maximum order IDs in the *Orders* table. The output of this query is shown here in abbreviated form.

```
n
-----------
10249
10251
10253
10255
10257
...
11067
11069
11071
11073
11075

(414 row(s) affected)
```

When you're done, run the following code for cleanup.

```
DROP TABLE dbo.Orders;
```

# Correlated Subqueries

Correlated subqueries are subqueries that refer to attributes from the table that appears in the outer query. This means that the subquery is dependent on the outer query and cannot be invoked independently. Logically, it's as if the subquery is evaluated separately for each outer row. For example, the query in Listing 4-1 returns orders with the maximum order ID for each customer.

**LISTING 4-1**  Correlated Subquery

```
USE TSQL2012;

SELECT custid, orderid, orderdate, empid
FROM Sales.Orders AS O1
WHERE orderid =
  (SELECT MAX(O2.orderid)
   FROM Sales.Orders AS O2
   WHERE O2.custid = O1.custid);
```

The outer query is against an instance of the *Orders* table called *O1*; it filters orders where the order ID is equal to the value returned by the subquery. The subquery filters orders from a second instance of the *Orders* table called *O2*, where the inner customer ID is equal to the outer customer ID, and returns the maximum order ID from the filtered orders. In simpler terms, for each row in *O1*, the subquery is in charge of returning the maximum order ID for the current customer. If the order ID in *O1* and the order ID returned by the subquery match, the order ID in *O1* is the maximum for the current customer, in which case the row from *O1* is returned by the query. This query returns the following output, shown here in abbreviated form.

```
custid       orderid      orderdate                   empid
-----------  -----------  --------------------------  -----------
91           11044        2008-04-23 00:00:00.000     4
90           11005        2008-04-07 00:00:00.000     2
89           11066        2008-05-01 00:00:00.000     7
88           10935        2008-03-09 00:00:00.000     4
87           11025        2008-04-15 00:00:00.000     6
...
5            10924        2008-03-04 00:00:00.000     3
4            11016        2008-04-10 00:00:00.000     9
3            10856        2008-01-28 00:00:00.000     3
2            10926        2008-03-04 00:00:00.000     4
1            11011        2008-04-09 00:00:00.000     3

(89 row(s) affected)
```

Correlated subqueries are usually much harder to figure out than self-contained subqueries. To better understand the concept of correlated subqueries, I find it useful to focus attention on a single row in the outer table and understand the logical processing that takes place for that row. For example, focus your attention on the order in the *Orders* table with order ID 10248.

```
custid        orderid       orderdate                    empid
-----------   -----------   --------------------------   -----------
85            10248         2006-07-04 00:00:00.000      5
```

With respect to this outer row, when the subquery is evaluated, the correlation or reference to *O1.custid* means *85*. After substituting the correlation with *85*, you get the following.

```
SELECT MAX(O2.orderid)
FROM Sales.Orders AS O2
WHERE O2.custid = 85;
```

This query returns the order ID 10739. The outer row's order ID—10248—is compared with the inner one—10739—and because there's no match in this case, the outer row is filtered out. The subquery returns the same value for all rows in *O1* with the same customer ID, and only in one case is there a match—when the outer row's order ID is the maximum for the current customer. Thinking in such terms will make it easier for you to grasp the concept of correlated subqueries.

The fact that correlated subqueries are dependent on the outer query makes them harder to debug than self-contained subqueries. You can't just highlight the subquery portion and run it. For example, if you try to highlight and run the subquery portion in Listing 4-1, you get the following error.

```
Msg 4104, Level 16, State 1, Line 1
The multi-part identifier "O1.custid" could not be bound.
```

This error indicates that the identifier *O1.custid* cannot be bound to an object in the query, because *O1* is not defined in the query. It is only defined in the context of the outer query. To debug correlated subqueries you need to substitute the correlation with a constant, and after ensuring that the code is correct, substitute the constant with the correlation.

As another example of a correlated subquery, suppose that you need to query the *Sales.OrderValues* view and return for each order the percentage that the current order value is of the total values of all of the customer's orders. In Chapter 7, "Beyond the Fundamentals of Querying," I provide a solution to this problem that uses window functions; here I'll explain how to solve the problem by using subqueries. It's always a good idea to try to come up with several solutions to each problem, because the different solutions will usually vary in complexity and performance.

You can write an outer query against an instance of the *OrderValues* view called *O1*; in the *SELECT* list, divide the current value by the result of a correlated subquery that returns the total value from a second instance of *OrderValues* called *O2* for the current customer. Here's the complete solution query.

```
SELECT orderid, custid, val,
  CAST(100. * val / (SELECT SUM(O2.val)
                     FROM Sales.OrderValues AS O2
                     WHERE O2.custid = O1.custid)
       AS NUMERIC(5,2)) AS pct
FROM Sales.OrderValues AS O1
ORDER BY custid, orderid;
```

The *CAST* function is used to convert the datatype of the expression to *NUMERIC* with a precision of 5 (the total number of digits) and a scale of 2 (the number of digits after the decimal point).

This query returns the following output.

```
orderid      custid       val          pct
-----------  -----------  -----------  ------
10643        1            814.50       19.06
10692        1            878.00       20.55
10702        1            330.00       7.72
10835        1            845.80       19.79
10952        1            471.20       11.03
11011        1            933.50       21.85
10308        2            88.80        6.33
10625        2            479.75       34.20
10759        2            320.00       22.81
10926        2            514.40       36.67
...

(830 row(s) affected)
```

## The *EXISTS* Predicate

T-SQL supports a predicate called *EXISTS* that accepts a subquery as input and returns *TRUE* if the subquery returns any rows and *FALSE* otherwise. For example, the following query returns customers from Spain who placed orders.

```
SELECT custid, companyname
FROM Sales.Customers AS C
WHERE country = N'Spain'
  AND EXISTS
    (SELECT * FROM Sales.Orders AS O
     WHERE O.custid = C.custid);
```

The outer query against the *Customers* table filters only customers from Spain for whom the *EXISTS* predicate returns *TRUE*. The *EXISTS* predicate returns *TRUE* if the current customer has related orders in the *Orders* table.

One of the benefits of using the *EXISTS* predicate is that it allows you to intuitively phrase English-like queries. For example, this query can be read just as you would say it in ordinary English: select the customer ID and company name attributes from the *Customers* table, where the country is equal to Spain, and at least one order exists in the *Orders* table with the same customer ID as the customer's customer ID.

This query returns the following output.

```
custid       companyname
-----------  ----------------
8            Customer QUHWH
29           Customer MDLWA
30           Customer KSLQF
69           Customer SIUIH
```

As with other predicates, you can negate the *EXISTS* predicate with the *NOT* logical operator. For example, the following query returns customers from Spain who did not place orders.

```
SELECT custid, companyname
FROM Sales.Customers AS C
WHERE country = N'Spain'
  AND NOT EXISTS
    (SELECT * FROM Sales.Orders AS O
     WHERE O.custid = C.custid);
```

This query returns the following output.

```
custid       companyname
-----------  ----------------
22           Customer DIDMN
```

Even though this book's focus is on logical query processing and not performance, I thought you might be interested to know that the *EXISTS* predicate lends itself to good optimization. That is, the Microsoft SQL Server engine knows that it is enough to determine whether the subquery returns at least one row or none, and it doesn't need to process all qualifying rows. You can think of this capability as a kind of short-circuit evaluation.

Unlike most other cases, in this case it's logically not a bad practice to use an asterisk (*) in the *SELECT* list of the subquery in the context of the *EXISTS* predicate. The *EXISTS* predicate only cares about the existence of matching rows regardless of the attributes specified in the *SELECT* list, as if the whole *SELECT* clause were superfluous. The SQL Server database engine knows this, and in terms of optimization, ignores the subquery's *SELECT* list. So in terms of optimization, specifying the column wildcard * in this case has no negative impact when compared to alternatives such as specifying a constant. However, some minor extra cost might be involved in the resolution process of expanding the wildcard against metadata info. But this extra resolution cost is so minor that you will probably barely notice it. My opinion on this matter is that queries should be natural and intuitive, unless there's a very compelling reason to sacrifice this aspect of the code. I find the form *EXISTS(SELECT * FROM ...)* much more intuitive than *EXISTS(SELECT 1 FROM ...)*. Saving the minor extra cost associated with the resolution of * is something that is not worth the cost of sacrificing the readability of the code.

Finally, another aspect of the *EXISTS* predicate that is interesting to note is that unlike most predicates in T-SQL, *EXISTS* uses two-valued logic and not three-valued logic. If you think about it, there's no situation where it is unknown whether a query returns rows.

# Beyond the Fundamentals of Subqueries

This section covers aspects of subqueries that you might consider to be beyond the fundamentals. I provide it as optional reading in case you feel very comfortable with the material covered so far in this chapter.

## Returning Previous or Next Values

Suppose that you need to query the *Orders* table in the *TSQL2012* database and return, for each order, information about the current order and also the previous order ID. The concept of "previous" implies logical ordering, but because you know that the rows in a table have no order, you need to come up with a logical equivalent to the concept of "previous" that can be phrased with a T-SQL expression. One example of such a logical equivalent is "the maximum value that is smaller than the current value." This phrase can be expressed in T-SQL with a correlated subquery like this.

```
SELECT orderid, orderdate, empid, custid,
  (SELECT MAX(O2.orderid)
   FROM Sales.Orders AS O2
   WHERE O2.orderid < O1.orderid) AS prevorderid
FROM Sales.Orders AS O1;
```

This query produces the following output, shown here in abbreviated form.

```
orderid     orderdate                   empid         custid        prevorderid
-----------  --------------------------  -----------   -----------   -----------
10248       2006-07-04 00:00:00.000     5             85            NULL
10249       2006-07-05 00:00:00.000     6             79            10248
10250       2006-07-08 00:00:00.000     4             34            10249
10251       2006-07-08 00:00:00.000     3             84            10250
10252       2006-07-09 00:00:00.000     4             76            10251
...
11073       2008-05-05 00:00:00.000     2             58            11072
11074       2008-05-06 00:00:00.000     7             73            11073
11075       2008-05-06 00:00:00.000     8             68            11074
11076       2008-05-06 00:00:00.000     4             9             11075
11077       2008-05-06 00:00:00.000     1             65            11076

(830 row(s) affected)
```

Notice that because there's no order before the first, the subquery returned a *NULL* for the first order.

Similarly, you can phrase the concept of "next" as "the minimum value that is greater than the current value." Here's the T-SQL query that returns for each order the next order ID.

```
SELECT orderid, orderdate, empid, custid,
  (SELECT MIN(O2.orderid)
   FROM Sales.Orders AS O2
   WHERE O2.orderid > O1.orderid) AS nextorderid
FROM Sales.Orders AS O1;
```

This query produces the following output, shown here in abbreviated form.

```
orderid    orderdate                   empid       custid      nextorderid
---------  --------------------------  ----------  ----------  -----------
10248      2006-07-04 00:00:00.000     5           85          10249
10249      2006-07-05 00:00:00.000     6           79          10250
10250      2006-07-08 00:00:00.000     4           34          10251
10251      2006-07-08 00:00:00.000     3           84          10252
10252      2006-07-09 00:00:00.000     4           76          10253
...
11073      2008-05-05 00:00:00.000     2           58          11074
11074      2008-05-06 00:00:00.000     7           73          11075
11075      2008-05-06 00:00:00.000     8           68          11076
11076      2008-05-06 00:00:00.000     4           9           11077
11077      2008-05-06 00:00:00.000     1           65          NULL
```

```
(830 row(s) affected)
```

Notice that because there's no order after the last, the subquery returned a *NULL* for the last order.

Note that SQL Server 2012 introduces new window functions called *LAG* and *LEAD* that allow the return of an element from a "previous" or "next" row based on specified ordering. I will cover these and other window functions in Chapter 7.

## Using Running Aggregates

*Running aggregates* are aggregates that accumulate values over time. In this section, I use the *Sales.OrderTotalsByYear* view to demonstrate the technique for calculating running aggregates. The view shows total order quantities by year. Query the view to examine its contents.

```
SELECT orderyear, qty
FROM Sales.OrderTotalsByYear;
```

You get the following output.

```
orderyear   qty
----------  -----------
2007        25489
2008        16247
2006        9581
```

Suppose you need to return for each year the order year, quantity, and running total quantity over the years. That is, for each year, return the sum of the quantity up to that year. So for the earliest year recorded in the view (2006), the running total is equal to that year's quantity. For the second year (2007), the running total is the sum of the first year plus the second year, and so on.

You can complete this task by querying one instance of the view (call it *O1*) to return for each year the order year and quantity, and then by using a correlated subquery against a second instance of the view (call it *O2*) to calculate the running-total quantity. The subquery should filter all years in *O2* that are smaller than or equal to the current year in *O1*, and sum the quantities from *O2*. Here's the solution query.

```
SELECT orderyear, qty,
  (SELECT SUM(O2.qty)
   FROM Sales.OrderTotalsByYear AS O2
   WHERE O2.orderyear <= O1.orderyear) AS runqty
FROM Sales.OrderTotalsByYear AS O1
ORDER BY orderyear;
```

This query returns the following output.

```
orderyear   qty         runqty
----------- ----------- -----------
2006        9581        9581
2007        25489       35070
2008        16247       51317
```

Note that SQL Server 2012 enhances the capabilities of window aggregate functions, allowing new, highly efficient solutions for running totals needs. As mentioned, I will discuss window functions in Chapter 7.

## Dealing with Misbehaving Subqueries

This section introduces cases in which subqueries might behave counter to your expectations, and provides best practices that you can follow to avoid logical bugs in your code that are associated with those cases.

### *NULL* Trouble

Remember that T-SQL uses three-valued logic. In this section, I will demonstrate problems that can evolve with subqueries when *NULL* marks are involved and you do not take into consideration the three-valued logic.

Consider the following apparently intuitive query that is supposed to return customers who did not place orders.

```
SELECT custid, companyname
FROM Sales.Customers
WHERE custid NOT IN(SELECT O.custid
                    FROM Sales.Orders AS O);
```

With the current sample data in the *Orders* table in the *TSQL2012* database, the query seems to work the way you expect it to; and indeed, it returns two rows for the two customers who did not place orders.

```
custid      companyname
----------- ----------------
22          Customer DTDMN
57          Customer WVAXS
```

Next, run the following code to insert a new order to the *Orders* table with a *NULL* customer ID.

```
INSERT INTO Sales.Orders
  (custid, empid, orderdate, requireddate, shippeddate, shipperid,
   freight, shipname, shipaddress, shipcity, shipregion,
   shippostalcode, shipcountry)
  VALUES(NULL, 1, '20090212', '20090212',
         '20090212', 1, 123.00, N'abc', N'abc', N'abc',
         N'abc', N'abc', N'abc');
```

Run the query that is supposed to return customers who did not place orders again.

```
SELECT custid, companyname
FROM Sales.Customers
WHERE custid NOT IN(SELECT O.custid
                    FROM Sales.Orders AS O);
```

This time, the query returns an empty set. Keeping in mind what you've read in the section about *NULL* marks in Chapter 2, "Single-Table Queries," try to explain why the query returns an empty set. Also try to think of ways to get customers 22 and 57 in the output, and in general, to figure out best practices you can follow to avoid such problems, assuming that there is a problem here.

Obviously, the culprit in this story is the *NULL* customer ID that was added to the *Orders* table and is now returned among the known customer IDs by the subquery.

Let's start with the part that behaves the way you expect it to. The *IN* predicate returns *TRUE* for a customer who placed orders (for example, customer 85), because such a customer is returned by the subquery. The *NOT* operator is used to negate the *IN* predicate; hence, the *NOT TRUE* becomes *FALSE*, and the customer is not returned by the outer query. This means that when a customer ID appears in the *Orders* table, you can tell for sure that the customer placed orders, and therefore you don't want to see it in the output. However, when you have a *NULL* customer ID in the *Orders* table, you can't tell for sure whether a certain customer ID does not appear in *Orders*, as explained shortly.

The *IN* predicate returns *UNKNOWN* (the truth value *UNKNOWN* like the truth values *TRUE* and *FALSE*) for a customer such as 22 that does not appear in the set of known customer IDs in *Orders*. The *IN* predicate returns *UNKNOWN* for such a customer, because comparing it with all known customer IDs yields *FALSE*, and comparing it with the *NULL* in the set yields *UNKNOWN*. *FALSE OR UNKNOWN* yields *UNKNOWN*. As a more tangible example, consider the expression *22 NOT IN (1, 2, NULL)*. This expression can be rephrased as *NOT 22 IN (1, 2, NULL)*. You can expand the last expression to *NOT (22 = 1 OR 22 = 2 OR 22 = NULL)*. Evaluate each individual expression in the parentheses to its truth value and you get *NOT (FALSE OR FALSE OR UNKNOWN)*, which translates to *NOT UNKNOWN*, which evaluates to *UNKNOWN*.

The logical meaning of *UNKNOWN* here before you apply the *NOT* operator is that it can't be determined whether the customer ID appears in the set, because the *NULL* could represent that customer ID as well as anything else. The tricky part is that negating the *UNKNOWN* with the *NOT* operator still yields *UNKNOWN*, and *UNKNOWN* in a query filter is filtered out. This means that in a case where it is unknown whether a customer ID appears in a set, it is also unknown whether it doesn't appear in the set.

In short, when you use the *NOT IN* predicate against a subquery that returns at least one *NULL*, the outer query always returns an empty set. Values from the outer table that are known to appear in the set are not returned because the outer query is supposed to return values that do not appear in the set. Values that do not appear in the set of known values are not returned because you can never tell for sure that the value is not in the set that includes the *NULL*.

So, what practices can you follow to avoid such trouble?

First, when a column is not supposed to allow *NULL* marks, it is important to define it as *NOT NULL*. Enforcing data integrity is much more important than many people realize.

Second, in all queries that you write, you should consider all three possible truth values of three-valued logic (*TRUE*, *FALSE*, and *UNKNOWN*). Think explicitly about whether the query might process *NULL* marks, and if so, whether the default treatment of *NULL* marks is suitable for your needs. When it isn't, you need to intervene. For example, in the example we've been working with, the outer query returns an empty set because of the comparison with *NULL*. If you want to check whether a customer ID appears in the set of known values and ignore the *NULL* marks, you should exclude the *NULL* marks—either explicitly or implicitly. One way to explicitly exclude the *NULL* marks is to add the predicate *O.custid IS NOT NULL* to the subquery, like this.

```
SELECT custid, companyname
FROM Sales.Customers
WHERE custid NOT IN(SELECT O.custid
                    FROM Sales.Orders AS O
                    WHERE O.custid IS NOT NULL);
```

You can also exclude the *NULL* marks implicitly by using the *NOT EXISTS* predicate instead of *NOT IN*, like this.

```
SELECT custid, companyname
FROM Sales.Customers AS C
WHERE NOT EXISTS
  (SELECT *
   FROM Sales.Orders AS O
   WHERE O.custid = C.custid);
```

Recall that unlike *IN*, *EXISTS* uses two-valued predicate logic. *EXISTS* always returns *TRUE* or *FALSE* and never *UNKNOWN*. When the subquery stumbles into a *NULL* in *O.custid*, the expression evaluates to *UNKNOWN* and the row is filtered out. As far as the *EXISTS* predicate is concerned, the *NULL* cases are eliminated naturally, as though they weren't there. So *EXISTS* ends up handling only known customer IDs. Therefore, it's safer to use *NOT EXISTS* than *NOT IN*.

When you're done experimenting, run the following code for cleanup.

```
DELETE FROM Sales.Orders WHERE custid IS NULL;
```

## Substitution Errors in Subquery Column Names

Logical bugs in your code can sometimes be very elusive. In this section, I describe an elusive bug that has to do with an innocent substitution error in a subquery column name. After explaining the bug, I provide best practices that can help you avoid such bugs in the future.

The examples in this section query a table called *MyShippers* in the *Sales* schema. Run the following code to create and populate this table.

```
IF OBJECT_ID('Sales.MyShippers', 'U') IS NOT NULL
  DROP TABLE Sales.MyShippers;

CREATE TABLE Sales.MyShippers
(
  shipper_id  INT          NOT NULL,
  companyname NVARCHAR(40) NOT NULL,
  phone       NVARCHAR(24) NOT NULL,
  CONSTRAINT PK_MyShippers PRIMARY KEY(shipper_id)
);

INSERT INTO Sales.MyShippers(shipper_id, companyname, phone)
  VALUES(1, N'Shipper GVSUA', N'(503) 555-0137'),
        (2, N'Shipper ETYNR', N'(425) 555-0136'),
        (3, N'Shipper ZHISN', N'(415) 555-0138');
```

Consider the following query, which is supposed to return shippers who shipped orders to customer 43.

```
SELECT shipper_id, companyname
FROM Sales.MyShippers
WHERE shipper_id IN
  (SELECT shipper_id
   FROM Sales.Orders
   WHERE custid = 43);
```

This query produces the following output.

```
shipper_id  companyname
----------- ---------------
1           Shipper GVSUA
2           Shipper ETYNR
3           Shipper ZHISN
```

Apparently, only shippers 2 and 3 shipped orders to customer 43, but for some reason, this query returned all shippers from the *MyShippers* table. Examine the query carefully and also the schemas of the tables involved, and see if you can explain why.

It turns out that the column name in the *Orders* table holding the shipper ID is not called *shipper_id*; it is called *shipperid* (no underscore). The column in the MyShippers table is called *shipper_id* with an underscore. The resolution of nonprefixed column names works in the context of a subquery from the current/inner scope outward. In our example, SQL Server first looks for the column *shipper_id* in the *Orders* table. Such a column is not found there, so SQL Server looks for it in the outer table in the query, *MyShippers*. Because one is found, it is the one used.

You can see that what was supposed to be a self-contained subquery unintentionally became a correlated subquery. As long as the *Orders* table has at least one row, all rows from the *MyShippers* table find a match when comparing the outer shipper ID with a query that returns the very same outer shipper ID for each row from the *Orders* table.

Some might argue that this behavior is a design flaw in standard SQL. However, it's not that the designers of this behavior in the ANSI SQL committee thought that it would be difficult to detect the "error;" rather, it's an intentional behavior designed to allow you to refer to column names from the outer table without needing to prefix them with the table name, as long as those column names are unambiguous (that is, as long as they appear only in one of the tables).

This problem is more common in environments that do not use consistent attribute names across tables. Sometimes the names are only slightly different, as in this case—*shipperid* in one table and *shipper_id* in another. That's enough for the bug to manifest itself.

You can follow a couple of best practices to avoid such problems—one to implement in the long run, and one that you can implement in the short run.

In the long run, your organization should as a policy not underestimate the importance of using consistent attribute names across tables. In the short run, of course, you don't want to start changing existing column names, which could break application code.

In the short run, you can adopt a very simple practice—prefix column names in subqueries with the source table alias. This way, the resolution process only looks for the column in the specified table, and if no such column is there, you get a resolution error. For example, try running the following code.

```
SELECT shipper_id, companyname
FROM Sales.MyShippers
WHERE shipper_id IN
  (SELECT O.shipper_id
   FROM Sales.Orders AS O
   WHERE O.custid = 43);
```

You get the following resolution error.

```
Msg 207, Level 16, State 1, Line 4
Invalid column name 'shipper_id'.
```

After getting this error, you of course can identify the problem and correct the query.

```
SELECT shipper_id, companyname
FROM Sales.MyShippers
WHERE shipper_id IN
  (SELECT O.shipperid
   FROM Sales.Orders AS O
   WHERE O.custid = 43);
```

This time, the query returns the expected result.

```
shipper_id  companyname
----------- ----------------
2           Shipper ETYNR
3           Shipper ZHISN
```

When you're done, run the following code for cleanup.

```
IF OBJECT_ID('Sales.MyShippers', 'U') IS NOT NULL
  DROP TABLE Sales.MyShippers;
```

# Conclusion

This chapter covered subqueries. It discussed self-contained subqueries, which are independent of their outer queries, and correlated subqueries, which are dependent on their outer queries. Regarding the results of subqueries, I discussed scalar and multivalued subqueries. I also provided a more advanced section as optional reading, in which I covered returning previous and next values, using running aggregates, and dealing with misbehaving subqueries. Remember to always think about the three-valued logic and the importance of prefixing column names in subqueries with the source table alias.

The next chapter focuses on table subqueries, also known as table expressions.

# Exercises

This section provides exercises to help you familiarize yourself with the subjects discussed in this chapter. The sample database *TSQL2012* is used in all exercises in this chapter.

## 1

Write a query that returns all orders placed on the last day of activity that can be found in the *Orders* table.

- Tables involved: *Sales.Orders*

- Desired output:

```
orderid     orderdate                        custid      empid
----------- -------------------------------- ----------- -----------
11077       2008-05-06 00:00:00.000          65          1
11076       2008-05-06 00:00:00.000          9           4
11075       2008-05-06 00:00:00.000          68          8
11074       2008-05-06 00:00:00.000          73          7
```

# 2 (Optional, Advanced)

Write a query that returns all orders placed by the customer(s) who placed the highest number of orders. Note that more than one customer might have the same number of orders.

- Tables involved: *Sales.Orders*

- Desired output (abbreviated):

```
custid        orderid       orderdate                   empid
-----------   -----------   -------------------------   -----------
71            10324         2006-10-08 00:00:00.000     9
71            10393         2006-12-25 00:00:00.000     1
71            10398         2006-12-30 00:00:00.000     2
71            10440         2007-02-10 00:00:00.000     4
71            10452         2007-02-20 00:00:00.000     8
71            10510         2007-04-18 00:00:00.000     6
71            10555         2007-06-02 00:00:00.000     6
71            10603         2007-07-18 00:00:00.000     8
71            10607         2007-07-22 00:00:00.000     5
71            10612         2007-07-28 00:00:00.000     1
71            10627         2007-08-11 00:00:00.000     8
71            10657         2007-09-04 00:00:00.000     2
71            10678         2007-09-23 00:00:00.000     7
71            10700         2007-10-10 00:00:00.000     3
71            10711         2007-10-21 00:00:00.000     5
71            10713         2007-10-22 00:00:00.000     1
71            10714         2007-10-22 00:00:00.000     5
71            10722         2007-10-29 00:00:00.000     8
71            10748         2007-11-20 00:00:00.000     3
71            10757         2007-11-27 00:00:00.000     6
71            10815         2008-01-05 00:00:00.000     2
71            10847         2008-01-22 00:00:00.000     4
71            10882         2008-02-11 00:00:00.000     4
71            10894         2008-02-18 00:00:00.000     1
71            10941         2008-03-11 00:00:00.000     7
71            10983         2008-03-27 00:00:00.000     2
71            10984         2008-03-30 00:00:00.000     1
71            11002         2008-04-06 00:00:00.000     4
71            11030         2008-04-17 00:00:00.000     7
71            11031         2008-04-17 00:00:00.000     6
71            11064         2008-05-01 00:00:00.000     1

(31 row(s) affected)
```

# 3

Write a query that returns employees who did not place orders on or after May 1, 2008.

- Tables involved: *HR.Employees* and *Sales.Orders*

- Desired output:

```
empid         FirstName       lastname
-----------   -------------   --------------------
3             Judy            Lew
5             Sven            Buck
6             Paul            Suurs
9             Zoya            Dolgopyatova
```

# 4

Write a query that returns countries where there are customers but not employees.

- Tables involved: *Sales.Customers* and *HR.Employees*

- Desired output:

```
country
---------------
Argentina
Austria
Belgium
Brazil
Canada
Denmark
Finland
France
Germany
Ireland
Italy
Mexico
Norway
Poland
Portugal
Spain
Sweden
Switzerland
Venezuela

(19 row(s) affected)
```

# 5

Write a query that returns for each customer all orders placed on the customer's last day of activity.

- Tables involved: *Sales.Orders*

- Desired output:

```
custid       orderid      orderdate                empid
-----------  -----------  -----------------------  -----------
1            11011        2008-04-09 00:00:00.000  3
2            10926        2008-03-04 00:00:00.000  4
3            10856        2008-01-28 00:00:00.000  3
4            11016        2008-04-10 00:00:00.000  9
5            10924        2008-03-04 00:00:00.000  3
...
87           11025        2008-04-15 00:00:00.000  6
88           10935        2008-03-09 00:00:00.000  4
89           11066        2008-05-01 00:00:00.000  7
90           11005        2008-04-07 00:00:00.000  2
91           11044        2008-04-23 00:00:00.000  4

(90 row(s) affected)
```

# 6

Write a query that returns customers who placed orders in 2007 but not in 2008.

- Tables involved: *Sales.Customers* and *Sales.Orders*

- Desired output:

```
custid       companyname
-----------  ----------------
21           Customer KIDPX
23           Customer WVFAF
33           Customer FVXPQ
36           Customer LVJSO
43           Customer UISOJ
51           Customer PVDZC
85           Customer ENQZT

(7 row(s) affected)
```

## 7 (Optional, Advanced)

Write a query that returns customers who ordered product 12.

- Tables involved: *Sales.Customers*, *Sales.Orders*, and *Sales.OrderDetails*

- Desired output:

```
custid       companyname
-----------  -------------------
48           Customer DVFMB
39           Customer GLLAG
71           Customer LCOUJ
65           Customer NYUHS
44           Customer OXFRU
51           Customer PVDZC
86           Customer SNXOJ
20           Customer THHDP
90           Customer XBBVR
46           Customer XPNIK
31           Customer YJCBX
87           Customer ZHYOS

(12 row(s) affected)
```

## 8 (Optional, Advanced)

Write a query that calculates a running-total quantity for each customer and month.

- Tables involved: *Sales.CustOrders*

- Desired output:

```
custid       ordermonth                  qty          runqty
-----------  --------------------------  -----------  ----------
1            2007-08-01 00:00:00.000     38           38
1            2007-10-01 00:00:00.000     41           79
1            2008-01-01 00:00:00.000     17           96
1            2008-03-01 00:00:00.000     18           114
1            2008-04-01 00:00:00.000     60           174
2            2006-09-01 00:00:00.000     6            6
2            2007-08-01 00:00:00.000     18           24
2            2007-11-01 00:00:00.000     10           34
2            2008-03-01 00:00:00.000     29           63
3            2006-11-01 00:00:00.000     24           24
3            2007-04-01 00:00:00.000     30           54
3            2007-05-01 00:00:00.000     80           134
3            2007-06-01 00:00:00.000     83           217
3            2007-09-01 00:00:00.000     102          319
3            2008-01-01 00:00:00.000     40           359
...

(636 row(s) affected)
```

# Solutions

This section provides solutions to the exercises in the preceding section.

## 1

You can write a self-contained subquery that returns the maximum order date from the *Orders* table. You can refer to the subquery in the *WHERE* clause of the outer query to return all orders that were placed on the last day of activity. Here's the solution query.

```
USE TSQL2012;

SELECT orderid, orderdate, custid, empid
FROM Sales.Orders
WHERE orderdate =
  (SELECT MAX(O.orderdate) FROM Sales.Orders AS O);
```

## 2

This problem is best solved in multiple steps. First, you can write a query that returns the customer or customers who placed the highest number of orders. You can achieve this by grouping the orders by customer, ordering the customers by *COUNT(\*)* descending, and using the *TOP(1) WITH TIES* option to return the IDs of the customers who placed the highest number of orders. If you don't remember how to use the *TOP* option, refer to Chapter 2. Here's the query that solves the first step.

```
SELECT TOP (1) WITH TIES O.custid
FROM Sales.Orders AS O
GROUP BY O.custid
ORDER BY COUNT(*) DESC;
```

This query returns the value 71, which is the customer ID of the customer who placed the highest number of orders, 31. With the sample data stored in the *Orders* table, only one customer placed the maximum number of orders. But the query uses the *WITH TIES* option to return all IDs of customers who placed the maximum number of orders, in case there are more than one.

The next step is to write a query against the *Orders* table returning all orders where the customer ID is in the set of customer IDs returned by the solution query for the first step.

```
SELECT custid, orderid, orderdate, empid
FROM Sales.Orders
WHERE custid IN
  (SELECT TOP (1) WITH TIES O.custid
   FROM Sales.Orders AS O
   GROUP BY O.custid
   ORDER BY COUNT(*) DESC);
```

# 3

You can write a self-contained subquery against the *Orders* table that filters orders placed on or after May 1, 2008 and returns only the employee IDs from those orders. Write an outer query against the *Employees* table returning employees whose IDs do not appear in the set of employee IDs returned by the subquery. Here's the complete solution query.

```
SELECT empid, FirstName, lastname
FROM HR.Employees
WHERE empid NOT IN
  (SELECT O.empid
   FROM Sales.Orders AS O
   WHERE O.orderdate >= '20080501');
```

# 4

You can write a self-contained subquery against the *Employees* table returning the country attribute from each employee row. Write an outer query against the *Customers* table that filters only customer rows where the country does not appear in the set of countries returned by the subquery. In the *SELECT* list of the outer query, specify *DISTINCT country* to return only distinct occurrences of countries, be cause the same country can have more than one customer. Here's the complete solution query.

```
SELECT DISTINCT country
FROM Sales.Customers
WHERE country NOT IN
  (SELECT E.country FROM HR.Employees AS E);
```

# 5

This exercise is similar to Exercise 1, except that in that exercise, you were asked to return orders placed on the last day of activity in general; in this exercise, you were asked to return orders placed on the last day of activity for the customer. The solutions for both exercises are similar, but here you need to correlate the subquery to match the inner customer ID with the outer customer ID, like this.

```
SELECT custid, orderid, orderdate, empid
FROM Sales.Orders AS O1
WHERE orderdate =
  (SELECT MAX(O2.orderdate)
   FROM Sales.Orders AS O2
   WHERE O2.custid = O1.custid)
ORDER BY custid;
```

You're not comparing the outer row's order date with the general maximum order date, but instead with the maximum order date for the current customer.

# 6

You can solve this problem by querying the *Customers* table and using *EXISTS* and *NOT EXISTS* predicates with correlated subqueries to ensure that the customer placed orders in 2007 but not in 2008. The *EXISTS* predicate returns *TRUE* only if at least one row exists in the *Orders* table with the same customer ID as in the outer row, within the date range representing the year 2007. The *NOT EXISTS* predicate returns *TRUE* only if no row exists in the *Orders* table with the same customer ID as in the outer row, within the date range representing the year 2008. Here's the complete solution query.

```
SELECT custid, companyname
FROM Sales.Customers AS C
WHERE EXISTS
  (SELECT *
   FROM Sales.Orders AS O
   WHERE O.custid = C.custid
     AND O.orderdate >= '20070101'
     AND O.orderdate < '20080101')
  AND NOT EXISTS
  (SELECT *
   FROM Sales.Orders AS O
   WHERE O.custid = C.custid
     AND O.orderdate >= '20080101'
     AND O.orderdate < '20090101');
```

# 7

You can solve this exercise by nesting *EXISTS* predicates with correlated subqueries. You write the outermost query against the *Customers* table. In the *WHERE* clause of the outer query, you can use the *EXISTS* predicate with a correlated subquery against the *Orders* table to filter only the current customer's orders. In the filter of the subquery against the *Orders* table, you can use a nested *EXISTS* predicate with a subquery against the *OrderDetails* table that filters only order details with product ID 12. This way, only customers who placed orders that contain product 12 in their order details are returned. Here's the complete solution query.

```
SELECT custid, companyname
FROM Sales.Customers AS C
WHERE EXISTS
  (SELECT *
   FROM Sales.Orders AS O
   WHERE O.custid = C.custid
     AND EXISTS
       (SELECT *
        FROM Sales.OrderDetails AS OD
        WHERE OD.orderid = O.orderid
          AND OD.ProductID = 12));
```

## 8

When I need to solve querying problems, I often find it useful to rephrase the original request in a more technical way so that it will be more convenient to translate the request to a T-SQL query. To solve the current exercise, you can first try to express the request "return a running total quantity for each customer and month" differently    in a more technical manner. For each customer, return the customer ID, month, the sum of the quantity for that month, and the sum of all months less than or equal to the current month. The rephrased request can be translated to the following T-SQL query quite literally.

```
SELECT custid, ordermonth, qty,
  (SELECT SUM(O2.qty)
   FROM Sales.CustOrders AS O2
   WHERE O2.custid = O1.custid
     AND O2.ordermonth <= O1.ordermonth) AS runqty
FROM Sales.CustOrders AS O1
ORDER BY custid, ordermonth;
```

This code defines a derived table called *D* based on a query against the *Orders* table that returns the order year and customer ID from all rows. The *SELECT* list of the inner query uses the inline aliasing form to assign the alias *orderyear* to the expression *YEAR(orderdate)*. The outer query can refer to the *orderyear* column alias in both the *GROUP BY* and *SELECT* clauses, because as far as the outer query is concerned, it queries a table called *D* with columns called *orderyear* and *custid*.

As I mentioned earlier, SQL Server expands the definition of the table expression and accesses the underlying objects directly. After expansion, the query in Listing 5-1 looks like the following.

```
SELECT YEAR(orderdate) AS orderyear, COUNT(DISTINCT custid) AS numcusts
FROM Sales.Orders
GROUP BY YEAR(orderdate);
```

This is just to emphasize that you use table expressions for logical (not performance-related) reasons. Generally speaking, table expressions have neither positive nor negative performance impact.

The code in Listing 5-1 uses the inline aliasing form to assign column aliases to expressions. The syntax for inline aliasing is *<expression> [AS] <alias>*. Note that the word *AS* is optional in the syntax for inline aliasing; however, I find that it helps the readability of the code and recommend using it.

In some cases, you might prefer to use a second supported form for assigning column aliases, which you can think of as an external form. With this form, you do not assign column aliases following the expressions in the *SELECT* list—you specify all target column names in parentheses following the table expression's name, like the following.

```
SELECT orderyear, COUNT(DISTINCT custid) AS numcusts
FROM (SELECT YEAR(orderdate), custid
      FROM Sales.Orders) AS D(orderyear, custid)
GROUP BY orderyear;
```

It is generally recommended that you use the inline form for a couple of reasons. If you need to debug the code when using the inline form, when you highlight the query defining the table expression and run it, the columns in the result appear with the aliases you assigned. With the external form, you cannot include the target column names when you highlight the table expression query, so the result appears with no column names in the case of the unnamed expressions. Also, when the table expression query is lengthy, using the external form can make it quite difficult to figure out which column alias belongs to which expression.

Even though it's a best practice to use the inline aliasing form, in some cases you may find the external form more convenient to work with. For example, when the query defining the table expression isn't going to undergo any further revisions and you want to treat it like a "black box"—that is, you want to focus your attention on the table expression name followed by the target column list when you look at the outer query. To use terminology from traditional programming languages, it allows you to specify a contract interface between the outer query and the table expression.

# CHAPTER 5

# Table Expressions

A table expression is a named query expression that represents a valid relational table. You can use table expressions in data manipulation statements much like you use other tables. Microsoft SQL Server supports four types of table expressions: derived tables, common table expressions (CTEs), views, and inline table-valued functions (inline TVFs), each of which I describe in detail in this chapter. The focus of this chapter is using SELECT queries against table expressions; Chapter 8, "Data Modification," covers modifications against table expressions.

Table expressions are not physically materialized anywhere—they are virtual. When you query a table expression, the inner query gets unnested. In other words, the outer query and the inner query are merged into one query directly against the underlying objects. The benefits of using table expressions are typically related to logical aspects of your code and not to performance. For example, table expressions help you simplify your solutions by using a modular approach. Table expressions also help you circumvent certain restrictions in the language, such as the inability to refer to column aliases assigned in the *SELECT* clause in query clauses that are logically processed before the *SELECT* clause.

This chapter also introduces the *APPLY* table operator as it is used in conjunction with a table expression. I explain how to use this operator to apply a table expression to each row of another table.

## Derived Tables

Derived tables (also known as *table subqueries*) are defined in the *FROM* clause of an outer query. Their scope of existence is the outer query. As soon as the outer query is finished, the derived table is gone.

You specify the query that defines the derived table within parentheses, followed by the AS clause and the derived table name. For example, the following code defines a derived table called *USACusts* based on a query that returns all customers from the United States, and the outer query selects all rows from the derived table.

```
USE TSQL2012;

SELECT *
FROM (SELECT custid, companyname
      FROM Sales.Customers
      WHERE country = N'USA') AS USACusts;
```

In this particular case, which is a simple example of the basic syntax, a derived table is not needed because the outer query doesn't apply any manipulation.

The code in this basic example returns the following output.

```
custid       companyname
-----------  ----------------
32           Customer YSIQX
36           Customer LVJSO
43           Customer UISOJ
45           Customer QXPPT
48           Customer DVFMB
55           Customer KZQZT
65           Customer NYUHS
71           Customer LCOUJ
75           Customer XOJYP
77           Customer LCYBZ
78           Customer NLTYP
82           Customer EYHKM
89           Customer YBQTI
```

A query must meet three requirements to be valid to define a table expression of any kind:

1. **Order is not guaranteed.** A table expression is supposed to represent a relational table, and the rows in a relational table have no guaranteed order. Recall that this aspect of a relation stems from set theory. For this reason, standard SQL disallows an *ORDER BY* clause in queries that are used to define table expressions, unless the *ORDER BY* serves another purpose besides presentation. An example for such an exception is when the query uses the *OFFSET-FETCH* filter. T-SQL enforces similar restrictions, with similar exceptions—when *TOP* or *OFFSET-FETCH* is also specified. In the context of a query with the *TOP* or *OFFSET-FETCH* filter, the *ORDER BY* clause serves as part of the specification of the filter. If you use a query with *TOP* or *OFFSET-FETCH* and *ORDER BY* to define a table expression, *ORDER BY* is only guaranteed to serve the filtering-related purpose and not the usual presentation purpose. If the outer query against the table expression does not have a presentation *ORDER BY*, the output is not guaranteed to be returned in any particular order. See the "Views and the *ORDER BY* Clause" section later in this chapter for more detail on this item.

2. **All columns must have names.** All columns in a table must have names; therefore, you must assign column aliases to all expressions in the *SELECT* list of the query that is used to define a table expression.

3. **All column names must be unique.** All column names in a table must be unique; therefore, a table expression that has multiple columns with the same name is invalid. This might happen when the query defining the table expression joins two tables, if both tables have a column with the same name. If you need to incorporate both columns in your table expression, they must have different column names. You can resolve this by assigning different column aliases to the two columns.

All three requirements have to do with the fact that the table expression is supposed to represent a relation. All relation attributes must have names; all attribute names must be unique; and the relation's body being a set of tuples, there's no order.

## Assigning Column Aliases

One of the benefits of using table expressions is that, in any clause of the outer query, you can refer to column aliases that were assigned in the *SELECT* clause of the inner query. This helps you get around the fact that you can't refer to column aliases assigned in the *SELECT* clause in query clauses that are logically processed prior to the *SELECT* clause (for example, *WHERE* or *GROUP BY*).

For example, suppose that you need to write a query against the *Sales.Orders* table and return the number of distinct customers handled in each order year. The following attempt is invalid because the *GROUP BY* clause refers to a column alias that was assigned in the *SELECT* clause, and the *GROUP BY* clause is logically processed prior to the *SELECT* clause.

```
SELECT
  YEAR(orderdate) AS orderyear,
  COUNT(DISTINCT custid) AS numcusts
FROM Sales.Orders
GROUP BY orderyear;
```

If you try running this query, you get the following error.

```
Msg 207, Level 16, State 1, Line 5
Invalid column name 'orderyear'.
```

You could solve the problem by referring to the expression *YEAR(orderdate)* in both the *GROUP BY* and the *SELECT* clauses, but this is an example with a short expression. What if the expression were much longer? Maintaining two copies of the same expression might hurt code readability and maintainability and is more prone to errors. To solve the problem in a way that requires only one copy of the expression, you can use a table expression like the one shown in Listing 5-1.

**LISTING 5-1** Query with a Derived Table Using Inline Aliasing Form

```
SELECT orderyear, COUNT(DISTINCT custid) AS numcusts
FROM (SELECT YEAR(orderdate) AS orderyear, custid
      FROM Sales.Orders) AS D
GROUP BY orderyear;
```

This query returns the following output.

```
orderyear    numcusts
-----------  -----------
2006         67
2007         86
2008         81
```

## Using Arguments

In the query that defines a derived table, you can refer to arguments. The arguments can be local variables and input parameters to a routine such as a stored procedure or function. For example, the following code declares and initializes a local variable called @empid, and the query in the code that is used to define the derived table D refers to the local variable in the WHERE clause.

```
DECLARE @empid AS INT = 3;

SELECT orderyear, COUNT(DISTINCT custid) AS numcusts
FROM (SELECT YEAR(orderdate) AS orderyear, custid
      FROM Sales.Orders
      WHERE empid = @empid) AS D
GROUP BY orderyear;
```

This query returns the number of distinct customers per year whose orders were handled by the input employee (the employee whose ID is stored in the variable @empid). Here's the output of this query.

```
orderyear    numcusts
-----------  -----------
2006         16
2007         46
2008         30
```

## Nesting

If you need to define a derived table by using a query that itself refers to a derived table, you end up nesting derived tables. Nesting of derived tables is a result of the fact that a derived table is defined in the FROM clause of the outer query and not separately. Nesting is a problematic aspect of programming in general, because it tends to complicate the code and reduce its readability.

For example, the code in Listing 5-2 returns order years and the number of customers handled in each year only for years in which more than 70 customers were handled.

**LISTING 5-2** Query with Nested Derived Tables

```
SELECT orderyear, numcusts
FROM (SELECT orderyear, COUNT(DISTINCT custid) AS numcusts
      FROM (SELECT YEAR(orderdate) AS orderyear, custid
            FROM Sales.Orders) AS D1
      GROUP BY orderyear) AS D2
WHERE numcusts > 70;
```

This code returns the following output.

```
orderyear    numcusts
-----------  -----------
2007         86
2008         81
```

The purpose of the innermost derived table, *D1*, is to assign the column alias *orderyear* to the expression *YEAR(orderdate)*. The query against *D1* refers to *orderyear* in both the *GROUP BY* and *SELECT* clauses and assigns the column alias *numcusts* to the expression *COUNT(DISTINCT custid)*. The query against *D1* is used to define the derived table *D2*. The query against *D2* refers to *numcusts* in the *WHERE* clause to filter order years in which more than 70 customers were handled.

The whole purpose of using table expressions in this example was to simplify the solution by reusing column aliases instead of repeating expressions. However, with the complexity added by the nesting aspect of derived tables, I'm not sure that the solution is simpler than the alternative, which does not make any use of derived tables but instead repeats expressions.

```
SELECT YEAR(orderdate) AS orderyear, COUNT(DISTINCT custid) AS numcusts
FROM Sales.Orders
GROUP BY YEAR(orderdate)
HAVING COUNT(DISTINCT custid) > 70;
```

In short, nesting is a problematic aspect of derived tables.

## Multiple References

Another problematic aspect of derived tables stems from the fact that derived tables are defined in the *FROM* clause of the outer query and not prior to the outer query. As far as the *FROM* clause of the outer query is concerned, the derived table doesn't exist yet; therefore, if you need to refer to multiple instances of the derived table, you can't. Instead, you have to define multiple derived tables based on the same query. The query in Listing 5-3 provides an example.

**LISTING 5-3** Multiple Derived Tables Based on the Same Query

```
SELECT Cur.orderyear,
  Cur.numcusts AS curnumcusts, Prv.numcusts AS prvnumcusts,
  Cur.numcusts - Prv.numcusts AS growth
FROM (SELECT YEAR(orderdate) AS orderyear,
        COUNT(DISTINCT custid) AS numcusts
      FROM Sales.Orders
      GROUP BY YEAR(orderdate)) AS Cur
  LEFT OUTER JOIN
    (SELECT YEAR(orderdate) AS orderyear,
       COUNT(DISTINCT custid) AS numcusts
     FROM Sales.Orders
     GROUP BY YEAR(orderdate)) AS Prv
  ON Cur.orderyear = Prv.orderyear + 1;
```

This query joins two instances of a table expression to create two derived tables: The first derived table, *Cur*, represents current years, and the second derived table, *Prv*, represents previous years. The join condition *Cur.orderyear = Prv.orderyear + 1* ensures that each row from the first derived table matches with the previous year of the second. Because the code makes the join a *LEFT* outer join, the first year that has no previous year is also returned from the *Cur* table. The *SELECT* clause of the outer query calculates the difference between the number of customers handled in the current and previous years.

The code in Listing 5-3 produces the following output.

```
orderyear   curnumcusts prvnumcusts growth
----------- ----------- ----------- -----------
2006        67          NULL        NULL
2007        86          67          19
2008        81          86          -5
```

The fact that you cannot refer to multiple instances of the same derived table forces you to maintain multiple copies of the same query definition. This leads to lengthy code that is hard to maintain and is prone to errors.

## Common Table Expressions

Common table expressions (CTEs) are another standard form of table expression very similar to derived tables, yet with a couple of important advantages.

CTEs are defined by using a *WITH* statement and have the following general form.

```
WITH <CTE_Name>[(<target_column_list>)]
AS
(
  <inner query defining CTE>
)
<outer_query_against_CTE>;
```

The inner query defining the CTE must follow all requirements mentioned earlier to be valid to define a table expression. As a simple example, the following code defines a CTE called *USACusts* based on a query that returns all customers from the United States, and the outer query selects all rows from the CTE.

```
WITH USACusts AS
(
  SELECT custid, companyname
  FROM Sales.Customers
  WHERE country = N'USA'
)
SELECT * FROM USACusts;
```

As with derived tables, as soon as the outer query finishes, the CTE goes out of scope.

**Note** The *WITH* clause is used in T-SQL for several different purposes. To avoid ambiguity, when the *WITH* clause is used to define a CTE, the preceding statement in the same batch—if one exists—must be terminated with a semicolon. And oddly enough, the semicolon for the entire CTE is not required, though I still recommend specifying it—as I do to terminate all T-SQL statements.

## Assigning Column Aliases in CTEs

CTEs also support two forms of column aliasing—inline and external. For the inline form, specify *<expression> AS <column_alias>*; for the external form, specify the target column list in parentheses immediately after the CTE name.

Here's an example of the inline form.

```
WITH C AS
(
  SELECT YEAR(orderdate) AS orderyear, custid
  FROM Sales.Orders
)
SELECT orderyear, COUNT(DISTINCT custid) AS numcusts
FROM C
GROUP BY orderyear;
```

And here's an example of the external form.

```
WITH C(orderyear, custid) AS
(
  SELECT YEAR(orderdate), custid
  FROM Sales.Orders
)
SELECT orderyear, COUNT(DISTINCT custid) AS numcusts
FROM C
GROUP BY orderyear;
```

The motivations for using one form or the other are similar to those described in the context of derived tables.

## Using Arguments in CTEs

As with derived tables, you can also use arguments in the query used to define a CTE. Here's an example.

```
DECLARE @empid AS INT = 3;

WITH C AS
(
  SELECT YEAR(orderdate) AS orderyear, custid
  FROM Sales.Orders
  WHERE empid = @empid
)
SELECT orderyear, COUNT(DISTINCT custid) AS numcusts
FROM C
GROUP BY orderyear;
```

## Defining Multiple CTEs

On the surface, the difference between derived tables and CTEs might seem to be merely semantic. However, the fact that you first define a CTE and then use it gives it several important advantages over derived tables. One of those advantages is that if you need to refer to one CTE from another, you don't end up nesting them as you do with derived tables. Instead, you simply define multiple CTEs separated by commas under the same *WITH* statement. Each CTE can refer to all previously defined CTEs, and the outer query can refer to all CTEs. For example, the following code is the CTE alternative to the nested derived tables approach In Listing 5-2.

```
WITH C1 AS
(
  SELECT YEAR(orderdate) AS orderyear, custid
  FROM Sales.Orders
),
C2 AS
(
  SELECT orderyear, COUNT(DISTINCT custid) AS numcusts
  FROM C1
  GROUP BY orderyear
)
SELECT orderyear, numcusts
FROM C2
WHERE numcusts > 70;
```

Because you define a CTE before you use it, you don't end up nesting CTEs. Each CTE appears separately in the code in a modular manner. This modular approach substantially improves the readability and maintainability of the code compared to the nested derived table approach.

Technically, you cannot nest CTEs, nor can you define a CTE within the parentheses of a derived table. However, nesting is a problematic practice; therefore, think of these restrictions as aids to code clarity rather than as obstacles.

## Multiple References in CTEs

The fact that a CTE is defined first and then queried has another advantage: As far as the *FROM* clause of the outer query is concerned, the CTE already exists; therefore, you can refer to multiple instances of the same CTE. For example, the following code is the logical equivalent of the code shown earlier in Listing 5-3, using CTEs instead of derived tables.

```
WITH YearlyCount AS
(
  SELECT YEAR(orderdate) AS orderyear,
    COUNT(DISTINCT custid) AS numcusts
  FROM Sales.Orders
  GROUP BY YEAR(orderdate)
)
SELECT Cur.orderyear,
  Cur.numcusts AS curnumcusts, Prv.numcusts AS prvnumcusts,
  Cur.numcusts - Prv.numcusts AS growth
FROM YearlyCount AS Cur
  LEFT OUTER JOIN YearlyCount AS Prv
    ON Cur.orderyear = Prv.orderyear + 1;
```

As you can see, the CTE *YearlyCount* is defined once and accessed twice in the *FROM* clause of the outer query—once as *Cur* and once as *Prv*. You need to maintain only one copy of the CTE query and not multiple copies as you would with derived tables. This leads to a query that is much clearer and easier to follow, and therefore less prone to errors.

If you're curious about performance, recall that earlier I mentioned that table expressions typically have no performance impact because they are not physically materialized anywhere. Both references to the CTE in the previous query are going to be expanded. Internally, this query has a self join between two instances of the *Orders* table, each of which involves scanning the table data and aggregating it before the join—the same physical processing that takes place with the derived table approach. If the work done per reference is very expensive and you want to avoid doing it multiple times, you should persist the inner query's result in a temporary table or a table variable. My focus in this discussion is on coding aspects and not performance, and clearly the ability to specify the inner query only once, and refer to the CTE name multiple times, is a great benefit over the counterpart that uses derived tables.

## Recursive CTEs

This section is optional because it covers subjects that are beyond the fundamentals.

CTEs are unique among table expressions because they have recursive capabilities. A recursive CTE is defined by at least two queries (more are possible)—at least one query known as the anchor member and at least one query known as the recursive member. The general form of a basic recursive CTE looks like the following.

```
WITH <CTE_Name>[(<target_column_list>)]
AS
(
  <anchor_member>
  UNION ALL
  <recursive_member>
)
<outer_query_against_CTE>;
```

The anchor member is a query that returns a valid relational result table—like a query that is used to define a nonrecursive table expression. The anchor member query is invoked only once.

The recursive member is a query that has a reference to the CTE name. The reference to the CTE name represents what is logically the previous result set in a sequence of executions. The first time that the recursive member is invoked, the previous result set represents whatever the anchor member returned. In each subsequent invocation of the recursive member, the reference to the CTE name represents the result set returned by the previous invocation of the recursive member. The recursive member has no explicit recursion termination check—the termination check is implicit. The recursive member is invoked repeatedly until it returns an empty set or exceeds some limit.

Both queries must be compatible in terms of the number of columns they return and the data types of the corresponding columns.

The reference to the CTE name in the outer query represents the unified result sets of the invocation of the anchor member and all invocations of the recursive member.

If this is your first encounter with recursive CTEs, you might find this explanation hard to understand. They are best explained with an example. The following code demonstrates how to use a recursive CTE to return information about an employee (Don Funk, employee ID 2) and all of the employee's subordinates in all levels (direct or indirect).

```
WITH EmpsCTE AS
(
  SELECT empid, mgrid, firstname, lastname
  FROM HR.Employees
  WHERE empid = 2

  UNION ALL

  SELECT C.empid, C.mgrid, C.firstname, C.lastname
  FROM EmpsCTE AS P
    JOIN HR.Employees AS C
      ON C.mgrid = P.empid
)
SELECT empid, mgrid, firstname, lastname
FROM EmpsCTE;
```

The anchor member queries the *HR.Employees* table and simply returns the row for employee 2.

```
SELECT empid, mgrid, firstname, lastname
FROM HR.Employees
WHERE empid = 2
```

The recursive member joins the CTE—representing the previous result set—with the *Employees* table to return the direct subordinates of the employees returned in the previous result set.

```
SELECT C.empid, C.mgrid, C.firstname, C.lastname
FROM EmpsCTE AS P
  JOIN HR.Employees AS C
    ON C.mgrid = P.empid
```

In other words, the recursive member is invoked repeatedly, and in each invocation it returns the next level of subordinates. The first time the recursive member is invoked, it returns the direct subordinates of employee 2—employees 3 and 5. The second time the recursive member is invoked, it returns the direct subordinates of employees 3 and 5—employees 4, 6, 7, 8, and 9. The third time the recursive member is invoked, there are no more subordinates; the recursive member returns an empty set, and therefore recursion stops.

The reference to the CTE name in the outer query represents the unified result sets; in other words, employee 2 and all of the employee's subordinates.

Here's the output of this code.

```
empid       mgrid       firstname   lastname
----------- ----------- ----------- --------------------
2           1           Don         Funk
3           2           Judy        Lew
5           2           Sven        Buck
6           5           Paul        Suurs
7           5           Russell     King
9           5           Zoya        Dolgopyatova
4           3           Yael        Peled
8           3           Maria       Cameron
```

In the event of a logical error in the join predicate in the recursive member, or problems with the data that result in cycles, the recursive member can potentially be invoked an infinite number of times. As a safety measure, by default SQL Server restricts the number of times that the recursive member can be invoked to 100. The code will fail upon the one hundred first invocation of the recursive member. You can change the default maximum recursion limit by specifying the hint *OPTION(MAXRECURSION n)* at the end of the outer query, where n is an integer in the range 0 through 32,767 representing the maximum recursion limit you want to set. If you want to remove the restriction altogether, specify *MAXRECURSION 0*. Note that SQL Server stores the intermediate result sets returned by the anchor and recursive members in a work table in *tempdb*; if you remove the restriction and have a runaway query, the work table will quickly get very large. If *tempdb* can't grow anymore—for example, when you run out of disk space—the query will fail.

# Views

The two types of table expressions discussed so far—derived tables and CTEs—have a very limited scope, which is the single-statement scope. As soon as the outer query against those table expressions is finished, they are gone. This means that derived tables and CTEs are not reusable.

Views and inline table-valued functions (inline TVFs) are two reusable types of table expressions; their definitions are stored as database objects. After they have been created, those objects are permanent parts of the database and are only removed from the database if they are explicitly dropped.

In most other respects, views and inline TVFs are treated like derived tables and CTEs. For example, when querying a view or an inline TVF, SQL Server expands the definition of the table expression and queries the underlying objects directly, as with derived tables and CTEs.

In this section, I describe views; in the next section, I describe inline TVFs.

As I mentioned earlier, a view is a reusable table expression whose definition is stored in the database. For example, the following code creates a view called *USACusts* in the *Sales* schema in the *TSQL2012* database, representing all customers from the United States.

```
IF OBJECT_ID('Sales.USACusts') IS NOT NULL
  DROP VIEW Sales.USACusts;
GO
CREATE VIEW Sales.USACusts
AS

SELECT
  custid, companyname, contactname, contacttitle, address,
  city, region, postalcode, country, phone, fax
FROM Sales.Customers
WHERE country = N'USA';
GO
```

Note that just as with derived tables and CTEs, instead of using inline column aliasing as shown in the preceding code, you can use external column aliasing by specifying the target column names in parentheses immediately after the view name.

After you have created this view, you can query it much like you query other tables in the database.

```
SELECT custid, companyname
FROM Sales.USACusts;
```

Because a view is an object in the database, you can control access to the view with permissions just as you can with other objects that can be queried (these permissions include *SELECT*, *INSERT*, *UPDATE*, and *DELETE* permissions). For example, you can deny direct access to the underlying objects while granting access to the view.

Note that the general recommendation to avoid using *SELECT* * has specific relevance in the context of views. The columns are enumerated in the compiled form of the view, and new table columns will not be automatically added to the view. For example, suppose you define a view based on the query *SELECT * FROM dbo.T1*, and at the view creation time the table *T1* has the columns *col1* and *col2*. SQL Server stores information only on those two columns in the view's metadata. If you alter the definition of the table to add new columns, those new columns will not be added to the view. You can refresh the view's metadata by using the stored procedure *sp_refreshview* or *sp_refreshsqlmodule*, but to avoid confusion, the best practice is to explicitly list the column names that you need in the definition of the view. If columns are added to the underlying tables and you need them in the view, use the *ALTER VIEW* statement to revise the view definition accordingly.

## Views and the *ORDER BY* Clause

The query that you use to define a view must meet all requirements mentioned earlier with respect to table expressions in the context of derived tables. The view should not guarantee any order to the rows, all view columns must have names, and all column names must be unique. In this section, I elaborate a bit about the ordering issue, which is a fundamental point that is crucial to understand.

Remember that a presentation *ORDER BY* clause is not allowed in the query defining a table expression because there's no order among the rows of a relational table. An attempt to create an ordered view is absurd because it violates fundamental properties of a relation as defined by the relational model. If you need to return rows from a view sorted for presentation purposes, you shouldn't try to make the view something it shouldn't be. Instead, you should specify a presentation *ORDER BY* clause in the outer query against the view, like this.

```
SELECT custid, companyname, region
FROM Sales.USACusts
ORDER BY region;
```

Try running the following code to create a view with a presentation *ORDER BY* clause.

```
ALTER VIEW Sales.USACusts
AS

SELECT
  custid, companyname, contactname, contacttitle, address,
  city, region, postalcode, country, phone, fax
FROM Sales.Customers
WHERE country = N'USA'
ORDER BY region;
GO
```

This attempt fails, and you get the following error.

```
Msg 1033, Level 15, State 1, Procedure USACusts, Line 9
The ORDER BY clause is invalid in views, inline functions, derived tables, subqueries, and
common table expressions, unless TOP, OFFSET or FOR XML is also specified.
```

The error message indicates that SQL Server allows the *ORDER BY* clause in three exceptional cases—when the *TOP*, *OFFSET-FETCH*, or *FOR XML* option is used. In all cases, the *ORDER BY* clause serves a purpose beyond the usual presentation purpose. Even standard SQL has a similar restriction, with a similar exception when the standard *OFFSET-FETCH* option is used.

Because T-SQL allows an *ORDER BY* clause in a view when *TOP* or *OFFSET-FETCH* is also specified, some people think that they can create "ordered views." One of the ways to try to achieve this is by using *TOP (100) PERCENT*, like the following.

```
ALTER VIEW Sales.USACusts
AS

SELECT TOP (100) PERCENT
  custid, companyname, contactname, contacttitle, address,
  city, region, postalcode, country, phone, fax
FROM Sales.Customers
WHERE country = N'USA'
ORDER BY region;
GO
```

Even though the code is technically valid and the view is created, you should be aware that because the query is used to define a table expression, the *ORDER BY* clause here is only guaranteed to serve the logical filtering purpose for the *TOP* option. If you query the view and don't specify an *ORDER BY* clause in the outer query, presentation order is not guaranteed.

For example, run the following query against the view.

```
SELECT custid, companyname, region
FROM Sales.USACusts;
```

Here is the output from one of my executions showing that the rows are not sorted by region.

```
custid       companyname               region
-----------  ------------------------  ----------------
32           Customer YSIQX            OR
36           Customer LVJSO            OR
43           Customer UISOJ            WA
45           Customer QXPPT            CA
48           Customer DVFMB            OR
55           Customer KZQZT            AK
65           Customer NYUHS            NM
71           Customer LCOUJ            ID
75           Customer XOJYP            WY
77           Customer LCYBZ            OR
78           Customer NLTYP            MT
82           Customer EYHKM            WA
89           Customer YBQTI            WA
```

In some cases, a query that is used to define a table expression has the *TOP* option with an *ORDER BY* clause, and the query against the table expression doesn't have an *ORDER BY* clause. In those cases, therefore, the output might or might not be returned in the specified order. If the results happen to be ordered, it may be due to optimization reasons, especially when you use values other than *TOP (100) PERCENT*. The point I'm trying to make is that any order of the rows in the output is considered valid, and no specific order is guaranteed; therefore, when querying a table expression, you should not assume any order unless you specify an *ORDER BY* clause in the outer query.

In SQL Server 2012, there's a new way to try to get a "sorted view," by using the *OFFSET* clause with *0 ROWS*, and without a *FETCH* clause, like the following.

```
ALTER VIEW Sales.USACusts
AS

SELECT
  custid, companyname, contactname, contacttitle, address,
  city, region, postalcode, country, phone, fax
FROM Sales.Customers
WHERE country = N'USA'
ORDER BY region
OFFSET 0 ROWS;
GO
```

At the moment, when I query the view and don't indicate an *ORDER BY* clause in the outer query, the result rows happen to be sorted by region. But I stress—*do not* assume that that's guaranteed. It happens to be the case due to current optimization. If you need a guarantee that the rows will be returned from the query against the view sorted, you need an *ORDER BY* clause in the outer query.

Do not confuse the behavior of a query that is used to define a table expression with a query that isn't. A query with an *ORDER BY* clause and a *TOP* or *OFFSET-FETCH* option does not guarantee presentation order only in the context of a table expression. In the context of a query that is not used to define a table expression, the *ORDER BY* clause serves both the filtering purpose for the *TOP* or *OFFSET-FETCH* option and the presentation purpose.

# View Options

When you create or alter a view, you can specify view attributes and options as part of the view definition. In the header of the view, under the *WITH* clause, you can specify attributes such as *ENCRYPTION* and *SCHEMABINDING*, and at the end of the query you can specify *WITH CHECK OPTION*. The following sections describe the purpose of these options.

## The *ENCRYPTION* Option

The *ENCRYPTION* option is available when you create or alter views, stored procedures, triggers, and user-defined functions (UDFs). The *ENCRYPTION* option indicates that SQL Server will internally store the text with the definition of the object in an obfuscated format. The obfuscated text is not directly visible to users through any of the catalog objects—only to privileged users through special means.

Before you look at the *ENCRYPTION* option, run the following code to alter the definition of the *USACusts* view to its original version.

```
ALTER VIEW Sales.USACusts
AS

SELECT
  custid, companyname, contactname, contacttitle, address,
  city, region, postalcode, country, phone, fax
FROM Sales.Customers
WHERE country = N'USA';
GO
```

To get the definition of the view, invoke the OBJECT_DEFINITION function like this.

```
SELECT OBJECT_DEFINITION(OBJECT_ID('Sales.USACusts'));
```

The text with the definition of the view is available because the view was created without the *ENCRYPTION* option. You get the following output.

```
CREATE VIEW Sales.USACusts
AS

SELECT
  custid, companyname, contactname, contacttitle, address,
  city, region, postalcode, country, phone, fax
FROM Sales.Customers
WHERE country = N'USA';
```

Next, alter the view definition—only this time, include the *ENCRYPTION* option.

```
ALTER VIEW Sales.USACusts WITH ENCRYPTION
AS

SELECT
  custid, companyname, contactname, contacttitle, address,
  city, region, postalcode, country, phone, fax
FROM Sales.Customers
WHERE country = N'USA';
GO
```

Try again to get the text with the definition of the view.

```
SELECT OBJECT_DEFINITION(OBJECT_ID('Sales.USACusts'));
```

This time you get a *NULL* back.

As an alternative to the OBJECT_DEFINITION function, you can use the *sp_helptext* stored procedure to get object definitions. For example, the following code requests the object definition of the *USACusts* view.

```
EXEC sp_helptext 'Sales.USACusts';
```

Because in our case the view was created with the *ENCRYPTION* option, you will not get the object definition back, but instead you will get the following message.

```
The text for object 'Sales.USACusts' is encrypted.
```

## The *SCHEMABINDING* Option

The *SCHEMABINDING* option is available to views and UDFs; it binds the schema of referenced objects and columns to the schema of the referencing object. It indicates that referenced objects cannot be dropped and that referenced columns cannot be dropped or altered.

For example, alter the *USACusts* view with the *SCHEMABINDING* option.

```
ALTER VIEW Sales.USACusts WITH SCHEMABINDING
AS

SELECT
  custid, companyname, contactname, contacttitle, address,
  city, region, postalcode, country, phone, fax
FROM Sales.Customers
WHERE country = N'USA';
GO
```

Now try to drop the *Address* column from the *Customers* table.

```
ALTER TABLE Sales.Customers DROP COLUMN address;
```

You get the following error.

```
Msg 5074, Level 16, State 1, Line 1
The object 'USACusts' is dependent on column 'address'.
Msg 4922, Level 16, State 9, Line 1
ALTER TABLE DROP COLUMN address failed because one or more objects access this column.
```

Without the *SCHEMABINDING* option, you would have been allowed to make such a schema change, as well as drop the *Customers* table altogether. This can lead to errors at run time when you try to query the view and referenced objects or columns do not exist. If you create the view with the *SCHEMABINDING* option, you can avoid these errors.

To support the *SCHEMABINDING* option, the object definition must meet a couple of technical requirements. The query is not allowed to use * in the *SELECT* clause; instead, you have to explicitly list column names. Also, you must use schema-qualified two-part names when referring to objects. Both requirements are actually good practices in general.

As you can imagine, creating your objects with the *SCHEMABINDING* option is a good practice.

## The *CHECK OPTION* Option

The purpose of *CHECK OPTION* is to prevent modifications through the view that conflict with the view's filter—assuming that one exists in the query defining the view.

The query defining the view *USACusts* filters customers whose country attribute is equal to *N'USA'*. The view is currently defined without *CHECK OPTION*. This means that you can currently insert rows through the view with customers from countries other than the United States, and you can update existing customers through the view, changing their country to one other than the United States. For example, the following code successfully inserts a customer with company name Customer ABCDE from the United Kingdom through the view.

```
INSERT INTO Sales.USACusts(
  companyname, contactname, contacttitle, address,
  city, region, postalcode, country, phone, fax)
VALUES(
  N'Customer ABCDE', N'Contact ABCDE', N'Title ABCDE', N'Address ABCDE',
  N'London', NULL, N'12345', N'UK', N'012-3456789', N'012-3456789');
```

The row was inserted through the view into the *Customers* table. However, because the view filters only customers from the United States, if you query the view looking for the new customer, you get an empty set back.

```
SELECT custid, companyname, country
FROM Sales.USACusts
WHERE companyname = N'Customer ABCDE';
```

Query the *Customers* table directly looking for the new customer.

```
SELECT custid, companyname, country
FROM Sales.Customers
WHERE companyname = N'Customer ABCDE';
```

You get the customer information in the output, because the new row made it to the *Customers* table.

```
custid       companyname          country
-----------  -------------------  ---------------
92           Customer ABCDE       UK
```

Similarly, if you update a customer row through the view, changing the country attribute to a country other than the United States, the update makes it to the table. But that customer information doesn't show up anymore in the view because it doesn't satisfy the view's query filter.

If you want to prevent modifications that conflict with the view's filter, add *WITH CHECK OPTION* at the end of the query defining the view.

```
ALTER VIEW Sales.USACusts WITH SCHEMABINDING
AS

SELECT
  custid, companyname, contactname, contacttitle, address,
  city, region, postalcode, country, phone, fax
FROM Sales.Customers
WHERE country = N'USA'
WITH CHECK OPTION;
GO
```

Now try to insert a row that conflicts with the view's filter.

```
INSERT INTO Sales.USACusts(
  companyname, contactname, contacttitle, address,
  city, region, postalcode, country, phone, fax)
VALUES(
  N'Customer FGHIJ', N'Contact FGHIJ', N'Title FGHIJ', N'Address FGHIJ',
  N'London', NULL, N'12345', N'UK', N'012-3456789', N'012-3456789');
```

You get the following error.

```
Msg 550, Level 16, State 1, Line 1
The attempted insert or update failed because the target view either specifies WITH CHECK
OPTION or spans a view that specifies WITH CHECK OPTION and one or more rows resulting from the
operation did not qualify under the CHECK OPTION constraint.
The statement has been terminated.
```

When you're done, run the following code for cleanup.

```
DELETE FROM Sales.Customers
WHERE custid > 91;

IF OBJECT_ID('Sales.USACusts') IS NOT NULL DROP VIEW Sales.USACusts;
```

# Inline Table-Valued Functions

Inline TVFs are reusable table expressions that support input parameters. In all respects except for the support for input parameters, inline TVFs are similar to views. For this reason, I like to think of inline TVFs as parameterized views, even though they are not called this formally.

For example, the following code creates an inline TVF called GetCustOrders in the *TSQL2012* database.

```
USE TSQL2012;
IF OBJECT_ID('dbo.GetCustOrders') IS NOT NULL
  DROP FUNCTION dbo.GetCustOrders;
GO
CREATE FUNCTION dbo.GetCustOrders
  (@cid AS INT) RETURNS TABLE
AS
RETURN
  SELECT orderid, custid, empid, orderdate, requireddate,
    shippeddate, shipperid, freight, shipname, shipaddress, shipcity,
    shipregion, shippostalcode, shipcountry
  FROM Sales.Orders
  WHERE custid = @cid;
GO
```

This inline TVF accepts an input parameter called @cid, representing a customer ID, and returns all orders that were placed by the input customer. You query inline TVFs by using DML statements, the same way you query other tables. If the function accepts input parameters, you specify those in parentheses following the function's name. Also, make sure you provide an alias for the table expression. Providing a table expression with an alias is not always a requirement, but it is a good practice because it makes your code more readable and less prone to errors. For example, the following code queries the function, requesting all orders that were placed by customer 1.

```
SELECT orderid, custid
FROM dbo.GetCustOrders(1) AS O;
```

This code returns the following output.

```
orderid      custid
-----------  -----------
10643        1
10692        1
10702        1
10835        1
10952        1
11011        1
```

As with other tables, you can refer to an inline TVF as part of a join. For example, the following query joins the inline TVF returning customer 1's orders with the *Sales.OrderDetails* table, matching customer 1's orders with the related order lines.

```
SELECT O.orderid, O.custid, OD.productid, OD.qty
FROM dbo.GetCustOrders(1) AS O
  JOIN Sales.OrderDetails AS OD
    ON O.orderid = OD.orderid;
```

This code returns the following output.

```
orderid      custid       productid    qty
-----------  -----------  -----------  ------
10643        1            28           15
10643        1            39           21
10643        1            46            2
10692        1            63           20
10702        1             3            6
10702        1            76           15
10835        1            59           15
10835        1            77            2
10952        1             6           16
10952        1            28            2
11011        1            58           40
11011        1            71           20
```

When you're done, run the following code for cleanup.

```
IF OBJECT_ID('dbo.GetCustOrders') IS NOT NULL
  DROP FUNCTION dbo.GetCustOrders;
```

# The *APPLY* Operator

The *APPLY* operator is a very powerful table operator. Like all table operators, this operator is used in the *FROM* clause of a query. The two supported types of *APPLY* operator are *CROSS APPLY* and *OUTER APPLY*. *CROSS APPLY* implements only one logical query processing phase, whereas *OUTER APPLY* implements two.

> **Note** *APPLY* isn't standard; the standard counterpart is called *LATERAL*, but the standard form wasn't implemented in SQL Server.

The *APPLY* operator operates on two input tables, the second of which can be a table expression; I'll refer to them as the "left" and "right" tables. The right table is usually a derived table or an inline TVF. The *CROSS APPLY* operator implements one logical query processing phase—it applies the right table expression to each row from the left table and produces a result table with the unified result sets.

So far it might sound like the *CROSS APPLY* operator is very similar to a cross join, and in a sense that's true. For example, the following two queries return the same result sets.

```
SELECT S.shipperid, E.empid
FROM Sales.Shippers AS S
  CROSS JOIN HR.Employees AS E;

SELECT S.shipperid, E.empid
FROM Sales.Shippers AS S
  CROSS APPLY HR.Employees AS E;
```

However, with the *CROSS APPLY* operator, the right table expression can represent a different set of rows per each row from the left table, unlike in a join. You can achieve this when you use a derived table in the right side, and in the derived table query refer to attributes from the left side. Alternatively, when you use an inline TVF, you can pass attributes from the left side as input arguments.

For example, the following code uses the *CROSS APPLY* operator to return the three most recent orders for each customer.

```
SELECT C.custid, A.orderid, A.orderdate
FROM Sales.Customers AS C
  CROSS APPLY
    (SELECT TOP (3) orderid, empid, orderdate, requireddate
     FROM Sales.Orders AS O
     WHERE O.custid = C.custid
     ORDER BY orderdate DESC, orderid DESC) AS A;
```

You can think of the table expression *A* as a correlated table subquery. In terms of logical query processing, the right table expression (a derived table, in this case) is applied to each row from the *Customers* table. Notice the reference to the attribute *C.custid* from the left table in the derived table's query filter. The derived table returns the three most recent orders for the customer from the current left row. Because the derived table is applied to each row from the left side, the *CROSS APPLY* operator returns the three most recent orders for each customer.

Here's the output of this query, shown in abbreviated form.

```
custid       orderid      orderdate
-----------  -----------  -----------------------
1            11011        2008-04-09 00:00:00.000
1            10952        2008-03-16 00:00:00.000
1            10835        2008-01-15 00:00:00.000
2            10926        2008-03-04 00:00:00.000
2            10759        2007-11-28 00:00:00.000
2            10625        2007-08-08 00:00:00.000
3            10856        2008-01-28 00:00:00.000
3            10682        2007-09-25 00:00:00.000
3            10677        2007-09-22 00:00:00.000
...

(263 row(s) affected)
```

Remember that, starting with SQL Server 2012, you can use the standard *OFFSET-FETCH* option instead of *TOP*, like the following.

```
SELECT C.custid, A.orderid, A.orderdate
FROM Sales.Customers AS C
  CROSS APPLY
    (SELECT orderid, empid, orderdate, requireddate
     FROM Sales.Orders AS O
     WHERE O.custid = C.custid
     ORDER BY orderdate DESC, orderid DESC
     OFFSET 0 ROWS FETCH FIRST 3 ROWS ONLY) AS A;
```

If the right table expression returns an empty set, the *CROSS APPLY* operator does not return the corresponding left row. For example, customers 22 and 57 did not place orders. In both cases, the derived table is an empty set; therefore, those customers are not returned in the output. If you want to return rows from the left table for which the right table expression returns an empty set, use the *OUTER APPLY* operator instead of *CROSS APPLY*. The *OUTER APPLY* operator adds a second logical phase that identifies rows from the left side for which the right table expression returns an empty set, and it adds those rows to the result table as outer rows with *NULL* marks in the right side's attributes as placeholders. In a sense, this phase is similar to the phase that adds outer rows in a left outer join.

For example, run the following code to return the three most recent orders for each customer, and include in the output customers with no orders as well.

```
SELECT C.custid, A.orderid, A.orderdate
FROM Sales.Customers AS C
  OUTER APPLY
    (SELECT TOP (3) orderid, empid, orderdate, requireddate
     FROM Sales.Orders AS O
     WHERE O.custid = C.custid
     ORDER BY orderdate DESC, orderid DESC) AS A;
```

This time, customers 22 and 57, who did not place orders, are included in the output, which is shown here in abbreviated form.

```
custid      orderid     orderdate
----------- ----------- -----------------------
1           11011       2008-04-09 00:00:00.000
1           10952       2008-03-16 00:00:00.000
1           10835       2008-01-15 00:00:00.000
2           10926       2008-03-04 00:00:00.000
2           10759       2007-11-28 00:00:00.000
2           10625       2007-08-08 00:00:00.000
3           10856       2008-01-28 00:00:00.000
3           10682       2007-09-25 00:00:00.000
3           10677       2007-09-22 00:00:00.000
...
22          NULL        NULL
...
57          NULL        NULL
...

(265 row(s) affected)
```

Here's the counterpart using *OFFSET-FETCH* instead of *TOP*.

```
SELECT C.custid, A.orderid, A.orderdate
FROM Sales.Customers AS C
  OUTER APPLY
    (SELECT orderid, empid, orderdate, requireddate
     FROM Sales.Orders AS O
     WHERE O.custid = C.custid
     ORDER BY orderdate DESC, orderid DESC
     OFFSET 0 ROWS FETCH FIRST 3 ROWS ONLY) AS A;
```

For encapsulation purposes, you might find it more convenient to work with inline TVFs instead of derived tables. if you do, your code will be simpler to follow and maintain. For example, the following code creates an inline TVF called TopOrders that accepts as inputs a customer ID (@custid) and a number (@n), and returns the @n most recent orders for customer @custid.

```
IF OBJECT_ID('dbo.TopOrders') IS NOT NULL
  DROP FUNCTION dbo.TopOrders;
GO
CREATE FUNCTION dbo.TopOrders
  (@custid AS INT, @n AS INT)
  RETURNS TABLE
AS
RETURN
  SELECT TOP (@n) orderid, empid, orderdate, requireddate
  FROM Sales.Orders
  WHERE custid = @custid
  ORDER BY orderdate DESC, orderid DESC;
GO
```

By using *OFFSET-FETCH* instead of *TOP*, you can replace the inner query in the function with this one.

```
SELECT orderid, empid, orderdate, requireddate
FROM Sales.Orders
WHERE custid = @custid
ORDER BY orderdate DESC, orderid DESC
OFFSET 0 ROWS FETCH FIRST @n ROWS ONLY;
```

You can now substitute the use of the derived table from the previous examples with the new function.

```
SELECT
  C.custid, C.companyname,
  A.orderid, A.empid, A.orderdate, A.requireddate
FROM Sales.Customers AS C
  CROSS APPLY dbo.TopOrders(C.custid, 3) AS A;
```

The code is much more readable and easier to maintain. In terms of physical processing, nothing really changed because, as I stated earlier, the definition of table expressions is expanded, and SQL Server will in any case end up querying the underlying objects directly.

# Conclusion

Table expressions can help you simplify your code, improve its maintainability, and encapsulate querying logic. When you need to use table expressions and are not planning to reuse their definitions, use derived tables or CTEs. CTEs have a couple of advantages over derived tables; you do not nest CTEs as you do derived tables, making CTEs more modular and easier to maintain. Also, you can refer to multiple instances of the same CTE, which you cannot do with derived tables.

When you need to define reusable table expressions, use views or inline TVFs. When you do not need to support input parameters, use views; otherwise, use inline TVFs.

Use the *APPLY* operator when you want to apply a table expression to each row from a source table and unify all result sets into one result table.

# Exercises

This section provides exercises to help you familiarize yourself with the subjects discussed in this chapter. All the exercises in this chapter require your session to be connected to the *TSQL2012* database.

## 1-1

Write a query that returns the maximum value in the orderdate column for each employee.

- Tables involved: *TSQL2012* database, *Sales.Orders* table

- Desired output:

```
empid       maxorderdate
----------- -----------------------
3           2008-04-30 00:00:00.000
6           2008-04-23 00:00:00.000
9           2008-04-29 00:00:00.000
7           2008-05-06 00:00:00.000
1           2008-05-06 00:00:00.000
4           2008-05-06 00:00:00.000
2           2008-05-05 00:00:00.000
5           2008-04-22 00:00:00.000
8           2008-05-06 00:00:00.000

(9 row(s) affected)
```

## 1-2

Encapsulate the query from Exercise 1-1 in a derived table. Write a join query between the derived table and the *Orders* table to return the orders with the maximum order date for each employee.

- Tables involved: *Sales.Orders*

- Desired output:

```
empid       orderdate                 orderid     custid
----------- ------------------------- ----------- -----------
9           2008-04-29 00:00:00.000   11058       6
8           2008-05-06 00:00:00.000   11075       68
7           2008-05-06 00:00:00.000   11074       73
6           2008-04-23 00:00:00.000   11045       10
5           2008-04-22 00:00:00.000   11043       74
4           2008-05-06 00:00:00.000   11076       9
3           2008-04-30 00:00:00.000   11063       37
2           2008-05-05 00:00:00.000   11073       58
2           2008-05-05 00:00:00.000   11070       44
1           2008-05-06 00:00:00.000   11077       65

(10 row(s) affected)
```

## 2-1

Write a query that calculates a row number for each order based on *orderdate, orderid* ordering.

- ■ Tables involved: *Sales.Orders*

- ■ Desired output (abbreviated):

```
orderid      orderdate                 custid        empid         rownum
-----------  ------------------------- -----------   -----------   -------
10248        2006-07-04 00:00:00.000   85            5             1
10249        2006-07-05 00:00:00.000   79            6             2
10250        2006-07-08 00:00:00.000   34            4             3
10251        2006-07-08 00:00:00.000   84            3             4
10252        2006-07-09 00:00:00.000   76            4             5
10253        2006-07-10 00:00:00.000   34            3             6
10254        2006-07-11 00:00:00.000   14            5             7
10255        2006-07-12 00:00:00.000   68            9             8
10256        2006-07-15 00:00:00.000   88            3             9
10257        2006-07-16 00:00:00.000   35            4             10
...

(830 row(s) affected)
```

## 2-2

Write a query that returns rows with row numbers 11 through 20 based on the row number definition in Exercise 2-1. Use a CTE to encapsulate the code from Exercise 2-1.

- ■ Tables involved: *Sales.Orders*

- ■ Desired output:

```
orderid      orderdate                 custid        empid         rownum
===========  ========================= ===========   ===========   =======
10258        2006-07-17 00:00:00.000   20            1             11
10259        2006-07-18 00:00:00.000   13            4             12
10260        2006-07-19 00:00:00.000   56            4             13
10261        2006-07-19 00:00:00.000   61            4             14
10262        2006-07-22 00:00:00.000   65            8             15
10263        2006-07-23 00:00:00.000   20            9             16
10264        2006-07-24 00:00:00.000   24            6             17
10265        2006-07-25 00:00:00.000   7             2             18
10266        2006-07-26 00:00:00.000   87            3             19
10267        2006-07-29 00:00:00.000   25            4             20

(10 row(s) affected)
```

# 3 (Optional, Advanced)

Write a solution using a recursive CTE that returns the management chain leading to Zoya Dolgopyatova (employee ID 9).

- Tables involved: *HR.Employees*

- Desired output:

```
empid        mgrid        firstname  lastname
-----------  -----------  ---------  --------------------
9            5            Zoya       Dolgopyatova
5            2            Sven       Buck
2            1            Don        Funk
1            NULL         Sara       Davis

(4 row(s) affected)
```

# 4-1

Create a view that returns the total quantity for each employee and year.

- Tables involved: *Sales.Orders* and *Sales.OrderDetails*

- When running the following code:

```
SELECT * FROM Sales.VEmpOrders ORDER BY empid, orderyear;
```

- Desired output:

```
empid        orderyear    qty
-----------  -----------  -----------
1            2006         1620
1            2007         3877
1            2008         2315
2            2006         1085
2            2007         2604
2            2008         2366
3            2006         940
3            2007         4436
3            2008         2476
4            2006         2212
4            2007         5273
4            2008         2313
5            2006         778
5            2007         1471
5            2008         787
6            2006         963
6            2007         1738
6            2008         826
7            2006         485
7            2007         2292
7            2008         1877
```

```
8        2006        923
8        2007        2843
8        2008        2147
9        2006        575
9        2007        955
9        2008        1140

(27 row(s) affected)
```

# 4-2 (Optional, Advanced)

Write a query against *Sales.VEmpOrders* that returns the running total quantity for each employee and year.

■ Tables involved: *Sales.VEmpOrders* view

■ Desired output:

```
empid        orderyear        qty        runqty
------------ ---------------- ---------- ----------
1            2006             1620       1620
1            2007             3877       5497
1            2008             2315       7812
2            2006             1085       1085
2            2007             2604       3689
2            2008             2366       6055
3            2006             940        940
3            2007             4436       5376
3            2008             2476       7852
4            2006             2212       2212
4            2007             5273       7485
4            2008             2313       9798
5            2006             778        778
5            2007             1471       2249
5            2008             787        3036
6            2006             963        963
6            2007             1738       2701
6            2008             826        3527
7            2006             485        485
7            2007             2292       2777
7            2008             1877       4654
8            2006             923        923
8            2007             2843       3766
8            2008             2147       5913
9            2006             575        575
9            2007             955        1530
9            2008             1140       2670

(27 row(s) affected)
```

## 5-1

Create an inline function that accepts as inputs a supplier ID (@supid AS INT) and a requested number of products (@n AS INT). The function should return @n products with the highest unit prices that are supplied by the specified supplier ID.

- ■ Tables involved: *Production.Products*

- ■ When issuing the following query:

    ```
    SELECT * FROM Production.TopProducts(5, 2);
    ```

- ■ Desired output:

    ```
    productid   productname         unitprice
    ----------- ------------------- ---------------
    12          Product OSFNS       38.00
    11          Product QMVUN       21.00

    (2 row(s) affected)
    ```

## 5-2

Using the *CROSS APPLY* operator and the function you created in Exercise 4-1, return, for each supplier, the two most expensive products.

- ■ Desired output (shown here in abbreviated form).

    ```
    supplierid  companyname       productid   productname       unitprice
    ----------- ----------------- ----------- ----------------- ----------
    8           Supplier BWGYE    20          Product QHFFP     81.00
    8           Supplier BWGYE    68          Product TBTBL     12.50
    20          Supplier CIYNM    43          Product ZZZHR     46.00
    20          Supplier CIYNM    44          Product VJIEO     19.45
    23          Supplier ELCRN    49          Product FPYPN     20.00
    23          Supplier ELCRN    76          Product JYGFE     18.00
    5           Supplier EQPNC    12          Product OSFNS     38.00
    5           Supplier EQPNC    11          Product QMVUN     21.00
    ...

    (55 row(s) affected)
    ```

- ■ When you're done, run the following code for cleanup.

    ```
    IF OBJECT_ID('Sales.VEmpOrders') IS NOT NULL
      DROP VIEW Sales.VEmpOrders;
    IF OBJECT_ID('Production.TopProducts') IS NOT NULL
      DROP FUNCTION Production.TopProducts;
    ```

# Solutions

This section provides solutions to the exercises in the preceding section.

## 1-1

This exercise is just a preliminary step required for the next exercise. This step involves writing a query that returns the maximum order date for each employee.

```
USE TSQL2012;

SELECT empid, MAX(orderdate) AS maxorderdate
FROM Sales.Orders
GROUP BY empid;
```

## 1-2

This exercise requires you to use the query from the previous step to define a derived table and join this derived table with the *Orders* table to return the orders with the maximum order date for each employee, like the following.

```
SELECT O.empid, O.orderdate, O.orderid, O.custid
FROM Sales.Orders AS O
  JOIN (SELECT empid, MAX(orderdate) AS maxorderdate
        FROM Sales.Orders
        GROUP BY empid) AS D
    ON O.empid = D.empid
    AND O.orderdate = D.maxorderdate;
```

## 2-1

This exercise is a preliminary step for the next exercise. It requires you to query the *Orders* table and calculate row numbers based on *orderdate, orderid* ordering, like the following.

```
SELECT orderid, orderdate, custid, empid,
  ROW_NUMBER() OVER(ORDER BY orderdate, orderid) AS rownum
FROM Sales.Orders;
```

## 2-2

This exercise requires you to define a CTE based on the query from the previous step, and filter only rows with row numbers in the range 11 through 20 from the CTE, like the following.

```
WITH OrdersRN AS
(
  SELECT orderid, orderdate, custid, empid,
    ROW_NUMBER() OVER(ORDER BY orderdate, orderid) AS rownum
  FROM Sales.Orders
)
SELECT * FROM OrdersRN WHERE rownum BETWEEN 11 AND 20;
```

You might wonder why you need a table expression here. Window functions (such as the ROW_NUMBER function) are only allowed in the *SELECT* and *ORDER BY* clauses of a query, and not directly in the *WHERE* clause. By using a table expression, you can invoke the ROW_NUMBER function in the *SELECT* clause, assign an alias to the result column, and refer to the result column in the *WHERE* clause of the outer query.

## 3

You can think of this exercise as the inverse of the request to return an employee and all subordinates in all levels. Here, the anchor member is a query that returns the row for employee 9. The recursive member joins the CTE (call it *C*)—representing the subordinate/child from the previous level—with the *Employees* table (call it *P*)—representing the manager/parent in the next level. This way, each invocation of the recursive member returns the manager from the next level, until no next-level manager is found (in the case of the CEO).

Here's the complete solution query.

```
WITH EmpsCTE AS
(
  SELECT empid, mgrid, firstname, lastname
  FROM HR.Employees
  WHERE empid = 9

  UNION ALL

  SELECT P.empid, P.mgrid, P.firstname, P.lastname
  FROM EmpsCTE AS C
    JOIN HR.Employees AS P
      ON C.mgrid = P.empid
)
SELECT empid, mgrid, firstname, lastname
FROM EmpsCTE;
```

## 4-1

This exercise is a preliminary step for the next exercise. Here you are required to define a view based on a query that joins the *Orders* and *OrderDetails* tables, group the rows by employee ID and order year, and return the total quantity for each group. The view definition should look like the following.

```
USE TSQL2012;
IF OBJECT_ID('Sales.VEmpOrders') IS NOT NULL
  DROP VIEW Sales.VEmpOrders;
GO
CREATE VIEW  Sales.VEmpOrders
AS

SELECT
  empid,
  YEAR(orderdate) AS orderyear,
  SUM(qty) AS qty
FROM Sales.Orders AS O
  JOIN Sales.OrderDetails AS OD
    ON O.orderid = OD.orderid
GROUP BY
  empid,
  YEAR(orderdate);
GO
```

## 4-2

In this exercise, you query the *VEmpOrders* view and return the running total quantity for each employee and order year. To achieve this, you can write a query against the *VEmpOrders* view (call it *V1*) that returns from each row the employee ID, order year, and quantity. In the SELECT list, you can incorporate a subquery against a second instance of *VEmpOrders* (call it *V2*), that returns the sum of all quantities from the rows where the employee ID is equal to the one in *V1*, and the order year is smaller than or equal to the one in *V1*. The complete solution query looks like the following.

```
SELECT empid, orderyear, qty,
  (SELECT SUM(qty)
   FROM  Sales.VEmpOrders AS V2
   WHERE V2.empid = V1.empid
     AND V2.orderyear <= V1.orderyear) AS runqty
FROM  Sales.VEmpOrders AS V1
ORDER BY empid, orderyear;
```

Note that in Chapter 7, "Beyond the Fundamentals of Querying," you will learn about new techniques to compute running totals by using window functions.

## 5-1

This exercise requires you to define a function called TopProducts that accepts a supplier ID (@supid) and a number (@n), and is supposed to return the @n most expensive products supplied by the input supplier ID. Here's how the function definition should look.

```
USE TSQL2012;
IF OBJECT_ID('Production.TopProducts') IS NOT NULL
  DROP FUNCTION Production.TopProducts;
GO
CREATE FUNCTION Production.TopProducts
  (@supid AS INT, @n AS INT)
  RETURNS TABLE
AS
RETURN
  SELECT TOP (@n) productid, productname, unitprice
  FROM Production.Products
  WHERE supplierid = @supid
  ORDER BY unitprice DESC;
GO
```

Starting with SQL Server 2012, you can use the *OFFSET-FETCH* filter instead of *TOP*. You would replace the inner query in the function with the following one.

```
SELECT productid, productname, unitprice
FROM Production.Products
WHERE supplierid = @supid
ORDER BY unitprice DESC
OFFSET 0 ROWS FETCH FIRST @n ROWS ONLY;
```

## 5-2

In this exercise, you write a query against the *Production.Suppliers* table and use the *CROSS APPLY* operator to apply the function you defined in the previous step to each supplier. Your query is supposed to return the two most expensive products for each supplier. Here's the solution query.

```
SELECT S.supplierid, S.companyname, P.productid, P.productname, P.unitprice
FROM Production.Suppliers AS S
  CROSS APPLY Production.TopProducts(S.supplierid, 2) AS P;
```

# CHAPTER 6

# Set Operators

Set operators are operators that are applied between two input sets—or, to use the more accurate SQL term, *multisets*—that result from two input queries. Remember, a multiset is not a true set, because it can contain duplicates. When I use the term multiset in this chapter, I'm referring to the intermediate results from two input queries that might contain duplicates. Although there are two multisets as inputs to an operator, depending on the flavor of the operator, the result is either a set or a multiset. If the operator is a true set operator (a *DISTINCT* flavor), the result is a set with no duplicates. If the operator is a multiset operator (an *ALL* flavor), the result is a multiset with possible duplicates. This chapter focuses on set operators but also covers multiset operators.

T-SQL supports three set operators: *UNION*, *INTERSECT*, and *EXCEPT*. In this chapter, I first introduce the general form and requirements of the operators, and then I describe each operator in detail.

The general form of a query with a set operator is as follows.

```
Input Query1
<set_operator>
Input Query2
[ORDER BY ...]
```

A set operator compares complete rows between the result sets of the two input queries involved. Whether a row will be returned in the result of the operator depends upon the outcome of the comparison and the operator used. Because by definition a set operator is applied to two sets (or, in SQL, multisets) and a set has no guaranteed order, the two queries involved cannot have *ORDER BY* clauses. Remember that a query with an *ORDER BY* clause guarantees presentation order and therefore does not return a set (or a multiset)—it returns a cursor. However, although the queries involved cannot have *ORDER BY* clauses, you can optionally add an *ORDER BY* clause that is applied to the result of the operator.

In terms of logical query processing, each of the individual queries can have all logical query processing phases except for a presentation *ORDER BY*, as I just explained. The set operator is applied to the results of the two queries, and the outer *ORDER BY* clause (if one exists) is applied to the result of the set operator.

The two queries involved in a set operator must produce results with the same number of columns, and corresponding columns must have compatible data types. By *compatible data types* I mean that the data type that is lower in terms of data type precedence must be implicitly convertible to the higher data type.

The names of the columns in the result of a set operator are determined by the first query; therefore, if you need to assign aliases to result columns, you should assign those in the first query.

An interesting aspect of set operators is that when it is comparing rows, a set operator considers two *NULLs* as equal. I'll demonstrate the importance of this point later in the chapter.

Standard SQL supports two "flavors" of each operator—*DISTINCT* (the default) and *ALL*. The *DISTINCT* flavor eliminates duplicates and returns a set. *ALL* doesn't attempt to remove duplicates and therefore returns a multiset. All three operators in Microsoft SQL Server support an implicit distinct version, but only the *UNION* operator supports the *ALL* version. In terms of syntax, you cannot explicitly specify the *DISTINCT* clause. Instead, it is implied when you don't specify *ALL* explicitly. I'll provide alternatives to the missing *INTERSECT ALL* and *EXCEPT ALL* operators in the "The *INTERSECT ALL* Multiset Operator" and "The *EXCEPT ALL* Multiset Operator" sections later in this chapter.

# The *UNION* Operator

In set theory, the union of two sets (call them A and B) is the set containing all elements of both A and B. In other words, if an element belongs to any of the input sets, it belongs to the result set. Figure 6-1 shows a set diagram (also known as a Venn diagram) with a graphical depiction of the union of two sets. The shaded area represents the result of the set operator.

Union: A U B

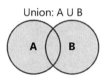

**FIGURE 6-1** A union of two sets.

In T-SQL, the *UNION* operator unifies the results of two input queries. If a row appears in any of the input sets, it will appear in the result of the *UNION* operator. T-SQL supports both the *UNION ALL* and *UNION* (implicit *DISTINCT*) flavors of the *UNION* operator.

## The *UNION ALL* Multiset Operator

The *UNION ALL* multiset operator returns all rows that appear in any of the input multisets resulting from the two input queries, without really comparing rows and without eliminating duplicates. Assuming that *Query1* returns m rows and *Query2* returns n rows, *Query1 UNION ALL Query2* returns m + n rows.

For example, the following code uses the *UNION ALL* operator to unify employee locations and customer locations.

```
USE TSQL2012;

SELECT country, region, city FROM HR.Employees
UNION ALL
SELECT country, region, city FROM Sales.Customers;
```

The result has 100 rows—9 from the *Employees* table and 91 from the *Customers* table—and is shown here in abbreviated form:

```
country          region           city
---------------  ---------------  ------------
USA              WA               Seattle
USA              WA               Tacoma
USA              WA               Kirkland
USA              WA               Redmond
UK               NULL             London
UK               NULL             London
UK               NULL             London
...
Finland          NULL             Oulu
Brazil           SP               Resende
USA              WA               Seattle
Finland          NULL             Helsinki
Poland           NULL             Warszawa

(100 row(s) affected)
```

Because *UNION ALL* doesn't eliminate duplicates, the result is a multiset and not a set. The same row can appear multiple times in the result, as is the case with *(UK, NULL, London)* in the result of this query.

## The *UNION* Distinct Set Operator

The *UNION* (implicit *DISTINCT*) set operator unifies the results of the two queries and eliminates duplicates. Note that if a row appears in both input sets, it will appear only once in the result; in other words, the result is a set and not a multiset.

For example, the following code returns distinct locations that are either employee locations or customer locations.

```
SELECT country, region, city FROM HR.Employees
UNION
SELECT country, region, city FROM Sales.Customers;
```

The difference between this example and the previous one with the *UNION ALL* operator is that in this example, the operator removed duplicates, whereas in the previous example, it didn't. Hence, the result of this query has 71 distinct rows, as shown here in abbreviated form.

```
country          region           city
---------------  ---------------  ---------------
Argentina        NULL             Buenos Aires
Austria          NULL             Graz
Austria          NULL             Salzburg
Belgium          NULL             Bruxelles
Belgium          NULL             Charleroi
...
USA              WY               Lander
Venezuela        DF               Caracas
Venezuela        Lara             Barquisimeto
Venezuela        Nueva Esparta    I. de Margarita
Venezuela        Táchira          San Cristóbal

(71 row(s) affected)
```

So when should you use *UNION ALL* and when should you use *UNION*? If a potential exists for duplicates after the two inputs of the operator have been unified, and you need to return the duplicates, use *UNION ALL*. If a potential exists for duplicates but you need to return distinct rows, use *UNION*. If no potential exists for duplicates after the two inputs have been unified, *UNION* and *UNION ALL* are logically equivalent. However, in such a case I'd recommend that you use *UNION ALL* because adding *ALL* removes the overhead incurred by SQL Server checking for duplicates.

## The *INTERSECT* Operator

In set theory, the intersection of two sets (call them A and B) is the set of all elements that belong to A and also belong to B. Figure 6-2 shows a graphical depiction of the intersection of two sets.

Intersection: A ∩ B

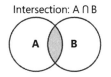

**FIGURE 6-2** The intersection of two sets.

In T-SQL, the *INTERSECT* set operator returns the intersection of the result sets of two input queries, returning only rows that appear in both inputs. After I describe *INTERSECT* (implicit *DISTINCT*), I provide an alternative solution to the *INTERSECT ALL* multiset operator that has not yet been implemented as of SQL Server 2012.

## The *INTERSECT* Distinct Set Operator

The *INTERSECT* set operator logically first eliminates duplicate rows from the two input multisets—turning them to sets—and then returns only rows that appear in both sets. In other words, a row is returned provided that it appears at least once in both input multisets.

For example, the following code returns distinct locations that are both employee locations and customer locations.

```
SELECT country, region, city FROM HR.Employees
INTERSECT
SELECT country, region, city FROM Sales.Customers;
```

This query returns the following output.

```
country          region          city
---------------- ------- ------- ---------------
UK               NULL            London
USA              WA              Kirkland
USA              WA              Seattle
```

It doesn't matter how many occurrences there are of an employee or customer location—if the location appears at least once in the *Employees* table and also at least once in the *Customers* table, the location is returned. The output of this query shows that three locations are both customer and employee locations.

I mentioned earlier that when it is comparing rows, a set operator considers two *NULL* marks as equal. There are both customers and employees with the location *(UK, NULL, London)*, but it's not trivial that this row appears in the output. The country and city attributes do not allow *NULL* marks, so the comparison that the set operator performs between these column values in an employee row and in a customer row is straightforward. What's not straightforward is that when the set operator compares the *NULL* region in the employee row and the *NULL* region in the customer row, it considers the two equal, and that's why it returns the row.

When this is the behavior of *NULL* comparison that you want—as it is in this case—set operators have a powerful advantage over alternatives. For example, one alternative to using the *INTERSECT* operator is to use an inner join, and another is to use the *EXISTS* predicate. In both cases, when the *NULL* in the region attribute of an employee is compared with the *NULL* in the region attribute of a customer, the comparison yields *UNKNOWN*, and such a row is filtered out. This means that unless you add extra logic that handles *NULL* marks in a special manner, neither the inner join nor the *EXISTS* alternative returns the row *(UK, NULL, London)*, even though it does appear in both sides.

## The *INTERSECT ALL* Multiset Operator

I provide this section as optional reading for those who feel very comfortable with the material covered so far in this chapter. Standard SQL supports an *ALL* flavor of the *INTERSECT* operator, but this flavor has not yet been implemented as of SQL Server 2012. After I describe the meaning of *INTERSECT ALL* in standard SQL, I'll provide an alternative in T-SQL.

Remember the meaning of the ALL keyword in the *UNION ALL* operator: it returns all duplicate rows. Similarly, the keyword ALL in the *INTERSECT ALL* operator means that duplicate intersections will not be removed. *INTERSECT ALL* is different from *UNION ALL* in that the former does not return all duplicates but only returns the number of duplicate rows, matching the lower of the counts in both multisets. Another way to look at it is that the *INTERSECT ALL* operator doesn't only care about the existence of a row in both sides—it also cares about the number of occurrences of the row in each side. It's as if this operator looks for matches per occurrence of each row. If there are x occurrences of a row R in the first input multiset and y occurrences of R in the second, R appears minimum(x, y) times in the result of the operator. For example, the location *(UK, NULL, London)* appears four times in *Employees* and six times in *Customers*; hence, an *INTERSECT ALL* operator between the employee locations and the customer locations should return four occurrences of *(UK, NULL, London)*, because at the logical level, four occurrences can be intersected.

Even though SQL Server does not support a built-in *INTERSECT ALL* operator, you can provide a solution that produces the same result. You can use the ROW_NUMBER function to number the occurrences of each row in each input query. To achieve this, specify all participating attributes in the *PARTITION BY* clause of the function, and use *(SELECT <constant>)* in the *ORDER BY* clause of the function to indicate that order doesn't matter.

> **Tip** Using *ORDER BY (SELECT <constant>)* as the ordering specification for a window function is one of several ways to tell SQL Server that order doesn't matter. SQL Server is smart enough to realize that the same constant will be assigned to all rows, and therefore it's not necessary to actually sort the data and incur the associated overhead.

Then apply the *INTERSECT* operator between the two queries with the ROW_NUMBER function. Because the occurrences of each row are numbered, the intersection is based on the row numbers in addition to the original attributes. For example, in the *Employees* table, which has four occurrences of the location *(UK, NULL, London)*, those occurrences would be numbered 1 through 4. In the *Customers* table, which has six occurrences of the location *(UK, NULL, London)*, those occurrences would be numbered 1 through 6. Occurrences 1 through 4 would all be intersected between the two.

Here's the complete solution code.

```
SELECT
  ROW_NUMBER()
    OVER(PARTITION BY country, region, city
         ORDER     BY (SELECT 0)) AS rownum,
  country, region, city
FROM HR.Employees

INTERSECT

SELECT
  ROW_NUMBER()
    OVER(PARTITION BY country, region, city
         ORDER     BY (SELECT 0)),
  country, region, city
FROM Sales.Customers;
```

This code produces the following output.

```
rownum                country          region           city
-------------------   --------------   --------------   --------------
1                     UK               NULL             London
1                     USA              WA               Kirkland
1                     USA              WA               Seattle
2                     UK               NULL             London
3                     UK               NULL             London
4                     UK               NULL             London
```

Of course, the *INTERSECT ALL* operator is not supposed to return any row numbers; those are used to support the solution. If you don't want to return those in the output, you can define a table expression such as a common table expression (CTE) based on this query and select only the original attributes from the table expression. Here's an example of how you can use *INTERSECT ALL* to return all occurrences of employee and customer locations that intersect.

```
WITH INTERSECT_ALL
AS
(
  SELECT
    ROW_NUMBER()
      OVER(PARTITION BY country, region, city
           ORDER     BY (SELECT 0)) AS rownum,
    country, region, city
  FROM HR.Employees

  INTERSECT

  SELECT
    ROW_NUMBER()
      OVER(PARTITION BY country, region, city
           ORDER     BY (SELECT 0)),
    country, region, city
  FROM Sales.Customers
)
SELECT country, region, city
FROM INTERSECT_ALL;
```

Here's the output of this query, which is equivalent to what the standard *INTERSECT ALL* would have returned.

```
country          region           city
--------------   --------------   --------------
UK               NULL             London
USA              WA               Kirkland
USA              WA               Seattle
UK               NULL             London
UK               NULL             London
UK               NULL             London
```

# The *EXCEPT* Operator

In set theory, the difference of sets A and B (A − B) is the set of elements that belong to A and do not belong to B. You can think of the set difference A − B as A minus the members of B also in A. Figure 6-3 shows a graphical depiction of the set difference A − B.

Difference: A − B

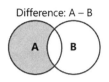

**FIGURE 6-3** Set difference.

In T-SQL, set difference is implemented with the *EXCEPT* set operator. *EXCEPT* operates on the result sets of two input queries and returns rows that appear in the first input but not the second. After I describe the *EXCEPT* (implicit *DISTINCT*) operator, I'll describe *EXCEPT ALL*, which has not yet been implemented as of SQL Server 2012, and how to provide an alternative to this operator.

## The *EXCEPT* Distinct Set Operator

The *EXCEPT* set operator logically first eliminates duplicate rows from the two input multisets—turning them to sets—and then returns only rows that appear in the first set but not the second. In other words, a row is returned provided that it appears at least once in the first input multiset and zero times in the second. Note that unlike the other two operators, *EXCEPT* is asymmetric; that is, with the other set operators, it doesn't matter which input query appears first and which second—with *EXCEPT*, it does.

For example, the following code returns distinct locations that are employee locations but not customer locations.

```
SELECT country, region, city FROM HR.Employees
EXCEPT
SELECT country, region, city FROM Sales.Customers;
```

This query returns the following two locations.

```
country          region           city
---------------- ---------------- ----------------
USA              WA               Redmond
USA              WA               Tacoma
```

The following query returns distinct locations that are customer locations but not employee locations.

```
SELECT country, region, city FROM Sales.Customers
EXCEPT
SELECT country, region, city FROM HR.Employees;
```

This query returns 66 locations, shown here in abbreviated form.

```
country          region           city
------------     ---------------  ---------------
Argentina        NULL             Buenos Aires
Austria          NULL             Graz
Austria          NULL             Salzburg
Belgium          NULL             Bruxelles
Belgium          NULL             Charleroi
...
USA              WY               Lander
Venezuela        DF               Caracas
Venezuela        Lara             Barquisimeto
Venezuela        Nueva Esparta    I. de Margarita
Venezuela        Tachira          San Cristóbal

(66 row(s) affected)
```

You can also use alternatives to the *EXCEPT* operator. One alternative is an outer join that filters only outer rows, which are rows that appear in one side but not the other. Another alternative is to use the *NOT EXISTS* predicate. However, if you want to consider two *NULL* marks as equal, set operators give you this behavior by default with no need for special treatment, whereas the alternatives don't.

## The *EXCEPT ALL* Multiset Operator

I provide this section as optional reading for those who feel very comfortable with the material covered so far in this chapter. The *EXCEPT ALL* operator is very similar to the *EXCEPT* operator, but it also takes into account the number of occurrences of each row. Provided that a row R appears x times in the first multiset and y times in the second, and x > y, R will appear x - y times in *Query1 EXCEPT ALL Query2*. In other words, at the logical level, *EXCEPT ALL* returns only occurrences of a row from the first multiset that do not have a corresponding occurrence in the second.

SQL Server does not provide a built-in *EXCEPT ALL* operator, but you can provide an alternative with a very similar solution to the one provided for *INTERSECT ALL*. Namely, add a *ROW_NUMBER* calculation to each of the input queries to number the occurrences of each row, and use the *EXCEPT* operator between the two input queries. Only occurrences that don't find matches will be returned.

The following example shows how you can use *EXCEPT ALL* to return occurrences of employee locations that have no corresponding occurrences of customer locations.

```
WITH EXCEPT_ALL
AS
(
  SELECT
    ROW_NUMBER()
      OVER(PARTITION BY country, region, city
           ORDER     BY (SELECT 0)) AS rownum,
    country, region, city
    FROM HR.Employees

  EXCEPT

  SELECT
    ROW_NUMBER()
      OVER(PARTITION BY country, region, city
           ORDER     BY (SELECT 0)),
    country, region, city
  FROM Sales.Customers
)
SELECT country, region, city
FROM EXCEPT_ALL;
```

This query returns the following output.

```
country          region           city
---------------  ---------------  ---------------
USA              WA               Redmond
USA              WA               Tacoma
USA              WA               Seattle
```

# Precedence

SQL defines precedence among set operators. The *INTERSECT* operator precedes *UNION* and *EXCEPT*, and *UNION* and *EXCEPT* are considered equal. In a query that contains multiple set operators, first *INTERSECT* operators are evaluated, and then operators with the same precedence are evaluated based on order of appearance.

Consider the following query, which shows how *INTERSECT* precedes *EXCEPT*.

```
SELECT country, region, city FROM Production.Suppliers
EXCEPT
SELECT country, region, city FROM HR.Employees
INTERSECT
SELECT country, region, city FROM Sales.Customers;
```

Because *INTERSECT* precedes *EXCEPT*, the *INTERSECT* operator is evaluated first, even though it appears second. Therefore, the meaning of this query is, "locations that are supplier locations but not (locations that are both employee and customer locations)."

This query returns the following output.

```
country          region           city
---------------  ---------------  ---------------
Australia        NSW              Sydney
Australia        Victoria         Melbourne
Brazil           NULL             Sao Paulo
Canada           Québec           Montréal
Canada           Québec           Ste-Hyacinthe
Denmark          NULL             Lyngby
Finland          NULL             Lappeenranta
France           NULL             Annecy
France           NULL             Montceau
France           NULL             Paris
Germany          NULL             Berlin
Germany          NULL             Cuxhaven
Germany          NULL             Frankfurt
Italy            NULL             Ravenna
Italy            NULL             Salerno
Japan            NULL             Osaka
Japan            NULL             Tokyo
Netherlands      NULL             Zaandam
Norway           NULL             Sandvika
Singapore        NULL             Singapore
Spain            Asturias         Oviedo
Sweden           NULL             Göteborg
Sweden           NULL             Stockholm
UK               NULL             Manchester
USA              LA               New Orleans
USA              MA               Boston
USA              MT               Ann Arbor
USA              OR               Bend
```

(28 row(s) affected)

To control the order of evaluation of set operators, use parentheses, because they have the highest precedence. Also, using parentheses increases the readability, thus reducing the chance for errors. For example, if you want to return "(locations that are supplier locations but not employee locations) and that are also customer locations," use the following code.

```
(SELECT country, region, city FROM Production.Suppliers
 EXCEPT
 SELECT country, region, city FROM HR.Employees)
INTERSECT
SELECT country, region, city FROM Sales.Customers;
```

This query returns the following output.

```
country          region           city
---------------  ---------------  ---------------
Canada           Québec           Montréal
France           NULL             Paris
Germany          NULL             Berlin
```

# Circumventing Unsupported Logical Phases

This section may be considered advanced for the book's target audience and is provided here as optional reading. The individual queries that are used as inputs to a set operator support all logical query processing phases (such as table operators, *WHERE*, *GROUP BY*, and *HAVING*) except for *ORDER BY*. However, only the *ORDER BY* phase is allowed on the result of the operator. What if you need to apply other logical phases besides *ORDER BY* to the result of the operator? This is not supported directly as part of the query that applies the operator, but you can easily circumvent this restriction by using table expressions. Define a table expression based on a query with a set operator, and apply any logical query processing phases that you want in the outer query against the table expression. For example, the following query returns the number of distinct locations that are either employee or customer locations in each country.

```
SELECT country, COUNT(*) AS numlocations
FROM (SELECT country, region, city FROM HR.Employees
      UNION
      SELECT country, region, city FROM Sales.Customers) AS U
GROUP BY country;
```

This query returns the following output.

```
country         numlocations
--------------- ------------
Argentina       1
Austria         2
Belgium         2
Brazil          4
Canada          3
Denmark         2
Finland         2
France          9
Germany         11
Ireland         1
Italy           3
Mexico          1
Norway          1
Poland          1
Portugal        1
Spain           3
Sweden          2
Switzerland     2
UK              2
USA             14
Venezuela       4

(21 row(s) affected)
```

This query demonstrates how to apply the *GROUP BY* logical query processing phase to the result of a *UNION* operator; similarly, you could of course apply any logical query processing phase in the outer query.

The fact that you cannot specify *ORDER BY* with the individual queries involved in the set operator might also cause logical problems. What if you need to restrict the number of rows in those queries with the *TOP* or *OFFSET-FETCH* option? Again, you can resolve this problem with table expressions. Recall that an *ORDER BY* clause is allowed in a query with *TOP* or *OFFSET-FETCH*, even when the query is used to define a table expression. In such a case, the *ORDER BY* clause serves only as part of the filtering specification and has no presentation meaning.

So if you need a query with *TOP* or *OFFSET-FETCH* to participate in a set operator, simply define a table expression and have an outer query against the table expression participate in the operator. For example, the following code uses *TOP* queries to return the two most recent orders for those employees with an employee ID of 3 or 5.

```
SELECT empid, orderid, orderdate
FROM (SELECT TOP (2) empid, orderid, orderdate
      FROM Sales.Orders
      WHERE empid = 3
      ORDER BY orderdate DESC, orderid DESC) AS D1

UNION ALL

SELECT empid, orderid, orderdate
FROM (SELECT TOP (2) empid, orderid, orderdate
      FROM Sales.Orders
      WHERE empid = 5
      ORDER BY orderdate DESC, orderid DESC) AS D2;
```

This query returns the following output.

```
empid        orderid      orderdate
-----------  -----------  -----------------------
3            11063        2008-04-30 00:00:00.000
3            11057        2008-04-29 00:00:00.000
5            11043        2008-04-22 00:00:00.000
5            10954        2008-03-17 00:00:00.000
```

Here's the logical equivalent using *OFFSET-FETCH*.

```
SELECT empid, orderid, orderdate
FROM (SELECT empid, orderid, orderdate
      FROM Sales.Orders
      WHERE empid = 3
      ORDER BY orderdate DESC, orderid DESC
      OFFSET 0 ROWS FETCH FIRST 2 ROWS ONLY) AS D1

UNION ALL

SELECT empid, orderid, orderdate
FROM (SELECT empid, orderid, orderdate
      FROM Sales.Orders
      WHERE empid = 5
      ORDER BY orderdate DESC, orderid DESC
      OFFSET 0 ROWS FETCH FIRST 2 ROWS ONLY) AS D2;
```

# Conclusion

This chapter covered set operators, including the general syntax and requirements of set operators, and describing in detail each supported set operator—*UNION*, *INTERSECT*, and *EXCEPT*. I explained that standard SQL supports two flavors of each operator—*DISTINCT* (set) and *ALL* (multiset)—and that as of SQL Server 2012, SQL Server implements the *ALL* flavor only with the *UNION* operator. I provided alternatives to the missing *INTERSECT ALL* and *EXCEPT ALL* operators that make use of the ROW_NUMBER function and table expressions. Finally, I introduced precedence among set operators, and explained how to circumvent unsupported logical query processing phases by using table expressions.

# Exercises

This section provides exercises to help you familiarize yourself with the subjects discussed in Chapter 6. All exercises except for the first require you to be connected to the sample database *TSQL2012*.

## 1

Write a query that generates a virtual auxiliary table of 10 numbers in the range 1 through 10 without using a looping construct. You do not need to guarantee any order of the rows in the output of your solution.

- Tables involved: None

- Desired output:

```
n
-----------
1
2
3
4
5
6
7
8
9
10

(10 row(s) affected)
```

## 2

Write a query that returns customer and employee pairs that had order activity in January 2008 but not in February 2008.

- Tables involved: *TSQL2012* database, *Sales.Orders* table

■ Desired output:

```
custid       empid
-----------  -----------
1            1
3            3
5            8
5            9
6            9
7            6
9            1
12           2
16           7
17           1
20           7
24           8
25           1
26           3
32           4
38           9
39           3
40           2
41           2
42           2
44           8
47           3
47           4
47           8
49           7
55           2
55           3
56           6
59           8
63           8
64           9
65           3
65           8
66           5
67           5
70           3
71           2
75           1
76           2
76           5
80           1
81           1
81           3
81           4
82           6
84           1
84           3
84           4
88           7
89           4

(50 row(s) affected)
```

# 3

Write a query that returns customer and employee pairs that had order activity in both January 2008 and February 2008.

- Tables involved: *Sales.Orders*

- Desired output:

```
custid      empid
----------- -----------
20          3
39          9
46          5
67          1
71          4

(5 row(s) affected)
```

# 4

Write a query that returns customer and employee pairs that had order activity in both January 2008 and February 2008 but not in 2007.

- Tables involved: *Sales.Orders*

- Desired output:

```
custid      empid
----------- -----------
67          1
46          5

(2 row(s) affected)
```

# 5 (Optional, Advanced)

You are given the following query.

```
SELECT country, region, city
FROM HR.Employees

UNION ALL

SELECT country, region, city
FROM Production.Suppliers;
```

You are asked to add logic to the query so that it guarantees that the rows from *Employees* are returned in the output before the rows from *Suppliers*. Also, within each segment, the rows should be sorted by country, region, and city.

- Tables involved: *HR.Employees* and *Production.Suppliers*

- Desired output:

```
country           region            city
----------------  ----------------  ---------------
UK                NULL              London
UK                NULL              London
UK                NULL              London
UK                NULL              London
USA               WA                Kirkland
USA               WA                Redmond
USA               WA                Seattle
USA               WA                Seattle
USA               WA                Tacoma
Australia         NSW               Sydney
Australia         Victoria          Melbourne
Brazil            NULL              Sao Paulo
Canada            Québec            Montréal
Canada            Québec            Ste-Hyacinthe
Denmark           NULL              Lyngby
Finland           NULL              Lappeenranta
France            NULL              Annecy
France            NULL              Montceau
France            NULL              Paris
Germany           NULL              Berlin
Germany           NULL              Cuxhaven
Germany           NULL              Frankfurt
Italy             NULL              Ravenna
Italy             NULL              Salerno
Japan             NULL              Osaka
Japan             NULL              Tokyo
Netherlands       NULL              Zaandam
Norway            NULL              Sandvika
Singapore         NULL              Singapore
Spain             Asturias          Oviedo
Sweden            NULL              Göteborg
Sweden            NULL              Stockholm
UK                NULL              London
UK                NULL              Manchester
USA               LA                New Orleans
USA               MA                Boston
USA               MI                Ann Arbor
USA               OR                Bend

(38 row(s) affected)
```

# Solutions

This section provides solutions to the Chapter 6 exercises.

## 1

T-SQL supports a *SELECT* statement based on constants with no *FROM* clause. Such a *SELECT* statement returns a table with a single row. For example, the following statement returns a row with a single column called *n* with the value 1.

> SELECT 1 AS n;

Here's the output of this statement.

```
n
-----------
1

(1 row(s) affected)
```

By using the *UNION ALL* operator, you can unify the result sets of multiple statements like the one just mentioned, each returning a row with a different number in the range 1 through 10, like the following.

```
SELECT 1 AS n
UNION ALL SELECT 2
UNION ALL SELECT 3
UNION ALL SELECT 4
UNION ALL SELECT 5
UNION ALL SELECT 6
UNION ALL SELECT 7
UNION ALL SELECT 8
UNION ALL SELECT 9
UNION ALL SELECT 10;
```

> **Tip** SQL Server supports an enhanced *VALUES* clause that you might be familiar with in the context of the *INSERT* statement. The *VALUES* clause is not restricted to representing a single row; it can represent multiple rows. Also, the *VALUES* clause is not restricted to *INSERT* statements but can be used to define a table expression with rows based on constants. As an example, here's how you can use the *VALUES* clause to provide a solution to this exercise instead of using the *UNION ALL* operator.
>
> ```
> SELECT n
> FROM (VALUES(1),(2),(3),(4),(5),(6),(7),(8),(9),(10)) AS Nums(n);
> ```
>
> I will provide details about the *VALUES* clause and row value constructors in Chapter 8, "Data Modification," as part of the discussion of the *INSERT* statement.

# 2

You can solve this exercise by using the *EXCEPT* set operator. The left input is a query that returns customer and employee pairs that had order activity in January 2008. The right input is a query that returns customer and employee pairs that had order activity in February 2008. Here's the solution query.

```
USE TSQL2012;

SELECT custid, empid
FROM Sales.Orders
WHERE orderdate >= '20080101' AND orderdate < '20080201'

EXCEPT

SELECT custid, empid
FROM Sales.Orders
WHERE orderdate >= '20080201' AND orderdate < '20080301';
```

# 3

Whereas Exercise 2 requested customer and employee pairs that had activity in one period but not another, this exercise concerns customer and employee pairs that had activity in both periods. So this time, instead of using the *EXCEPT* operator, you need to use the *INTERSECT* operator, like this.

```
SELECT custid, empid
FROM Sales.Orders
WHERE orderdate >= '20080101' AND orderdate < '20080201'

INTERSECT

SELECT custid, empid
FROM Sales.Orders
WHERE orderdate >= '20080201' AND orderdate < '20080301';
```

# 4

This exercise requires you to combine set operators. To return customer and employee pairs that had order activity in both January 2008 and February 2008, you need to use the *INTERSECT* operator, as in Exercise 3. To exclude customer and employee pairs that had order activity in 2007 from the result, you need to use the *EXCEPT* operator between the result and a third query. The solution query looks like this.

```
SELECT custid, empid
FROM Sales.Orders
WHERE orderdate >= '20080101' AND orderdate < '20080201'

INTERSECT
```

```
SELECT custid, empid
FROM Sales.Orders
WHERE orderdate >= '20080201' AND orderdate < '20080301'

EXCEPT

SELECT custid, empid
FROM Sales.Orders
WHERE orderdate >= '20070101' AND orderdate < '20080101';
```

Keep in mind that the *INTERSECT* operator precedes *EXCEPT*. In this case, the default precedence is also the precedence you want, so you don't need to intervene by using parentheses. But you might prefer to add them for clarity, as shown here.

```
(SELECT custid, empid
 FROM Sales.Orders
 WHERE orderdate >= '20080101' AND orderdate < '20080201'

 INTERSECT

 SELECT custid, empid
 FROM Sales.Orders
 WHERE orderdate >= '20080201' AND orderdate < '20080301')

EXCEPT

SELECT custid, empid
FROM Sales.Orders
WHERE orderdate >= '20070101' AND orderdate < '20080101';
```

# 5

The problem here is that the individual queries are not allowed to have *ORDER BY* clauses, and for a good reason. You can solve the problem by adding a result column based on a constant to each of the queries involved in the operator (call it *sortcol*). In the query against *Employees*, specify a smaller constant than the one you specify in the query against *Suppliers*. Define a table expression based on the query with the operator, and in the *ORDER BY* clause of the outer query, specify *sortcol* as the first sort column, followed by country, region, and city. Here's the complete solution query.

```
SELECT country, region, city
FROM (SELECT 1 AS sortcol, country, region, city
      FROM HR.Employees

      UNION ALL

      SELECT 2, country, region, city
      FROM Production.Suppliers) AS D
ORDER BY sortcol, country, region, city;
```

# CHAPTER 7

# Beyond the Fundamentals of Querying

This chapter starts with the profound window functions, which allow you to apply calculations against sets in a flexible and efficient manner. The chapter then proceeds with techniques for pivoting and unpivoting data. Pivoting means rotating data from a state of rows to a state of columns. Unpivoting means rotating data from a state of columns to a state of rows. The chapter then finishes with a discussion of grouping sets. Grouping sets are sets of attributes by which data can be grouped. This chapter covers techniques for requesting multiple grouping sets in the same query.

Note that all subjects covered in this chapter may be considered advanced for readers who are new to T-SQL; therefore, the chapter is optional reading. If you already feel comfortable with the material discussed in the book so far, you may want to tackle this chapter; otherwise, feel free to skip it at this point and return to it later after you've gained more experience.

## Window Functions

A *window function* is a function that, for each row, computes a scalar result value based on a calculation against a subset of the rows from the underlying query. The subset of rows is known as a *window* and is based on a window descriptor that relates to the current row. The syntax for window functions uses a clause called *OVER*, in which you provide the window specification.

If this sounds too technical, simply think of the need to perform a calculation against a set and return a single value. A classic example would be aggregate calculations such as *SUM*, *COUNT*, and *AVG*, but there are others as well, such as ranking functions. If you're reading this chapter, you should be familiar already with a couple of ways to apply such calculations—one is by using grouped queries, and another is by using subqueries. However, both options have shortcomings that window functions elegantly resolve.

Grouped queries do provide insights into new information in the form of aggregates, but they also cause you to lose something—the detail. After you group the rows, all computations in the query have to be done in the context of the defined groups. Often you need to perform calculations that involve both a detail element and the result of a set calculation such as an aggregate. Window functions are not limited in the same way. A window function has an *OVER* clause that defines the set of rows for the function to work with, without imposing the same arrangement of rows on the query itself. In other words, grouped queries define the sets, or groups, in the query, and therefore all calculations in the query have to be done in the context of those groups. With window functions, the set is defined for each function, not for the entire query.

As for subqueries, they do allow you to apply a calculation against a set, but a subquery starts from a fresh view of the data. If the query has table operators or filters, for example, and you need the subquery to operate on a subset of rows from the underlying query, you have to repeat a lot of logic from the underlying query also in the subquery. In contrast, a window function is applied to a subset of rows from the underlying query's result set—not a fresh view of the data. Therefore, anything you add to the underlying query is automatically applicable to all window functions used in the query. Then, different elements in the window function's *OVER* clause allow you to further restrict the window as a subset of the underlying query's result set.

Another benefit of window functions is the ability to define order, when applicable, as part of the specification of the calculation, without conflicting with relational aspects of the result set. That is, order is defined for the calculation, and not confused with presentation ordering. The ordering specification for the window function, if applicable, is different from the ordering specification for presentation. If you don't include a presentation *ORDER BY* clause, there are no assurances that the result will be returned in a particular order. If you do decide to force certain presentation ordering, the resulting ordering can be different than the ordering for the window function.

Following is an example of a query against the *Sales.EmpOrders* view in the *TSQL2012* database that uses a window aggregate function to compute the running total values for each employee and month.

```
USE TSQL2012;

SELECT empid, ordermonth, val,
  SUM(val) OVER(PARTITION BY empid
                ORDER BY ordermonth
                ROWS BETWEEN UNBOUNDED PRECEDING
                      AND CURRENT ROW) AS runval
FROM Sales.EmpOrders;
```

Here's the output of this query, shown in abbreviated form.

```
empid  ordermonth   val       runval
------ -----------  --------  ----------
1      2006-07-01   1614.88   1614.88
1      2006-08-01   5555.90   7170.78
1      2006-09-01   6651.00   13821.78
1      2006-10-01   3933.18   17754.96
1      2006-11-01   9562.65   27317.61
...
2      2006-07-01   1176.00   1176.00
2      2006-08-01   1814.00   2990.00
2      2006-09-01   2950.80   5940.80
2      2006-10-01   5164.00   11104.80
2      2006-11-01   4614.58   15719.38
...

(192 row(s) affected)
```

The window specification in the *OVER* clause has three main parts: partitioning, ordering, and framing. An empty *OVER()* clause exposes to the function a window made of all rows from the underlying query's result set. Then anything you add to the window specification essentially further restricts the window.

The window partition clause (*PARTITION BY*) restricts the window to the subset of rows from the underlying query's result set that share the same values in the partitioning columns as in the current row. In the example, the window is partitioned by *empid*. Consider, for example, a row in which the *empid* value is 1. The window exposed to the function in respect to that row will have only the subset of rows in which the *empid* value is 1.

The window order clause (*ORDER BY*) defines ordering in the window, but don't confuse this with presentation ordering; the window ordering is what gives meaning to window framing. In this case, the window ordering is based on *ordermonth*.

After order has been defined in the window, a window frame clause (*ROWS BETWEEN <top delimiter> AND <bottom delimiter>*) filters a frame, or a subset, of rows from the window partition between the two specified delimiters. In this example, the frame is between the beginning of the partition (*UNBOUNDED PRECEDING*) and the current row (*CURRENT ROW*). In addition to the window frame unit *ROWS*, there's another called *RANGE*, but it was implemented in a very limited form as of Microsoft SQL Server 2012.

Putting all of these together, what you get from the function in the example is the running total values for each employee and month.

Note that because the starting point of a window function is the underlying query's result set, and the underlying query's result set is generated only when you reach the *SELECT* phase, window functions are allowed only in the *SELECT* and *ORDER BY* clauses of a query. If you need to refer to a window function in an earlier logical query processing phase (such as *WHERE*), you need to use a table expression. You specify the window function in the *SELECT* list of the inner query and assign it with an alias. Then in the outer query, you can refer to that alias anywhere you like.

As with any new concept, the windowing concept can take some getting used to, but when you are comfortable with it, you'll realize that it's actually much better aligned with the way we humans tend to think of calculations. Hence, in the long run, window functions will allow you to phrase what you want in a natural and intuitive manner. Window functions also lend themselves to very efficient optimization for common-use cases.

There were two major milestones in SQL Server's support for window functions. SQL Server 2005 introduced ranking window functions with complete implementation (partitioning and ordering), and partial support for window aggregate functions (only partitioning, without ordering and framing). SQL Server 2012 adds a lot of functionality, including support for ordering and framing for aggregates, as well as new types of functions: offset and distribution. There are still standard windowing capabilities that were not yet implemented in SQL Server, and I hope very much to see Microsoft continuing the investment in this area.

In the next sections, I provide more specifics about ranking, offset, and aggregate window functions. Because this book is about fundamentals, there are some things that I will not get into here. Those include optimization of window functions, distribution functions, and the *RANGE* window frame unit.

**See Also** *Because window functions are so profound and so useful, I wrote an entire book on the subject called Microsoft SQL Server 2012 High-Performance T-SQL Using Window Functions (Microsoft Press, 2012). In that book, I do get into the gory details, optimization, and lots of practical uses.*

## Ranking Window Functions

Ranking window functions allow you to rank each row in respect to others in several different ways. SQL Server supports four ranking functions: ROW_NUMBER, RANK, DENSE_RANK, and NTILE. The following query demonstrates the use of these functions.

```
SELECT orderid, custid, val,
  ROW_NUMBER() OVER(ORDER BY val) AS rownum,
  RANK()       OVER(ORDER BY val) AS rank,
  DENSE_RANK() OVER(ORDER BY val) AS dense_rank,
  NTILE(100)   OVER(ORDER BY val) AS ntile
FROM Sales.OrderValues
ORDER BY val;
```

This query generates the following output, shown here in abbreviated form.

| orderid | custid | val | rownum | rank | dense_rank | ntile |
|---------|--------|-----|--------|------|------------|-------|
| 10782 | 12 | 12.50 | 1 | 1 | 1 | 1 |
| 10807 | 27 | 18.40 | 2 | 2 | 2 | 1 |
| 10586 | 66 | 23.80 | 3 | 3 | 3 | 1 |
| 10767 | 76 | 28.00 | 4 | 4 | 4 | 1 |
| 10898 | 54 | 30.00 | 5 | 5 | 5 | 1 |
| 10900 | 88 | 33.75 | 6 | 6 | 6 | 1 |
| 10883 | 48 | 36.00 | 7 | 7 | 7 | 1 |
| 11051 | 41 | 36.00 | 8 | 7 | 7 | 1 |
| 10815 | 71 | 40.00 | 9 | 9 | 8 | 1 |
| 10674 | 38 | 45.00 | 10 | 10 | 9 | 1 |
| ... | | | | | | |
| 10691 | 63 | 10164.80 | 821 | 821 | 786 | 10 |
| 10540 | 63 | 10191.70 | 822 | 822 | 787 | 10 |
| 10479 | 65 | 10495.60 | 823 | 823 | 788 | 10 |
| 10897 | 37 | 10835.24 | 824 | 824 | 789 | 10 |
| 10817 | 39 | 10952.85 | 825 | 825 | 790 | 10 |
| 10417 | 73 | 11188.40 | 826 | 826 | 791 | 10 |
| 10889 | 65 | 11380.00 | 827 | 827 | 792 | 10 |
| 11030 | 71 | 12615.05 | 828 | 828 | 793 | 10 |
| 10981 | 34 | 15810.00 | 829 | 829 | 794 | 10 |
| 10865 | 63 | 16387.50 | 830 | 830 | 795 | 10 |

```
(830 row(s) affected)
```

I already described the ROW_NUMBER function in Chapter 2, "Single-Table Queries," but for the sake of completeness, I'll describe it here again. This function assigns incrementing sequential integers to the rows in the result set of a query, based on logical order that is specified in the *ORDER BY* subclause of the *OVER* clause. In the sample query, the logical order is based on the *val* column; therefore, you can see in the output that when the value increases, the row number increases as well. However, even when the ordering value doesn't increase, the row number still must increase. Therefore, if the ROW_NUMBER function's *ORDER BY* list is non-unique, as in the preceding example, the query is nondeterministic. That is, more than one correct result is possible. For example, observe that two rows with the value 36.00 got the row numbers 7 and 8. Any arrangement of these row numbers would have been considered correct. If you want to make a row number calculation deterministic, you need to add elements to the *ORDER BY* list to make it unique; meaning that the list of elements in the *ORDER BY* clause would uniquely identify rows. For example, you can add the *orderid* column as a tiebreaker to the *ORDER BY* list to make the row number calculation deterministic.

As mentioned, the ROW_NUMBER function must produce unique values even when there are ties in the ordering values. If you want to treat ties in the ordering values the same way, you will probably want to use the RANK or DENSE_RANK function instead. Both are similar to the ROW_NUMBER function, but they produce the same ranking value in all rows that have the same logical ordering value. The difference between RANK and DENSE_RANK is that RANK indicates how many rows have a lower ordering value, whereas DENSE_RANK indicates how many distinct ordering values are lower. For example, in the sample query, a rank of 9 indicates eight rows with lower values. A dense rank of 9 indicates eight distinct lower values.

The NTILE function allows you to associate the rows in the result with tiles (equally sized groups of rows) by assigning a tile number to each row. You specify the number of tiles you are after as input to the function, and in the *OVER* clause, you specify the logical ordering. The sample query has 830 rows and the request was for 10 tiles; therefore, the tile size is 83 (830 divided by 10). Logical ordering is based on the *val* column. This means that the 83 rows with the lowest values are assigned with tile number 1, the next 83 with tile number 2, the next 83 with tile number 3, and so on. The NTILE function is logically related to the ROW_NUMBER function. It's as if you assigned row numbers to the rows based on *val* ordering, and based on the calculated tile size of 83, you assigned tile number 1 to rows 1 through 83, tile number 2 to rows 84 through 166, and so on. If the number of rows doesn't divide evenly by the number of tiles, an extra row is added to each of the first tiles from the remainder. For example, if there had been 102 rows and five tiles were requested, the first two tiles would have had 21 rows instead of 20.

Ranking functions support window partition clauses. Remember that window partitioning restricts the window to only those rows that share the same values in the partitioning attributes as in the current row. For example, the expression *ROW_NUMBER() OVER(PARTITION BY custid ORDER BY val)* independently assigns row numbers for each subset of rows that have the same *custid*, as opposed to assigning those row numbers across the whole set. Here's the expression in a query.

```
SELECT orderid, custid, val,
  ROW_NUMBER() OVER(PARTITION BY custid
                    ORDER BY val) AS rownum
FROM Sales.OrderValues
ORDER BY custid, val;
```

This query generates the following output , shown here in abbreviated form.

```
orderid       custid        val            rownum
-----------   -----------   ------------   -------
10702         1             330.00         1
10952         1             471.20         2
10643         1             814.50         3
10835         1             845.80         4
10692         1             878.00         5
11011         1             933.50         6
10308         2             88.80          1
10759         2             320.00         2
10625         2             479.75         3
10926         2             514.40         4
10682         3             375.50         1
...
```

(830 row(s) affected)

As you can see in the output, the row numbers are calculated independently for each customer, as though the calculation were reset for each customer.

Remember that window ordering has nothing to do with presentation ordering and does not change the nature of the result from being relational. If you need to guarantee presentation ordering, you have to add a presentation *ORDER BY* clause, as I did in the last two queries demonstrating the use of ranking functions.

As you saw in Chapter 2, window functions are evaluated as part of the evaluation of the expressions in the *SELECT* list, before the *DISTINCT* clause is evaluated. If you're wondering why it matters, I'll explain with an example. Currently the *OrderValues* view has 830 rows with 795 distinct values in the *val* column. Consider the following query and its output, shown here in abbreviated form.

```
SELECT DISTINCT val, ROW_NUMBER() OVER(ORDER BY val) AS rownum
FROM Sales.OrderValues;
```

```
val         rownum
----------  -------
12.50       1
18.40       2
23.80       3
28.00       4
30.00       5
33.75       6
36.00       7
36.00       8
40.00       9
45.00       10
...
12615.05    828
15810.00    829
16387.50    830
```

(830 row(s) affected)

The ROW_NUMBER function is processed before the *DISTINCT* clause. First, unique row numbers are assigned to the 830 rows from the *OrderValues* view. Then the *DISTINCT* clause is processed—therefore, there are no duplicate rows to remove. You can consider it a best practice not to specify both *DISTINCT* and *ROW_NUMBER* in the same *SELECT* clause, because the *DISTINCT* clause has no effect in such a case. If you want to assign row numbers to the 795 unique values, you need to come up with a different solution. For example, because the *GROUP BY* phase is processed before the *SELECT* phase, you could use the following query.

```
SELECT val, ROW_NUMBER() OVER(ORDER BY val) AS rownum
FROM Sales.OrderValues
GROUP BY val;
```

This query generates the following output, shown here in abbreviated form.

```
val        rownum
---------  -------
12.50      1
18.40      2
23.80      3
28.00      4
30.00      5
33.75      6
36.00      7
40.00      8
45.00      9
48.00      10
...
12615.05   793
15810.00   794
16387.50   795

(795 row(s) affected)
```

Here, the *GROUP BY* phase produces 795 groups for the 795 distinct values, and then the *SELECT* phase produces a row for each group with *val* and a row number based on *val* order.

## Offset Window Functions

Offset window functions allow you to return an element from a row that is at a certain offset from the current row or from the beginning or end of a window frame. SQL Server 2012 supports four offset functions: *LAG* and *LEAD*, and *FIRST_VALUE* and *LAST_VALUE*.

The *LAG* and *LEAD* functions support window partition and window order clauses. There's no relevance to window framing here. These functions allow you to obtain an element from a row that is at a certain offset from the current row within the partition, based on the indicated ordering. The *LAG* function looks before the current row, and the *LEAD* function looks ahead. The first argument to the functions (which is mandatory) is the element you want to return; the second argument (optional) is the offset (1 if not specified); the third argument (optional) is the default value to return in case there is no row at the requested offset (*NULL* if not specified).

As an example, the following query returns order information from the *OrderValues* view. For each customer order, the query uses the *LAG* function to return the value of the previous customer's order and the *LEAD* function to return the value of the next customer's order.

```
SELECT custid, orderid, val,
  LAG(val)  OVER(PARTITION BY custid
                   ORDER BY orderdate, orderid) AS prevval,
  LEAD(val) OVER(PARTITION BY custid
                   ORDER BY orderdate, orderid) AS nextval
FROM Sales.OrderValues;
```

Here's the output of this query in abbreviated form.

```
custid  orderid  val       prevval   nextval
-------  --------  --------  --------  --------
1        10643    814.50    NULL      878.00
1        10692    878.00    814.50    330.00
1        10702    330.00    878.00    845.80
1        10835    845.80    330.00    471.20
1        10952    471.20    845.80    933.50
1        11011    933.50    471.20    NULL
2        10308    88.80     NULL      479.75
2        10625    479.75    88.80     320.00
2        10759    320.00    479.75    514.40
2        10926    514.40    320.00    NULL
3        10365    403.20    NULL      749.06
3        10507    749.06    403.20    1940.85
3        10535    1940.85   749.06    2082.00
3        10573    2082.00   1940.85   813.37
3        10677    813.37    2082.00   375.50
3        10682    375.50    813.37    660.00
3        10856    660.00    375.50    NULL
...
```

(830 row(s) affected)

Because you didn't indicate the offset, the functions assumed 1 by default; in other words, *LAG* obtained the value of the immediately previous customer's order, and *LEAD* from the immediately next. Also, because you didn't specify a third argument, *NULL* was assumed by default when there was no previous or next row. The expression *LAG(val, 3, 0)* would obtain the value from three rows back and would return 0 if a row wasn't found.

In this example, I just returned the values from the previous and next orders, but normally you would compute something based on the returned values. For example, you could compute the difference between the current customer's order value and that of the previous customer's: *val - LAG(val) OVER(...)*, or the difference from the next: *val - LEAD(val) OVER(...)*.

The *FIRST_VALUE* and *LAST_VALUE* functions allow you to return an element from the first and last rows in the window frame, respectively. Therefore, these functions support window partition, order, and frame clauses. If you want the element from the first row in the window partition, use *FIRST_VALUE* with the window frame extent *ROWS BETWEEN UNBOUNDED PRECEDING AND CURRENT ROW*. If you want the element from the last row in the window partition, use *LAST_VALUE* with the window frame extent *ROWS BETWEEN CURRENT ROW AND UNBOUNDED FOLLOWING*. Note that if you specify *ORDER BY* without a window frame unit (such as *ROWS*), the bottom delimiter will by default be *CURRENT ROW*, and clearly that's not what you want with *LAST_VALUE*. Also, for reasons that are beyond the scope of this book, you should be explicit about the window frame extent even for *FIRST_VALUE*.

As an example, the following query uses the *FIRST_VALUE* function to return the value of the first customer's order and the *LAST_VALUE* function to return the value of the last customer's order.

```
SELECT custid, orderid, val,
  FIRST_VALUE(val) OVER(PARTITION BY custid
                        ORDER BY orderdate, orderid
                        ROWS BETWEEN UNBOUNDED PRECEDING
                             AND CURRENT ROW) AS firstval,
  LAST_VALUE(val)  OVER(PARTITION BY custid
                        ORDER BY orderdate, orderid
                        ROWS BETWEEN CURRENT ROW
                             AND UNBOUNDED FOLLOWING) AS lastval
FROM Sales.OrderValues
ORDER BY custid, orderdate, orderid;
```

This query generates the following output, shown here in abbreviated form.

```
custid  orderid  val      firstval  lastval
------- -------- -------- --------- -------
1       10643    814.50   814.50    933.50
1       10692    878.00   814.50    933.50
1       10702    330.00   814.50    933.50
1       10835    845.80   814.50    933.50
1       10952    471.20   814.50    933.50
1       11011    933.50   814.50    933.50
2       10308    88.80    88.80     514.40
2       10625    479.75   88.80     514.40
2       10759    320.00   88.80     514.40
2       10926    514.40   88.80     514.40
3       10365    403.20   403.20    660.00
3       10507    749.06   403.20    660.00
3       10535    1940.85  403.20    660.00
3       10573    2082.00  403.20    660.00
3       10677    813.37   403.20    660.00
3       10682    375.50   403.20    660.00
3       10856    660.00   403.20    660.00
...

(830 row(s) affected)
```

As with *LAG* and *LEAD*, normally you would compute something based on the returned values. For example, you could compute the difference between the current customer's order value and the first: *val – FIRST_VALUE(val) OVER(...)* or the difference from the last: *val – LAST_VALUE(val) OVER(...)*.

# Aggregate Window Functions

Prior to SQL Server 2012, window aggregate functions supported only a window partition clause. In SQL Server 2012, they also support window order and frame clauses, advancing their usefulness dramatically.

I'll start with an example that doesn't involve ordering and framing. Recall that using an *OVER* clause with empty parentheses exposes a window of all rows from the underlying query's result set to the function. So, for example, *SUM(val) OVER()* returns the grand total of all values. If you do add a window partition clause, you expose a restricted window to the function, with only those rows from the underlying query's result set that share the same values in the partitioning elements as in the current row. So, for example, *SUM(val) OVER(PARTITION BY custid)* returns the total values for the current customer.

Here's a query against *OrderValues* that returns, along with each order, the grand total of all order values, as well as the customer total.

```
SELECT orderid, custid, val,
  SUM(val) OVER() AS totalvalue,
  SUM(val) OVER(PARTITION BY custid) AS custtotalvalue
FROM Sales.OrderValues;
```

This query returns the following output, shown here in abbreviated form.

```
orderid      custid       val          totalvalue         custtotalvalue
-----------  -----------  -----------  -----------------  ---------------
10643        1            814.50       1265793.22         4273.00
10692        1            878.00       1265793.22         4273.00
10702        1            330.00       1265793.22         4273.00
10835        1            845.80       1265793.22         4273.00
10952        1            471.20       1265793.22         4273.00
11011        1            933.50       1265793.22         4273.00
10926        2            514.40       1265793.22         1402.95
10759        2            320.00       1265793.22         1402.95
10625        2            479.75       1265793.22         1402.95
10308        2            88.80        1265793.22         1402.95
10365        3            403.20       1265793.22         7023.98
...

(830 row(s) affected)
```

The *totalvalue* column shows, for each row, the total value calculated for all rows. The column *custtotalvalue* has the total value for all rows that have the same *custid* value as in the current row.

As mentioned, one of the great advantages of window functions is that by enabling you to return detail elements and aggregate them in the same row, they also enable you to write expressions that mix detail and aggregates. For example, the following query calculates for each row the percentage that the current value is of the grand total, and also the percentage that the current value is of the customer total.

```
SELECT orderid, custid, val,
  100. * val / SUM(val) OVER() AS pctall,
  100. * val / SUM(val) OVER(PARTITION BY custid) AS pctcust
FROM Sales.OrderValues;
```

This query returns the following output, shown here in abbreviated form.

```
orderid     custid val         pctall                          pctcust
----------- ------ ----------- ------------------------------- -------------------------------
10643       1      814.50      0.0643470029014691672941        19.0615492628130119354083
10692       1      878.00      0.0693636200705830925528        20.5476246197051252047741
10702       1      330.00      0.0260706089103558320528        7.72291130353381699040448
10835       1      845.80      0.0668197606556938265161        19.7940556985724315469225
10952       1      471.20      0.0372256694501808123130        11.0273812309852562602387
11011       1      933.50      0.0737482224782338461253        21.8464778843903580622513
10926       2      514.40      0.0406385491620819394181        36.6655974910011048148544
10759       2      320.00      0.0252805904585268674452        22.8090808653195053280587
10625       2      479.75      0.0379011352264945770526        34.1958017035532271285505
10308       2      88.80       0.0070153638522412057160        6.32951994012616272855362
10365       3      403.20      0.0318535439777438529809        5.74033525152406470405566
...
```

(830 row(s) affected)

SQL Server 2012 adds support for window ordering and framing for aggregate functions. This allows for more sophisticated calculations such as running and moving aggregates, YTD calculations, and others. Let's re-examine the query I used in the introduction to the section about window functions.

```
SELECT empid, ordermonth, val,
  SUM(val) OVER(PARTITION BY empid
                ORDER BY ordermonth
                ROWS BETWEEN UNBOUNDED PRECEDING
                        AND CURRENT ROW) AS runval
FROM Sales.EmpOrders;
```

This query generates the following output (abbreviated).

```
empid  ordermonth   val       runval
------ ------------ -------- ----------
1      2006-07-01   1614.88  1614.88
1      2006-08-01   5555.90  7170.78
1      2006-09-01   6651.00  13821.78
1      2006-10-01   3933.18  17754.96
1      2006-11-01   9562.65  27317.61
...
2      2006-07-01   1176.00  1176.00
2      2006-08-01   1814.00  2990.00
2      2006-09-01   2950.80  5940.80
2      2006-10-01   5164.00  11104.80
2      2006-11-01   4614.58  15719.38
...
```

(192 row(s) affected)

Each row in the *EmpOrders* view holds information about the order activity for each employee and month. The query returns for each employee and month the monthly total, plus the running-total values from the beginning of the employee's activity through the current month. To apply the calculation to each employee independently, you partition the window by *empid*. Then you define ordering based on *ordermonth*, giving meaning to the window frame extent: *ROWS BETWEEN UNBOUNDED PRECEDING AND CURRENT ROW*. This frame means "all activity from the beginning of the partition through the current month."

SQL Server supports other delimiters for the *ROWS* window frame unit. You can indicate an offset back from the current row as well as an offset forward. For example, to capture all rows from two rows before the current row and through one row ahead, you would use *ROWS BETWEEN 2 PRECEDING AND 1 FOLLOWING*. Also, if you want no upper bound, you can use *UNBOUNDED FOLLOWING*. SQL Server also supports a window frame unit called *RANGE*, but in a very limited form. This option is beyond the scope of this book, but I will say that at least with the current implementation, you should avoid it.

Because window functions are so profound and have so many practical uses, I urge you to invest the time and effort to get to know the concept well. The investment is worth its weight in gold.

# Pivoting Data

Pivoting data involves rotating data from a state of rows to a state of columns, possibly aggregating values along the way. Don't worry that this description isn't enough to clarify exactly what pivoting data means; this is a subject best explained through examples. In many cases, pivoting of data is handled by the presentation layer. This section teaches you how to handle pivoting with T-SQL for those cases that you do decide to handle in the database.

For the rest of the topics in this chapter, I use a sample table called *dbo.Orders* that you create and populate in the *TSQL2012* database by running the code in Listing 7-1.

**LISTING 7-1** Code to Create and Populate the *dbo.Orders* Table

```
USE TSQL2012;

IF OBJECT_ID('dbo.Orders', 'U') IS NOT NULL DROP TABLE dbo.Orders;

CREATE TABLE dbo.Orders


(
  orderid   INT        NOT NULL,
  orderdate DATE       NOT NULL,
  empid     INT        NOT NULL,
  custid    VARCHAR(5) NOT NULL,
  qty       INT        NOT NULL,
  CONSTRAINT PK_Orders PRIMARY KEY(orderid)
);
```

```
INSERT INTO dbo.Orders(orderid, orderdate, empid, custid, qty)
VALUES
  (30001, '20070802', 3, 'A', 10),
  (10001, '20071224', 2, 'A', 12),
  (10005, '20071224', 1, 'B', 20),
  (40001, '20080109', 2, 'A', 40),
  (10006, '20080118', 1, 'C', 14),
  (20001, '20080212', 2, 'B', 12),
  (40005, '20090212', 3, 'A', 10),
  (20002, '20090216', 1, 'C', 20),
  (30003, '20090418', 2, 'B', 15),
  (30004, '20070418', 3, 'C', 22),
  (30007, '20090907', 3, 'D', 30);

SELECT * FROM dbo.Orders;
```

The query at the end of the code in Listing 7-1 produces the following output showing the contents of the *dbo.Orders* table.

```
orderid      orderdate     empid           custid     qty
-----------  ------------  --------------  ---------  -----------
10001        2007-12-24    2               A          12
10005        2007-12-24    1               B          20
10006        2008-01-18    1               C          14
20001        2008-02-12    2               B          12
20002        2009-02-16    1               C          20
30001        2007-08-02    3               A          10
30003        2009-04-18    2               B          15
30004        2007-04-18    3               C          22
30007        2009-09-07    3               D          30
40001        2008-01-09    2               A          40
40005        2009-02-12    3               A          10
```

Before I further explain what pivoting is, consider a request to produce a report with the total order quantity for each employee and customer. The request is satisfied with the following simple query.

```
SELECT empid, custid, SUM(qty) AS sumqty
FROM dbo.Orders
GROUP BY empid, custid;
```

This query generates the following output.

```
empid        custid    sumqty
-----------  --------- -----------
2            A         52
3            A         20
1            B         20
2            B         27
1            C         34
3            C         22
3            D         30
```

Suppose, however, that you have a requirement to produce the output in the form shown in Table 7-1.

**TABLE 7-1** Pivoted View of Total Quantity per Employee (on Rows) and Customer (on Columns)

| empid | A | B | C | D |
|-------|------|------|------|------|
| 1 | NULL | 20 | 34 | NULL |
| 2 | 52 | 27 | NULL | NULL |
| 3 | 20 | NULL | 22 | 30 |

What you see in Table 7-1 is an aggregated and pivoted view of the data from the *dbo.Orders* table; the technique for generating this view of the data is called *pivoting*.

Every pivoting request involves three logical processing phases, each with associated elements: a grouping phase with an associated grouping or on rows element, a spreading phase with an associated spreading or on cols element, and an aggregation phase with an associated aggregation element and aggregate function.

In this example, you need to produce a single row in the result for each unique employee ID. This means that the rows from the *dbo.Orders* table need to be grouped by the *empid* attribute, and therefore the grouping element in this case is the *empid* attribute.

The *dbo.Orders* table has a single column that holds all customer ID values and a single column that holds their ordered quantities. The pivoting process is supposed to produce a different result column for each unique customer ID, and each column contains the aggregated quantities for that customer. You can think of this process as "spreading" quantities by customer ID. The spreading element in this case is the *custid* attribute.

Finally, because pivoting involves grouping, you need to aggregate data to produce the result values in the "intersection" of the grouping and spreading elements. You need to identify the aggregate function (SUM, in this case) and the aggregation element (the *qty* attribute, in this case).

To recap, pivoting involves grouping, spreading, and aggregating. In this example, you group by *empid*, spread (quantities) by *custid*, and aggregate with *SUM(qty)*. After you have identified the elements involved in pivoting, the rest is just a matter of incorporating those elements in the right places in a generic query template for pivoting.

This chapter presents two solutions for pivoting—a standard solution and a solution that uses a T-SQL–specific *PIVOT* operator.

## Pivoting with Standard SQL

The standard solution for pivoting handles all three phases involved in a very straightforward manner.

The grouping phase is achieved with a *GROUP BY* clause; in this case, *GROUP BY empid*.

The spreading phase is achieved in the *SELECT* clause with a *CASE* expression for each target column. You need to know the spreading element values ahead of time and specify a separate expression for each. Because in this case you need to "spread" the quantities of four customers (A, B, C, and D), there are four *CASE* expressions. For example, here's the *CASE* expression for customer A.

```
CASE WHEN custid = 'A' THEN qty END
```

This expression returns the quantity from the current row only when the current row represents an order for customer A; otherwise the expression returns a *NULL*. Remember that if an *ELSE* clause is not specified in a *CASE* expression, the default is *ELSE NULL*. This means that in the target column for customer A, only quantities associated with customer A appear as column values, and in all other cases the column values are *NULL*.

If you don't know the values that you need to spread by ahead of time (the distinct customer IDs in this case) and you want to query them from the data, you need to use dynamic SQL to construct the query string and execute it. Dynamic pivoting is demonstrated in Chapter 10, "Programmable Objects."

Finally, the aggregation phase is achieved by applying the relevant aggregate function (SUM, in this case) to the result of each *CASE* expression. For example, here's the expression that produces the result column for customer A.

```
SUM(CASE WHEN custid = 'A' THEN qty END) AS A
```

Of course, depending on the request, you might need to use another aggregate function (such as MAX, MIN, or COUNT).

Here's the complete solution query that pivots order data, returning the total quantity for each employee (on rows) and customer (on columns).

```
SELECT empid,
  SUM(CASE WHEN custid = 'A' THEN qty END) AS A,
  SUM(CASE WHEN custid = 'B' THEN qty END) AS B,
  SUM(CASE WHEN custid = 'C' THEN qty END) AS C,
  SUM(CASE WHEN custid = 'D' THEN qty END) AS D
FROM dbo.Orders
GROUP BY empid;
```

This query produces the output shown earlier in Table 7-1.

## Pivoting with the Native T-SQL *PIVOT* Operator

SQL Server supports a T-SQL–specific table operator called *PIVOT*. The *PIVOT* operator operates in the context of the *FROM* clause of a query like other table operators (for example, *JOIN*). It operates on a source table or table expression, pivots the data, and returns a result table. The *PIVOT* operator involves the same logical processing phases as described earlier (grouping, spreading, and aggregating) with the same pivoting elements, but it uses different, native syntax.

The general form of a query with the *PIVOT* operator is shown here.

```
SELECT ...
FROM <source_table_or_table_expression>
  PIVOT(<agg_func>(<aggregation_element>)
        FOR <spreading_element>
          IN (<list_of_target_columns>)) AS <result_table_alias>
...;
```

In the parentheses of the *PIVOT* operator, you specify the aggregate function (SUM, in this example), aggregation element (*qty*), spreading element (*custid*), and the list of target column names (A, B, C, D). Following the parentheses of the *PIVOT* operator, you specify an alias for the result table.

It is important to note that with the *PIVOT* operator, you do not explicitly specify the grouping elements, removing the need for *GROUP BY* in the query. The *PIVOT* operator figures out the grouping elements implicitly as all attributes from the source table (or table expression) that were not specified as either the spreading element or the aggregation element. You must ensure that the source table for the *PIVOT* operator has no attributes besides the grouping, spreading, and aggregation elements, so that after specifying the spreading and aggregation elements, the only attributes left are those you intend as grouping elements. You achieve this by not applying the *PIVOT* operator to the original table directly (*Orders* in this case), but instead to a table expression that includes only the attributes representing the pivoting elements and no others. For example, here's the solution query to the original pivoting request, using the native *PIVOT* operator.

```
SELECT empid, A, B, C, D
FROM (SELECT empid, custid, qty
      FROM dbo.Orders) AS D
  PIVOT(SUM(qty) FOR custid IN(A, B, C, D)) AS P;
```

Instead of operating directly on the *dbo.Orders* table, the *PIVOT* operator operates on a derived table called D that includes only the pivoting elements *empid*, *custid*, and *qty*. When you account for the spreading element, which is *custid*, and the aggregation element, which is *qty*, what's left is *empid*, which will be considered the grouping element.

This query returns the output shown earlier in Table 7-1.

To understand why you're required to use a table expression here, consider the following query that applies the *PIVOT* operator directly to the *dbo.Orders* table.

```
SELECT empid, A, B, C, D
FROM dbo.Orders
  PIVOT(SUM(qty) FOR custid IN(A, B, C, D)) AS P;
```

The dbo.Orders table contains the attributes *orderid*, *orderdate*, *empid*, *custid*, and *qty*. Because the query specified *custid* as the spreading element and *qty* as the aggregation element, the remaining attributes (*orderid*, *orderdate*, and *empid*) are all considered the grouping elements. This query, therefore, returns the following output.

```
empid        A            B            C            D
-----------  -----------  -----------  -----------  -----------
2            12           NULL         NULL         NULL
1            NULL         20           NULL         NULL
1            NULL         NULL         14           NULL
2            NULL         12           NULL         NULL
1            NULL         NULL         20           NULL
3            10           NULL         NULL         NULL
2            NULL         15           NULL         NULL
3            NULL         NULL         22           NULL
3            NULL         NULL         NULL         30
2            40           NULL         NULL         NULL
3            10           NULL         NULL         NULL
```

(11 row(s) affected)

Because *orderid* is part of the grouping elements, you get a row for each order instead of a row for each employee. The logical equivalent of this query that uses the standard solution for pivoting has *orderid*, *orderdate*, and *empid* listed in the *GROUP BY* list as follows.

```
SELECT empid,
  SUM(CASE WHEN custid = 'A' THEN qty END) AS A,
  SUM(CASE WHEN custid = 'B' THEN qty END) AS B,
  SUM(CASE WHEN custid = 'C' THEN qty END) AS C,
  SUM(CASE WHEN custid = 'D' THEN qty END) AS D
FROM dbo.Orders
GROUP BY orderid, orderdate, empid;
```

I strongly recommend that you never operate on the base table directly, even when the table contains only columns used as pivoting elements. You never know whether new columns will be added to the table in the future, rendering your queries incorrect. I recommend considering the use of a table expression as the input table to the *PIVOT* operator as if it were part of the requirement of the operator's syntax.

As another example of a pivoting request, suppose that instead of returning employees on rows and customers on columns, you want it the other way around: the grouping element is *custid*, the spreading element is *empid*, and the aggregation element and aggregate function remain SUM(*qty*). After you learn the "template" for a pivoting solution (standard or native), it's just a matter of fitting those elements in the right places. The following solution query uses the native *PIVOT* operator to achieve the result.

```
SELECT custid, [1], [2], [3]
FROM (SELECT empid, custid, qty
      FROM dbo.Orders) AS D
  PIVOT(SUM(qty) FOR empid IN([1], [2], [3])) AS P;
```

The employee IDs 1, 2, and 3 are values in the *empid* column in the source table, but in terms of the result, these values become target column names. Therefore, in the *PIVOT IN* clause, you must refer to them as identifiers. When identifiers are irregular (for example, when they start with a digit), you need to delimit them—hence the use of square brackets.

This query returns the following output.

```
custid    1             2             3
-------   -----------   -----------   -----------
A         NULL          52            20
B         20            27            NULL
C         34            NULL          22
D         NULL          NULL          30
```

# Unpivoting Data

*Unpivoting* is a technique to rotate data from a state of columns to a state of rows. Usually it involves querying a pivoted state of the data, producing from each source row multiple result rows, each with a different source column value. In other words, each source row of the pivoted table becomes potentially many rows, one row for each of the specified source column values. This may be difficult to understand at first, but an example should help.

Run the following code to create and populate a table called *EmpCustOrders* in the *TSQL2012* sample database.

```
USE TSQL2012;

IF OBJECT_ID('dbo.EmpCustOrders', 'U') IS NOT NULL DROP TABLE dbo.EmpCustOrders;

CREATE TABLE dbo.EmpCustOrders
(
  empid INT NOT NULL
    CONSTRAINT PK_EmpCustOrders PRIMARY KEY,
  A VARCHAR(5) NULL,
  B VARCHAR(5) NULL,
  C VARCHAR(5) NULL,
  D VARCHAR(5) NULL
);

INSERT INTO dbo.EmpCustOrders(empid, A, B, C, D)
  SELECT empid, A, B, C, D
  FROM (SELECT empid, custid, qty
        FROM dbo.Orders) AS D
    PIVOT(SUM(qty) FOR custid IN(A, B, C, D)) AS P;

SELECT * FROM dbo.EmpCustOrders;
```

Here's the output of the query against *EmpCustOrders* showing its contents.

```
empid         A             B             C             D
-----------   -----------   -----------   -----------   -----------
1             NULL          20            34            NULL
2             52            27            NULL          NULL
3             20            NULL          22            30
```

The table has a row for each employee; a column for each of the four customers A, B, C, and D; and the order quantity for each employee and customer in the employee-customer intersections. Notice that irrelevant intersections (employee-customer combinations that had no intersecting order activity) are represented by *NULL* marks. Suppose that you receive a request to unpivot the data, requiring you to return a row for each employee and customer, along with the order quantity. The resulting output should look like this.

```
empid        custid    qty
-----------  --------- -----------
1            B         20
1            C         34
2            A         52
2            B         27
3            A         20
3            C         22
3            D         30
```

In the following sections, I'll discuss two techniques for solving this problem—a technique that follows the SQL standard and a technique that uses a T-SQL–specific *UNPIVOT* operator.

## Unpivoting with Standard SQL

The standard solution to unpivoting involves implementing three logical processing phases in a very explicit manner: producing copies, extracting elements, and eliminating irrelevant intersections.

The first step in the solution involves producing multiple copies of each source row—one for each column that you need to unpivot. In this case, you need to produce a copy for each of the columns A, B, C, and D, which represent customer IDs. In relational algebra and in SQL, the operation used to produce multiple copies of each row is a Cartesian product (a cross join). You need to apply a cross join between the *EmpCustOrders* table and a table that has a row for each customer.

You can use a table value constructor in the form of a *VALUES* clause to create a virtual table with a row for each customer. The query implementing the first step in the solution looks like this.

```
SELECT *
FROM dbo.EmpCustOrders
  CROSS JOIN (VALUES('A'),('B'),('C'),('D')) AS Custs(custid);
```

Note that if you're not familiar yet with the *VALUES* clause, it is described in detail in Chapter 8, "Data Modification."

In this example, the query that implements the first step in the solution returns the following output.

```
empid        A            B            C            D            custid
-----------  -----------  -----------  -----------  -----------  ------
1            NULL         20           34           NULL         A
1            NULL         20           34           NULL         B
1            NULL         20           34           NULL         C
1            NULL         20           34           NULL         D
2            52           27           NULL         NULL         A
2            52           27           NULL         NULL         B
2            52           27           NULL         NULL         C
2            52           27           NULL         NULL         D
3            20           NULL         22           30           A
3            20           NULL         22           30           B
3            20           NULL         22           30           C
3            20           NULL         22           30           D
```

As you can see, four copies were produced for each source row—one each for customers A, B, C, and D.

The second step in the solution is to produce a column (call it *qty* in this case) that returns the value from the column that corresponds to the customer represented by the current copy. More specifically in this case, if the current *custid* value is A, the *qty* column should return the value from column A, if *custid* is B, *qty* should return the value from column B, and so on. You can implement this step with a simple *CASE* expression like this.

```
SELECT empid, custid,
  CASE custid
    WHEN 'A' THEN A
    WHEN 'B' THEN B
    WHEN 'C' THEN C
    WHEN 'D' THEN D
  END AS qty
FROM dbo.EmpCustOrders
  CROSS JOIN (VALUES('A'),('B'),('C'),('D')) AS Custs(custid);
```

This query returns the following output.

```
empid        custid    qty
-----------  --------  -----------
1            A         NULL
1            B         20
1            C         34
1            D         NULL
2            A         52
2            B         27
2            C         NULL
2            D         NULL
3            A         20
3            B         NULL
3            C         22
3            D         30
```

Recall that in the original table, *NULL* marks represent irrelevant intersections. To eliminate irrelevant intersections, define a table expression based on the query that implements step 2 in the solution, and in the outer query, filter out *NULL* marks. Here's the complete solution query.

```
SELECT *
FROM (SELECT empid, custid,
         CASE custid
            WHEN 'A' THEN A
            WHEN 'B' THEN B
            WHEN 'C' THEN C
            WHEN 'D' THEN D
         END AS qty
      FROM dbo.EmpCustOrders
         CROSS JOIN (VALUES('A'),('B'),('C'),('D')) AS Custs(custid)) AS D
WHERE qty IS NOT NULL;
```

This query returns the following output.

```
empid       custid    qty
----------- --------- ----------
1           B         20
1           C         34
2           A         52
2           B         27
3           A         20
3           C         22
3           D         30
```

## Unpivoting with the Native T-SQL *UNPIVOT* Operator

Unpivoting data involves producing two result columns from any number of source columns that you unpivot. In this example, you need to unpivot the source columns A, B, C and D, producing two result columns called *custid* and *qty*. The former will hold the source column names (A, B, C, and D), and the latter will hold the source column values (quantities in this case). SQL Server supports a very elegant, minimalistic native *UNPIVOT* table operator. The general form of a query with the *UNPIVOT* operator is as follows.

```
SELECT ...
FROM <source_table_or_table_expression>
  UNPIVOT(<target_col_to_hold_source_col_values>
    FOR <target_col_to_hold_source_col_names> IN(<list_of_source_columns>)) AS
<result_table_alias>
...;
```

Like the *PIVOT* operator, *UNPIVOT* was also implemented as a table operator in the context of the *FROM* clause. It operates on a source table or table expression (*EmpCustOrders* in this case). Within the parentheses of the *UNPIVOT* operator, you specify the name you want to assign to the column that will hold the source column values (*qty* here), the name you want to assign to the column that will hold the source column names (*custid*), and the list of source column names (A, B, C, and D). Following the parentheses, you provide an alias to the table resulting from the table operator.

Here's the complete solution query that uses the *UNPIVOT* operator to satisfy the unpivoting request in the example.

```
SELECT empid, custid, qty
FROM dbo.EmpCustOrders
  UNPIVOT(qty FOR custid IN(A, B, C, D)) AS U;
```

Note that the *UNPIVOT* operator implements the same logical processing phases described earlier—generating copies, extracting elements, and eliminating *NULL* intersections. The last phase is not an optional phase as in the solution based on standard SQL.

Also note that unpivoting a pivoted table cannot bring back the original table. Rather, unpivoting is just a rotation of the pivoted values into a new format. However, the table that has been unpivoted can be pivoted back to its original pivoted state. In other words, the aggregation results in a loss of detail information in the original pivoting. After the initial pivot, all the aggregations can be preserved between the operations, provided that the unpivot does not lose information.

When you are done, run the following code for cleanup.

```
IF OBJECT_ID('dbo.EmpCustOrders', 'U') IS NOT NULL DROP TABLE dbo.EmpCustOrders;
```

# Grouping Sets

This section describes both what grouping sets are and the features in SQL Server that support grouping sets.

A grouping set is simply a set of attributes by which you group. Traditionally in SQL, a single aggregate query defines a single grouping set. For example, each of the following four queries defines a single grouping set.

```
SELECT empid, custid, SUM(qty) AS sumqty
FROM dbo.Orders
GROUP BY empid, custid;

SELECT empid, SUM(qty) AS sumqty
FROM dbo.Orders
GROUP BY empid;

SELECT custid, SUM(qty) AS sumqty
FROM dbo.Orders
GROUP BY custid;

SELECT SUM(qty) AS sumqty
FROM dbo.Orders;
```

The first query defines the grouping set *(empid, custid)*; the second *(empid)*, the third *(custid)*, and the last query define what's known as the empty grouping set, *()*. This code returns four result sets—one for each of the four queries.

Suppose that instead of four separate result sets, you wanted a single unified result set with the aggregated data for all four grouping sets. You could achieve this by using the *UNION ALL* set operation to unify the result sets of all four queries. Because set operations require all result sets to have compatible schemas with the same number of columns, you need to adjust the queries by adding placeholders (for example, *NULL* marks) to account for missing columns. Here's what the code would look like.

```
SELECT empid, custid, SUM(qty) AS sumqty
FROM dbo.Orders
GROUP BY empid, custid

UNION ALL

SELECT empid, NULL, SUM(qty) AS sumqty
FROM dbo.Orders
GROUP BY empid

UNION ALL

SELECT NULL, custid, SUM(qty) AS sumqty
FROM dbo.Orders
GROUP BY custid

UNION ALL

SELECT NULL, NULL, SUM(qty) AS sumqty
FROM dbo.Orders;
```

This code generates a single result set, with the aggregates for all four grouping sets being unified.

```
empid       custid    sumqty
----------- --------- -----------
2           A         52
3           A         20
1           B         20
2           B         27
1           C         34
3           C         22
3           D         30
1           NULL      54
2           NULL      79
3           NULL      72
NULL        A         72
NULL        B         47
NULL        C         56
NULL        D         30
NULL        NULL      205

(15 row(s) affected)
```

Even though you managed to get what you were after, this solution has two main problems—the length of the code and the performance. This solution requires you to specify a whole *GROUP BY* query for each grouping set. When you have a large number of grouping sets, the query can get quite long. Also, to process the query, SQL Server will scan the source table separately for each query, which is inefficient.

SQL Server supports several features that follow standard SQL and address the need to define multiple grouping sets in the same query. Those are the *GROUPING SETS*, *CUBE*, and *ROLLUP* subclauses of the *GROUP BY* clause and the GROUPING and GROUPING_ID functions.

## The *GROUPING SETS* Subclause

The *GROUPING SETS* subclause is a powerful enhancement to the *GROUP BY* clause that is used mainly in reporting and data warehousing. By using this subclause, you can define multiple grouping sets in the same query. Simply list the grouping sets that you want to define, separated by commas within the parentheses of the *GROUPING SETS* subclause, and for each grouping set list the members separated by commas within parentheses. For example, the following query defines four grouping sets: *(empid, custid)*, *(empid)*, *(custid)*, and *()*.

```
SELECT empid, custid, SUM(qty) AS sumqty
FROM dbo.Orders
GROUP BY
  GROUPING SETS
  (
    (empid, custid),
    (empid),
    (custid),
    ()
  );
```

This query is a logical equivalent of the previous solution that unified the result sets of four aggregate queries, returning the same output. This query, though, has two main advantages over the previous solution—obviously it requires much less code, and SQL Server will optimize the number of times it scans the source table and won't necessarily scan it separately for each grouping set.

## The *CUBE* Subclause

The *CUBE* subclause of the *GROUP BY* clause provides an abbreviated way to define multiple grouping sets. In the parentheses of the *CUBE* subclause, you provide a list of members separated by commas, and you get all possible grouping sets that can be defined based on the input members. For example, *CUBE(a, b, c)* is equivalent to *GROUPING SETS( (a, b, c), (a, b), (a, c), (b, c), (a), (b), (c), () )*. In set theory, the set of all subsets of elements that can be produced from a particular set is called the power set. You can think of the *CUBE* subclause as producing the power set of grouping sets that can be formed from the given set of elements.

Instead of using the *GROUPING SETS* subclause in the previous query to define the four grouping sets *(empid, custid)*, *(empid)*, *(custid)*, and *()*, you can simply use *CUBE(empid, custid)*. Here's the complete query.

```
SELECT empid, custid, SUM(qty) AS sumqty
FROM dbo.Orders
GROUP BY CUBE(empid, custid);
```

# The *ROLLUP* Subclause

The *ROLLUP* subclause of the *GROUP BY* clause also provides an abbreviated way to define multiple grouping sets. However, unlike the *CUBE* subclause, *ROLLUP* doesn't produce all possible grouping sets that can be defined based on the input members—it produces a subset of those. *ROLLUP* assumes a hierarchy among the input members and produces all grouping sets that make sense considering the hierarchy. In other words, whereas *CUBE(a, b, c)* produces all eight possible grouping sets from the three input members, *ROLLUP(a, b, c)* produces only four grouping sets, assuming the hierarchy a>b>c, and is the equivalent of specifying *GROUPING SETS( (a, b, c), (a, b), (a), () )*.

For example, suppose that you want to return total quantities for all grouping sets that can be defined based on the time hierarchy order year > order month > order day. You could use the *GROUPING SETS* subclause and explicitly list all four possible grouping sets.

```
GROUPING SETS(
  (YEAR(orderdate), MONTH(orderdate), DAY(orderdate)),
  (YEAR(orderdate), MONTH(orderdate)),
  (YEAR(orderdate)),
  () )
```

The logical equivalent that uses the *ROLLUP* subclause is much more economical.

```
ROLLUP(YEAR(orderdate), MONTH(orderdate), DAY(orderdate))
```

Here's the complete query that you need to run.

```
SELECT
  YEAR(orderdate) AS orderyear,
  MONTH(orderdate) AS ordermonth,
  DAY(orderdate) AS orderday,
  SUM(qty) AS sumqty
FROM dbo.Orders
GROUP BY ROLLUP(YEAR(orderdate), MONTH(orderdate), DAY(orderdate));
```

This query produces the following output.

| orderyear | ordermonth | orderday | sumqty |
|-----------|------------|----------|--------|
| 2007 | 4 | 18 | 22 |
| 2007 | 4 | NULL | 22 |
| 2007 | 8 | 2 | 10 |
| 2007 | 8 | NULL | 10 |
| 2007 | 12 | 24 | 32 |
| 2007 | 12 | NULL | 32 |
| 2007 | NULL | NULL | 64 |
| 2008 | 1 | 9 | 40 |
| 2008 | 1 | 18 | 14 |
| 2008 | 1 | NULL | 54 |
| 2008 | 2 | 12 | 12 |
| 2008 | 2 | NULL | 12 |
| 2008 | NULL | NULL | 66 |

| 2009 | 2    | 12   | 10  |
|------|------|------|-----|
| 2009 | 2    | 16   | 20  |
| 2009 | 2    | NULL | 30  |
| 2009 | 4    | 18   | 15  |
| 2009 | 4    | NULL | 15  |
| 2009 | 9    | 7    | 30  |
| 2009 | 9    | NULL | 30  |
| 2009 | NULL | NULL | 75  |
| NULL | NULL | NULL | 205 |

## The *GROUPING* and *GROUPING_ID* Functions

When you have a single query that defines multiple grouping sets, you might need to be able to associate result rows and grouping sets—that is, to identify for each result row the grouping set it is associated with. As long as all grouping elements are defined as *NOT NULL*, this is easy. For example, consider the following query.

```
SELECT empid, custid, SUM(qty) AS sumqty
FROM dbo.Orders
GROUP BY CUBE(empid, custid);
```

This query produces the following output.

| empid | custid | sumqty |
|-------|--------|--------|
| 2     | A      | 52     |
| 3     | A      | 20     |
| NULL  | A      | 72     |
| 1     | B      | 20     |
| 2     | B      | 27     |
| NULL  | B      | 47     |
| 1     | C      | 34     |
| 3     | C      | 22     |
| NULL  | C      | 56     |
| 3     | D      | 30     |
| NULL  | D      | 30     |
| NULL  | NULL   | 205    |
| 1     | NULL   | 54     |
| 2     | NULL   | 79     |
| 3     | NULL   | 72     |

Because both the *empid* and *custid* columns were defined in the *dbo.Orders* table as *NOT NULL*, a *NULL* in those columns can only represent a placeholder, indicating that the column did not participate in the current grouping set. So, for example, all rows in which *empid* is not *NULL* and *custid* is not *NULL* are associated with the grouping set *(empid, custid)*. All rows in which *empid* is not *NULL* and *custid* is *NULL* are associated with the grouping set *(empid)*, and so on. Some people override the presentation of *NULL* marks with *ALL* or a similar designator, provided that the original columns are not nullable. This helps for reporting.

However, if a grouping column is defined as allowing *NULL* marks in the table, you cannot tell for sure whether a *NULL* in the result set originated from the data or is a placeholder for a nonpartici- pating member in a grouping set. One way to determine grouping set association in a deterministic manner, even when grouping columns allow *NULL* marks, is to use the GROUPING function. This function accepts a name of a column and returns 0 if it is a member of the current grouping set and 1 otherwise.

> **Note** I find it counterintuitive that the *GROUPING* function returns 1 when the element isn't part of the grouping set and 0 when it is. To me, it would have made more sense for the function to return 1 (meaning true) when the element is part of the grouping set and 0 otherwise. But that's the implementation, so you just need to make sure that you realize this fact.

For example, the following query invokes the GROUPING function for each of the grouping elements.

```
SELECT
  GROUPING(empid) AS grpemp,
  GROUPING(custid) AS grpcust,
  empid, custid, SUM(qty) AS sumqty
FROM dbo.Orders
GROUP BY CUBE(empid, custid);
```

This query returns the following output.

| grpemp | grpcust | empid | custid | sumqty |
| --- | --- | --- | --- | --- |
| 0 | 0 | 2 | A | 52 |
| 0 | 0 | 3 | A | 20 |
| 1 | 0 | NULL | A | 72 |
| 0 | 0 | 1 | B | 20 |
| 0 | 0 | 2 | B | 27 |
| 1 | 0 | NULL | B | 47 |
| 0 | 0 | 1 | C | 34 |
| 0 | 0 | 3 | C | 22 |
| 1 | 0 | NULL | C | 56 |
| 0 | 0 | 3 | D | 30 |
| 1 | 0 | NULL | D | 30 |
| 1 | 1 | NULL | NULL | 205 |
| 0 | 1 | 1 | NULL | 54 |
| 0 | 1 | 2 | NULL | 79 |
| 0 | 1 | 3 | NULL | 72 |

(15 row(s) affected)

Now you don't need to rely on the *NULL* marks anymore to figure out the association between result rows and grouping sets. For example, all rows in which *grpemp* is 0 and *grpcust* is 0 are associated with the grouping set *(empid, custid)*. All rows in which *grpemp* is 0 and *grpcust* is 1 are associated with the grouping set *(empid)*, and so on.

SQL Server supports another function called GROUPING_ID that can further simplify the process of associating result rows and grouping sets. You provide the function with all elements that participate in any grouping set as inputs—for example, GROUPING_ID*(a, b, c, d)*—and the function returns an integer bitmap in which each bit represents a different input element—the rightmost element represented by the rightmost bit. For example, the grouping set *(a, b, c, d)* is represented by the integer 0 (0×8 + 0×4 + 0×2 + 0×1). The grouping set *(a, c)* is represented by the integer 5 (0×8 + 1×4 + 0×2 + 1×1), and so on.

Instead of calling the GROUPING function for each grouping element as in the previous query, you can call the GROUPING_ID function once and provide it with all grouping elements as input, as shown here.

```
SELECT
  GROUPING_ID(empid, custid) AS groupingset,
  empid, custid, SUM(qty) AS sumqty
FROM dbo.Orders
GROUP BY CUBE(empid, custid);
```

This query produces the following output.

| groupingset | empid | custid | sumqty |
| --- | --- | --- | --- |
| 0 | 2 | A | 52 |
| 0 | 3 | A | 20 |
| 2 | NULL | A | 72 |
| 0 | 1 | B | 20 |
| 0 | 2 | B | 27 |
| 2 | NULL | B | 47 |
| 0 | 1 | C | 34 |
| 0 | 3 | C | 22 |
| 2 | NULL | C | 56 |
| 0 | 3 | D | 30 |
| 2 | NULL | D | 30 |
| 3 | NULL | NULL | 205 |
| 1 | 1 | NULL | 54 |
| 1 | 2 | NULL | 79 |
| 1 | 3 | NULL | 72 |

Now you can easily figure out which grouping set each row is associated with. The integer 0 (binary 00) represents the grouping set *(empid, custid)*; the integer 1 (binary 01) represents *(empid)*; the integer 2 (binary 10) represents *(custid)*; and the integer 3 (binary (11) represents *()*.

# Conclusion

This chapter covered window functions, pivoting and unpivoting data, and features related to grouping sets.

Window functions allow you to perform calculations against sets in a more flexible and efficient manner when compared to alternative methods. Window functions have numerous practical uses, so it's well worth your time to get to know them well.

I provided both standard and nonstandard techniques to achieve pivoting and unpivoting. The nonstandard techniques use the T-SQL–specific *PIVOT* and *UNPIVOT* operators; the main advantage of these is that they require less code than standard techniques.

SQL Server supports several important features that make the handling of grouping sets flexible and efficient: the *GROUPING SETS*, *CUBE*, and *ROLLUP* subclauses and the GROUPING and GROUPING_ID function.

# Exercises

This section provides exercises to help you familiarize yourself with the subjects discussed in Chapter 7. All exercises for this chapter involve querying the *dbo.Orders* table in the *TSQL2012* database that you created and populated earlier in this chapter by running the code in Listing 7-1.

## 1

Write a query against the *dbo.Orders* table that computes for each customer order both a rank and a dense rank, partitioned by *custid* and ordered by *qty*.

■ Tables involved: *TSQL2012* database and *dbo.Orders* table

■ Desired output:

```
custid orderid     qty         rnk                   drnk
------ ----------- ----------- --------------------- --------------------
A      30001       10          1                     1
A      40005       10          1                     1
A      10001       12          3                     2
A      40001       40          4                     3
B      20001       12          1                     1
B      30003       15          2                     2
B      10005       20          3                     3
C      10006       14          1                     1
C      20002       20          2                     2
C      30004       22          3                     3
D      30007       30          1                     1
```

# 2

Write a query against the *dbo.Orders* table that computes for each customer order both the difference between the current order quantity and the customer's previous order quantity *and* the difference between the current order quantity and the customer's next order quantity.

- Tables involved: *TSQL2012* database and *dbo.Orders* table

- Desired output:

```
custid orderid    qty        diffprev    diffnext
------ ---------- ---------- ----------- -----------
A      30001      10         NULL        -2
A      10001      12         2           -28
A      40001      40         28          30
A      40005      10         -30         NULL
B      10005      20         NULL        8
B      20001      12         -8          -3
B      30003      15         3           NULL
C      30004      22         NULL        8
C      10006      14         -8          -6
C      20002      20         6           NULL
D      30007      30         NULL        NULL
```

# 3

Write a query against the *dbo.Orders* table that returns a row for each employee, a column for each order year, and the count of orders for each employee and order year.

- Tables involved: *TSQL2012* database and *dbo.Orders* table

- Desired output:

```
empid       cnt2007     cnt2008     cnt2009
----------- ----------- ----------- -----------
1           1           1           1
2           1           2           1
3           2           0           2
```

## 4

Run the following code to create and populate the *EmpYearOrders* table.

```
USE TSQL2012;

IF OBJECT_ID('dbo.EmpYearOrders', 'U') IS NOT NULL DROP TABLE dbo.EmpYearOrders;

CREATE TABLE dbo.EmpYearOrders
(
  empid INT NOT NULL
    CONSTRAINT PK_EmpYearOrders PRIMARY KEY,
  cnt2007 INT NULL,
  cnt2008 INT NULL,
  cnt2009 INT NULL
);

INSERT INTO dbo.EmpYearOrders(empid, cnt2007, cnt2008, cnt2009)
  SELECT empid, [2007] AS cnt2007, [2008] AS cnt2008, [2009] AS cnt2009
  FROM (SELECT empid, YEAR(orderdate) AS orderyear
        FROM dbo.Orders) AS D
    PIVOT(COUNT(orderyear)
          FOR orderyear IN([2007], [2008], [2009])) AS P;

SELECT * FROM dbo.EmpYearOrders;
```

Here is the output for the query.

```
empid        cnt2007      cnt2008      cnt2009
-----------  -----------  -----------  -----------
1            1            1            1
2            1            2            1
3            2            0            2
```

Write a query against the *EmpYearOrders* table that unpivots the data, returning a row for each employee and order year with the number of orders. Exclude rows in which the number of orders is 0 (in this example, employee 3 in the year 2008).

- Desired output:

```
empid        orderyear    numorders
-----------  -----------  -----------
1            2007         1
1            2008         1
1            2009         1
2            2007         1
2            2008         2
2            2009         1
3            2007         2
3            2009         2
```

# 5

Write a query against the *dbo.Orders* table that returns the total quantities for each: (employee, customer, and order year), (employee and order year), and (customer and order year). Include a result column in the output that uniquely identifies the grouping set with which the current row is associated.

- Tables involved: *TSQL2012* database and *dbo.Orders* table

- Desired output:

```
groupingset    empid        custid     orderyear    sumqty
-------------- ------------ ---------- ------------ -----------
0              2            A          2007         12
0              3            A          2007         10
4              NULL         A          2007         22
0              2            A          2008         40
4              NULL         A          2008         40
0              3            A          2009         10
4              NULL         A          2009         10
0              1            B          2007         20
4              NULL         B          2007         20
0              2            B          2008         12
4              NULL         B          2008         12
0              2            B          2009         15
4              NULL         B          2009         15
0              3            C          2007         22
4              NULL         C          2007         22
0              1            C          2008         14
4              NULL         C          2008         14
0              1            C          2009         20
4              NULL         C          2009         20
0              3            D          2009         30
4              NULL         D          2009         30
2              1            NULL       2007         20
2              2            NULL       2007         12
2              3            NULL       2007         32
2              1            NULL       2008         14
2              2            NULL       2008         52
2              1            NULL       2009         20
2              2            NULL       2009         15
2              3            NULL       2009         40
```

(29 row(s) affected)

When you are done with the exercises in this chapter, run the following code for cleanup.

```
IF OBJECT_ID('dbo.Orders', 'U') IS NOT NULL DROP TABLE dbo.Orders;
```

# Solutions

This section provides solutions to the Chapter 7 exercises.

## 1

This exercise is very technical. It's just a matter of being familiar with the syntax for window ranking functions. Here's the solution query, returning for each order both the rank and the dense rank, partitioned by *custid* and ordered by *qty*.

```
SELECT custid, orderid, qty,
  RANK() OVER(PARTITION BY custid ORDER BY qty) AS rnk,
  DENSE_RANK() OVER(PARTITION BY custid ORDER BY qty) AS drnk
FROM dbo.Orders;
```

## 2

The window offset functions *LAG* and *LEAD* allow you to return an element from a previous and next row, respectively, based on the indicated partitioning and ordering specification. In this exercise, you need to perform the calculations within each customer's orders, hence the window partitioning should be based on *custid*. As for ordering, use *orderdate* as the first ordering column and *orderid* as the tiebreaker. Here's the complete solution query.

```
SELECT custid, orderid, qty,
  qty - LAG(qty) OVER(PARTITION BY custid
                      ORDER BY orderdate, orderid) AS diffprev,
  qty - LEAD(qty) OVER(PARTITION BY custid
                       ORDER BY orderdate, orderid) AS diffnext
FROM dbo.Orders;
```

This query is a good example that shows that you can mix detail elements from the row with window functions in the same expression.

## 3

Solving a pivoting problem is all about identifying the elements involved: the grouping element, the spreading element, the aggregation element, and the aggregate function. After you identify the elements involved, you simply fit them into the "template" query for pivoting—whether it is the standard solution or the solution using the native *PIVOT* operator.

In this exercise, the grouping element is the employee (*empid*), the spreading element is order year (*YEAR(orderdate)*), and the aggregate function is COUNT; however, identifying the aggregation element is not that straightforward. You want the COUNT aggregate function to count matching rows and orders—you don't really care which attribute it counts. In other words, you can use any attribute that you want, as long as the attribute does not allow *NULL* marks, because aggregate functions ignore *NULL* marks, and counting an attribute that allows *NULL* marks would result in an incorrect count of the orders.

If it doesn't really matter which attribute you use as the input to the COUNT aggregate, why not use the same attribute that you already use as the spreading element? In this case, you can use the order year as both the spreading and aggregation element.

Now that you've identified all pivoting elements, you're ready to write the complete solution. Here's the solution query without using the *PIVOT* operator.

```
USE TSQL2012;

SELECT empid,
  COUNT(CASE WHEN orderyear = 2007 THEN orderyear END) AS cnt2007,
  COUNT(CASE WHEN orderyear = 2008 THEN orderyear END) AS cnt2008,
  COUNT(CASE WHEN orderyear = 2009 THEN orderyear END) AS cnt2009
FROM (SELECT empid, YEAR(orderdate) AS orderyear
      FROM dbo.Orders) AS D
GROUP BY empid;
```

Recall that if you do not specify an *ELSE* clause in a *CASE* expression, an implicit *ELSE NULL* is assumed. Thus the *CASE* expression produces non-*NULL* marks only for matching orders (orders placed by the current employee in the current order year), and only those matching orders are taken into consideration by the *COUNT* aggregate.

Notice that even though the standard solution does not require you to use a table expression, I used one here to alias the *YEAR(orderdate)* expression as *orderyear* to avoid repeating the expression *YEAR(orderdate)* multiple times in the outer query.

Here's the solution query that uses the native *PIVOT* operator.

```
SELECT empid, [2007] AS cnt2007, [2008] AS cnt2008, [2009] AS cnt2009
FROM (SELECT empid, YEAR(orderdate) AS orderyear
      FROM dbo.Orders) AS D
  PIVOT(COUNT(orderyear)
        FOR orderyear IN([2007], [2008], [2009])) AS P;
```

As you can see, it's just a matter of fitting the pivoting elements in the right places.

If you prefer to use your own target column names and not the ones based on the actual data, of course you can provide your own aliases in the *SELECT* list. In this query, I aliased the result columns *[2007]*, *[2008]*, and *[2009]* as *cnt2007*, *cnt2008*, and *cnt2009*, respectively.

# 4

This exercise involves a request to unpivot the source columns *cnt2007*, *cnt2008*, and *cnt2009* to two target columns—*orderyear* to hold the year that the source column name represents and *numorders* to hold the source column value. You can use the solutions that I showed in the chapter as the basis for solving this exercise with a couple of small revisions.

In the examples I used in the chapter, *NULL* marks in the table represented irrelevant column values. The unpivoting solutions I presented filtered out rows with *NULL* marks. The *EmpYearOrders* table has no *NULL* marks, but it does have zeros in some cases, and the request is to filter out rows with 0 number of orders. With the standard solution, simply use the predicate *numorders* <> 0 instead of using *IS NOT NULL*. Here's the version that uses the *VALUES* clause.

```
SELECT *
FROM (SELECT empid, orderyear,
        CASE orderyear
          WHEN 2007 THEN cnt2007
          WHEN 2008 THEN cnt2008
          WHEN 2009 THEN cnt2009
        END AS numorders
      FROM dbo.EmpYearOrders
        CROSS JOIN (VALUES(2007),(2008),(2009)) AS Years (orderyear)) AS D
WHERE numorders <> 0;
```

As for the solution that uses the native *UNPIVOT* operator, remember that it eliminates *NULL* marks as an integral part of its logic. However, it does not eliminate zeros—you have to take care of eliminating zeros yourself by adding a *WHERE* clause, like this.

```
SELECT empid, CAST(RIGHT(orderyear, 4) AS INT) AS orderyear, numorders
FROM dbo.EmpYearOrders
  UNPIVOT(numorders FOR orderyear IN(cnt2007, cnt2008, cnt2009)) AS U
WHERE numorders <> 0;
```

Notice the expression used in the *SELECT* list to produce the *orderyear* result column: *CAST(RIGHT(orderyear, 4) AS INT)*. The original column names that the query unpivots are *cnt2007*, *cnt2008*, and *cnt2009*. These column names become the values *'cnt2007'*, *'cnt2008'*, and *'cnt2009'*, respectively, in the *orderyear* column in the result of the *UNPIVOT* operator. The purpose of this expression is to extract the four rightmost characters representing the order year and convert the value to an integer. This manipulation was not required in the standard solution because the constants used to construct the table expression *Years* were specified as the integer order years to begin with.

# 5

If you understand the concept of grouping sets, this exercise should be straightforward for you. You can use the *GROUPING SETS* subclause to list the requested grouping sets and the GROUPING_ID function to produce a unique identifier for the grouping set with which each row is associated. Here's the complete solution query.

```
SELECT
  GROUPING_ID(empid, custid, YEAR(Orderdate)) AS groupingset,
  empid, custid, YEAR(Orderdate) AS orderyear, SUM(qty) AS sumqty
FROM dbo.Orders
GROUP BY
  GROUPING SETS
  (
    (empid, custid, YEAR(orderdate)),
    (empid, YEAR(orderdate)),
    (custid, YEAR(orderdate))
  );
```

The requested grouping sets are neither a power set nor a rollup of some set of attributes. Therefore, you cannot use either the *CUBE* or the *ROLLUP* subclause to further abbreviate the code.

CHAPTER 8

# Data Modification

SQL has a set of statements known as Data Manipulation Language (DML) that deals with, well, data manipulation. Some people think that DML involves only statements that modify data, but in fact it also involves data retrieval. DML includes the statements *SELECT, INSERT, UPDATE, DELETE, TRUNCATE,* and *MERGE*. Up to this point in the book, I've focused on the *SELECT* statement. This chapter focuses on data modification statements. In addition to covering standard aspects of data modification, in this chapter, I'll also cover aspects specific to T-SQL.

To avoid changing data in your existing sample databases, for demonstration purposes, most of the examples in this chapter create, populate, and operate against tables in the *TSQL2012* database that use the *dbo* schema.

## Inserting Data

T-SQL provides several statements for inserting data into tables: *INSERT VALUES, INSERT SELECT, INSERT EXEC, SELECT INTO,* and *BULK INSERT*. I'll first describe those statements, and then I'll talk about tools for automatically generating keys, such as the *identity* column property and the sequence object.

### The *INSERT VALUES* Statement

You use the *INSERT VALUES* statement to insert rows into a table based on specified values. To practice using this statement and others, you will work with a table called *Orders* in the *dbo* schema in the *TSQL2012* database. Run the following code to create the *Orders* table.

```
USE TSQL2012;

IF OBJECT_ID('dbo.Orders', 'U') IS NOT NULL DROP TABLE dbo.Orders;

CREATE TABLE dbo.Orders
(
  orderid   INT       NOT NULL
    CONSTRAINT PK_Orders PRIMARY KEY,
  orderdate DATE      NOT NULL
    CONSTRAINT DFT_orderdate DEFAULT(SYSDATETIME()),
  empid     INT       NOT NULL,
  custid    VARCHAR(10) NOT NULL
)
```

The following example demonstrates how to use the *INSERT VALUES* statement to insert a single row into the *Orders* table.

```
INSERT INTO dbo.Orders(orderid, orderdate, empid, custid)
  VALUES(10001, '20090212', 3, 'A');
```

Specifying the target column names right after the table name is optional, but by doing so, you control the value-column associations instead of relying on the order in which the columns appeared when the table was defined (or the table structure was last altered).

If you specify a value for a column, Microsoft SQL Server will use that value. If you don't, SQL Server will check whether a default value is defined for the column, and if so, the default will be used. If a default value isn't defined and the column allows *NULL* marks, a *NULL* will be used. If you do not specify a value for a column that does not allow *NULL* marks and does not somehow get its value automatically, your *INSERT* statement will fail. As an example of relying on a default value or expression, the following statement inserts a row into the *Orders* table without specifying a value for the *orderdate* column, but because this column has a default expression defined for it (*SYSDATETIME*), that default will be used.

```
INSERT INTO dbo.Orders(orderid, empid, custid)
  VALUES(10002, 5, 'B');
```

SQL Server 2008 and SQL Server 2012 support an enhanced *VALUES* clause that allows you to specify multiple rows separated by commas. For example, the following statement inserts four rows into the *Orders* table.

```
INSERT INTO dbo.Orders
  (orderid, orderdate, empid, custid)
VALUES
  (10003, '20090213', 4, 'B'),
  (10004, '20090214', 1, 'A'),
  (10005, '20090213', 1, 'C'),
  (10006, '20090215', 3, 'C');
```

This statement is processed as an atomic operation, meaning that if any row fails to enter the table, none of the rows in the statement enters the table.

There's more to this enhanced *VALUES* clause. You can use it in a standard way as a table value constructor to construct a derived table. Here's an example.

```
SELECT *
FROM ( VALUES
        (10003, '20090213', 4, 'B'),
        (10004, '20090214', 1, 'A'),
        (10005, '20090213', 1, 'C'),
        (10006, '20090215', 3, 'C') )
    AS O(orderid, orderdate, empid, custid);
```

Following the parentheses that contain the table value constructor, you assign an alias to the table (*O* in this case), and following the table alias, you assign aliases to the target columns in parentheses. This query generates the following output.

```
orderid      orderdate    empid        custid
-----------  -----------  -----------  ------
10003        20090213     4            B
10004        20090214     1            A
10005        20090213     1            C
10006        20090215     3            C
```

## The *INSERT SELECT* Statement

The *INSERT SELECT* statement inserts a set of rows returned by a *SELECT* query into a target table. The syntax is very similar to that of an *INSERT VALUES* statement, but instead of the *VALUES* clause, you specify a *SELECT* query. For example, the following code inserts into the *dbo.Orders* table the result of a query against the *Sales.Orders* table returning orders that were shipped to the United Kingdom.

```
INSERT INTO dbo.Orders(orderid, orderdate, empid, custid)
  SELECT orderid, orderdate, empid, custid
  FROM Sales.Orders
  WHERE shipcountry = 'UK';
```

The *INSERT SELECT* statement also allows you the option of specifying the target column names, and the recommendations I gave earlier regarding specifying those names remain the same. The requirement to provide values for all columns that do not somehow get their values automatically and the implicit use of default values or *NULL* marks when a value is not provided are also the same as with the *INSERT VALUES* statement. The *INSERT SELECT* statement is performed as an atomic operation, so if any row fails to enter the target table, none of the rows enters the table.

Before SQL Server enhanced the *VALUES* clause, if you wanted to construct a virtual table based on values, you had to use multiple *SELECT* statements, each returning a single row based on values, and unify the rows with *UNION ALL* set operations. In the context of an *INSERT SELECT* statement, you could use this technique to insert multiple rows based on values in a single statement that is considered an atomic operation. For example, the following statement inserts four rows based on values into the *Orders* table.

```
INSERT INTO dbo.Orders(orderid, orderdate, empid, custid)
  SELECT 10007, '20090215', 2, 'B' UNION ALL
  SELECT 10008, '20090215', 1, 'C' UNION ALL
  SELECT 10009, '20090216', 2, 'C' UNION ALL
  SELECT 10010, '20090216', 3, 'A';
```

However, this syntax isn't standard because it uses *SELECT* statements without *FROM* clauses. Use of a table value constructor based on the *VALUES* clause is standard, and hence it is the preferred option.

# The *INSERT EXEC* Statement

You use the *INSERT EXEC* statement to insert a result set returned from a stored procedure or a dynamic SQL batch into a target table. You'll find information about stored procedures, batches, and dynamic SQL in Chapter 10, "Programmable Objects." The *INSERT EXEC* statement is very similar in syntax and concept to the *INSERT SELECT* statement, but instead of a *SELECT* statement, you specify an *EXEC* statement.

For example, the following code creates a stored procedure called *Sales.usp_getorders*, returning orders that were shipped to a specified input country (with the *@country* parameter).

```
IF OBJECT_ID('Sales.usp_getorders', 'P') IS NOT NULL
  DROP PROC Sales.usp_getorders;
GO

CREATE PROC Sales.usp_getorders
  @country AS NVARCHAR(40)
AS

SELECT orderid, orderdate, empid, custid
FROM Sales.Orders
WHERE shipcountry = @country;
GO
```

To test the stored procedure, execute it with the input country France.

```
EXEC Sales.usp_getorders @country = 'France';
```

You get the following output.

```
orderid     orderdate                empid       custid
----------- ------------------------ ----------- -----------
10248       2006-07-04 00:00:00.000  5           85
10251       2006-07-08 00:00:00.000  3           84
10265       2006-07-25 00:00:00.000  2           7
10274       2006-08-06 00:00:00.000  6           85
10295       2006-09-02 00:00:00.000  2           85
10297       2006-09-04 00:00:00.000  5           7
10311       2006-09-20 00:00:00.000  1           18
10331       2006-10-16 00:00:00.000  9           9
10334       2006-10-21 00:00:00.000  8           84
10340       2006-10-29 00:00:00.000  1           9
...

(77 row(s) affected)
```

By using an *INSERT EXEC* statement, you can direct the result set returned from the procedure to the *dbo.Orders* table.

```
INSERT INTO dbo.Orders(orderid, orderdate, empid, custid)
  EXEC Sales.usp_getorders @country = 'France';
```

# The *SELECT INTO* Statement

The *SELECT INTO* statement is a nonstandard T-SQL statement that creates a target table and populates it with the result set of a query. By "nonstandard," I mean that it is not part of the ISO and ANSI SQL standards. You cannot use this statement to insert data into an existing table. In terms of syntax, simply add *INTO <target_table_name>* right before the *FROM* clause of the *SELECT* query that you want to use to produce the result set. For example, the following code creates a table called *dbo.Orders* and populates it with all rows from the *Sales.Orders* table.

```
IF OBJECT_ID('dbo.Orders', 'U') IS NOT NULL DROP TABLE dbo.Orders;

SELECT orderid, orderdate, empid, custid
INTO dbo.Orders
FROM Sales.Orders;
```

The target table's structure and data are based on the source table. The *SELECT INTO* statement copies from the source the base structure (column names, types, nullability, and identity property) and the data. There are four things that the statement does not copy from the source: constraints, indexes, triggers, and permissions. If you need those in the target, you will need to create them yourself.

**Note** At the date of this writing, Windows Azure SQL Database doesn't support heaps (tables without clustered indexes). *SELECT INTO* creates a heap because it doesn't copy indexes—including clustered ones. For this reason, SQL Database doesn't support *SELECT INTO*. You will need to issue a *CREATE TABLE* statement followed by an *INSERT SELECT* statement to achieve the same result.

One of the benefits of the *SELECT INTO* statement is that as long as a database property called *Recovery Model* is not set to *FULL*, the *SELECT INTO* operation is performed in a minimally logged mode. This translates to a very fast operation compared to a fully logged one. Note also that the *INSERT SELECT* statement can benefit from minimal logging, but the list of requirements it needs to meet is longer. For details, see "Prerequisites for Minimal Logging in Bulk Import" in SQL Server Books Online at the following URL: *http://msdn.microsoft.com/en-us/library/ms190422.aspx*.

If you need to use a *SELECT INTO* statement with set operations, you specify the *INTO* clause right in front of the *FROM* clause of the first query. For example, the following *SELECT INTO* statement creates a table called *Locations* and populates it with the result of an *EXCEPT* set operation, returning locations where there are customers but not employees.

```
IF OBJECT_ID('dbo.Locations', 'U') IS NOT NULL DROP TABLE dbo.Locations;

SELECT country, region, city
INTO dbo.Locations
FROM Sales.Customers

EXCEPT

SELECT country, region, city
FROM HR.Employees;
```

# The *BULK INSERT* Statement

You use the *BULK INSERT* statement to insert into an existing table data originating from a file. In the statement, you specify the target table, the source file, and options. You can specify many options, including the data file type (for example, *char* or *native*), the field terminator, the row terminator, and others—all of which are fully documented.

For example, the following code bulk inserts the contents of the file *c:\temp\orders.tx*t into the table *dbo.Orders*, specifying that the data file type is *char*, the field terminator is a comma, and the row terminator is the newline character.

```
BULK INSERT dbo.Orders FROM 'c:\temp\orders.txt'
  WITH
    (
        DATAFILETYPE    = 'char',
        FIELDTERMINATOR = ',',
        ROWTERMINATOR   = '\n'
    );
```

Note that if you want to actually run this statement, you need to place the *orders.txt* file provided along with the source code for this book into the c:\temp folder.

You can run the *BULK INSERT* statement in a fast, minimally logged mode in certain scenarios provided that certain requirements are met. For details, see "Prerequisites for Minimal Logging in Bulk Import" in SQL Server Books Online.

# The Identity Property and the Sequence Object

SQL Server supports two built-in solutions to automatically generate keys: the identity column property and the sequence object. The identity property has been supported for as long as I can remember in SQL Server. It works well for some scenarios, but it also has many shortcomings. The sequence object was added in SQL Server 2012, and it resolves many of the identity property's limitations. I'll start with identity.

## Identity

SQL Server allows you to define a property called *identity* for a column with any numeric type with a scale of zero (no fraction). This property generates values automatically upon *INSERT* based on a seed (first value) and an increment (step value) that are provided in the column's definition. Typically, you would use this property to generate *surrogate keys*, which are keys that are produced by the system and are not derived from the application data.

For example, the following code creates a table called *dbo.T1*.

```
IF OBJECT_ID('dbo.T1', 'U') IS NOT NULL DROP TABLE dbo.T1;

CREATE TABLE dbo.T1
(
  keycol  INT          NOT NULL IDENTITY(1, 1)
    CONSTRAINT PK_T1 PRIMARY KEY,
  datacol VARCHAR(10) NOT NULL
    CONSTRAINT CHK_T1_datacol CHECK(datacol LIKE '[A-Za-z]%')
);
```

The table contains a column called *keycol* that is defined with an *identity* property using 1 as the seed and 1 as the increment. The table also contains a character string column called *datacol*, whose data is restricted with a *CHECK* constraint to strings starting with an alphabetical character.

In your *INSERT* statements, you should completely ignore the identity column, pretending as though it isn't in the table. For example, the following code inserts three rows into the table, specifying values only for the *datacol* column.

```
INSERT INTO dbo.T1(datacol) VALUES('AAAAA');
INSERT INTO dbo.T1(datacol) VALUES('CCCCC');
INSERT INTO dbo.T1(datacol) VALUES('BBBBB');
```

SQL Server produced the values for *keycol* automatically. To see the values that SQL Server produced, query the table.

```
SELECT * FROM dbo.T1;
```

You get the following output.

```
keycol      datacol
----------- ----------
1           AAAAA
2           CCCCC
3           BBBBB
```

When you query the table, naturally you can refer to the identity column by its name (*keycol* in this case). SQL Server also provides a way to refer to the identity column by using the more generic form *$identity*.

For example, the following query selects the identity column from *T1* by using the generic form.

```
SELECT $identity FROM dbo.T1;
```

This query returns the following output.

```
keycol
-----------
1
2
3
```

When you insert a new row into the table, SQL Server generates a new identity value based on the current identity value in the table and the increment. If you need to obtain the newly generated identity value—for example, to insert child rows into a referencing table—you query one of two functions called @@*identity* and *SCOPE_IDENTITY*. The @@*identity* function is an old feature that returns the last identity value generated by the session, regardless of scope (for example, the current procedure and the trigger fired by *INSERT* are different scopes). *SCOPE_IDENTITY* returns the last identity value generated by the session in the current scope (for example, the same procedure). Except for very special cases when you don't really care about scope, you should use the *SCOPE_IDENTITY* function.

For example, the following code inserts a row into table *T1*, obtains the newly generated identity value into a variable by querying the *SCOPE_IDENTITY* function, and queries the variable.

```
DECLARE @new_key AS INT;

INSERT INTO dbo.T1(datacol) VALUES('AAAAA');

SET @new_key = SCOPE_IDENTITY();

SELECT @new_key AS new_key
```

If you ran all previous code samples provided in this section, this code returns the following output.

```
new_key
-----------
4
```

Remember that both @@*identity* and *SCOPE_IDENTITY* return the last identity value produced by the current session. Neither is affected by inserts issued by other sessions. However, if you want to know the current identity value in a table (the last value produced) regardless of session, you should use the *IDENT_CURRENT* function and provide the table name as input. For example, run the following code from a new session (not the one from which you ran the previous *INSERT* statements).

```
SELECT
  SCOPE_IDENTITY() AS [SCOPE_IDENTITY],
  @@identity AS [@@identity],
  IDENT_CURRENT('dbo.T1') AS [IDENT_CURRENT];
```

You get the following output.

```
SCOPE_IDENTITY    @@identity    IDENT_CURRENT
----------------  ------------  -------------
NULL              NULL          4
```

Both *@@identity* and *SCOPE_IDENTITY* returned *NULL* marks because no identity values were created in the session in which this query ran. *IDENT_CURRENT* returned the value 4 because it returns the current identity value in the table, regardless of the session in which it was produced.

The rest of this section provides several important details regarding the identity property.

The change to the current identity value in a table is not undone if the *INSERT* that generated the change fails or the transaction in which the statement runs is rolled back. For example, run the following *INSERT* statement, which contradicts the *CHECK* constraint defined in the table.

```
INSERT INTO dbo.T1(datacol) VALUES('12345');
```

The insert fails, and you get the following error.

```
Msg 547, Level 16, State 0, Line 1
The INSERT statement conflicted with the CHECK constraint "CHK_T1_datacol". The conflict
occurred in database "TSQL2012", table "dbo.T1", column 'datacol'.
The statement has been terminated.
```

Even though the insert failed, the current identity value in the table changed from 4 to 5, and this change was not undone because of the failure. This means that the next insert will produce the value 6.

```
INSERT INTO dbo.T1(datacol) VALUES('EEEEE');
```

Query the table.

```
SELECT * FROM dbo.T1;
```

Notice a gap between the values 4 and 6 in the output.

```
keycol       datacol
----------- ----------
1            AAAAA
2            CCCCC
3            BBBBB
4            AAAAA
6            EEEEE
```

Of course, this means that you should only rely on the identity property to automatically generate values when you don't care about having gaps. Otherwise, you should consider using your own alternative mechanism.

Another important aspect of the identity property is that you cannot add it to an existing column or remove it from an existing column; you can only define the property along with a column as part of a *CREATE TABLE* statement or an *ALTER TABLE* statement that adds a new column. However, SQL Server does allow you to explicitly specify your own values for the identity column in *INSERT* statements, provided that you set a session option called *IDENTITY_INSERT* against the table involved. No option allows you to update an identity column, though.

For example, the following code demonstrates how to insert a row into *T1* with the explicit value 5 in *keycol*.

```
SET IDENTITY_INSERT dbo.T1 ON;
INSERT INTO dbo.T1(keycol, datacol) VALUES(5, 'FFFFF');
SET IDENTITY_INSERT dbo.T1 OFF;
```

Interestingly, SQL Server changes the current identity value in the table only if the explicit value provided for the identity column is higher than the current identity value in the table. Because the current identity value in the table prior to running the preceding code was 6, and the *INSERT* statement in this code used the lower explicit value 5, the current identity value in the table did not change. So if, at this point, after running the preceding code, you query the *IDENT_CURRENT* function for this table, you will get 6 and not 5. This way the next *INSERT* statement against the table will produce the value 7.

```
INSERT INTO dbo.T1(datacol) VALUES('GGGGG');
```

Query the current contents of the table T1.

```
SELECT * FROM dbo.T1;
```

You get the following output.

```
keycol      datacol
----------- ----------
1           AAAAA
2           CCCCC
3           BBBBB
4           AAAAA
5           FFFFF
6           EEEEE
7           GGGGG
```

It is important to understand that the identity property itself does not enforce uniqueness in the column. I already explained that you can provide your own explicit values after setting the *IDENTITY_INSERT* option to *ON*, and those values can be ones that already exist in rows in the table. Also, you can reseed the current identity value in the table by using the *DBCC CHECKIDENT* command. For details about the syntax of the *DBCC CHECKIDENT* command, see "*DBCC CHECKIDENT* (Transact-SQL)" in SQL Server Books Online. In short, the identity property does not enforce uniqueness. If you need to guarantee uniqueness in an identity column, make sure you also define a primary key or a unique constraint on that column.

## Sequence

The sequence object is a feature that was added in SQL Server 2012 as an alternative key-generating mechanism for identity. It is a standard feature that some of the other database platforms had already implemented, and now migrations from those platforms are easier. The sequence object is more flexible than identity in many ways, making it the preferred choice in many cases.

One of the advantages of the sequence object is that, unlike identity, it is not tied to a particular column in a particular table; rather, it is an independent object in the database. Whenever you need to generate a new value, you invoke a function against the object, and use the returned value wherever you like. This means that you can use one sequence object that will help you maintain keys that would not conflict across multiple tables.

To create a sequence object, use the *CREATE SEQUENCE* command. The minimum required information is just the sequence name, but note that the defaults in such a case might not be what you want. If you don't indicate the type, SQL Server will use *BIGINT* by default. If you want a different type, indicate *AS <type>*. The type can be any numeric type with a scale of zero. For example, if you need your sequence to be of an *INT* type, indicate *AS INT*.

Unlike the identity property, the sequence object supports the specification of a minimum value (*MINVALUE <val>*) and a maximum value (*MAXVALUE <val>*) within the type. If you don't indicate what the minimum and maximum values are, the sequence object will assume the minimum and maximum values supported by the type. For example, for an *INT* type, those would be -2,147,483,648 and 2,147,483,647, respectively.

Also, unlike identity, the sequence object supports cycling. Note, though, that the default is not to cycle, so if you want the sequence object to cycle, you will need to be explicit about it by using the *CYCLE* option.

Like identity, the sequence object allows you to specify the starting value (*START WITH <val>*) and the increment (*INCREMENET BY <val>*). If you don't indicate the starting value, the default will be the same as the minimum value (*MINVALUE*). If you don't indicate the increment value, it will be 1 by default.

So, for example, suppose you want to create a sequence that will help you generate order IDs. You want it to be of an *INT* type, have a minimum value of 1 and a maximum value that is the maximum supported by the type, start with 1, increment by 1, and allow cycling. Here's the *CREATE SEQUENCE* command you could use to create such a sequence.

```
CREATE SEQUENCE dbo.SeqOrderIDs AS INT
  MINVALUE 1
  CYCLE;
```

You had to be explicit about the type, minimum value, and cycling option, because they are different than the defaults. You didn't need to indicate the maximum, start with, and increment values because you wanted the defaults.

The sequence object also supports a caching option (*CACHE <val>* | *NO CACHE*) that tells SQL Server how many values to write to disk. If you write less frequently to disk, you'll get better performance when generating a value (on average), but you'll risk losing more values in case of an unexpected shutdown of the SQL Server process. SQL Server has a default cache value that Microsoft prefers not to publish so that they can change it.

In addition to the type, you can change any of the other options with an *ALTER SEQUENCE* command (*MINVAL <val>*, *MAXVAL <val>*, *RESTART WITH <val>*, *INCREMENT BY <val>*, *CYCLE | NO CYCLE*, or *CACHE <val> | NO CACHE*). For example, suppose you wanted to prevent the *dbo.SeqOrderIDs* from cycling. You would change the current sequence definition with the following *ALTER SEQUENCE* command.

```
ALTER SEQUENCE dbo.SeqOrderIDs
  NO CYCLE;
```

To generate a new sequence value, you need to invoke the function *NEXT VALUE FOR <sequence name>*. It might seem strange that the aforementioned expression is a function, but nevertheless, it is. You can just call it in a *SELECT* statement, like this.

```
SELECT NEXT VALUE FOR dbo.SeqOrderIDs;
```

This code generates the following output.

```
-----------
1
```

Notice that unlike with identity, you didn't need to insert a row into a table in order to generate a new value. Some applications need to generate the new value before using it. With sequences, you can store the result of the function in a variable, and then use it wherever you like. To demonstrate this, first create a table called *T1* with the following code.

```
IF OBJECT_ID('dbo.T1', 'U') IS NOT NULL DROP TABLE dbo.T1;

CREATE TABLE dbo.T1
(
  keycol  INT         NOT NULL
    CONSTRAINT PK_T1 PRIMARY KEY,
  datacol VARCHAR(10) NOT NULL
);
```

The following code generates a new sequence value, stores it in a variable, and then uses the variable in an *INSERT* statement to insert a row into the table.

```
DECLARE @neworderid AS INT = NEXT VALUE FOR dbo.SeqOrderIDs;
INSERT INTO dbo.T1(keycol, datacol) VALUES(@neworderid, 'a');

SELECT * FROM dbo.T1;
```

This code returns the following output.

```
keycol      datacol
----------- ----------
2           a
```

If you need to use the new key in related rows that you need to insert into another table, you could use the variable in those *INSERT* statements as well.

If you don't need to generate the new sequence value before using it, you can specify the *NEXT VALUE FOR* function directly as part of your *INSERT* statement, like this.

```
INSERT INTO dbo.T1(keycol, datacol)
  VALUES(NEXT VALUE FOR dbo.SeqOrderIDs, 'b');

SELECT * FROM dbo.T1;
```

This code returns the following output.

```
keycol      datacol
----------- ----------
2           a
3           b
```

Unlike with identity, you can generate new sequence values in an *UPDATE* statement, like this.

```
UPDATE dbo.T1
  SET keycol = NEXT VALUE FOR dbo.SeqOrderIDs;

SELECT * FROM dbo.T1;
```

This code returns the following output.

```
keycol      datacol
----------- ----------
4           a
5           b
```

To get information about your sequences, query a view called *sys.sequences*. For example, to find the current sequence value in the *SeqOrderIDs* sequence, you would use the following code.

```
SELECT current_value
FROM sys.sequences
WHERE OBJECT_ID = OBJECT_ID('dbo.SeqOrderIDs');
```

This code generates the following output.

```
current_value
--------------
5
```

SQL Server extends its support for the sequence option with capabilities beyond what the competitors and the standard currently support. One of the extensions enables you to control the order of the assigned sequence values in a multi-row insert by using an *OVER* clause similar to the one window functions use. Here's an example.

```
INSERT INTO dbo.T1(keycol, datacol)
  SELECT
    NEXT VALUE FOR dbo.SeqOrderIDs OVER(ORDER BY hiredate),
    LEFT(firstname, 1) + LEFT(lastname, 1)
  FROM HR.Employees;

SELECT * FROM dbo.T1;
```

This code returns the following output.

```
keycol      datacol
----------- ----------
4           a
5           b
6           JL
7           SD
8           DF
9           YP
10          SB
11          PS
12          RK
13          MC
14          ZD
```

Another extension allows the use of the *NEXT VALUE FOR* function in a default constraint. Here's an example.

```
ALTER TABLE dbo.T1
  ADD CONSTRAINT DFT_T1_keycol
    DEFAULT (NEXT VALUE FOR dbo.SeqOrderIDs)
    FOR keycol;
```

Now when you insert rows into the table, you don't have to indicate a value for keycol.

```
INSERT INTO dbo.T1(datacol) VALUES('c');
```

```
SELECT * FROM dbo.T1;
```

This code returns the following output.

```
keycol      datacol
----------- ----------
4           a
5           b
6           JL
7           SD
8           DF
9           YP
10          SB
11          PS
12          RK
13          MC
14          ZD
15          C
```

This is a great advantage over identity—you can add a default constraint to an existing table and remove it from an existing table as well.

Finally, another extension allows you to allocate a whole range of sequence values at once by using a stored procedure called *sp_sequence_get_range*. The idea is that if the application needs to assign a range of sequence values, it is easiest to update the sequence only once, incrementing it by the size of the range. You call the procedure, indicate the size of the range you want, and collect the first value in the range, as well as other information, by using output parameters. Here's an example of calling the procedure and asking for a range of 1,000 sequence values.

```
DECLARE @first AS SQL_VARIANT;

EXEC sys.sp_sequence_get_range
  @sequence_name       = N'dbo.SeqOrderIDs',
  @range_size          = 1000,
  @range_first_value = @first OUTPUT ;

SELECT @first;
```

If you run the code twice, you will find that the returned first value in the second call is greater than the first by 1,000.

Note that like identity, the sequence object does not guarantee that you will have no gaps. If a new sequence value was generated by a transaction that failed, the sequence change is not undone.

When you're done, run the following code for cleanup.

```
IF OBJECT_ID('dbo.T1', 'U') IS NOT NULL DROP TABLE dbo.T1;
IF OBJECT_ID('dbo.SeqOrderIDs', 'So') IS NOT NULL DROP SEQUENCE dbo.SeqOrderIDs;
```

## Deleting Data

T-SQL provides two statements for deleting rows from a table—*DELETE* and *TRUNCATE*. In this section, I'll describe those statements. The examples I provide in this section are against copies of the *Customers* and *Orders* tables from the *Sales* schema created in the *dbo* schema. Run the following code to create and populate those tables.

```
IF OBJECT_ID('dbo.Orders', 'U') IS NOT NULL DROP TABLE dbo.Orders;
IF OBJECT_ID('dbo.Customers', 'U') IS NOT NULL DROP TABLE dbo.Customers;

CREATE TABLE dbo.Customers
(
  custid       INT          NOT NULL,
  companyname  NVARCHAR(40) NOT NULL,
  contactname  NVARCHAR(30) NOT NULL,
  contacttitle NVARCHAR(30) NOT NULL,
  address      NVARCHAR(60) NOT NULL,
  city         NVARCHAR(15) NOT NULL,
  region       NVARCHAR(15) NULL,
  postalcode   NVARCHAR(10) NULL,
  country      NVARCHAR(15) NOT NULL,
  phone        NVARCHAR(24) NOT NULL,
  fax          NVARCHAR(24) NULL,
  CONSTRAINT PK_Customers PRIMARY KEY(custid)
);
```

```
CREATE TABLE dbo.Orders
(
  orderid         INT          NOT NULL,
  custid          INT          NULL,
  empid           INT          NOT NULL,
  orderdate       DATETIME     NOT NULL,
  requireddate    DATETIME     NOT NULL,
  shippeddate     DATETIME     NULL,
  shipperid       INT          NOT NULL,
  freight         MONEY        NOT NULL
    CONSTRAINT DFT_Orders_freight DEFAULT(0),
  shipname        NVARCHAR(40) NOT NULL,
  shipaddress     NVARCHAR(60) NOT NULL,
  shipcity        NVARCHAR(15) NOT NULL,
  shipregion      NVARCHAR(15) NULL,
  shippostalcode  NVARCHAR(10) NULL,
  shipcountry     NVARCHAR(15) NOT NULL,
  CONSTRAINT PK_Orders PRIMARY KEY(orderid),
  CONSTRAINT FK_Orders_Customers FOREIGN KEY(custid)
    REFERENCES dbo.Customers(custid)
);
GO

INSERT INTO dbo.Customers SELECT * FROM Sales.Customers;
INSERT INTO dbo.Orders SELECT * FROM Sales.Orders;
```

## The *DELETE* Statement

The *DELETE* statement is a standard statement used to delete data from a table based on a predicate. The standard statement has only two clauses—the *FROM* clause, in which you specify the target table name, and a *WHERE* clause, in which you specify a predicate. Only the subset of rows for which the predicate evaluates to *TRUE* will be deleted.

For example, the following statement deletes, from the *dbo.Orders* table, all orders that were placed prior to 2007.

```
DELETE FROM dbo.Orders
WHERE orderdate < '20070101';
```

Run this statement. SQL Server will report that it deleted 152 rows.

```
(152 row(s) affected)
```

Note that the message indicating the number of rows that were affected appears only if the *NOCOUNT* session option is *OFF*, which it is by default. If it is *ON*, SQL Server Management Studio will only state that the command completed successfully.

The *DELETE* statement is fully logged. Therefore, you should expect it to run for a while when you delete a large number of rows.

# The *TRUNCATE* Statement

The *TRUNCATE* statement deletes all rows from a table. Unlike the *DELETE* statement, *TRUNCATE* has no filter. For example, to delete all rows from a table called *dbo.T1*, you run the following code.

```
TRUNCATE TABLE dbo.T1;
```

The advantage that *TRUNCATE* has over *DELETE* is that the former is minimally logged, whereas the latter is fully logged, resulting in significant performance differences. For example, if you use the *TRUNCATE* statement to delete all rows from a table with millions of rows, the operation will finish in a matter of seconds. If you use the *DELETE* statement, the operation can take minutes or even hours. Note that I said that *TRUNCATE* is *minimally* logged, as opposed to not being logged at all. This means that it's fully transactional (despite the common misconception), and in case of a *ROLLBACK*, SQL Server can undo the truncation.

*TRUNCATE* and *DELETE* also have a functional difference when the table has an identity column. *TRUNCATE* resets the identity value back to the original seed, but *DELETE* doesn't.

The *TRUNCATE* statement is not allowed when the target table is referenced by a foreign key constraint, even if the referencing table is empty and even if the foreign key is disabled. The only way to allow a *TRUNCATE* statement is to drop all foreign keys referencing the table.

Accidents such as truncating or dropping the incorrect table can happen. For example, let's say you have connections open against both the production and the development environments, and you submit your code in the wrong connection. Both the *TRUNCATE* and *DROP* statements are so fast that before you realize your mistake, the transaction is committed. To prevent such accidents, you can protect a production table by simply creating a dummy table with a foreign key pointing to the production table. You can even disable the foreign key so that it won't have any impact on performance. As I mentioned earlier, even when disabled, this foreign key prevents you from truncating or dropping the referenced table.

# *DELETE* Based on a Join

T-SQL supports a nonstandard *DELETE* syntax based on joins. The join itself serves a filtering purpose because it has a filter based on a predicate (the *ON* clause). The join also gives you access to attributes of related rows from another table that you can refer to in the *WHERE* clause. This means that you can delete rows from one table based on a filter against attributes in related rows from another table.

For example, the following statement deletes orders placed by customers from the United States.

```
DELETE FROM O
FROM dbo.Orders AS O
  JOIN dbo.Customers AS C
    ON O.custid = C.custid
WHERE C.country = N'USA';
```

Very much like in a *SELECT* statement, the first clause that is logically processed in a *DELETE* statement is the *FROM* clause (the second one that appears in this statement). Then the *WHERE* clause is processed, and finally the *DELETE* clause. The way to "read" or interpret this query is, "The query joins the *Orders* table (aliased as *O*) with the *Customers* table (aliased as *C*) based on a match between the order's customer ID and the customer's customer ID. The query then filters only orders placed by customers from the United States. Finally, the query deletes all qualifying rows from *O* (the alias representing the *Orders* table)."

The two *FROM* clauses in a *DELETE* statement based on a join might be confusing. But when you develop the code, develop it as if it were a *SELECT* statement with a join. That is, start with the *FROM* clause with the joins, move on to the *WHERE* clause, and finally, instead of specifying a *SELECT* clause, specify a *DELETE* clause with the alias of the side of the join that is supposed to be the target for the deletion.

As I mentioned earlier, a *DELETE* statement based on a join is nonstandard. If you want to stick to standard code, you can use subqueries instead of joins. For example, the following *DELETE* statement uses a subquery to achieve the same task.

```
DELETE FROM dbo.Orders
WHERE EXISTS
  (SELECT *
   FROM dbo.Customers AS C
   WHERE Orders.Custid = C.Custid
     AND C.Country = 'USA');
```

This code deletes all rows from the *Orders* table for which a related customer in the *Customers* table from the United States exists.

SQL Server will most likely process the two queries the same way; therefore, you shouldn't expect any performance difference between the two. So why do people even consider using the nonstandard syntax? Some people feel more comfortable with joins, whereas others feel more comfortable with subqueries. I usually recommend sticking to the standard as much as possible unless you have a very compelling reason to do otherwise—for example, in the case of a big performance difference.

When you're done, run the following code for cleanup.

```
IF OBJECT_ID('dbo.Orders', 'U') IS NOT NULL DROP TABLE dbo.Orders;
IF OBJECT_ID('dbo.Customers', 'U') IS NOT NULL DROP TABLE dbo.Customers;
```

# Updating Data

T-SQL supports a standard *UPDATE* statement that allows you to update rows in a table. T-SQL also supports nonstandard uses of the *UPDATE* statement with joins and with variables. This section describes the various uses of the *UPDATE* statement.

The examples I provide in this section are against copies of the *Orders* and *OrderDetails* tables from the *Sales* schema created in the *dbo* schema. Run the following code to create and populate those tables.

```
IF OBJECT_ID('dbo.OrderDetails', 'U') IS NOT NULL DROP TABLE dbo.OrderDetails;
IF OBJECT_ID('dbo.Orders', 'U') IS NOT NULL DROP TABLE dbo.Orders;

CREATE TABLE dbo.Orders
(
  orderid        INT           NOT NULL,
  custid         INT           NULL,
  empid          INT           NOT NULL,
  orderdate      DATETIME      NOT NULL,
  requireddate   DATETIME      NOT NULL,
  shippeddate    DATETIME      NULL,
  shipperid      INT           NOT NULL,
  freight        MONEY         NOT NULL
    CONSTRAINT DFT_Orders_freight DEFAULT(0),
  shipname       NVARCHAR(40) NOT NULL,
  shipaddress    NVARCHAR(60) NOT NULL,
  shipcity       NVARCHAR(15) NOT NULL,
  shipregion     NVARCHAR(15) NULL,
  shippostalcode NVARCHAR(10) NULL,
  shipcountry    NVARCHAR(15) NOT NULL,
  CONSTRAINT PK_Orders PRIMARY KEY(orderid)
);

CREATE TABLE dbo.OrderDetails
(
  orderid   INT              NOT NULL,
  productid INT              NOT NULL,
  unitprice MONEY            NOT NULL
    CONSTRAINT DFT_OrderDetails_unitprice DEFAULT(0),
  qty       SMALLINT         NOT NULL
    CONSTRAINT DFT_OrderDetails_qty DEFAULT(1),
  discount  NUMERIC(4, 3) NOT NULL
    CONSTRAINT DFT_OrderDetails_discount DEFAULT(0),
  CONSTRAINT PK_OrderDetails PRIMARY KEY(orderid, productid),
  CONSTRAINT FK_OrderDetails_Orders FOREIGN KEY(orderid)
    REFERENCES dbo.Orders(orderid),
  CONSTRAINT CHK_discount  CHECK (discount BETWEEN 0 AND 1),
  CONSTRAINT CHK_qty  CHECK (qty > 0),
  CONSTRAINT CHK_unitprice CHECK (unitprice >= 0)
);
GO

INSERT INTO dbo.Orders SELECT * FROM Sales.Orders;
INSERT INTO dbo.OrderDetails SELECT * FROM Sales.OrderDetails;
```

# The *UPDATE* Statement

The *UPDATE* statement is a standard statement that allows you to update a subset of rows in a table. To identify the subset of rows that are the target of the update, you specify a predicate in a *WHERE* clause. You specify the assignment of values or expressions to columns in a *SET* clause, separated by commas.

For example, the following *UPDATE* statement increases the discount of all order details for product 51 by 5 percent.

```
UPDATE dbo.OrderDetails
  SET discount = discount + 0.05
WHERE productid = 51;
```

Of course, you can run a *SELECT* statement with the same filter before and after the update to see the changes. Later in this chapter, I'll show you another way to see the changes, by using a clause called *OUTPUT* that you can add to modification statements.

SQL Server 2008 and SQL Server 2012 support compound assignment operators: += (plus equal), −= (minus equal), *= (multiplication equal), /= (division equal), and %= (modulo equal), allowing you to shorten assignment expressions such as the one in the preceding query. Instead of the expression *discount = discount + 0.05*, you can use the shorter form: *discount += 0.05*. The full *UPDATE* statement looks like this.

```
UPDATE dbo.OrderDetails
  SET discount += 0.05
WHERE productid = 51;
```

All-at-once operations are an important aspect of SQL that you should keep in mind when writing *UPDATE* statements. I explained the concept in Chapter 2, "Single-Table Queries," in the context of *SELECT* statements, but it's just as applicable with *UPDATE* statements. Remember the concept that says that all expressions in the same logical phase are evaluated logically at the same point in time. To understand the relevance of this concept, consider the following *UPDATE* statement.

```
UPDATE dbo.T1
  SET col1 = col1 + 10, col2 = col1 + 10;
```

Suppose that one row in the table has the values 100 in *col1* and 200 in *col2* prior to the update. Can you determine the values of those columns after the update?

If you do not consider the all-at-once concept, you would think that *col1* will be set to 110 and *col2* to 120, as if the assignments were performed from left to right. However, the assignments take place all at once, meaning that both assignments use the same value of *col1*—the value before the update. The result of this update is that both *col1* and *col2* will end up with the value 110.

With the concept of all-at-once in mind, can you figure out how to write an *UPDATE* statement that swaps the values in the columns *col1* and *col2*? In most programming languages where expressions and assignments are evaluated in some order (typically left to right), you need a temporary variable. However, because in SQL all assignments take place as if at the same point in time, the solution is very simple.

```
UPDATE dbo.T1
  SET col1 = col2, col2 = col1;
```

In both assignments, the source column values used are those prior to the update, so you don't need a temporary variable.

## UPDATE Based on a Join

Similar to the DELETE statement, the UPDATE statement is also supported by T-SQL in a nonstandard syntax for statements based on joins. As with DELETE statements, the join serves a filtering purpose.

The syntax is very similar to a SELECT statement based on a join; that is, the FROM and WHERE clauses are the same, but instead of the SELECT clause, you specify an UPDATE clause. The UPDATE keyword is followed by the alias of the table that is the target of the update (you can't update more than one table in the same statement), followed by the SET clause with the column assignments.

For example, the UPDATE statement in Listing 8-1 increases the discount of all order details of orders placed by customer 1 by 5 percent.

**LISTING 8-1** UPDATE Based on a Join

```
UPDATE OD
  SET discount += 0.05
FROM dbo.OrderDetails AS OD
  JOIN dbo.Orders AS O
    ON OD.orderid = O.orderid
WHERE O.custid = 1;
```

To "read" or interpret the query, start with the FROM clause, move on to the WHERE clause, and finally go to the UPDATE clause. The query joins the OrderDetails table (aliased as OD) with the Orders table (aliased as O) based on a match between the order detail's order ID and the order's order ID. The query then filters only the rows where the order's customer ID is 1. The query then specifies in the UPDATE clause that OD (the alias of the OrderDetails table) is the target of the update, and increases the discount by 5 percent.

If you want to achieve the same task by using standard code, you would need to use a subquery instead of a join, like this.

```
UPDATE dbo.OrderDetails
  SET discount += 0.05
WHERE EXISTS
  (SELECT * FROM dbo.Orders AS O
   WHERE O.orderid = OrderDetails.orderid
     AND O.custid = 1);
```

The query's WHERE clause filters only order details in which a related order is placed by customer 1. With this particular task, SQL Server will most likely interpret both versions the same way; therefore, you shouldn't expect performance differences between the two. Again, the version you feel more comfortable with probably depends on whether you feel more comfortable with joins or subqueries. But as I mentioned earlier in regard to the DELETE statement, I recommend sticking to standard code unless you have a compelling reason to do otherwise. With the current task, I do not see a compelling reason.

However, in some cases, the join version will have a performance advantage over the subquery version. In addition to filtering, the join also gives you access to attributes from other tables that you can use in the column assignments in the *SET* clause. The same access to the other table can allow you to both filter and obtain attribute values from the other table for the assignments. However, with the subquery approach, each subquery involves a separate access to the other table—that's at least the way subqueries are processed today by SQL Server's engine.

For example, consider the following nonstandard *UPDATE* statement based on a join.

```
UPDATE T1
  SET col1 = T2.col1,
      col2 = T2.col2,
      col3 = T2.col3
FROM dbo.T1 JOIN dbo.T2
  ON T2.keycol = T1.keycol
WHERE T2.col4 = 'ABC';
```

This statement joins the tables *T1* and *T2* based on a match between *T1.keycol* and *T2.keycol*. The *WHERE* clause filters only rows where *T2.col4* is equal to 'ABC'. The *UPDATE* statement marks the *T1* table as the target for the *UPDATE*, and the *SET* clause sets the values of the columns *col1*, *col2*, and *col3* in *T1* to the values of the corresponding columns from *T2*.

An attempt to express this task by using standard code with subqueries yields the following lengthy query.

```
UPDATE dbo.T1
  SET col1 = (SELECT col1
                FROM dbo.T2
                WHERE T2.keycol = T1.keycol),

      col2 = (SELECT col2
                FROM dbo.T2
                WHERE T2.keycol = T1.keycol),

      col3 = (SELECT col3
                FROM dbo.T2
                WHERE T2.keycol = T1.keycol)
WHERE EXISTS
  (SELECT *
   FROM dbo.T2
   WHERE T2.keycol = T1.keycol
     AND T2.col4 = 'ABC');
```

Not only is this version convoluted (unlike the join version), but each subquery also involves separate access to table *T2*. So this version is less efficient than the join version.

Standard SQL has support for *row constructors* (also known as *vector expressions*) that were only implemented partially as of SQL Server 2012. Many aspects of row constructors have not yet been implemented in SQL Server, including the ability to use them in the *SET* clause of an *UPDATE* statement like this.

```
UPDATE dbo.T1

  SET (col1, col2, col3) =

      (SELECT col1, col2, col3
       FROM dbo.T2
       WHERE T2.keycol = T1.keycol)

WHERE EXISTS
  (SELECT *
   FROM dbo.T2
   WHERE T2.keycol = T1.keycol
     AND T2.col4 = 'ABC');
```

But as you can see, this version would still be more complicated than the join version, because it requires separate subqueries for the filtering part and for obtaining the attributes from the other table for the assignments.

## Assignment *UPDATE*

T-SQL supports a proprietary *UPDATE* syntax that both updates data in a table and assigns values to variables at the same time. This syntax saves you the need to use separate *UPDATE* and *SELECT* statements to achieve the same task.

One of the common cases for which you can use this syntax is in maintaining a custom sequence/autonumbering mechanism when the identity column property and the sequence object don't work for you. One example where this might be the case is if you need a sequencing mechanism that guarantees no gaps. The idea is to keep the last-used value in a table, and to use this special *UPDATE* syntax to increment the value in the table and assign the new value to a variable.

Run the following code to first create the *Sequence* table with the column *val*, and then populate it with a single row with the value 0—one less than the first value that you want to use.

```
IF OBJECT_ID('dbo.Sequences', 'U') IS NOT NULL DROP TABLE dbo.Sequences;

CREATE TABLE dbo.Sequences
(
  id VARCHAR(10) NOT NULL
    CONSTRAINT PK_Sequences PRIMARY KEY(id),
  val INT NOT NULL
);
INSERT INTO dbo.Sequences VALUES('SEQ1', 0);
```

Now, whenever you need to obtain a new sequence value, use the following code.

```
DECLARE @nextval AS INT;

UPDATE dbo.Sequences
  SET @nextval = val += 1
WHERE id = 'SEQ1';

SELECT @nextval;
```

The code declares a local variable called *@nextval*. Then it uses the special *UPDATE* syntax to incre-ment the column value by 1, assigns the updated column value to the variable, and presents the value in the variable. The assignments in the *SET* clause take place from right to left. That is, first *val* is set to *val* + 1, then the result (*val* + 1) is set to the variable *@nextval*.

The specialized *UPDATE* syntax is run as an atomic operation, and it is more efficient than using separate *UPDATE* and *SELECT* statements because it accesses the data only once.

When you're done, run the following code for cleanup.

```
IF OBJECT_ID('dbo.Sequences', 'U') IS NOT NULL DROP TABLE dbo.Sequences;
```

# Merging Data

SQL Server 2008 and SQL Server 2012 support a statement called *MERGE* that allows you to modify data, applying different actions (*INSERT*, *UPDATE*, and *DELETE*) based on conditional logic. The *MERGE* statement is part of the SQL standard, although the T-SQL version adds a few nonstandard extensions to the statement.

A task achieved by a single *MERGE* statement will typically translate to a combination of several other DML statements (*INSERT*, *UPDATE*, and *DELETE*) without *MERGE*. The benefit of using *MERGE* over the alternatives is that it allows you to express the request with less code and run it more ef-ficiently because it requires fewer accesses to the tables involved.

To demonstrate the *MERGE* statement, I'll use tables called *dbo.Customers* and *dbo.Customers-Stage*. Run the code in Listing 8-2 to create those tables and populate them with sample data.

**LISTING 8-2** Code That Creates and Populates *Customers* and *CustomersStage*

```
IF OBJECT_ID('dbo.Customers', 'U') IS NOT NULL DROP TABLE dbo.Customers;
GO

CREATE TABLE dbo.Customers
(
  custid      INT         NOT NULL,
  companyname VARCHAR(25) NOT NULL,
  phone       VARCHAR(20) NOT NULL,
  address     VARCHAR(50) NOT NULL,
  CONSTRAINT PK_Customers PRIMARY KEY(custid)
);
```

```
INSERT INTO dbo.Customers(custid, companyname, phone, address)
VALUES
  (1, 'cust 1', '(111) 111-1111', 'address 1'),
  (2, 'cust 2', '(222) 222-2222', 'address 2'),
  (3, 'cust 3', '(333) 333-3333', 'address 3'),
  (4, 'cust 4', '(444) 444-4444', 'address 4'),
  (5, 'cust 5', '(555) 555-5555', 'address 5');

IF OBJECT_ID('dbo.CustomersStage', 'U') IS NOT NULL DROP TABLE dbo.
CustomersStage;
GO

CREATE TABLE dbo.CustomersStage
(
  custid       INT         NOT NULL,
  companyname  VARCHAR(25) NOT NULL,
  phone        VARCHAR(20) NOT NULL,
  address      VARCHAR(50) NOT NULL,
  CONSTRAINT PK_CustomersStage PRIMARY KEY(custid)
);

INSERT INTO dbo.CustomersStage(custid, companyname, phone, address)
VALUES
  (2, 'AAAAA', '(222) 222-2222', 'address 2'),
  (3, 'cust 3', '(333) 333-3333', 'address 3'),
  (5, 'BBBBB', 'CCCCC', 'DDDDD'),
  (6, 'cust 6 (new)', '(666) 666-6666', 'address 6'),
  (7, 'cust 7 (new)', '(777) 777-7777', 'address 7');
```

Run the following query to examine the contents of the *Customers* table.

```
SELECT * FROM dbo.Customers;
```

This query returns the following output.

```
custid      companyname       phone                 address
----------- ----------------- --------------------- ------------
1           cust 1            (111) 111-1111        address 1
2           cust 2            (222) 222-2222        address 2
3           cust 3            (333) 333-3333        address 3
4           cust 4            (444) 444-4444        address 4
5           cust 5            (555) 555-5555        address 5
```

Run the following query to examine the contents of the *CustomersStage* table.

```
SELECT * FROM dbo.CustomersStage;
```

This query returns the following output.

```
custid        companyname        phone                    address
-----------   ----------------   --------------------     ------------
2             AAAAA              (222) 222-2222           address 2
3             cust 3             (333) 333-3333           address 3
5             BBBBB              CCCCC                    DDDDD
6             cust 6 (new)       (666) 666-6666           address 6
7             cust 7 (new)       (777) 777-7777           address 7
```

The purpose of the first example of the *MERGE* statement that I'll demonstrate is to merge the contents of the *CustomersStage* table (the source) into the *Customers* table (the target). More specifically, the example will add customers that do not exist, and update the attributes of customers that already exist.

If you already feel comfortable with the sections that covered deletions and updates based on joins, you should feel quite comfortable with *MERGE*, which is based on join semantics. You specify the target table name in the *MERGE* clause and the source table name in the *USING* clause. You define a merge condition by specifying a predicate in the *ON* clause, very much as you do in a join. The merge condition defines which rows in the source table have matches in the target and which don't. You define the action to take when a match is found in a clause called *WHEN MATCHED THEN*, and the action to take when a match is not found in the *WHEN NOT MATCHED THEN* clause.

Here's the first example for the *MERGE* statement: adding nonexistent customers and updating existing ones.

```
MERGE INTO dbo.Customers AS TGT
USING dbo.CustomersStage AS SRC
  ON TGT.custid = SRC.custid
WHEN MATCHED THEN
  UPDATE SET
    TGT.companyname = SRC.companyname,
    TGT.phone = SRC.phone,
    TGT.address = SRC.address
WHEN NOT MATCHED THEN
  INSERT (custid, companyname, phone, address)
  VALUES (SRC.custid, SRC.companyname, SRC.phone, SRC.address);
```

**Note** It is mandatory to terminate the *MERGE* statement with a semicolon, whereas in most other statements in T-SQL, this is optional. But if you follow best practices to terminate all statements with a semicolon (as I mentioned earlier in this book), this shouldn't concern you.

This *MERGE* statement defines the *Customers* table as the target (in the *MERGE* clause) and the *CustomersStage* table as the source (in the *USING* clause). Notice that you can assign aliases to the target and source tables for brevity (TGT and SRC in this case). The predicate *TGT.custid = SRC.custid* is used to define what is considered a match and what is considered a nonmatch. In this case, if a customer ID that exists in the source also exists in the target, that's a match. If a customer ID in the source does not exist in the target, that's a nonmatch.

The *MERGE* statement defines an *UPDATE* action when a match is found, setting the target *companyname*, *phone*, and *address* values to those of the corresponding row from the source. Notice that the syntax of the *UPDATE* action is similar to a normal *UPDATE* statement, except that you don't need to provide the name of the table that is the target of the update because it was already defined in the *MERGE* clause.

The *MERGE* statement defines an *INSERT* action when a match is not found, inserting the row from the source to the target. Again, the syntax of the *INSERT* action is similar to a normal *INSERT* statement, except that you don't need to provide the name of the table that is the target of the activity because it was already defined in the *MERGE* clause.

The *MERGE* statement reports that five rows were modified.

```
(5 row(s) affected)
```

This includes three rows that were updated (customers 2, 3, and 5) and two that were inserted (customers 6 and 7). Query the *Customers* table to get the new contents.

```
SELECT * FROM dbo.Customers;
```

This query returns the following output.

```
custid      companyname          phone                 address
----------  -------------------  --------------------  --------
1           cust 1               (111) 111-1111        address 1
2           AAAAA                (222) 222-2222        address 2
3           cust 3               (333) 333-3333        address 3
4           cust 4               (444) 444-4444        address 4
5           BBBBB                CCCCC                 DDDDD
6           cust 6 (new)         (666) 666-6666        address 6
7           cust 7 (new)         (777) 777-7777        address 7
```

The *WHEN MATCHED* clause defines what action to take when a source row is matched by a target row. The *WHEN NOT MATCHED* clause defines what action to take when a source row is not matched by a target row. T-SQL also supports a third clause that defines what action to take when a target row is not matched by a source row; this clause is called *WHEN NOT MATCHED BY SOURCE*. For example, suppose that you want to add logic to the *MERGE* example to delete rows from the target when the target row is not matched by a source row. All you need to do is add the *WHEN NOT MATCHED BY SOURCE* clause with a *DELETE* action, like this.

```
MERGE dbo.Customers AS TGT
USING dbo.CustomersStage AS SRC
  ON TGT.custid = SRC.custid
WHEN MATCHED THEN
  UPDATE SET
    TGT.companyname = SRC.companyname,
    TGT.phone = SRC.phone,
    TGT.address = SRC.address
WHEN NOT MATCHED THEN
  INSERT (custid, companyname, phone, address)
  VALUES (SRC.custid, SRC.companyname, SRC.phone, SRC.address)
WHEN NOT MATCHED BY SOURCE THEN
  DELETE;
```

Query the Customers table to see the result of this *MERGE* statement.

```
SELECT * FROM dbo.Customers;
```

This query returns the following output, showing that customers 1 and 4 were deleted.

```
custid       companyname          phone                 address
-----------  -------------------  --------------------  ----------
2            AAAAA                (222) 222-2222        address 2
3            cust 3               (333) 333-3333        address 3
5            BBBBB                CCCCC                 DDDDD
6            cust 6 (new)         (666) 666-6666        address 6
7            cust 7 (new)         (777) 777-7777        address 7
```

Going back to the first *MERGE* example, which updates existing customers and adds nonexistent ones, you can see that it is not written in the most efficient way. The statement doesn't check whether column values have actually changed before overwriting the attributes of an existing customer. This means that a customer row is modified even when the source and target rows are identical. You can address this by adding predicates to the different action clauses by using the *AND* option; except for the original condition, action will take place only if the additional predicate evaluates to *TRUE*. In this case, you need to add a predicate under the *WHEN MATCHED AND* clause that checks whether at least one of the attributes changed to justify the *UPDATE* action. The complete *MERGE* statement looks like this.

```
MERGE dbo.Customers AS TGT
USING dbo.CustomersStage AS SRC
  ON TGT.custid = SRC.custid
WHEN MATCHED AND
        (   TGT.companyname <> SRC.companyname
         OR TGT.phone       <> SRC.phone
         OR TGT.address      <> SRC.address) THEN
  UPDATE SET
    TGT.companyname = SRC.companyname,
    TGT.phone = SRC.phone,
    TGT.address = SRC.address
WHEN NOT MATCHED THEN
  INSERT (custid, companyname, phone, address)
  VALUES (SRC.custid, SRC.companyname, SRC.phone, SRC.address);
```

As you can see, the *MERGE* statement is very powerful, allowing you to express modification logic with less code and more efficiently than the alternatives.

# Modifying Data Through Table Expressions

SQL Server doesn't limit the actions against table expressions (derived tables, common table expressions [CTEs], views, and inline table-valued user-defined functions [UDFs]) to *SELECT* only, but also allows other DML statements (*INSERT*, *UPDATE*, *DELETE*, and *MERGE*) against those expressions. Think about it: a table expression doesn't really contain data—it's a reflection of underlying data in base tables. With this in mind, think of a modification against a table expression as modifying the data in the underlying tables through the table expression. Just as with a *SELECT* statement against a table expression, and also with a data modification statement, the definition of the table expression is expanded, so in practice the activity is done against the underlying tables.

Modifying data through table expressions has a few logical restrictions. For example:

- If the query defining the table expression joins tables, you're only allowed to affect one of the sides of the join and not both in the same modification statement.

- You cannot update a column that is a result of a calculation; SQL Server doesn't try to reverse-engineer the values.

- *INSERT* statements must specify values for any columns in the underlying table that do not have implicit values. A column can get a value implicitly if it allows *NULL* marks, has a default value, has an identity property, or is typed as *ROWVERSION*.

You can find other requirements in SQL Server Books Online, but as you can see, the requirements make sense.

Now that you know that you can modify data through table expressions, the question is, why would you want to? One reason is for better debugging and troubleshooting. For example, Listing 8-1 contained the following *UPDATE* statement.

```
UPDATE OD
  SET discount += 0.05
FROM dbo.OrderDetails AS OD
  JOIN dbo.Orders AS O
    ON OD.orderid = O.orderid
WHERE O.custid = 1;
```

Suppose that for troubleshooting purposes, you first want to see which rows would be modified by this statement without actually modifying them. One option is to revise the code to a *SELECT* statement, and after troubleshooting the code, change it back to an *UPDATE* statement. But instead of making such revisions back and forth between *SELECT* and *UPDATE* statements, you can simply use a table expression. That is, you can define a table expression based on a *SELECT* statement with the join query, and issue an *UPDATE* statement against the table expression. The following example uses a CTE.

```
WITH C AS
(
  SELECT custid, OD.orderid,
    productid, discount, discount + 0.05 AS newdiscount
  FROM dbo.OrderDetails AS OD
    JOIN dbo.Orders AS O
      ON OD.orderid = O.orderid
  WHERE O.custid = 1
)
UPDATE C
  SET discount = newdiscount;
```

And here's an example using a derived table.

```
UPDATE D
  SET discount = newdiscount
FROM ( SELECT custid, OD.orderid,
         productid, discount, discount + 0.05 AS newdiscount
       FROM dbo.OrderDetails AS OD
         JOIN dbo.Orders AS O
           ON OD.orderid = O.orderid
       WHERE O.custid = 1 ) AS D;
```

With the table expression, troubleshooting is simpler because you can always highlight just the *SELECT* statement that defines the table expression and run it without making any data changes. With this example, the use of table expressions is for convenience. However, with some problems, using a table expression is the only option. To demonstrate such a problem, I'll use a table called *T1* that you create and populate by running the following code.

```
IF OBJECT_ID('dbo.T1', 'U') IS NOT NULL DROP TABLE dbo.T1;
CREATE TABLE dbo.T1(col1 INT, col2 INT);
GO

INSERT INTO dbo.T1(col1) VALUES(10),(20),(30);

SELECT * FROM dbo.T1;
```

The *SELECT* statement returns the following output showing the current contents of the table *T1*.

```
col1        col2
----------- -----------
10          NULL
20          NULL
30          NULL
```

Suppose that you want to update the table, setting *col2* to the result of an expression with the *ROW_NUMBER* function. The problem is that the *ROW_NUMBER* function is not allowed in the SET clause of an *UPDATE* statement. Try running the following code.

```
UPDATE dbo.T1
  SET col2 = ROW_NUMBER() OVER(ORDER BY col1);
```

You get the following error.

```
Msg 4108, Level 15, State 1, Line 2
Windowed functions can only appear in the SELECT or ORDER BY clauses.
```

To get around this problem, define a table expression that returns both the column that you need to update (*col2*) and a result column based on an expression with the *ROW_NUMBER* function (call it *rownum*). The outer statement against the table expression would then be an *UPDATE* statement setting *col2* to *rownum*. Here's how the code would look if you were using a CTE.

```
WITH C AS
(
  SELECT col1, col2, ROW_NUMBER() OVER(ORDER BY col1) AS rownum
  FROM dbo.T1
)
UPDATE C
  SET col2 = rownum;
```

Query the table to see the result of the update.

```
SELECT * FROM dbo.T1;
```

You get the following output.

```
col1        col2
----------- -----------
10          1
20          2
30          3
```

# Modifications with *TOP* and *OFFSET-FETCH*

SQL Server supports using the *TOP* option directly in *INSERT, UPDATE, DELETE*, and *MERGE* statements. When you use the *TOP* option, SQL Server stops processing the modification statement as soon as the specified number or percentage of rows are processed. Unfortunately, unlike with the *SELECT* statement, you cannot specify an *ORDER BY* clause for the *TOP* option with modification statements. Essentially, whichever rows SQL Server happens to access first will be the rows affected by the modification.

An example for a typical usage scenario for modifications with *TOP* is when you have a large modification, such as a large deletion operation, and you want to split it into multiple smaller chunks.

The new alternative to *TOP, OFFSET-FETCH*, is considered to be part of the *ORDER BY* clause in T-SQL. Because modification statements do not support an *ORDER BY* clause, they do not support the *OFFSET-FETCH* option either—at least not directly.

I'll demonstrate modifications with *TOP* by using a table called *dbo.Orders* that you create and populate by running the following code.

```
IF OBJECT_ID('dbo.OrderDetails', 'U') IS NOT NULL DROP TABLE dbo.OrderDetails;
IF OBJECT_ID('dbo.Orders', 'U') IS NOT NULL DROP TABLE dbo.Orders;

CREATE TABLE dbo.Orders
(
  orderid         INT           NOT NULL,
  custid          INT           NULL,
  empid           INT           NOT NULL,
  orderdate       DATETIME      NOT NULL,
  requireddate    DATETIME      NOT NULL,
  shippeddate     DATETIME      NULL,
  shipperid       INT           NOT NULL,
  freight         MONEY         NOT NULL
    CONSTRAINT DFT_Orders_freight DEFAULT(0),
  shipname        NVARCHAR(40)  NOT NULL,
  shipaddress     NVARCHAR(60)  NOT NULL,
  shipcity        NVARCHAR(15)  NOT NULL,
  shipregion      NVARCHAR(15)  NULL,
  shippostalcode  NVARCHAR(10)  NULL,
  shipcountry     NVARCHAR(15)  NOT NULL,
  CONSTRAINT PK_Orders PRIMARY KEY(orderid)
);
GO

INSERT INTO dbo.Orders SELECT * FROM Sales.Orders;
```

The following example demonstrates the use of a *DELETE* statement with the *TOP* option to delete 50 rows from the *Orders* table.

```
DELETE TOP(50) FROM dbo.Orders;
```

Because you are not allowed to specify a logical *ORDER BY* for the *TOP* option in a modification statement, this query is problematic in the sense that you can't control which 50 rows will be deleted. They will be the first 50 rows from the table that SQL Server happens to access first. This problem demonstrates the limitations of using *TOP* for modifications.

Similarly, you can use the *TOP* option with *UPDATE* and *INSERT* statements, but again, an *ORDER BY* is not allowed. As an example of an *UPDATE* statement with *TOP*, the following code updates 50 rows from the *Orders* table, increasing their *freight* values by 10.

```
UPDATE TOP(50) dbo.Orders
  SET freight += 10.00;
```

Again, you cannot control which 50 rows will be updated; they are the first 50 rows that SQL Server happens to access first.

In practice, of course, you would usually care which rows are affected and you wouldn't want them to be chosen arbitrarily. To get around this problem, you can rely on the fact that you can modify data through table expressions. You can define a table expression based on a *SELECT* query with the

*TOP* option based on a logical *ORDER BY* clause that defines precedence among rows. You can then issue the modification statement against the table expression.

For example, the following code deletes the 50 orders with the lowest order ID values rather than just any 50 rows.

```
WITH C AS
(
  SELECT TOP(50) *
  FROM dbo.Orders
  ORDER BY orderid
)
DELETE FROM C;
```

Similarly, the following code updates the 50 orders with the highest order ID values, increasing their *freight* values by 10.

```
WITH C AS
(
  SELECT TOP(50) *
  FROM dbo.Orders
  ORDER BY orderid DESC
)
UPDATE C
  SET freight += 10.00;
```

In SQL Server 2012, you can use the *OFFSET-FETCH* option instead of *TOP* in the inner *SELECT* queries. Here's the revised *DELETE* example.

```
WITH C AS
(
  SELECT *
  FROM dbo.Orders
  ORDER BY orderid
  OFFSET 0 ROWS FETCH FIRST 50 ROWS ONLY
)
DELETE FROM C;
```

And here's the revised *UPDATE* example.

```
WITH C AS
(
  SELECT *
  FROM dbo.Orders
  ORDER BY orderid DESC
  OFFSET 0 ROWS FETCH FIRST 50 ROWS ONLY
)
UPDATE C
  SET freight += 10.00;
```

# The *OUTPUT* Clause

Normally, you would not expect a modification statement to do more than modify data. That is, you would not expect a modification statement to return any output. However, in some scenarios, being able to get data back from the modified rows can be useful. For example, think about the advantages of requesting an *UPDATE* statement to not only modify data, but to also return the old and new values of the updated columns. This can be useful for troubleshooting, auditing, and other purposes.

SQL Server supports this capability via a clause called *OUTPUT* that you add to the modification statement. In this *OUTPUT* clause, you specify the attributes and expressions that you want to return from the modified rows.

You can think of the *OUTPUT* clause in terms very similar to those you use to think about the *SELECT* clause. That is, you list the attributes and expressions based on existing attributes that you want to return. What's special in terms of the *OUTPUT* clause syntax is that you need to prefix the attribute names with either the *inserted* or the *deleted* keyword. In an *INSERT* statement, you refer to *inserted*; in a *DELETE* statement, you refer to *deleted*; and in an *UPDATE* statement, you refer to *deleted* when you're after the image of the row before the change and *inserted* when you're after the image of the row after the change.

The *OUTPUT* clause will return the requested attributes from the modified rows as a result set, very much like a *SELECT* statement does. If you want to direct the result set to a table, add an *INTO* clause with the target table name. If you want to return modified rows back to the caller and also direct a copy to a table, specify two *OUTPUT* clauses—one with the *INTO* clause and one without it.

The following sections provide examples of using the *OUTPUT* clause with the different modification statements.

## *INSERT* with *OUTPUT*

An example of an *INSERT* statement for which the *OUTPUT* clause can be useful is when you need to insert a row set into a table with an identity column, and you need to get back all identity values that were generated. The *SCOPE_IDENTITY* function returns only the very last identity value that was generated by your session; it doesn't help you much in obtaining all identity values that were generated by an insert of a row set. The *OUTPUT* clause makes the task very simple. To demonstrate the technique, first create a table called *T1* with an identity column called *keycol* and another column called *datacol* by running the following code.

```
IF OBJECT_ID('dbo.T1', 'U') IS NOT NULL DROP TABLE dbo.T1;

CREATE TABLE dbo.T1
(
  keycol  INT           NOT NULL IDENTITY(1, 1) CONSTRAINT PK_T1 PRIMARY KEY,
  datacol NVARCHAR(40) NOT NULL
);
```

Suppose you want to insert into *T1* the result of a query against the *HR.Employees* table. To return all newly generated identity values from the *INSERT* statement, simply add the *OUTPUT* clause and specify the attributes you want to return.

```
INSERT INTO dbo.T1(datacol)
  OUTPUT inserted.keycol, inserted.datacol
    SELECT lastname
    FROM HR.Employees
    WHERE country = N'USA';
```

This statement returns the following result set.

```
keycol      datacol
----------- ---------
1           Davis
2           Funk
3           Lew
4           Peled
5           Cameron

(5 row(s) affected)
```

As you can guess, you can use a similar technique to return sequence values generated for an *INSERT* statement by the *NEXT VALUE FOR* function (either directly or in a default constraint).

As I mentioned earlier, you can also direct the result set into a table. The table can be a real table, a temporary table, or a table variable. When the result set is stored in the target table, you can manipulate the data by querying that table. For example, the following code declares a table variable called *@NewRows*, inserts another result set into *T1*, and directs the result set returned by the *OUTPUT* clause into the table variable. The code then queries the table variable just to show the data that was stored in it.

```
DECLARE @NewRows TABLE(keycol INT, datacol NVARCHAR(40));

INSERT INTO dbo.T1(datacol)
  OUTPUT inserted.keycol, inserted.datacol
  INTO @NewRows
    SELECT lastname
    FROM HR.Employees
    WHERE country = N'UK';

SELECT * FROM @NewRows;
```

This code returns the following output showing the contents of the table variable.

```
keycol      datacol
----------- -------------
6           Buck
7           Suurs
8           King
9           Dolgopyatova

(4 row(s) affected)
```

## DELETE with OUTPUT

The next example demonstrates the use of the *OUTPUT* clause with a *DELETE* statement. First, run the following code to create a copy of the *Orders* table from the *Sales* schema in the *dbo* schema.

```
IF OBJECT_ID('dbo.Orders', 'U') IS NOT NULL DROP TABLE dbo.Orders;

CREATE TABLE dbo.Orders
(
  orderid         INT           NOT NULL,
  custid          INT           NULL,
  empid           INT           NOT NULL,
  orderdate       DATETIME      NOT NULL,
  requireddate    DATETIME      NOT NULL,
  shippeddate     DATETIME      NULL,
  shipperid       INT           NOT NULL,
  freight         MONEY         NOT NULL
    CONSTRAINT DFT_Orders_freight DEFAULT(0),
  shipname        NVARCHAR(40) NOT NULL,
  shipaddress     NVARCHAR(60) NOT NULL,
  shipcity        NVARCHAR(15) NOT NULL,
  shipregion      NVARCHAR(15) NULL,
  shippostalcode NVARCHAR(10) NULL,
  shipcountry     NVARCHAR(15) NOT NULL,
  CONSTRAINT PK_Orders PRIMARY KEY(orderid)
);
GO

INSERT INTO dbo.Orders SELECT * FROM Sales.Orders;
```

The following code deletes all orders that were placed prior to 2008 and, using the *OUTPUT* clause, returns attributes from the deleted rows.

```
DELETE FROM dbo.Orders
  OUTPUT
    deleted.orderid,
    deleted.orderdate,
    deleted.empid,
    deleted.custid
WHERE orderdate < '20080101';
```

This *DELETE* statement returns the following result set.

```
orderid     orderdate                   empid       custid
----------- --------------------------- ----------- -----------
10248       2006-07-04 00:00:00.000     5           85
10249       2006-07-05 00:00:00.000     6           79
10250       2006-07-08 00:00:00.000     4           34
10251       2006-07-08 00:00:00.000     3           84
10252       2006-07-09 00:00:00.000     4           76
...
10400       2007-01-01 00:00:00.000     1           19
10401       2007-01-01 00:00:00.000     1           65
10402       2007-01-02 00:00:00.000     8           20
```

```
10403       2007-01-03 00:00:00.000    4       20
10404       2007-01-03 00:00:00.000    2       49
...
```

```
(560 row(s) affected)
```

If you want to archive the rows that are deleted, simply add an *INTO* clause and specify the archive table name as the target.

## UPDATE with OUTPUT

By using the *OUTPUT* clause with an *UPDATE* statement, you can refer to both the image of the modified row before the change (by prefixing the attribute names with the *deleted* keyword) and to the image after the change (by prefixing the attribute names with the *inserted* keyword). This way, you can return both old and new images of the updated attributes.

Before I demonstrate how to use the *OUTPUT* clause in an *UPDATE* statement, you should first run the following code to create a copy of the *Sales.OrderDetails* table from the *Sales* schema in the *dbo* schema.

```
IF OBJECT_ID('dbo.OrderDetails', 'U') IS NOT NULL DROP TABLE dbo.OrderDetails;

CREATE TABLE dbo.OrderDetails
(
  orderid   INT          NOT NULL,
  productid INT          NOT NULL,
  unitprice MONEY        NOT NULL
    CONSTRAINT DFT_OrderDetails_unitprice DEFAULT(0),
  qty        SMALLINT     NOT NULL
    CONSTRAINT DFT_OrderDetails_qty DEFAULT(1),
  discount  NUMERIC(4, 3) NOT NULL
    CONSTRAINT DFT_OrderDetails_discount DEFAULT(0),
  CONSTRAINT PK_OrderDetails PRIMARY KEY(orderid, productid),
  CONSTRAINT CHK_discount  CHECK (discount BETWEEN 0 AND 1),
  CONSTRAINT CHK_qty  CHECK (qty > 0),
  CONSTRAINT CHK_unitprice CHECK (unitprice >= 0)
);
GO

INSERT INTO dbo.OrderDetails SELECT * FROM Sales.OrderDetails;
```

The following *UPDATE* statement increases the discount of all order details for product 51 by 5 percent and uses the *OUTPUT* clause to return the product ID, old discount, and new discount from the modified rows.

```
UPDATE dbo.OrderDetails
  SET discount += 0.05
OUTPUT
  inserted.productid,
  deleted.discount AS olddiscount,
  inserted.discount AS newdiscount
WHERE productid = 51;
```

This statement returns the following output.

```
productid    olddiscount   newdiscount
-----------  ------------  ------------
51           0.000         0.050
51           0.150         0.200
51           0.100         0.150
51           0.200         0.250
51           0.000         0.050
51           0.150         0.200
51           0.000         0.050
51           0.000         0.050
51           0.000         0.050
51           0.000         0.050
...

(39 row(s) affected)
```

## MERGE with OUTPUT

You can also use the *OUTPUT* clause with the *MERGE* statement, but remember that a single *MERGE* statement can invoke multiple different DML actions based on conditional logic. This means that a single *MERGE* statement might return through the *OUTPUT* clause rows that were produced by different DML actions. To identify which DML action produced the output row, you can invoke a function called *$action* in the *OUTPUT* clause, which will return a string representing the action (INSERT, UPDATE, or DELETE). To demonstrate the use of the *OUTPUT* clause with the *MERGE* statement, I'll use one of the examples from the "Merging Data" section earlier in this chapter. To run this example, make sure you rerun Listing 8-2 to re-create the *dbo.Customers* and *dbo.CustomersStage* tables.

The following code merges the contents of *CustomersStage* into *Customers*, updating the attributes of customers who already exist in the target and adding customers who don't.

```
MERGE INTO dbo.Customers AS TGT
USING dbo.CustomersStage AS SRC
  ON TGT.custid = SRC.custid
WHEN MATCHED THEN
  UPDATE SET
    TGT.companyname = SRC.companyname,
    TGT.phone = SRC.phone,
    TGT.address = SRC.address
WHEN NOT MATCHED THEN
  INSERT (custid, companyname, phone, address)
  VALUES (SRC.custid, SRC.companyname, SRC.phone, SRC.address)
OUTPUT $action AS theaction, inserted.custid,
  deleted.companyname AS oldcompanyname,
  inserted.companyname AS newcompanyname,
  deleted.phone AS oldphone,
  inserted.phone AS newphone,
  deleted.address AS oldaddress,
  inserted.address AS newaddress;
```

This *MERGE* statement uses the *OUTPUT* clause to return the old and new values of the modified rows. Of course, with *INSERT* actions, there are no old values, so all references to deleted attributes return *NULL* marks. The *$action* function tells you whether an *UPDATE* or an *INSERT* action produced the output row. Here's the output of this *MERGE* statement.

```
theaction custid oldcompanyname newcompanyname
--------- ------ -------------- --------------
UPDATE    2      cust 2         AAAAA
UPDATE    3      cust 3         cust 3
UPDATE    5      cust 5         BBBBB
INSERT    6      NULL           cust 6 (new)
INSERT    7      NULL           cust 7 (new)

theaction custid oldphone        newphone        oldaddress newaddress
--------- ------ --------------- --------------- ---------- ----------
UPDATE    2      (222) 222-2222  (222) 222-2222  address 2  address 2
UPDATE    3      (333) 333-3333  (333) 333-3333  address 3  address 3
UPDATE    5      (555) 555-5555  CCCCC           address 5  DDDDD
INSERT    6      NULL            (666) 666-6666  NULL       address 6
INSERT    7      NULL            (777) 777-7777  NULL       address 7

(5 row(s) affected)
```

## Composable DML

The *OUTPUT* clause returns an output row for every modified row. But what if you need to direct only a subset of the modified rows to a table, perhaps for auditing purposes? SQL Server supports a feature called *composable DML* that allows you to directly insert into the final target table only the subset of rows that you need from the full set of modified rows.

To demonstrate this capability, first create a copy of the *Products* table from the *Production* schema in the *dbo* schema, as well as the *dbo.ProductsAudit* table, by running the following code.

```
IF OBJECT_ID('dbo.ProductsAudit', 'U') IS NOT NULL DROP TABLE dbo.ProductsAudit;
IF OBJECT_ID('dbo.Products', 'U') IS NOT NULL DROP TABLE dbo.Products;

CREATE TABLE dbo.Products
(
  productid    INT          NOT NULL,
  productname  NVARCHAR(40) NOT NULL,
  supplierid   INT          NOT NULL,
  categoryid   INT          NOT NULL,
  unitprice    MONEY        NOT NULL
    CONSTRAINT DFT_Products_unitprice DEFAULT(0),
  discontinued BIT          NOT NULL
    CONSTRAINT DFT_Products_discontinued DEFAULT(0),
  CONSTRAINT PK_Products PRIMARY KEY(productid),
  CONSTRAINT CHK_Products_unitprice CHECK(unitprice >= 0)
);

INSERT INTO dbo.Products SELECT * FROM Production.Products;

CREATE TABLE dbo.ProductsAudit
```

```
(
  LSN INT NOT NULL IDENTITY PRIMARY KEY,
  TS  DATETIME NOT NULL DEFAULT(CURRENT_TIMESTAMP),
  productid INT NOT NULL,
  colname SYSNAME NOT NULL,
  oldval SQL_VARIANT NOT NULL,
  newval SQL_VARIANT NOT NULL
);
```

Suppose that you now need to update all products that are supplied by supplier 1, increasing their price by 15 percent. You also need to audit the old and new values of updated products, but only those with an old price that was less than 20 and a new price that is greater than or equal to 20.

You can achieve this by using composable DML. You write an *UPDATE* statement with an *OUTPUT* clause and define a derived table based on the *UPDATE* statement. You write an *INSERT SELECT* statement that queries the derived table, filtering only the subset of rows that is needed. Here's the complete solution code.

```
INSERT INTO dbo.ProductsAudit(productid, colname, oldval, newval)
  SELECT productid, N'unitprice', oldval, newval
  FROM (UPDATE dbo.Products
          SET unitprice *= 1.15
        OUTPUT
          inserted.productid,
          deleted.unitprice AS oldval,
          inserted.unitprice AS newval
        WHERE supplierid = 1) AS D
  WHERE oldval < 20.0 AND newval >= 20.0;
```

Recall earlier discussions in the book about logical query processing and table expressions—the multiset output of one query can be used as input to subsequent SQL statements. Here, the output of the *OUTPUT* clause is a multiset input for the *SELECT* statement, and then the output of the *SELECT* statement is inserted into a table.

Run the following code to query the *ProductsAudit* table.

```
SELECT * FROM dbo.ProductsAudit;
```

You get the following output.

```
LSN TS                       ProductID  ColName      OldVal   NewVal
--- ------------------------ ---------- ----------- -------- ------
1   2008-08-05 18:56:04.793  1          unitprice    18.00    20.70
2   2008-08-05 18:56:04.793  2          unitprice    19.00    21.85
```

Three products were updated, but only two were filtered by the outer query; therefore, only those two were audited.

When you're done, run the following code for cleanup.

```
IF OBJECT_ID('dbo.OrderDetails', 'U') IS NOT NULL DROP TABLE dbo.OrderDetails;
IF OBJECT_ID('dbo.ProductsAudit', 'U') IS NOT NULL DROP TABLE dbo.ProductsAudit;
IF OBJECT_ID('dbo.Products', 'U') IS NOT NULL DROP TABLE dbo.Products;
IF OBJECT_ID('dbo.Orders', 'U') IS NOT NULL DROP TABLE dbo.Orders;
IF OBJECT_ID('dbo.Customers', 'U') IS NOT NULL DROP TABLE dbo.Customers;
IF OBJECT_ID('dbo.T1', 'U') IS NOT NULL DROP TABLE dbo.T1;
IF OBJECT_ID('dbo.Sequences', 'U') IS NOT NULL DROP TABLE dbo.Sequences;
IF OBJECT_ID('dbo.CustomersStage', 'U') IS NOT NULL DROP TABLE dbo.CustomersStage;
```

# Conclusion

In this chapter, I covered various aspects of data modification. I described inserting, updating, deleting, and merging data. I also discussed modifying data through table expressions, using *TOP* (and indirectly *OFFSET-FETCH*) with modification statements, and returning modified rows using the *OUTPUT* clause.

# Exercises

This section provides exercises so you can practice the subjects discussed in this chapter. The database assumed in the exercise is *TSQL2012*.

## 1

Run the following code to create the *dbo.Customers* table in the *TSQL2012* database.

```
USE TSQL2012;

IF OBJECT_ID('dbo.Customers', 'U') IS NOT NULL DROP TABLE dbo.Customers;

CREATE TABLE dbo.Customers
(
  custid      INT          NOT NULL PRIMARY KEY,
  companyname NVARCHAR(40) NOT NULL,
  country     NVARCHAR(15) NOT NULL,
  region      NVARCHAR(15) NULL,
  city        NVARCHAR(15) NOT NULL
);
```

## 1-1

Insert into the *dbo.Customers* table a row with:

- *custid*: 100

- *companyname*: Coho Winery

- *country*: USA

- *region*: WA

- *city*: Redmond

## 1-2

Insert into the *dbo.Customers* table all customers from *Sales.Customers* who placed orders.

## 1-3

Use a *SELECT INTO* statement to create and populate the *dbo.Orders* table with orders from the *Sales.Orders* table that were placed in the years 2006 through 2008. Note that this exercise can only be practiced in an on-premises SQL Server, because SQL Database doesn't support the *SELECT INTO* statement. In SQL Database, use a *CREATE TABLE* and *INSERT SELECT* statements instead.

## 2

Delete from the *dbo.Orders* table orders that were placed before August 2006. Use the *OUTPUT* clause to return the *orderid* and *orderdate* of the deleted orders.

- Desired output:

```
orderid      orderdate
-----------  -----------------------
10248        2006-07-04 00:00:00.000
10249        2006-07-05 00:00:00.000
10250        2006-07-08 00:00:00.000
10251        2006-07-08 00:00:00.000
10252        2006-07-09 00:00:00.000
10253        2006-07-10 00:00:00.000
10254        2006-07-11 00:00:00.000
10255        2006-07-12 00:00:00.000
10256        2006-07-15 00:00:00.000
10257        2006-07-16 00:00:00.000
10258        2006-07-17 00:00:00.000
10259        2006-07-18 00:00:00.000
10260        2006-07-19 00:00:00.000
10261        2006-07-19 00:00:00.000
10262        2006-07-22 00:00:00.000
10263        2006-07-23 00:00:00.000
10264        2006-07-24 00:00:00.000
```

```
10265          2006-07-25 00:00:00.000
10266          2006-07-26 00:00:00.000
10267          2006-07-29 00:00:00.000
10268          2006-07-30 00:00:00.000
10269          2006-07-31 00:00:00.000

(22 row(s) affected)
```

## 3

Delete from the *dbo.Orders* table orders placed by customers from Brazil.

## 4

Run the following query against *dbo.Customers*, and notice that some rows have a *NULL* in the region column.

```
SELECT * FROM dbo.Customers;
```

The output from this query is as follows.

```
custid       companyname       country          region       city
-----------  ----------------  ---------------- ------------  ---------------
1            Customer NRZBB    Germany          NULL         Berlin
2            Customer MLTDN    Mexico           NULL         México D.F.
3            Customer KBUDE    Mexico           NULL         México D.F.
4            Customer HFBZG    UK               NULL         London
5            Customer IIGVLZ   Sweden           NULL         Luleå
6            Customer XHXJV    Germany          NULL         Mannheim
7            Customer QXVLA    France           NULL         Strasbourg
8            Customer QUHWH    Spain            NULL         Madrid
9            Customer RTXGC    France           NULL         Marseille
10           Customer EEALV    Canada           BC           Tsawassen
...

(90 row(s) affected)
```

Update the *dbo.Customers* table and change all *NULL* region values to *<None>*. Use the *OUTPUT* clause to show the *custid*, *oldregion*, and *newregion*.

- Desired output:

```
custid       oldregion        newregion
-----------  ---------------- ----------------
1            NULL             <None>
2            NULL             <None>
3            NULL             <None>
4            NULL             <None>
5            NULL             <None>
6            NULL             <None>
7            NULL             <None>
8            NULL             <None>
9            NULL             <None>
```

```
11          NULL            <None>
12          NULL            <None>
13          NULL            <None>
14          NULL            <None>
16          NULL            <None>
17          NULL            <None>
18          NULL            <None>
19          NULL            <None>
20          NULL            <None>
23          NULL            <None>
24          NULL            <None>
25          NULL            <None>
26          NULL            <None>
27          NULL            <None>
28          NULL            <None>
29          NULL            <None>
30          NULL            <None>
39          NULL            <None>
40          NULL            <None>
41          NULL            <None>
44          NULL            <None>
49          NULL            <None>
50          NULL            <None>
52          NULL            <None>
53          NULL            <None>
54          NULL            <None>
56          NULL            <None>
58          NULL            <None>
59          NULL            <None>
60          NULL            <None>
63          NULL            <None>
64          NULL            <None>
66          NULL            <None>
68          NULL            <None>
69          NULL            <None>
70          NULL            <None>
72          NULL            <None>
73          NULL            <None>
74          NULL            <None>
76          NULL            <None>
79          NULL            <None>
80          NULL            <None>
83          NULL            <None>
84          NULL            <None>
85          NULL            <None>
86          NULL            <None>
87          NULL            <None>
90          NULL            <None>
91          NULL            <None>

(58 row(s) affected)
```

## 5

Update all orders in the *dbo.Orders* table that were placed by United Kingdom customers and set their *shipcountry*, *shipregion*, and *shipcity* values to the *country*, *region*, and *city* values of the corresponding customers.

## 6

When you're done, run the following code for cleanup.

```
IF OBJECT_ID('dbo.Orders', 'U') IS NOT NULL DROP TABLE dbo.Orders;
IF OBJECT_ID('dbo.Customers', 'U') IS NOT NULL DROP TABLE dbo.Customers;
```

# Solutions

This section provides solutions to the preceding exercises.

## 1-1

Make sure that you are connected to the *TSQL2012* database.

```
USE TSQL2012;
```

Use the following *INSERT VALUES* statement to insert a row into the *Customers* table with the values provided in the exercise.

```
INSERT INTO dbo.Customers(custid, companyname, country, region, city)
  VALUES(100, N'Coho Winery', N'USA', N'WA', N'Redmond');
```

## 1-2

One way to identify customers who placed orders is to use the *EXISTS* predicate, as the following query shows.

```
SELECT custid, companyname, country, region, city
FROM Sales.Customers AS C
WHERE EXISTS
  (SELECT * FROM Sales.Orders AS O
   WHERE O.custid = C.custid);
```

To insert the rows returned from this query into the *dbo.Customers* table, you can use an *INSERT SELECT* statement as follows.

```
INSERT INTO dbo.Customers(custid, companyname, country, region, city)
  SELECT custid, companyname, country, region, city
  FROM Sales.Customers AS C
  WHERE EXISTS
    (SELECT * FROM Sales.Orders AS O
     WHERE O.custid = C.custid);
```

## 1-3

The following code first ensures that the session is connected to the *TSQL2012* database, then it drops the *dbo.Orders* table if it already exists, and then it uses the *SELECT INTO* statement to create a new *dbo.Orders* table and populate it with orders from the *Sales.Orders* table placed in the years 2006 through 2008.

```
USE TSQL2012;

IF OBJECT_ID('dbo.Orders', 'U') IS NOT NULL DROP TABLE dbo.Orders;

SELECT *
INTO dbo.Orders
FROM Sales.Orders
WHERE orderdate >= '20060101'
  AND orderdate < '20090101';
```

In SQL Database, you use *CREATE TABLE* and *INSERT SELECT* statements instead.

```
CREATE TABLE dbo.Orders
(
  orderid        INT          NOT NULL,
  custid         INT          NULL,
  empid          INT          NOT NULL,
  orderdate      DATETIME     NOT NULL,
  requireddate   DATETIME     NOT NULL,
  shippeddate    DATETIME     NULL,
  shipperid      INT          NOT NULL,
  freight        MONEY        NOT NULL,
  shipname       NVARCHAR(40) NOT NULL,
  shipaddress    NVARCHAR(60) NOT NULL,
  shipcity       NVARCHAR(15) NOT NULL,
  shipregion     NVARCHAR(15) NULL,
  shippostalcode NVARCHAR(10) NULL,
  shipcountry    NVARCHAR(15) NOT NULL,
  CONSTRAINT PK_Orders PRIMARY KEY(orderid)
);

INSERT INTO dbo.Orders
  (orderid, custid, empid, orderdate, requireddate, shippeddate,
   shipperid, freight, shipname, shipaddress, shipcity, shipregion,
   shippostalcode, shipcountry)
SELECT
  orderid, custid, empid, orderdate, requireddate, shippeddate,
  shipperid, freight, shipname, shipaddress, shipcity, shipregion,
  shippostalcode, shipcountry
FROM Sales.Orders
WHERE orderdate >= '20060101'
  AND orderdate < '20090101';
```

## 2

To delete orders placed before August 2006, you need a *DELETE* statement with a filter based on the predicate *orderdate < '20060801'*. As requested, use the *OUTPUT* clause to return attributes from the deleted rows.

```
DELETE FROM dbo.Orders
  OUTPUT deleted.orderid, deleted.orderdate
WHERE orderdate < '20060801';
```

## 3

This exercise requires you to write a *DELETE* statement that deletes rows from one table (*dbo.Orders*) based on the existence of a matching row in another table (*dbo.Customers*). One way to solve the problem is to use a standard *DELETE* statement with an *EXISTS* predicate in the *WHERE* clause, like this.

```
DELETE FROM dbo.Orders
WHERE EXISTS
  (SELECT *
   FROM dbo.Customers AS C
   WHERE Orders.custid = C.custid
     AND C.country = N'Brazil');
```

This *DELETE* statement deletes the rows from the *dbo.Orders* table for which a related row exists in the *dbo.Customers* table with the same customer ID as the order's customer ID and the customer's country is Brazil.

Another way to solve this problem is to use the T-SQL-specific *DELETE* syntax based on a join, like this.

```
DELETE FROM O
FROM dbo.Orders AS O
  JOIN dbo.Customers AS C
    ON O.custid = C.custid
WHERE country = N'Brazil';
```

Note that there are no matched rows, of course, if the previous *DELETE* is executed.

The join between the *dbo.Orders* and *dbo.Customers* tables serves a filtering purpose. The join matches each order with the customer who placed the order. The *WHERE* clause filters only rows for which the customer's country is Brazil. The *DELETE FROM* clause refers to the alias *O* representing the table *Orders*, indicating that *Orders* is the target of the *DELETE* operation.

As a standard alternative, you can use the *MERGE* statement to solve this problem. Even though you would normally think of using *MERGE* when you need to apply different actions based on conditional logic, you can also use it when you need to apply one action when a certain predicate is *TRUE*. In other words, you can use the *MERGE* statement with the *WHEN MATCHED* clause alone; you don't have to have a *WHEN NOT MATCHED* clause as well. The following *MERGE* statement handles the request in the exercise.

```
MERGE INTO dbo.Orders AS O
USING dbo.Customers AS C
  ON O.custid = C.custid
  AND country = N'Brazil'
WHEN MATCHED THEN DELETE;
```

Again, note that there are no matched rows if either of the previous *DELETE* statements is executed.

This *MERGE* statement defines the *dbo.Orders* table as the target and the *dbo.Customers* table as the source. An order is deleted from the target (*dbo.Orders*) when a matching row is found in the source (*dbo.Customers*) with the same customer ID and the country Brazil.

## 4

This exercise involves writing an *UPDATE* statement that filters only rows for which the region attribute is *NULL*. Make sure you use the *IS NULL* predicate and not an equality operator when looking for *NULL* marks. Use the *OUTPUT* clause to return the requested information. Here's the complete *UPDATE* statement.

```
UPDATE dbo.Customers
  SET region = '<None>'
OUTPUT
  deleted.custid,
  deleted.region AS oldregion,
  inserted.region AS newregion
WHERE region IS NULL;
```

## 5

One way to solve this exercise is to use the T-SQL–specific *UPDATE* syntax based on a join. You can join *dbo.Orders* and *dbo.Customers* based on a match between the order's customer ID and the customer's customer ID. In the *WHERE* clause, you can filter only the rows where the customer's country is the United Kingdom. In the *UPDATE* clause, specify the alias you assigned to the *dbo.Orders* table to indicate that it's the target of the modification. In the *SET* clause, assign the values of the shipping location attributes of the order to the location attributes of the corresponding customer. Here's the complete *UPDATE* statement.

```
UPDATE O
  SET shipcountry = C.country,
      shipregion = C.region,
      shipcity = C.city
FROM dbo.Orders AS O
  JOIN dbo.Customers AS C
    ON O.custid = C.custid
WHERE C.country = 'UK';
```

Another solution to this exercise uses CTEs. You can define a CTE based on a *SELECT* query that joins *dbo.Orders* and *dbo.Customers* and returns both the target location attributes from *dbo.Orders* and the source location attributes from *dbo.Customers*. The outer query would then be an *UPDATE* statement modifying the target attributes with the values of the source attributes. Here's the complete solution statement.

```
WITH CTE_UPD AS
(
  SELECT
    O.shipcountry AS ocountry, C.country AS ccountry,
    O.shipregion  AS oregion,  C.region  AS cregion,
    O.shipcity    AS ocity,    C.city    AS ccity
  FROM dbo.Orders AS O
    JOIN dbo.Customers AS C
      ON O.custid = C.custid
  WHERE C.country = 'UK'
)
UPDATE CTE_UPD
  SET ocountry = ccountry, oregion = cregion, ocity = ccity;
```

You can also use the *MERGE* statement to achieve this task. As explained earlier, even though in a *MERGE* statement you usually want to specify both the *WHEN MATCHED* and *WHEN NOT MATCHED* clauses, the statement supports specifying only one of the clauses. Using only a *WHEN MATCHED* clause with an *UPDATE* action, you can write a solution that is logically equivalent to the last two solutions. Here's the complete solution statement.

```
MERGE INTO dbo.Orders AS O
USING dbo.Customers AS C
  ON O.custid = C.custid
  AND C.country = 'UK'
WHEN MATCHED THEN
  UPDATE SET shipcountry = C.country,
             shipregion = C.region,
             shipcity = C.city;
```

# CHAPTER 9

# Transactions and Concurrency

This chapter covers transactions and their properties and describes how Microsoft SQL Server handles users who are concurrently trying to access the same data. I explain how SQL Server uses locks to isolate inconsistent data, how you can troubleshoot blocking situations, and how you can control the level of consistency when you are querying data with isolation levels. This chapter also covers deadlocks and ways to mitigate their occurrence.

## Transactions

A *transaction* is a unit of work that might include multiple activities that query and modify data and that can also change data definition.

You can define transaction boundaries either explicitly or implicitly. You define the beginning of a transaction explicitly with a *BEGIN TRAN* (or *BEGIN TRANSACTION*) statement. You define the end of a transaction explicitly with a *COMMIT TRAN* statement if you want to confirm it and with a *ROLLBACK TRAN* (or *ROLLBACK TRANSACTION*) statement if you do not want to confirm it (that is, if you want to undo its changes). Here's an example of marking the boundaries of a transaction with two *INSERT* statements.

```
BEGIN TRAN;
  INSERT INTO dbo.T1(keycol, col1, col2) VALUES(4, 101, 'C');
  INSERT INTO dbo.T2(keycol, col1, col2) VALUES(4, 201, 'X');
COMMIT TRAN;
```

If you do not mark the boundaries of a transaction explicitly, by default, SQL Server treats each individual statement as a transaction; in other words, by default, SQL Server automatically commits the transaction at the end of each individual statement. You can change the way SQL Server handles implicit transactions with a session option called IMPLICIT_TRANSACTIONS. This option is off by default. When this option is on, you do not have to specify the *BEGIN TRAN* statement to mark the beginning of a transaction, but you have to mark the transaction's end with a *COMMIT TRAN* or a *ROLLBACK TRAN* statement.

Transactions have four properties—atomicity, consistency, isolation, and durability—abbreviated with the acronym *ACID*.

- **Atomicity**   A transaction is an atomic unit of work. Either all changes in the transaction take place or none do. If the system fails before a transaction is completed (before the commit instruction is recorded in the transaction log), upon restart, SQL Server undoes the changes that took place. Also, if errors are encountered during the transaction, normally SQL Server automatically rolls back the transaction, with a few exceptions. Some errors, such as primary key violation and lock expiration timeout (discussed later in this chapter, in the "Troubleshooting Blocking" section), are not considered severe enough to justify an automatic rollback of the transaction. You can use error-handling code to capture such errors and apply some course of action (for example, log the error and roll back the transaction). Chapter 10, "Programmable Objects," provides an overview of error handling.

> **Tip**   At any point in your code, you can tell programmatically whether you are in an open transaction by querying a function called *@@TRANCOUNT*. This function returns 0 if you're not in an open transaction and returns a value greater than 0 if you are.

- **Consistency**   The term consistency refers to the state of the data that the RDBMS gives you access to as concurrent transactions modify and query it. As you can probably imagine, consistency is a subjective term, which depends on your application's needs. The "Isolation Levels" section later in this chapter explains the level of consistency that SQL Server provides by default and how you can control consistency if the default behavior is not suitable for your application. Consistency also refers to the fact that the database must adhere to all integrity rules that have been defined within it by constraints (such as primary keys, unique constraints, and foreign keys). The transaction transitions the database from one consistent state to another.

- **Isolation**   *Isolation* is a mechanism used to control access to data and ensure that transactions access data only if the data is in the level of consistency that those transactions expect. SQL Server supports two different models to handle isolation: a traditional one based on locking and a newer one based on row versioning. The model based on locking is the default in an on-premises SQL Server installation. In this model, readers require shared locks. If the current state of the data is inconsistent, readers are blocked until the state of the data becomes consistent. The model based on row versioning is the default in Windows Azure SQL Database. In this model, readers don't take shared locks and don't need to wait. If the current state of the data is inconsistent, the reader gets an older consistent state. The "Isolation Levels" section later in this chapter provides more details about both ways of handling isolation.

- **Durability**   Data changes are always written to the database's transaction log on disk before they are written to the data portion of the database on disk. After the commit instruction is recorded in the transaction log on disk, the transaction is considered durable even if the change hasn't yet made it to the data portion on disk. When the system starts, either normally or after a system failure, SQL Server inspects the transaction log of each database and runs a recovery process with two phases—redo and undo. The redo phase involves rolling forward (replaying) all of the changes from any transaction whose commit instruction is written to the log but whose changes haven't yet made it to the data portion. The undo phase involves rolling back (undoing) the changes from any transaction whose commit instruction was not recorded in the log.

For example, the following code defines a transaction that records information about a new order in the *TSQL2012* database.

```
USE TSQL2012;

-- Start a new transaction
BEGIN TRAN;

  -- Declare a variable
  DECLARE @neworderid AS INT;

  -- Insert a new order into the Sales.Orders table
  INSERT INTO Sales.Orders
      (custid, empid, orderdate, requireddate, shippeddate,
       shipperid, freight, shipname, shipaddress, shipcity,
       shippostalcode, shipcountry)
    VALUES
      (85, 5, '20090212', '20090301', '20090216',
       3, 32.38, N'Ship to 85-B', N'6789 rue de l''Abbaye', N'Reims',
       N'10345', N'France');

  -- Save the new order ID in a variable
  SET @neworderid = SCOPE_IDENTITY();

  -- Return the new order ID
  SELECT @neworderid AS neworderid;

  -- Insert order lines for the new order into Sales.OrderDetails
  INSERT INTO Sales.OrderDetails
      (orderid, productid, unitprice, qty, discount)
    VALUES(@neworderid, 11, 14.00, 12, 0.000),
          (@neworderid, 42, 9.80, 10, 0.000),
          (@neworderid, 72, 34.80, 5, 0.000);

-- Commit the transaction
COMMIT TRAN;
```

The transaction's code inserts a row with the order header information into the *Sales.Orders* table and a few rows with the order lines information into the *Sales.OrderDetails* table. The new order ID is produced automatically by SQL Server because the *orderid* column has an identity property. Immediately after the code inserts the new row into the *Sales.Orders* table, it stores the newly generated order ID in a local variable, and then it uses that local variable when inserting rows into the *Sales.OrderDetails* table. For test purposes, I added a *SELECT* statement that returns the order ID of the newly generated order. Here's the output from the *SELECT* statement after the code runs.

```
neworderid
-----------
11078
```

Note that this example has no error handling and does not make any provision for a *ROLLBACK* in case of an error. To handle errors, you can enclose a transaction in a *TRY/CATCH* construct. You can find an overview of error handling in Chapter 10.

When you're done, run the following code for cleanup.

```
DELETE FROM Sales.OrderDetails
WHERE orderid > 11077;

DELETE FROM Sales.Orders
WHERE orderid > 11077;
```

# Locks and Blocking

SQL Server uses locks to enforce the isolation property of transactions. The following sections provide details about locking and explain how to troubleshoot blocking situations that are caused by conflicting lock requests.

## Locks

Locks are control resources obtained by a transaction to guard data resources, preventing conflicting or incompatible access by other transactions. I'll first cover the important lock modes supported by SQL Server and their compatibility, and then I'll describe the lockable resource types.

### Lock Modes and Compatibility

As you start learning about transactions and concurrency, you should first familiarize yourself with two main lock modes—*exclusive* and *shared*.

When you try to modify data, your transaction requests an exclusive lock on the data resource, regardless of your isolation level (you'll learn more about isolation levels later in this chapter). If granted, the exclusive lock is held until the end of the transaction. For single-statement transactions, this means that the lock is held until the statement completes. For multistatement transactions, this means that the lock is held until all statements complete and the transaction is ended by a *COMMIT TRAN* or *ROLLBACK TRAN* command.

Exclusive locks are called "exclusive" because you cannot obtain an exclusive lock on a resource if another transaction is holding any lock mode on the resource, and no lock mode can be obtained on a resource if another transaction is holding an exclusive lock on the resource. This is the way modifications behave by default, and this default behavior cannot be changed—not in terms of the lock mode required to modify a data resource (exclusive) and not in terms of the duration of the lock (until the end of the transaction). In practical terms, this means that if one transaction modifies rows, until the transaction is completed, another transaction cannot modify the same rows. However, whether another transaction can read the same rows or not depends on its isolation level.

As for reading data, the defaults are different for on-premises SQL Server installations and SQL Database. In an on-premises SQL Server installation, the default isolation level is called *READ COMMITTED*. In this isolation, when you try to read data, by default your transaction requests a shared lock on the data resource and releases the lock as soon as the read statement is done with that resource. This lock mode is called "shared" because multiple transactions can hold shared locks on the same data resource simultaneously. Although you cannot change the lock mode and duration required when you are modifying data, you can control the way locking is handled when you are reading data by changing your isolation level. As mentioned, I will elaborate on this later in this chapter.

In SQL Database, the default isolation level is called *READ COMMITTED SNAPSHOT*. Instead of relying on locking, this isolation relies on a row-versioning technology. Under this isolation level, readers do not require shared locks, and therefore they never wait; they rely on the row-versioning technology to provide the expected isolation. In practical terms, this means that under the *READ COMMITTED* isolation level, if a transaction modifies rows, until the transaction completes, another transaction can't read the same rows. This approach to concurrency control is known as the *pessimistic concurrency* approach. Under the *READ COMMITTED SNAPSHOT* isolation level, if a transaction modifies rows, another transaction trying to read the data will get the last committed state of the rows that was available when the statement started. This approach to concurrency control is known as the *optimistic concurrency* approach.

This lock interaction between transactions is known as *lock compatibility*. Table 9-1 shows the lock compatibility of exclusive and shared locks (when you are working with an isolation level that generates these locks). The columns represent granted lock modes, and the rows represent requested lock modes.

**TABLE 9-1** Lock Compatibility of Exclusive and Shared Locks

| Requested Mode | Granted Exclusive (X) | Granted Shared (S) |
|---|---|---|
| Grant request for exclusive? | No | No |
| Grant request for shared? | No | Yes |

A "No" in the intersection means that the locks are incompatible and the requested mode is denied; the requester must wait. A "Yes" in the intersection means that the locks are compatible and the requested mode is accepted.

The following summarizes lock interaction between transactions in simple terms: data that was modified by one transaction can neither be modified nor read (at least by default in an on-premises SQL Server installation) by another transaction until the first transaction finishes. And while data is being read by one transaction, it cannot be modified by another (at least by default in an on-premises SQL Server installation).

## Lockable Resource Types

SQL Server can lock different types of resources. The types of resources that can be locked include RIDs or keys (row), pages, objects (for example, tables), databases, and others. Rows reside within pages, and pages are the physical data blocks that contain table or index data. You should first familiarize yourself with these resource types, and at a more advanced stage, you might want to familiarize yourself with other lockable resource types such as extents, allocation units, and heaps or B-trees.

To obtain a lock on a certain resource type, your transaction must first obtain intent locks of the same mode on higher levels of granularity. For example, to get an exclusive lock on a row, your transaction must first acquire an intent exclusive lock on the page where the row resides and an intent exclusive lock on the object that owns the page. Similarly, to get a shared lock on a certain level of granularity, your transaction first needs to acquire intent shared locks on higher levels of granularity. The purpose of intent locks is to efficiently detect incompatible lock requests on higher levels of granularity and prevent the granting of those. For example, if one transaction holds a lock on a row and another asks for an incompatible lock mode on the whole page or table where that row resides, it is easy for SQL Server to identify the conflict because of the intent locks that the first transaction acquired on the page and table. Intent locks do not interfere with requests for locks on lower levels of granularity. For example, an intent lock on a page doesn't prevent other transactions from acquiring incompatible lock modes on rows within the page. Table 9-2 expands on the lock compatibility table shown in Table 9-1, adding intent exclusive and intent shared locks.

**TABLE 9-2** Lock Compatibility Including Intent Locks

| Requested Mode | Granted Exclusive (X) | Granted Shared (S) | Granted Intent Exclusive (IX) | Granted Intent Shared (IS) |
|---|---|---|---|---|
| Grant request for exclusive? | No | No | No | No |
| Grant request for shared? | No | Yes | No | Yes |
| Grant request for intent exclusive? | No | No | Yes | Yes |
| Grant request for intent shared? | No | Yes | Yes | Yes |

SQL Server determines dynamically which resource types to lock. Naturally, for ideal concurrency, it is best to lock only what needs to be locked, namely only the affected rows. However, locks require memory resources and internal management overhead. So SQL Server considers both concurrency and system resources when it is choosing which resource types to lock.

SQL Server might first acquire fine-grained locks (such as row or page locks), and in certain circumstances, try to escalate the fine-grained locks to more coarse-grained locks (such as table locks). For example, lock escalation is triggered when a single statement acquires at least 5,000 locks, and then for every 1,250 new locks, if previous attempts at lock escalation were unsuccessful.

In SQL Server 2008 and SQL Server 2012, you can set a table option called *LOCK_ESCALATION* by using the *ALTER TABLE* statement to control the way lock escalation behaves. You can disable lock escalation if you like, or determine whether escalation takes place at a table level (default) or a partition level. (A table can be physically organized into multiple smaller units called *partitions*.)

# Troubleshooting Blocking

When one transaction holds a lock on a data resource and another transaction requests an incompatible lock on the same resource, the request is blocked and the requester enters a wait state. By default, the blocked request keeps waiting until the blocker releases the interfering lock. Later in this section, I'll explain how you can define a lock expiration time-out in your session if you want to restrict the amount of time that a blocked request waits before it times out.

Blocking is normal in a system as long as requests are satisfied within a reasonable amount of time. However, if some requests end up waiting too long, you might need to troubleshoot the blocking situation and see whether you can do something to prevent such long latencies. For example, long-running transactions result in locks being held for long periods. You can try to shorten such transactions, moving activities that are not supposed to be part of the unit of work outside the transaction. A bug in the application might result in a transaction that remains open in certain circumstances. If you identify such a bug, you can fix it and ensure that the transaction is closed in all circumstances.

This section demonstrates a blocking situation and walks you through the process of troubleshooting it. Note that this demonstration assumes that you're connected to an on-premises SQL Server instance and using the *READ COMMITTED* isolation level, meaning that by default *SELECT* statements will request a shared lock. Remember that in SQL Database the default isolation is *READ COMMITTED SNAPSHOT*, in which *SELECT* statements do not ask for a shared lock by default. If you want to run the demo in SQL Database, to work under *READ COMMITTED*, you will need to add a table hint called *READCOMMITTEDLOCK* to your *SELECT* statements, as in *SELECT \* FROM T1 WITH (READCOMMITTEDLOCK)*. Also, by default, connections to SQL Database time out quite quickly. So if a demo you're running doesn't work as expected, it could be that a connection involved in that demo timed out.

Open three separate query windows in SQL Server Management Studio. (For this example, I will refer to them as Connection 1, Connection 2, and Connection 3.) Make sure that in all of them you are connected to the sample database *TSQL2012*.

```
USE TSQL2012;
```

Run the following code in Connection 1 to update a row in the *Production.Products* table, adding 1.00 to the current unit price of 19.00 for product 2.

```
BEGIN TRAN;

  UPDATE Production.Products
    SET unitprice += 1.00
  WHERE productid = 2;
```

To update the row, your session had to acquire an exclusive lock, and if the update was successful, SQL Server granted your session the lock. Recall that exclusive locks are kept until the end of the transaction, and because the transaction remains open, the lock is still held.

Run the following code in Connection 2 to try to query the same row (uncomment the hint *WITH (READCOMMITTEDLOCK)* in this and subsequent queries if you're running this on SQL Database).

```
SELECT productid, unitprice
FROM Production.Products -- WITH (READCOMMITTEDLOCK)
WHERE productid = 2;
```

Your session needs a shared lock to read the data, but because the row is exclusively locked by the other session, and a shared lock is incompatible with an exclusive lock, your session is blocked and has to wait.

Assuming that such a blocking situation happens in your system, and the blocked session ends up waiting for a long time, you probably want to troubleshoot the situation. The rest of this section provides queries against dynamic management objects, including views and functions, that you should run from Connection 3 when you troubleshoot the blocking situation.

To get lock information, including both locks that are currently granted to sessions and locks that sessions are waiting for, query the dynamic management view (DMV) *sys.dm_tran_locks* in Connection 3.

```
SELECT -- use * to explore other available attributes
    request_session_id              AS spid,
    resource_type                   AS restype,
    resource_database_id            AS dbid,
    DB_NAME(resource_database_id)   AS dbname,
    resource_description            AS res,
    resource_associated_entity_id   AS resid,
    request_mode                    AS mode,
    request_status                  AS status
FROM sys.dm_tran_locks;
```

When I run this code in my on-premises system (with no other query window open), I get the following output.

| spid | restype | dbid | dbname | res | resid | mode | status |
|------|---------|------|--------|-----|-------|------|--------|
| 53 | DATABASE | 8 | TSQL2012 | | 0 | S | GRANT |
| 52 | DATABASE | 8 | TSQL2012 | | 0 | S | GRANT |
| 51 | DATABASE | 8 | TSQL2012 | | 0 | S | GRANT |
| 54 | DATABASE | 8 | TSQL2012 | | 0 | S | GRANT |
| 53 | PAGE | 8 | TSQL2012 | 1:127 | 72057594038845440 | IS | GRANT |
| 52 | PAGE | 8 | TSQL2012 | 1:127 | 72057594038845440 | IX | GRANT |
| 53 | OBJECT | 8 | TSQL2012 | | 133575514 | IS | GRANT |
| 52 | OBJECT | 8 | TSQL2012 | | 133575514 | IX | GRANT |
| 52 | KEY | 8 | TSQL2012 | (020068e8b274) | 72057594038845440 | X | GRANT |
| 53 | KEY | 8 | TSQL2012 | (020068e8b274) | 72057594038845440 | S | WAIT |

Each session is identified by a unique server process ID (SPID). You can determine your session's SPID by querying the function @@SPID. If you're working with SQL Server Management Studio, you will find the session SPID in parentheses to the right of the logon name in the status bar at the bottom of the screen, and also in the caption of the connected query window. For example, Figure 9-1 shows a screen shot of SQL Server Management Studio, where the SPID 53 appears to the right of the logon name K2\Gandalf.

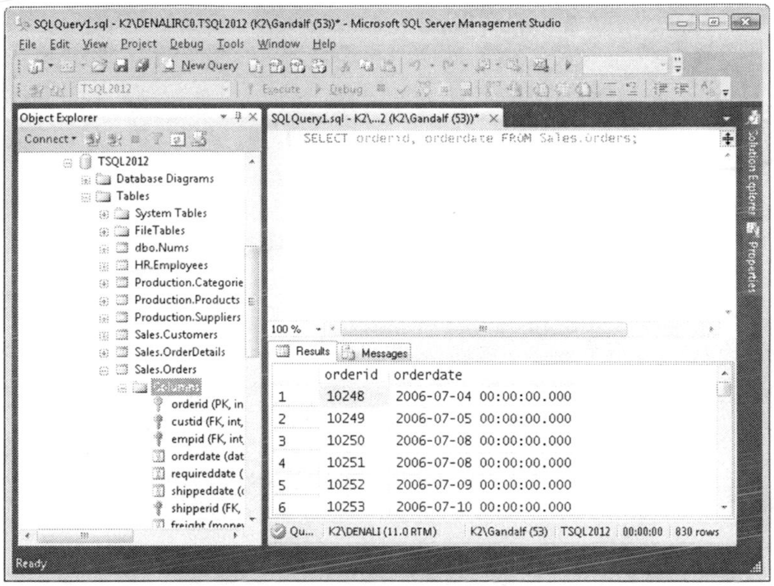

**FIGURE 9-1** The SSID shown in SQL Server Management Studio.

As you can see in the output of the query against *sys.dm_tran_locks*, four sessions (51, 52, 53, and 54) are currently holding locks. You can see the following:

- The resource type that is locked (for example, *KEY* for a row in an index)

- The ID of the database in which it is locked, which you can translate to the database name by using the DB_NAME function

- The resource and resource ID

- The lock mode

- Whether the lock was granted or the session is waiting for it

Note that this is only a subset of the view's attributes; I recommend that you explore the other attributes of the view to learn what other information about locks is available.

In the output from my query, you can observe that process 53 is waiting for a shared lock on a row in the sample database *TSQL2012*. (The database name is obtained with the DB_NAME function.) Notice that process 52 is holding an exclusive lock on the same row. You can determine this by observing that both processes lock a row with the same res and resid values. You can figure out which table is involved by moving upward in the lock hierarchy for either process 52 or 53 and inspecting the intent locks on the page and the object (table) where the row resides. You can use the OBJECT_NAME function to translate the object ID (133575514 in this example) that appears under the *resid* attribute in the object lock. You will find that the table involved is *Production.Product*.

The *sys.dm_tran_locks* view only gives you information about the IDs of the processes involved in the blocking chain and nothing else. To get information about the connections associated with the processes involved in the blocking chain, query a view called *sys.dm_exec_connections,* and filter only the SPIDs that are involved.

```
SELECT -- use * to explore
  session_id AS spid,
  connect_time,
  last_read,
  last_write,
  most_recent_sql_handle
FROM sys.dm_exec_connections
WHERE session_id IN(52, 53);
```

Note that the process IDs that were involved in the blocking chain in my system were 52 and 53. Depending on what else you are doing in your system, you might get different process IDs. When you run the queries that I demonstrate here in your system, make sure that you substitute the process IDs with those you find involved in your blocking chain.

This query returns the following output (split into several parts for display purposes here).

```
spid   connect_time             last_read
------ ------------------------ -----------------------
52     2012-06-25 15:20:03.360  2012-06-25 15:20:15.750
53     2012-06-25 15:20:07.300  2012-06-25 15:20:20.950

spid   last_write               most_recent_sql_handle
------ ------------------------ -----------------------------------------------------
52     2012-06-25 15:20:15.817  0x01000800DE2DB71FB0936F0500000000000000000000000000
53     2012-06-25 15:20:07.327  0x0200000063FC7D052E09844778CDD615CFE7A2D1FB411802
```

The information that this query gives you about the connections includes:

- The time they connected.

- The time of their last read and write.

- A binary value holding a handle to the most recent SQL batch run by the connection. You provide this handle as an input parameter to a table function called sys.dm_exec_sql_text, and the function returns the batch of code represented by the handle. You can query the table function passing the binary handle explicitly, but you will probably find it more convenient to use the *APPLY* table operator described in Chapter 5, "Table Expressions," to apply the table function to each connection row like this (run in Connection 3).

    ```
    SELECT session_id, text
    FROM sys.dm_exec_connections
      CROSS APPLY sys.dm_exec_sql_text(most_recent_sql_handle) AS ST
    WHERE session_id IN(52, 53);
    ```

When I run this query, I get the following output, showing the last batch of code invoked by each connection involved in the blocking chain.

```
session_id  text
----------  ---------------------------------------
52              BEGIN TRAN;

                UPDATE Production.Products
                  SET unitprice += 1.00
                WHERE productid = 2;

53              (@1 tinyint)
                SELECT [productid],[unitprice]
                FROM [Production].[Products]
                WHERE [productid]=@1
```

The blocked process—53—shows the query that is waiting because that's the last thing that the process ran. As for the blocker, in this example, you can see the statement that caused the problem, but keep in mind that the blocker might continue working and that the last thing you see in the code isn't necessarily the statement that caused the trouble.

You can also find a lot of useful information about the sessions involved in a blocking situation in the DMV *sys.dm_exec_sessions*. The following query returns only a small subset of the attributes available about those sessions.

```
SELECT -- use * to explore
  session_id AS spid,
  login_time,
  host_name,
  program_name,
  login_name,
  nt_user_name,
  last_request_start_time,
  last_request_end_time
FROM sys.dm_exec_sessions
WHERE session_id IN(52, 53);
```

This query returns the following output in this example, split here into several parts.

```
spid login_time               host_name
---- ------------------------ ---------
52   2012-06-25 15:20:03.407  K2
53   2012-06-25 15:20:07.303  K2

spid  program_name                                       login_name
----- -------------------------------------------------- --------------
52    Microsoft SQL Server Management Studio - Query     K2\Gandalf
53    Microsoft SQL Server Management Studio - Query     K2\Gandalf

spid  nt_user_name  last_request_start_time  last_request_end_time
----- ------------- ------------------------ -----------------------
52    Gandalf       2012-06-25 15:20:15.703  2012-06-25 15:20:15.750
53    Gandalf       2012-06-25 15:20:20.693  2012-06-25 15:20:07.320
```

This output contains information such as the session's logon time, host name, program name, logon name, Windows NT user name, the time that the last request started, and the time that the last request ended. This kind of information gives you a good idea of what those sessions are doing.

Another DMV that you will probably find very useful for troubleshooting blocking situations is *sys.dm_exec_requests*. This view has a row for each active request, including blocked requests. In fact, you can easily isolate blocked requests because the attribute *blocking_session_id* is greater than zero. For example, the following query filters only blocked requests.

```
SELECT -- use * to explore
  session_id AS spid,
  blocking_session_id,
  command,
  sql_handle,
  database_id,
  wait_type,
  wait_time,
  wait_resource
FROM sys.dm_exec_requests
WHERE blocking_session_id > 0;
```

This query returns the following output, split across several lines.

```
spid    blocking_session_id    command
------  --------------------   -------
53      52                     SELECT

spid    sql_handle                                                  database_id
------  ----------------------------------------------------------  -----------
53      0x0200000063FC7D052E09844778CDD615CFE7A2D1FB411802          8

spid    wait_type    wait_time    wait_resource
------  -----------  -----------  -------------------------------------
53      LCK_M_S      1383760      KEY: 8:72057594038845440 (020068e8b274)
```

You can easily identify the sessions that participate in the blocking chain, the resource in dispute, how long the blocked session is waiting in milliseconds, and more.

If you need to terminate the blocker—for example, if you realize that as a result of a bug in the application the transaction remained open and nothing in the application can close it—you can do so by using the KILL *<spid>* command. (Don't do so yet.) Note that at the date of this writing, the *KILL* command is not available in SQL Database.

Earlier, I mentioned that by default the session has no lock timeout set. If you want to restrict the amount of time your session waits for a lock, you can set a session option called *LOCK_TIMEOUT*. You specify a value in milliseconds—such as 5000 for 5 seconds, 0 for an immediate timeout, and -1 for no timeout (which is the default). To see how this option works, first stop the query in Connection 2 by choosing Cancel Executing Query from the Query menu (or by using Alt+Break). Then run the following code to set the lock timeout to five seconds, and run the query again.

```
SET LOCK_TIMEOUT 5000;

SELECT productid, unitprice
FROM Production.Products -- WITH (READCOMMITTEDLOCK)
WHERE productid = 2;
```

The query is still blocked because Connection 1 hasn't yet ended the update transaction, but if after 5 seconds the lock request is not satisfied, SQL Server terminates the query and you get the following error.

```
Msg 1222, Level 16, State 51, Line 3
Lock request time out period exceeded.
```

Note that lock timeouts do not roll back transactions.

To remove the lock timeout value, set it back to the default (indefinite), and issue the query again, run the following code in Connection 2.

```
SET LOCK_TIMEOUT -1;

SELECT productid, unitprice
FROM Production.Products -- WITH (READCOMMITTEDLOCK)
WHERE productid = 2;
```

To terminate the update transaction in Connection 1, run the following code from Connection 3 (assuming you're connected to an on-premises SQL Server instance).

```
KILL 52;
```

This statement causes a rollback of the transaction in Connection 1, meaning that the price change of product 2 from 19.00 to 20.00 is undone, and the exclusive lock is released. Go to Connection 2. Notice that you get the data after the change is undone—namely, before the price change.

```
productid    unitprice
-----------  --------------------
2            19.00
```

## Isolation Levels

Isolation levels determine the behavior of concurrent users who read or write data. A reader is any statement that selects data, using a shared lock by default. A writer is any statement that makes a modification to a table and requires an exclusive lock. You cannot control the way writers behave in terms of the locks that they acquire and the duration of the locks, but you can control the way readers behave. Also, as a result of controlling the behavior of readers, you can have an implicit influence on the behavior of writers. You do so by setting the isolation level, either at the session level with a session option or at the query level with a table hint.

SQL Server supports four traditional isolation levels that are based on pessimistic concurrency control (locking): *READ UNCOMMITTED*, *READ COMMITTED* (the default in on-premises SQL Server instances), *REPEATABLE READ*, and *SERIALIZABLE*. SQL Server also supports two isolation levels that are based on optimistic concurrency control (row versioning): *SNAPSHOT* and *READ COMMITTED SNAPSHOT* (the default in SQL Database). *SNAPSHOT* and *READ COMMITTED SNAPSHOT* are in a sense the optimistic-concurrency-based counterparts of *READ COMMITTED* and *SERIALIZABLE*, respectively.

Note that some texts refer to *READ COMMITTED* and *READ COMMITTED SNAPSHOT* as one isolation level with two different semantic treatments.

You can set the isolation level of the whole session by using the following command.

```
SET TRANSACTION ISOLATION LEVEL <isolation name>;
```

You can use a table hint to set the isolation level of a query.

```
SELECT ... FROM <table> WITH (<isolationname>);
```

Note that with the session option, you specify a space between the words in case the name of the isolation level is made of more than one word, such as *REPEATABLE READ*. With the query hint, you don't specify a space between the words—for example, *WITH (REPEATABLEREAD)*. Also, some of the isolation level names used as table hints have synonyms. For example, *NOLOCK* is the equivalent of specifying *READUNCOMMITTED*, and *HOLDLOCK* is the equivalent of specifying *SERIALIZABLE*.

The default isolation level in an on-premises SQL Server instance is *READ COMMITTED* (based on locking). The default in SQL Database is *READ COMMITTED SNAPSHOT* (based on row versioning). If you choose to override the default isolation level, your choice affects both the concurrency of the database users and the consistency they get from the data.

With the first four isolation levels, the higher the isolation level, the tougher the locks that readers request and the longer their duration; therefore, the higher the isolation level, the higher the consistency and the lower the concurrency. The converse is also true, of course.

With the two snapshot-based isolation levels, SQL Server is able to store previous committed versions of rows in *tempdb*. Readers do not request shared locks; instead, if the current version of the rows is not what they are supposed to see, SQL Server provides them with an older version.

The following sections describe each of the six supported isolation levels and demonstrate their behavior.

## The *READ UNCOMMITTED* Isolation Level

*READ UNCOMMITTED* is the lowest available isolation level. In this isolation level, a reader doesn't ask for a shared lock. A reader that doesn't ask for a shared lock can never be in conflict with a writer that is holding an exclusive lock. This means that the reader can read uncommitted changes (also known as dirty reads). It also means that the reader won't interfere with a writer that asks for an exclusive lock. In other words, a writer can change data while a reader that is running under the *READ UNCOMMITTED* isolation level reads data.

To see how an uncommitted read (dirty read) works, open two query windows (I will refer to them as Connection 1 and Connection 2). Make sure that in all connections your database context is that of the sample database *TSQL2012*.

Run the following code in Connection 1 to open a transaction, update the unit price of product 2 by adding 1.00 to its current price (19.00), and then query the product's row.

```
BEGIN TRAN;

  UPDATE Production.Products
    SET unitprice += 1.00
  WHERE productid = 2;

  SELECT productid, unitprice
  FROM Production.Products
  WHERE productid = 2;
```

Note that the transaction remains open, meaning that the product's row is locked exclusively by Connection 1. The code in Connection 1 returns the following output showing the product's new price.

```
productid    unitprice
----------- ----------------------
2            20.00
```

In Connection 2, run the following code to set the isolation level to *READ UNCOMMITTED* and query the row for product 2.

```
SET TRANSACTION ISOLATION LEVEL READ UNCOMMITTED;

SELECT productid, unitprice
FROM Production.Products
WHERE productid = 2;
```

Because the query did not request a shared lock, it was not in conflict with the other transaction. This query returned the state of the row after the change, even though the change was not committed.

```
productid    unitprice
----------- ---------------------- -----
2            20.00
```

Keep in mind that Connection 1 might apply further changes to the row later in the transaction or even roll back at some point. For example, run the following code in Connection 1 to roll back the transaction.

```
ROLLBACK TRAN;
```

This rollback undoes the update of product 2, changing its price back to 19.00. The value 20.00 that the reader got was never committed. That's an example of a dirty read.

## The *READ COMMITTED* Isolation Level

If you want to prevent readers from reading uncommitted changes, you need to use a stronger isolation level. The lowest isolation level that prevents dirty reads is *READ COMMITTED*, which is also the default isolation level in an on-premises SQL Server installation. As the name indicates, this isolation level allows readers to read only committed changes. It prevents uncommitted reads by requiring a reader to obtain a shared lock. This means that if a writer is holding an exclusive lock, the reader's shared lock request will be in conflict with the writer, and it has to wait. As soon as the writer commits the transaction, the reader can get its shared lock, but what it reads are necessarily only committed changes.

The following example demonstrates that, in this isolation level, a reader can only read committed changes.

Run the following code in Connection 1 to open a transaction, update the price of product 2, and query the row to show the new price.

```
BEGIN TRAN;

  UPDATE Production.Products
    SET unitprice += 1.00
  WHERE productid = 2;

  SELECT productid, unitprice
  FROM Production.Products
  WHERE productid = 2;
```

This code returns the following output.

```
productid   unitprice
----------- ---------------------
2           20.00
```

Connection 1 now locks the row for product 2 exclusively.

Run the following code in Connection 2 to set the session's isolation level to *READ COMMITTED* and query the row for product 2 (remember to uncomment the hint in SQL Database to use *READ COMMITTED* instead of *READ COMMITTED SNAPSHOT*).

```
SET TRANSACTION ISOLATION LEVEL READ COMMITTED;

SELECT productid, unitprice
FROM Production.Products -- WITH (READCOMMITTEDLOCK)
WHERE productid = 2;
```

Keep in mind that this isolation level is the default, so unless you previously changed the session's isolation level, you don't need to set it explicitly. The *SELECT* statement is currently blocked because it needs a shared lock to be able to read, and this shared lock request is in conflict with the exclusive lock held by the writer in Connection 1.

Next, run the following code in Connection 1 to commit the transaction.

```
COMMIT TRAN;
```

Now go to Connection 2 and notice that you get the following output.

```
productid   unitprice
----------- ---------------------
2           20.00
```

Unlike in *READ UNCOMMITTED*, in the *READ COMMITTED* isolation level, you don't get dirty reads. Instead, you can only read committed changes.

In terms of the duration of locks, in the *READ COMMITTED* isolation level, a reader only holds the shared lock until it is done with the resource. It doesn't keep the lock until the end of the transaction; in fact, it doesn't even keep the lock until the end of the statement. This means that in between two reads of the same data resource in the same transaction, no lock is held on the resource. Therefore, another transaction can modify the resource in between those two reads, and the reader might get different values in each read. This phenomenon is called non-repeatable reads or inconsistent analysis. For many applications, this phenomenon is acceptable, but for some it isn't.

When you are done, run the following code for cleanup in any of the open connections.

```
UPDATE Production.Products
  SET unitprice - 19.00
WHERE productid = 2;
```

## The *REPEATABLE READ* Isolation Level

If you want to ensure that no one can change values in between reads that take place in the same transaction, you need to move up in the isolation levels to *REPEATABLE READ*. In this isolation level, not only does a reader need a shared lock to be able to read, but it also holds the lock until the end of the transaction. This means that as soon as the reader has acquired a shared lock on a data resource to read it, no one can obtain an exclusive lock to modify that resource until the reader ends the transaction. This way, you're guaranteed to get repeatable reads, or consistent analysis.

The following example demonstrates getting repeatable reads. Run the following code in Connection 1 to set the session's isolation level to *REPEATABLE READ*, open a transaction, and read the row for product 2.

```
SET TRANSACTION ISOLATION LEVEL REPEATABLE READ;

BEGIN TRAN;

  SELECT productid, unitprice
  FROM Production.Products
  WHERE productid = 2;
```

This code returns the following output showing the current price of product 2.

```
productid   unitprice
----------- ---------------------
2           19.00
```

Connection 1 still holds a shared lock on the row for product 2 because in *REPEATABLE READ*, shared locks are held until the end of the transaction. Run the following code from Connection 2 to try to modify the row for product 2.

```
UPDATE Production.Products
  SET unitprice += 1.00
WHERE productid = 2;
```

Notice that the attempt is blocked because the modifier's request for an exclusive lock is in conflict with the reader's granted shared lock. If the reader was running under the READ UNCOMMITTED or READ COMMITTED isolation level, it wouldn't have held the shared lock at this point, and the attempt to modify the row would have been successful.

Back in Connection 1, run the following code to read the row for product 2 a second time and commit the transaction.

```
SELECT productid, unitprice
FROM Production.Products
WHERE productid = 2;

COMMIT TRAN;
```

This code returns the following output.

```
productid   unitprice
----------- ---------------------
2           19.00
```

Notice that the second read got the same unit price for product 2 as the first read. Now that the reader's transaction has been committed and the shared lock is released, the modifier in Connection 2 can obtain the exclusive lock it was waiting for and update the row.

Another phenomenon prevented by REPEATABLE READ but not by lower isolation levels is called a lost update. A lost update happens when two transactions read a value, make calculations based on what they read, and then update the value. Because in isolation levels lower than REPEATABLE READ no lock is held on the resource after the read, both transactions can update the value, and whichever transaction updates the value last "wins," overwriting the other transaction's update. In REPEATABLE READ, both sides keep their shared locks after the first read, so neither can acquire an exclusive lock later in order to update. The situation results in a deadlock, and the update conflict is prevented. I'll provide more details on deadlocks later in this chapter, in the "Deadlocks" section.

When you're done, run the following code for cleanup.

```
UPDATE Production.Products
  SET unitprice = 19.00
WHERE productid = 2;
```

## The *SERIALIZABLE* Isolation Level

Running under the REPEATABLE READ isolation level, readers keep shared locks until the end of the transaction. Therefore, you are guaranteed to get a repeatable read of the rows that you read the first time in the transaction. However, your transaction locks resources (for example, rows) that the query found the first time it ran, not rows that weren't there when the query ran. Therefore, a second read in the same transaction might return new rows as well. Those new rows are called phantoms, and such reads are called phantom reads. This happens if, in between the reads, another transaction adds new rows that qualify for the reader's query filter.

To prevent phantom reads, you need to move up in the isolation levels to *SERIALIZABLE*. For the most part, the *SERIALIZABLE* isolation level behaves similarly to *REPEATABLE READ*: namely, it requires a reader to obtain a shared lock to be able to read, and keeps the lock until the end of the transaction. But the *SERIALIZABLE* isolation level adds another facet—logically, this isolation level causes a reader to lock the whole range of keys that qualify for the query's filter. This means that the reader locks not only the existing rows that qualify for the query's filter, but also future ones. Or, more accurately, it blocks attempts made by other transactions to add rows that qualify for the reader's query filter.

The following example demonstrates that the *SERIALIZABLE* isolation level prevents phantom reads. Run the following code in Connection 1 to set the transaction isolation level to *SERIALIZABLE*, open a transaction, and query all products with category 1.

```
SET TRANSACTION ISOLATION LEVEL SERIALIZABLE;

BEGIN TRAN

  SELECT productid, productname, categoryid, unitprice
  FROM Production.Products
  WHERE categoryid = 1;
```

You get the following output, showing 12 products in category 1.

```
productid    productname      categoryid    unitprice
-----------  ---------------  -----------   -------------------
1            Product HHYDP    1             18.00
2            Product RECZE    1             19.00
24           Product QOGNU    1             4.50
34           Product SWNJY    1             14.00
35           Product NEVTJ    1             18.00
38           Product QDOMO    1             263.50
39           Product LSOFL    1             18.00
43           Product ZZZHR    1             46.00
67           Product XLXQF    1             14.00
70           Product TOONT    1             15.00
75           Product BWRLG    1             7.75
76           Product JYGFE    1             18.00
```

(12 row(s) affected)

From Connection 2, run the following code in an attempt to insert a new product with category 1.

```
INSERT INTO Production.Products
    (productname, supplierid, categoryid,
     unitprice, discontinued)
  VALUES('Product ABCDE', 1, 1, 20.00, 0);
```

In all isolation levels that are lower than *SERIALIZABLE*, such an attempt would have been success-ful. In the *SERIALIZABLE* isolation level, the attempt is blocked.

Back in Connection 1, run the following code to query products with category 1 a second time and commit the transaction.

```
SELECT productid, productname, categoryid, unitprice
FROM Production.Products
WHERE categoryid = 1;

COMMIT TRAN;
```

You get the same output as before, with no phantoms. Now that the reader's transaction is committed, and the shared key-range lock is released, the modifier in Connection 2 can obtain the exclusive lock it was waiting for and insert the row.

When you're done, run the following code for cleanup.

```
DELETE FROM Production.Products
WHERE productid > 77;
```

Run the following code in all open connections to set the isolation level back to the default.

```
SET TRANSACTION ISOLATION LEVEL READ COMMITTED;
```

## Isolation Levels Based on Row Versioning

With SQL Server, you can store previous versions of committed rows in *tempdb*. SQL Server supports two isolation levels called *SNAPSHOT* and *READ COMMITTED SNAPSHOT* based on this row-versioning technology. The *SNAPSHOT* isolation level is logically similar to the *SERIALIZABLE* isolation level in terms of the types of consistency problems that can or cannot happen; the *READ COMMITTED SNAPSHOT* isolation level is similar to the *READ COMMITTED* isolation level. However, readers using isolation levels based on row versioning do not issue shared locks, so they don't wait when the requested data is exclusively locked. Readers still get levels of consistency similar to *SERIALIZABLE* and *READ COMMITTED*. SQL Server provides readers with an older version of the row if the current version is not the one they are supposed to see.

Note that if you enable any of the snapshot-based isolation levels (which are enabled in SQL Database by default), the *DELETE* and *UPDATE* statements need to copy the version of the row before the change to *tempdb*; *INSERT* statements don't need to be versioned in *tempdb* because no earlier version of the row exists. But it is important to be aware that enabling any of the isolation levels that are based on row versioning may have a negative impact on the performance of data updates and deletes. The performance of readers usually improves because they do not acquire shared locks and don't need to wait when data is exclusively locked or its version is not the expected one. The next sections cover snapshot-based isolation levels and demonstrate their behavior.

## The *SNAPSHOT* Isolation Level

Under the *SNAPSHOT* isolation level, when the reader is reading data, it is guaranteed to get the last committed version of the row that was available when the transaction started. This means that you are guaranteed to get committed reads and repeatable reads, and also guaranteed not to get phantom reads—just as in the *SERIALIZABLE* isolation level. But instead of using shared locks, this isolation level relies on row versioning. As mentioned, snapshot isolation levels incur a performance penalty, mainly when updating and deleting data, regardless of whether or not the modification is executed from a session running under one of the snapshot-based isolation levels. For this reason, to allow your transactions to work with the *SNAPSHOT* isolation level in an on-premises SQL Server instance (this behavior is enabled by default in SQL Database), you need to first enable the option at the database level by running the following code in any open query window.

```
ALTER DATABASE TSQL2012 SET ALLOW_SNAPSHOT_ISOLATION ON;
```

The following example demonstrates the behavior of the *SNAPSHOT* isolation level. Run the following code from Connection 1 to open a transaction, update the price of product 2 by adding 1.00 to its current price of 19.00, and query the product's row to show the new price.

```
BEGIN TRAN;

  UPDATE Production.Products
    SET unitprice += 1.00
  WHERE productid = 2;

  SELECT productid, unitprice
  FROM Production.Products
  WHERE productid = 2;
```

Here the output of this code shows that the product's price was updated to 20.00.

```
productid   unitprice
----------- ---------------------
2           20.00
```

Note that even if the transaction in Connection 1 runs under the *READ COMMITTED* isolation level, SQL Server has to copy the version of the row before the update (with the price of 19.00) to *tempdb*. That's because the *SNAPSHOT* isolation level is enabled at the database level. If someone begins a transaction using the *SNAPSHOT* isolation level, they can request the version before the update. For example, run the following code from Connection 2 to set the isolation level to *SNAPSHOT*, open a transaction, and query the row for product 2.

```
SET TRANSACTION ISOLATION LEVEL SNAPSHOT;

BEGIN TRAN;

  SELECT productid, unitprice
  FROM Production.Products
  WHERE productid = 2;
```

If your transaction had been under the *SERIALIZABLE* isolation level, the query would have been blocked. But because it is running under *SNAPSHOT*, you get the last committed version of the row that was available when the transaction started. That version (with the price of 19.00) is not the current version (with the price of 20.00), so SQL Server pulls the appropriate version from the version store, and the code returns the following output.

```
productid   unitprice
----------- ---------------------
2           19.00
```

Go back to Connection 1 and commit the transaction that modified the row.

```
COMMIT TRAN;
```

At this point, the current version of the row with the price of 20.00 is a committed version. However, if you read the data again in Connection 2, you should still get the last committed version of the row that was available when the transaction started (with a price of 19.00). Run the following code in Connection 2 to read the data again, and then commit the transaction.

```
SELECT productid, unitprice
FROM Production.Products
WHERE productid = 2;
```

```
COMMIT TRAN;
```

As expected, you get the following output with a price of 19.00.

```
productid   unitprice
----------- ---------------------
2           19.00
```

Run the following code in Connection 2 to open a new transaction, query the data, and commit the transaction.

```
BEGIN TRAN
```

```
SELECT productid, unitprice
FROM Production.Products
WHERE productid = 2;
```

```
COMMIT TRAN;
```

This time, the last committed version of the row that was available when the transaction started is the one with a price of 20.00. Therefore, you get the following output.

```
productid   unitprice
----------- ---------------------
2           20.00
```

Now that no transaction needs the version of the row with the price of 19.00, a cleanup thread that runs once a minute can remove it from *tempdb* the next time it runs.

When you're done, run the following code for cleanup.

```
UPDATE Production.Products
  SET unitprice = 19.00
WHERE productid = 2;
```

## Conflict Detection

The *SNAPSHOT* isolation level prevents update conflicts, but unlike the *REPEATABLE READ* and *SERIALIZABLE* isolation levels that do so by generating a deadlock, the *SNAPSHOT* isolation level fails the transaction, indicating that an update conflict was detected. The *SNAPSHOT* isolation level can detect update conflicts by examining the version store. It can figure out whether another transaction modified the data between a read and a write that took place in your transaction.

The following example demonstrates a scenario with no update conflict, followed by an example of a scenario with an update conflict.

Run the following code in Connection 1 to set the transaction isolation level to *SNAPSHOT*, open a transaction, and read the row for product 2.

```
SET TRANSACTION ISOLATION LEVEL SNAPSHOT;

BEGIN TRAN;

  SELECT productid, unitprice
  FROM Production.Products
  WHERE productid = 2;
```

You get the following output.

```
productid    unitprice
-----------  --------------------
2            19.00
```

Assuming you have made some calculations based on what you read, run the following code while still in Connection 1 to update the price of the product you queried previously to 20.00, and commit the transaction.

```
  UPDATE Production.Products
    SET unitprice = 20.00
  WHERE productid = 2;

COMMIT TRAN;
```

No other transaction modified the row between your read, calculation, and write; therefore, there was no update conflict and SQL Server allowed the update to take place.

Run the following code to modify the price of product 2 back to 19.00.

```
UPDATE Production.Products
  SET unitprice = 19.00
WHERE productid = 2;
```

Next, run the following code in Connection 1, again, to open a transaction, and read the row for product 2.

```
BEGIN TRAN;

  SELECT productid, unitprice
  FROM Production.Products
  WHERE productid = 2;
```

You get the following output, indicating that the price of the product is 19.00.

```
productid    unitprice
-----------  --------------------
2            19.00
```

This time, run the following code in Connection 2 to update the price of product 2 to 25.00.

```
UPDATE Production.Products
  SET unitprice = 25.00
WHERE productid = 2;
```

Assume that you have made calculations in Connection 1 based on the price of 19.00 that you read. Based on your calculations, try to update the price of the product to 20.00 in Connection 1.

```
  UPDATE Production.Products
    SET unitprice = 20.00
  WHERE productid = 2;
```

SQL Server detected that this time another transaction modified the data between your read and write; therefore, it fails your transaction with the following error.

```
Msg 3960, Level 16, State 2, Line 1
Snapshot isolation transaction aborted due to update conflict. You cannot use snapshot isolation
to access table 'Production.Products' directly or indirectly in database 'TSQL2012' to update,
delete, or insert the row that has been modified or deleted by another transaction. Retry the
transaction or change the isolation level for the update/delete statement.
```

Of course, you can use error handling code to retry the whole transaction when an update conflict is detected.

When you're done, run the following code for cleanup.

```
UPDATE Production.Products
  SET unitprice = 19.00
WHERE productid = 2;
```

Close all connections. Note that if all connections aren't closed, your example results might not match those in the chapter examples.

## The *READ COMMITTED SNAPSHOT* Isolation Level

The *READ COMMITTED SNAPSHOT* isolation level is also based on row versioning. It differs from the *SNAPSHOT* isolation level in that instead of providing a reader with the last committed version of the row that was available when the *transaction* started, a reader gets the last committed version of the row that was available when the *statement* started. The *READ COMMITTED SNAPSHOT* isolation level also does not detect update conflicts. This results in logical behavior very similar to the *READ COMMITTED* isolation level, except that readers do not acquire shared locks and do not wait when the requested resource is exclusively locked.

To enable the use of the *READ COMMITTED SNAPSHOT* isolation level in an on-premises SQL Server database (the behavior is enabled by default in SQL Database), you need to turn on a different database flag than the one required to enable the *SNAPSHOT* isolation level. Run the following code to enable the use of the *READ COMMITTED SNAPSHOT* isolation level in the *TSQL2012* database.

```
ALTER DATABASE TSQL2012 SET READ_COMMITTED_SNAPSHOT ON;
```

Note that for this code to run successfully, this connection must be the only connection open to the *TSQL2012* database.

An interesting aspect of enabling this database flag is that unlike with the *SNAPSHOT* isolation level, this flag actually changes the meaning, or semantics, of the *READ COMMITTED* isolation level to *READ COMMITTED SNAPSHOT*. This means that when this database flag is turned on, unless you explicitly change the session's isolation level, *READ COMMITTED SNAPSHOT* is the default.

For a demonstration of using the *READ COMMITTED SNAPSHOT* isolation level, open two connections. Run the following code in Connection 1 to open a transaction, update the row for product 2, and read the row, leaving the transaction open.

```
USE TSQL2012;

BEGIN TRAN;

  UPDATE Production.Products
    SET unitprice += 1.00
  WHERE productid = 2;

  SELECT productid, unitprice
  FROM Production.Products
  WHERE productid = 2;
```

You get the following output, indicating that the product's price was changed to 20.00.

```
productid   unitprice
----------- ---------------------
2           20.00
```

In Connection 2, open a transaction and read the row for product 2, leaving the transaction open.

```
BEGIN TRAN;

  SELECT productid, unitprice
  FROM Production.Products
  WHERE productid = 2;
```

You get the last committed version of the row that was available when the statement started (19.00).

```
productid   unitprice
----------- ---------------------
2           19.00
```

Run the following code in Connection 1 to commit the transaction.

```
COMMIT TRAN;
```

Now run the code in Connection 2 to read the row for product 2 again, and commit the transaction.

```
  SELECT productid, unitprice
  FROM Production.Products
  WHERE productid = 2;
```

```
COMMIT TRAN;
```

If this code had been running under the *SNAPSHOT* isolation level, you would have gotten a price of 19.00; however, because the code is running under the *READ COMMITTED SNAPSHOT* isolation level, you get the last committed version of the row that was available when the statement started (20.00) and not when the transaction started (19.00).

```
productid   unitprice
----------- ---------------------
2           20.00
```

Recall that this phenomenon is called a non-repeatable read, or inconsistent analysis.

When you're done, run the following code for cleanup.

```
UPDATE Production.Products
  SET unitprice = 19.00
WHERE productid = 2;
```

Close all connections. If you ran this demo in an on-premises SQL Server instance, open a new connection and run the following code to disable the isolation levels that are based on row versioning in the *TSQL2012* database.

```
ALTER DATABASE TSQL2012 SET ALLOW_SNAPSHOT_ISOLATION OFF;
ALTER DATABASE TSQL2012 SET READ_COMMITTED_SNAPSHOT OFF;
```

## Summary of Isolation Levels

Table 9-3 provides a summary of the logical consistency problems that can or cannot happen in each isolation level and indicates whether the isolation level detects update conflicts for you and whether the isolation level uses row versioning.

**TABLE 9-3** Summary of Isolation Levels

| Isolation Level | Allows Uncommitted Reads? | Allows Non-repeatable Reads? | Allows Lost Updates? | Allows Phantom Reads? | Detects Update Conflicts? | Uses Row Versioning? |
|---|---|---|---|---|---|---|
| READ UNCOMMITTED | Yes | Yes | Yes | Yes | No | No |
| READ COMMITTED | No | Yes | Yes | Yes | No | No |
| READ COMMITTED SNAPSHOT | No | Yes | Yes | Yes | No | Yes |
| REPEATABLE READ | No | No | No | Yes | No | No |
| SERIALIZABLE | No | No | No | No | No | No |
| SNAPSHOT | No | No | No | No | Yes | Yes |

# Deadlocks

A deadlock is a situation in which two or more processes block each other. An example of a two-process deadlock is when process A blocks process B and process B blocks process A. An example of a deadlock involving more than two processes is when process A blocks process B, process B blocks process C, and process C blocks process A. In either case, SQL Server detects the deadlock and intervenes by terminating one of the transactions. If SQL Server does not intervene, the processes involved would remain deadlocked forever.

Unless otherwise specified, SQL Server chooses to terminate the transaction that did the least work, because it is cheapest to roll that transaction's work back. However, SQL Server allows you to set a session option called *DEADLOCK_PRIORITY* to one of 21 values in the range –10 through 10. The process with the lowest deadlock priority is chosen as the deadlock "victim" regardless of how much work is done; in the event of a tie, the amount of work is used as a tiebreaker.

The following example demonstrates a simple deadlock. Then I'll explain how you can mitigate deadlock occurrences in the system.

Open two connections and make sure that you are connected to the *TSQL2012* database in both. Run the following code in Connection 1 to open a new transaction, update a row in the *Production.Products* table for product 2, and leave the transaction open.

```
USE TSQL2012;

BEGIN TRAN;

  UPDATE Production.Products
    SET unitprice += 1.00
  WHERE productid = 2;
```

Run the following code in Connection 2 to open a new transaction, update a row in the *Sales.OrderDetails* table for product 2, and leave the transaction open.

```
BEGIN TRAN;

  UPDATE Sales.OrderDetails
    SET unitprice += 1.00
  WHERE productid = 2;
```

At this point, the transaction in Connection 1 is holding an exclusive lock on the row for product 2 in the *Production.Products* table, and the transaction in Connection 2 is now holding locks on the rows for product 2 in the *Sales.OrderDetails* table. Both queries succeed, and no blocking has occurred yet.

Run the following code in Connection 1 to attempt to query the rows for product 2 in the *Sales.OrderDetails* table and commit the transaction (remember to uncomment the hint if you are running the transaction against SQL Database).

```
SELECT orderid, productid, unitprice
FROM Sales.OrderDetails -- WITH (READCOMMITTEDLOCK)
WHERE productid = 2;

COMMIT TRAN;
```

The transaction in Connection 1 needs a shared lock to be able to perform its read. Because the other transaction holds an exclusive lock on the same resource, the transaction in Connection 1 is blocked. At this point, you have a blocking situation, not yet a deadlock. Of course, a chance remains that Connection 2 will end the transaction, releasing all locks and allowing the transaction in Connection 1 to get the requested locks.

Next, run the following code in Connection 2 to attempt to query the row for product 2 in the *Product.Production* table and commit the transaction.

```
SELECT productid, unitprice
FROM Production.Products -- WITH (READCOMMITTEDLOCK)
WHERE productid = 2;

COMMIT TRAN;
```

To be able to perform its read, the transaction in Connection 2 needs a shared lock on the row for product 2 in the *Product.Production* table, so this request is now in conflict with the exclusive lock held on the same resource by Connection 1. Each of the processes blocks the other—you have a deadlock. SQL Server identifies the deadlock (typically within a few seconds), chooses one of the two processes as the deadlock victim, and terminates its transaction with the following error.

```
Msg 1205, Level 13, State 51, Line 1
Transaction (Process ID 52) was deadlocked on lock resources with another process and has been
chosen as the deadlock victim. Rerun the transaction.
```

In this example, SQL Server chose to terminate the transaction in Connection 1 (shown here as process ID 52). Because you didn't set a deadlock priority and both transactions did a similar amount of work, either transaction could have been terminated.

Deadlocks are expensive because they involve undoing work that has already been done. You can follow a few practices to mitigate deadlock occurrences in your system.

Obviously, the longer the transactions are, the longer locks are kept, increasing the probability of deadlocks. You should try to keep transactions as short as possible, taking activities out of the transaction that aren't logically supposed to be part of the same unit of work.

A deadlock happens when transactions access resources in inverse order. For example, in the example, Connection 1 first accessed a row in *Production.Products* and then accessed a row in *Sales.OrderDetails*, whereas Connection 2 first accessed a row in *Sales.OrderDetails* and then accessed a row in *Production.Products*. This type of deadlock can't happen if both transactions access resources in the same order. By swapping the order in one of the transactions, you can prevent this type of deadlock from happening—assuming that it makes no logical difference to your application.

The deadlock example has a real logical conflict because both sides try to access the same rows. However, deadlocks often happen when there is no real logical conflict, because of a lack of good indexing to support query filters. For example, suppose that both statements in the transaction in Connection 2 were to filter product 5. Now that the statements in Connection 1 handle product 2 and the statements in Connection 2 handle product 5, there shouldn't be any conflict. However, if no indexes on the *productid* column in the tables support the filter, SQL Server has to scan (and lock) all rows in the table. This, of course, can lead to a deadlock. In short, good index design can help mitigate the occurrences of deadlocks that have no real logical conflict.

Another option to consider when mitigating deadlock occurrences is the choice of isolation level. The *SELECT* statements in the example needed shared locks because they ran under the *READ COMMITTED* isolation level. If you use the *READ COMMITTED SNAPSHOT* isolation level, readers will not need shared locks, and such deadlocks that evolve due to the involvement of shared locks can be eliminated.

When you're done, run the following code for cleanup in any connection.

```
UPDATE Production.Products
  SET unitprice = 19.00
WHERE productid = 2;

UPDATE Sales.OrderDetails
  SET unitprice = 19.00
WHERE productid = 2
  AND orderid >= 10500;

UPDATE Sales.OrderDetails
  SET unitprice = 15.20
WHERE productid = 2
  AND orderid < 10500;
```

# Conclusion

This chapter introduced you to transactions and concurrency. I described what transactions are and how SQL Server manages them. I explained how SQL Server isolates data accessed by one transaction from inconsistent use by other transactions, and how to troubleshoot blocking scenarios. I described how you can control the level of consistency that you get from the data by choosing an isolation level, and the impact that your choice has on concurrency. I described four isolation levels that do not rely on row versioning and two that do. Finally, I covered deadlocks and explained practices that you can follow to reduce the frequency of their occurrence.

To practice what you've learned, perform the practice exercises.

# Exercises

This section provides exercises to help you familiarize yourself with the subjects discussed in this chapter. The exercises for most of the previous chapters involve requests for which you have to figure out a solution in the form of a T-SQL query or statement. The exercises for this chapter are different. You will be provided with instructions to follow to troubleshoot blocking and deadlock situations, and to observe the behavior of different isolation levels. Therefore, this chapter's exercises have no separate "Solutions" section, as in other chapters.

For all exercises in this chapter, make sure you are connected to the *TSQL2012* sample database by running the following code.

```
USE TSQL2012;
```

Exercises 1-1 through 1-6 deal with blocking.

## 1-1

Open three connections in SQL Server Management Studio (the exercises will refer to them as Connection 1, Connection 2, and Connection 3). Run the following code in Connection 1 to update rows in *Sales.OrderDetails*.

```
BEGIN TRAN;

  UPDATE Sales.OrderDetails
    SET discount = 0.05
  WHERE orderid = 10249;
```

## 1-2

Run the following code in Connection 2 to query *Sales.OrderDetails*; Connection 2 will be blocked (remember to uncomment the hint if you are running against SQL Database).

```
SELECT orderid, productid, unitprice, qty, discount
FROM Sales.OrderDetails -- WITH (READCOMMITTEDLOCK)
WHERE orderid = 10249;
```

## 1-3

Run the following code in Connection 3 and identify the locks and process IDs involved in the blocking chain.

```
SELECT -- use * to explore
  request_session_id                AS spid,
  resource_type                     AS restype,
  resource_database_id              AS dbid,
  resource_description              AS res,
  resource_associated_entity_id AS resid,
  request_mode                      AS mode,
  request_status                    AS status
FROM sys.dm_tran_locks;
```

## 1-4

Replace the process IDs 52 and 53 with the ones you found to be involved in the blocking chain in the previous exercise. Run the following code to obtain connection, session, and blocking information about the processes involved in the blocking chain.

```
-- Connection info:
SELECT -- use * to explore
  session_id AS spid,
  connect_time,
  last_read,
  last_write,
  most_recent_sql_handle
FROM sys.dm_exec_connections
WHERE session_id IN(52, 53);

-- Session info
SELECT -- use * to explore
  session_id AS spid,
  login_time,
  host_name,
  program_name,
  login_name,
  nt_user_name,
  last_request_start_time,
  last_request_end_time
FROM sys.dm_exec_sessions
WHERE session_id IN(52, 53);
```

```
-- Blocking
SELECT -- use * to explore
  session_id AS spid,
  blocking_session_id,
  command,
  sql_handle,
  database_id,
  wait_type,
  wait_time,
  wait_resource
FROM sys.dm_exec_requests
WHERE blocking_session_id > 0;
```

## 1-5

Run the following code to obtain the SQL text of the connections involved in the blocking chain.

```
SELECT session_id, text
FROM sys.dm_exec_connections
  CROSS APPLY sys.dm_exec_sql_text(most_recent_sql_handle) AS ST
WHERE session_id IN(52, 53);
```

## 1-6

Run the following code in Connection 1 to roll back the transaction.

```
ROLLBACK TRAN;
```

Observe in Connection 2 that the *SELECT* query returned the two order detail rows, and that those rows were not modified.

Remember that if you need to terminate the blocker's transaction, you can use the KILL command. Close all connections.

Exercises 2-1 through 2-6 deal with isolation levels.

## 2-1

In this exercise, you will practice using the *READ UNCOMMITTED* isolation level.

### 2-1a

Open two new connections. (This exercise will refer to them as Connection 1 and Connection 2.)

## 2-1b

Run the following code in Connection 1 to update rows in *Sales.OrderDetails* and query it.

```
BEGIN TRAN;

  UPDATE Sales.OrderDetails
    SET discount += 0.05
  WHERE orderid = 10249;

  SELECT orderid, productid, unitprice, qty, discount
  FROM Sales.OrderDetails
  WHERE orderid = 10249;
```

## 2-1c

Run the following code in Connection 2 to set the isolation level to *READ UNCOMMITTED* and query *Sales.OrderDetails*.

```
SET TRANSACTION ISOLATION LEVEL READ UNCOMMITTED;

SELECT orderid, productid, unitprice, qty, discount
FROM Sales.OrderDetails
WHERE orderid = 10249;
```

Notice that you get the modified, uncommitted version of the rows.

## 2-1d

Run the following code in Connection 1 to roll back the transaction.

```
ROLLBACK TRAN;
```

## 2-2

In this exercise, you will practice using the *READ COMMITTED* isolation level.

## 2-2a

Run the following code in Connection 1 to update rows in *Sales.OrderDetails* and query it.

```
BEGIN TRAN;

  UPDATE Sales.OrderDetails
    SET discount += 0.05
  WHERE orderid = 10249;

  SELECT orderid, productid, unitprice, qty, discount
  FROM Sales.OrderDetails
  WHERE orderid = 10249;
```

## 2-2b

Run the following code in Connection 2 to set the isolation level to *READ COMMITTED* and query *Sales.OrderDetails*. (Remember to uncomment the hint if you are running against SQL Database.)

```
SET TRANSACTION ISOLATION LEVEL READ COMMITTED;

SELECT orderid, productid, unitprice, qty, discount
FROM Sales.OrderDetails -- WITH (READCOMMITTEDLOCK)
WHERE orderid = 10249;
```

Notice that you are now blocked.

## 2-2c

Run the following code in Connection 1 to commit the transaction.

```
COMMIT TRAN;
```

## 2-2d

Go to Connection 2 and notice that you get the modified, committed version of the rows.

## 2-2e

Run the following code for cleanup.

```
UPDATE Sales.OrderDetails
  SET discount = 0.00
WHERE orderid = 10249;
```

# 2-3

In this exercise, you will practice using the *REPEATABLE READ* isolation level.

## 2-3a

Run the following code in Connection 1 to set the isolation level to *REPEATABLE READ*, open a transaction, and read data from *Sales.OrderDetails*.

```
SET TRANSACTION ISOLATION LEVEL REPEATABLE READ;

BEGIN TRAN;

  SELECT orderid, productid, unitprice, qty, discount
  FROM Sales.OrderDetails
  WHERE orderid = 10249;
```

You get two rows with discount values of 0.00.

## 2-3b

Run the following code in Connection 2 and notice that you are blocked.

```
UPDATE Sales.OrderDetails
  SET discount += 0.05
WHERE orderid = 10249;
```

## 2-3c

Run the following code in Connection 1 to read the data again and commit the transaction.

```
  SELECT orderid, productid, unitprice, qty, discount
  FROM Sales.OrderDetails
  WHERE orderid = 10249;

COMMIT TRAN;
```

You get the two rows with discount values of 0.00 again, giving you repeatable reads. Note that if your code was running under a lower isolation level (such as *READ UNCOMMITTED* or *READ COMMITTED*), the *UPDATE* statement wouldn't have been blocked, and you would have gotten non-repeatable reads.

## 2-3d

Go to Connection 2 and notice that the update has finished.

## 2-3e

Run the following code for cleanup.

```
UPDATE Sales.OrderDetails
  SET discount = 0.00
WHERE orderid = 10249;
```

## 2-4

In this exercise, you will practice using the *SERIALIZABLE* isolation level.

## 2-4a

Run the following code in Connection 1 to set the isolation level to *SERIALIZABLE* and query *Sales.OrderDetails*.

```
SET TRANSACTION ISOLATION LEVEL SERIALIZABLE;

BEGIN TRAN;

  SELECT orderid, productid, unitprice, qty, discount
  FROM Sales.OrderDetails
  WHERE orderid = 10249;
```

## 2-4b

Run the following code in Connection 2 to attempt to insert a row to *Sales.OrderDetails* with the same order ID that is filtered by the previous query and notice that you are blocked.

```
INSERT INTO Sales.OrderDetails
    (orderid, productid, unitprice, qty, discount)
  VALUES(10249, 2, 19.00, 10, 0.00);
```

Note that in lower isolation levels (such as *READ UNCOMMITTED, READ COMMITTED,* or *REPEATABLE READ*), this *INSERT* statement wouldn't have been blocked.

## 2-4c

Run the following code in Connection 1 to query *Sales.OrderDetails* again and commit the transaction.

```
SELECT orderid, productid, unitprice, qty, discount
FROM Sales.OrderDetails
WHERE orderid = 10249;
```

```
COMMIT TRAN;
```

You get the same result set that you got from the previous query in the same transaction, and because the *INSERT* statement was blocked, you get no phantom reads.

## 2-4d

Go back to Connection 2 and notice that the *INSERT* statement has finished.

## 2-4e

Run the following code for cleanup.

```
DELETE FROM Sales.OrderDetails
WHERE orderid = 10249
  AND productid = 2;
```

## 2-4f

Run the following code in both Connection 1 and Connection 2 to set the isolation level to the default.

```
SET TRANSACTION ISOLATION LEVEL READ COMMITTED;
```

## 2-5

In this exercise, you will practice using the *SNAPSHOT* isolation level.

## 2-5a

If you're doing the exercises against an on-premises SQL Server instance, run the following code to set the *SNAPSHOT* isolation level in the *TSQL2012* database (enabled in SQL Database by default):

```
ALTER DATABASE TSQL2012 SET ALLOW_SNAPSHOT_ISOLATION ON;
```

## 2-5b

Run the following code in Connection 1 to open a transaction, update rows in *Sales.OrderDetails*, and query it.

```
BEGIN TRAN;

  UPDATE Sales.OrderDetails
    SET discount += 0.05
  WHERE orderid = 10249;

  SELECT orderid, productid, unitprice, qty, discount
  FROM Sales.OrderDetails
  WHERE orderid = 10249;
```

## 2-5c

Run the following code in Connection 2 to set the isolation level to *SNAPSHOT* and query *Sales.OrderDetails*. Notice that you're not blocked—instead, you get an earlier, consistent version of the data that was available when the transaction started (with discount values of 0.00).

```
SET TRANSACTION ISOLATION LEVEL SNAPSHOT;

BEGIN TRAN;

  SELECT orderid, productid, unitprice, qty, discount
  FROM Sales.OrderDetails
  WHERE orderid = 10249;
```

## 2-5d

Go to Connection 1 and commit the transaction.

```
COMMIT TRAN;
```

## 2-5e

Go to Connection 2 and query the data again; notice that you still get discount values of 0.00.

```
  SELECT orderid, productid, unitprice, qty, discount
  FROM Sales.OrderDetails
  WHERE orderid = 10249;
```

## 2-5f

In Connection 2, commit the transaction and query the data again; notice that now you get discount values of 0.05.

```
COMMIT TRAN;

SELECT orderid, productid, unitprice, qty, discount
FROM Sales.OrderDetails
WHERE orderid = 10249;
```

## 2-5g

Run the following code for cleanup.

```
UPDATE Sales.OrderDetails
  SET discount = 0.00
WHERE orderid = 10249;
```

Close all connections.

# 2-6

In this exercise, you will practice using the *READ COMMITTED SNAPSHOT* isolation level.

## 2-6a

If you are running against an on-premises SQL Server instance, turn on *READ_COMMITTED_SNAPSHOT* in the *TSQL2012* database (on by default in SQL Database).

```
ALTER DATABASE TSQL2012 SET READ_COMMITTED_SNAPSHOT ON;
```

## 2-6b

Open two new connections. (This exercise will refer to them as Connection 1 and Connection 2.)

## 2-6c

Run the following code in Connection 1 to open a transaction, update rows in *Sales.OrderDetails*, and query it.

```
BEGIN TRAN;

  UPDATE Sales.OrderDetails
    SET discount += 0.05
  WHERE orderid = 10249;

  SELECT orderid, productid, unitprice, qty, discount
  FROM Sales.OrderDetails
  WHERE orderid = 10249;
```

## 2-6d

Run the following code in Connection 2, which is now running under the *READ COMMITTED SNAPSHOT* isolation level because the database flag *READ_COMMITTED_SNAPSHOT* is turned on. Notice that you're not blocked—instead, you get an earlier, consistent version of the data that was available when the statement started (with discount values of 0.00).

```
BEGIN TRAN;

  SELECT orderid, productid, unitprice, qty, discount
  FROM Sales.OrderDetails
  WHERE orderid = 10249;
```

## 2-6e

Go to Connection 1 and commit the transaction.

```
COMMIT TRAN;
```

## 2-6f

Go to Connection 2, query the data again, and commit the transaction; notice that you get the new discount values of 0.05.

```
  SELECT orderid, productid, unitprice, qty, discount
  FROM Sales.OrderDetails
  WHERE orderid = 10249;

COMMIT TRAN;
```

## 2-6g

Run the following code for cleanup.

```
UPDATE Sales.OrderDetails
  SET discount = 0.00
WHERE orderid = 10249;
```

Close all connections.

## 2-6h

If you are running against an on-premises SQL Server instance, change the database flags back to the defaults, disabling isolation levels based on row versioning.

```
ALTER DATABASE TSQL2012 SET ALLOW_SNAPSHOT_ISOLATION OFF;
ALTER DATABASE TSQL2012 SET READ_COMMITTED_SNAPSHOT OFF;
```

Exercise 3 (steps 1 through 7) deals with deadlocks.

## 3-1

Open two new connections. (This exercise will refer to them as Connection 1 and Connection 2.)

## 3-2

Run the following code in Connection 1 to open a transaction and update the row for product 2 in *Production.Products.*

```
BEGIN TRAN;

  UPDATE Production.Products
    SET unitprice += 1.00
  WHERE productid = 2;
```

## 3-3

Run the following code in Connection 2 to open a transaction and update the row for product 3 in *Production.Products.*

```
BEGIN TRAN;

  UPDATE Production.Products
    SET unitprice += 1.00
  WHERE productid = 3;
```

## 3-4

Run the following code in Connection 1 to query product 3. You will be blocked. (Remember to un-comment the hint if you are connected to SQL Database.)

```
  SELECT productid, unitprice
  FROM Production.Products -- WITH (READCOMMITTEDLOCK)
  WHERE productid = 3;

COMMIT TRAN;
```

## 3-5

Run the following code in Connection 2 to query product 2. You will be blocked, and a deadlock error will be generated either in Connection 1 or Connection 2.

```
  SELECT productid, unitprice
  FROM Production.Products -- WITH (READCOMMITTEDLOCK)
  WHERE productid = 2;

COMMIT TRAN;
```

## 3-6

Can you suggest a way to prevent this deadlock? Hint: Refer back to what you read in the "Deadlocks" section.

## 3-7

Run the following code for cleanup.

```
UPDATE Production.Products
  SET unitprice = 19.00
WHERE productid = 2;

UPDATE Production.Products
  SET unitprice = 10.00
WHERE productid = 3;
```

# Programmable Objects

This chapter provides a brief overview of programmable objects to familiarize you with the capabilities of Microsoft SQL Server in this area and with the concepts involved. The chapter covers variables; batches; flow elements; cursors; temporary tables; routines such as user-defined functions, stored procedures, and triggers; and dynamic SQL. The purpose of this chapter is to provide a high-level overview, not to delve into technical details. Try to focus on the logical aspects and capabilities of programmable objects rather than trying to understand all code elements and their technicalities.

## Variables

Variables allow you to temporarily store data values for later use in the same batch in which they were declared. I describe batches later in this chapter, but for now, the important thing for you to know is that a batch is one T-SQL statement or more sent to SQL Server for execution as a single unit.

Use a *DECLARE* statement to declare one or more variables, and use a *SET* statement to assign a value to a single variable. For example, the following code declares a variable called @i of an *INT* data type and assigns it the value 10.

```
DECLARE @i AS INT;
SET @i = 10;
```

SQL Server 2008 and SQL Server 2012 support the declaration and initialization of variables in the same statement, like this.

```
DECLARE @i AS INT = 10;
```

When you are assigning a value to a scalar variable, the value must be the result of a scalar expression. The expression can be a scalar subquery. For example, the following code declares a variable called @*empname* and assigns it the result of a scalar subquery that returns the full name of the employee with an ID of 3.

```
USE TSQL2012;

DECLARE @empname AS NVARCHAR(31);

SET @empname = (SELECT firstname + N' ' + lastname
                FROM HR.Employees
                WHERE empid = 3);

SELECT @empname AS empname;
```

This code returns the following output.

```
empname
----------
Judy Lew
```

The *SET* statement can operate only on one variable at a time, so if you need to assign values to multiple attributes, you need to use multiple *SET* statements. This can involve unnecessary overhead when you need to pull multiple attribute values from the same row. For example, the following code uses two separate *SET* statements to pull both the first and the last names of the employee with the ID of 3 to two separate variables.

```
DECLARE @firstname AS NVARCHAR(10), @lastname AS NVARCHAR(20);

SET @firstname = (SELECT firstname
                  FROM HR.Employees
                  WHERE empid = 3);
SET @lastname = (SELECT lastname
                 FROM HR.Employees
                 WHERE empid = 3);

SELECT @firstname AS firstname, @lastname AS lastname;
```

This code returns the following output.

```
firstname   lastname
----------  ---------
Judy        Lew
```

SQL Server also supports a nonstandard assignment *SELECT* statement, which allows you to query data and assign multiple values obtained from the same row to multiple variables by using a single statement. Here's an example.

```
DECLARE @firstname AS NVARCHAR(10), @lastname AS NVARCHAR(20);

SELECT
  @firstname = firstname,
  @lastname  = lastname
FROM HR.Employees
WHERE empid = 3;

SELECT @firstname AS firstname, @lastname AS lastname;
```

The assignment *SELECT* has predictable behavior when exactly one row qualifies. However, note that if the query has more than one qualifying row, the code doesn't fail. The assignments take place per each qualifying row, and with each row accessed, the values from the current row overwrite the existing values in the variables. When the assignment *SELECT* finishes, the values in the variables are those from the last row that SQL Server happened to access. For example, the following assignment *SELECT* has two qualifying rows.

```
DECLARE @empname AS NVARCHAR(31);

SELECT @empname = firstname + N' ' + lastname
FROM HR.Employees
WHERE mgrid = 2;

SELECT @empname AS empname;
```

The employee information that ends up in the variable after the assignment *SELECT* finishes depends on the order in which SQL Server happens to access those rows—and you have no control over this order. When I ran this code I got the following output.

```
empname
----------
Sven Buck
```

The *SET* statement is safer than assignment *SELECT* because it requires you to use a scalar subquery to pull data from a table. Remember that a scalar subquery fails at run time if it returns more than one value. For example, the following code fails.

```
DECLARE @empname AS NVARCHAR(31);

SET @empname = (SELECT firstname + N' ' + lastname
                FROM HR.Employees
                WHERE mgrid = 2);

SELECT @empname AS empname;
```

Because the variable was not assigned a value, it remains *NULL*, which is the default for variables that were not initialized. This code returns the following output.

```
Msg 512, Level 16, State 1, Line 3
Subquery returned more than 1 value. This is not permitted when the subquery follows =, !=, <,
<= , >, >= or when the subquery is used as an expression.
empname
--------
NULL
```

# Batches

A batch is one or more T-SQL statements sent by a client application to SQL Server for execution as a single unit. The batch undergoes parsing (syntax checking), resolution (checking the existence of referenced objects and columns), permissions checking, and optimization as a unit.

Don't confuse transactions and batches. A transaction is an atomic unit of work. A batch can have multiple transactions, and a transaction can be submitted in parts as multiple batches. When a transaction is canceled or rolled back in midstream, SQL Server undoes the partial activity that has taken place since the beginning of the transaction, regardless of where the batch began.

Client application programming interfaces (APIs) such as ADO.NET provide you with methods for submitting a batch of code to SQL Server for execution. SQL Server utilities such as SQL Server Management Studio, SQLCMD, and OSQL provide a client command called *GO* that signals the end of a batch. Note that the *GO* command is a client command and not a T-SQL server command.

## A Batch As a Unit of Parsing

A batch is a set of commands that are parsed and executed as a unit. If the parsing is successful, SQL Server will then attempt to execute the batch. In the event of a syntax error in the batch, the whole batch is not submitted to SQL Server for execution. For example, the following code has three batches, the second of which has a syntax error (*FOM* instead of *FROM* in the second query).

```
-- Valid batch
PRINT 'First batch';
USE TSQL2012;
GO
-- Invalid batch
PRINT 'Second batch';
SELECT custid FROM Sales.Customers;
SELECT orderid FOM Sales.Orders;
GO
-- Valid batch
PRINT 'Third batch';
SELECT empid FROM HR.Employees;
```

Because the second batch has a syntax error, the whole batch is not submitted to SQL Server for execution. The first and third batches pass syntax validation and therefore are submitted for execution. This code produces the following output, showing that the whole second batch was not executed.

```
First batch
Msg 102, Level 15, State 1, Line 4
Incorrect syntax near 'Sales'.
Third batch
empid
-----------
2
7
1
5
6
8
3
9
4

(9 row(s) affected)
```

## Batches and Variables

A variable is local to the batch in which it is defined. If you try to refer to a variable that was defined in another batch, you will get an error saying that the variable was not defined. For example, the following code declares a variable and prints its content in one batch, and then tries to print its content from another batch.

```
DECLARE @i AS INT;
SET @i = 10;
-- Succeeds
PRINT @i;
GO

-- Fails
PRINT @i;
```

The reference to the variable in the first *PRINT* statement is valid because it appears in the same batch where the variable was declared, but the second reference is invalid. Therefore, the first *PRINT* statement returns the variable's value (10), whereas the second fails. Here's the output returned from this code.

```
10
Msg 137, Level 15, State 2, Line 3
Must declare the scalar variable "@i".
```

## Statements That Cannot Be Combined in the Same Batch

The following statements cannot be combined with other statements in the same batch: *CREATE DEFAULT, CREATE FUNCTION, CREATE PROCEDURE, CREATE RULE, CREATE SCHEMA, CREATE TRIGGER,* and *CREATE VIEW.* For example, the following code has an *IF* statement followed by a *CREATE VIEW* statement in the same batch and therefore is invalid.

```
IF OBJECT_ID('Sales.MyView', 'V') IS NOT NULL DROP VIEW Sales.MyView;

CREATE VIEW Sales.MyView
AS

SELECT YEAR(orderdate) AS orderyear, COUNT(*) AS numorders
FROM Sales.Orders
GROUP BY YEAR(orderdate);
GO
```

An attempt to run this code generates the following error.

```
Msg 111, Level 15, State 1, Line 3
'CREATE VIEW' must be the first statement in a query batch.
```

To get around the problem, separate the *IF* and *CREATE VIEW* statements into different batches by adding a *GO* command after the *IF* statement.

## A Batch As a Unit of Resolution

A batch is a unit of resolution. This means that checking the existence of objects and columns happens at the batch level. Keep this fact in mind when you are designing batch boundaries. When you apply schema changes to an object and try to manipulate the object data in the same batch, SQL Server might not be aware of the schema changes yet and fail the data manipulation statement with a resolution error. I'll demonstrate the problem through an example and then recommend best practices.

Run the following code to create a table called *T1* in the current database, with one column called *col1*.

```
IF OBJECT_ID('dbo.T1', 'U') IS NOT NULL DROP TABLE dbo.T1;
CREATE TABLE dbo.T1(col1 INT);
```

Next, try to add a column called *col2* to *T1* and query the new column in the same batch.

```
ALTER TABLE dbo.T1 ADD col2 INT;
SELECT col1, col2 FROM dbo.T1;
```

Even though the code might seem to be perfectly valid, the batch fails during the resolution phase with the following error.

```
Msg 207, Level 16, State 1, Line 2
Invalid column name 'col2'.
```

At the time the *SELECT* statement was resolved, *T1* had only one column, and the reference to the *col2* column caused the error. One best practice you can follow to avoid such problems is to separate DDL and DML statements into different batches, as in the following example.

```
ALTER TABLE dbo.T1 ADD col2 INT;
GO
SELECT col1, col2 FROM dbo.T1;
```

## The *GO n* Option

The *GO* command is not really a T-SQL command; it's actually a command used by SQL Server's client tools, such as SSMS, to denote the end of a batch. This command supports an argument indicating how many times you want to execute the batch. To see how the *GO* command with the argument works, first create the table *T1* by using the following code.

```
IF OBJECT_ID('dbo.T1', 'U') IS NOT NULL DROP TABLE dbo.T1;
CREATE TABLE dbo.T1(col1 INT IDENTITY);
```

The *col1* column gets its values automatically from an identity property. Note that the demo would work just as well if you used a default constraint to generate values from a sequence object. Next, run the following code to suppress the default output produced by DML statements that indicates how many rows were affected.

```
SET NOCOUNT ON;
```

Finally, run the following code to define a batch with an *INSERT DEFAULT VALUES* statement and to execute the batch 100 times.

```
INSERT INTO dbo.T1 DEFAULT VALUES;
GO 100

SELECT * FROM dbo.T1;
```

The query returns 100 rows with the values 1 through 100 in *col1*.

# Flow Elements

Flow elements allow you to control the flow of your code. T-SQL provides very basic forms of control with flow elements, including the *IF ... ELSE* element and the *WHILE* element.

## The *IF ... ELSE* Flow Element

The *IF ... ELSE* element allows you to control the flow of your code based on a predicate. You specify a statement or statement block that is executed if the predicate is *TRUE*, and optionally a statement or statement block that is executed if the predicate is *FALSE* or *UNKNOWN*.

For example, the following code checks whether today is the last day of the year (in other words, whether today's year is different than tomorrow's year). If this is true, the code prints a message saying that today is the last day of the year; if it is not true ("else"), the code prints a message saying that today is not the last day of the year.

```
IF YEAR(SYSDATETIME()) <> YEAR(DATEADD(day, 1, SYSDATETIME()))
  PRINT 'Today is the last day of the year.';
ELSE
  PRINT 'Today is not the last day of the year.';
```

In this example, I use *PRINT* statements to demonstrate which parts of the code were executed and which weren't, but of course you can specify other statements as well.

Keep in mind that T-SQL uses three-valued logic and that the *ELSE* block is activated when the predicate is either *FALSE* or *UNKNOWN*. In cases for which both *FALSE* and *UNKNOWN* are possible outcomes of the predicate (for example, when *NULL* marks are involved) and you need different treatment for each case, make sure you have an explicit test for *NULL* marks with the *IS NULL* predicate.

If the flow you need to control involves more than two cases, you can nest *IF ... ELSE* elements. For example, the next code handles the following three cases differently:

1. Today is the last day of the year.

2. Today is the last day of the month but not the last day of the year.

3. Today is not the last day of the month.

```
IF YEAR(SYSDATETIME()) <> YEAR(DATEADD(day, 1, SYSDATETIME()))
  PRINT 'Today is the last day of the year.';
ELSE
  IF MONTH(SYSDATETIME()) <> MONTH(DATEADD(day, 1, SYSDATETIME()))
    PRINT 'Today is the last day of the month but not the last day of the year.';
  ELSE
    PRINT 'Today is not the last day of the month.';
```

If you need to run more than one statement in the *IF* or *ELSE* sections, you need to use a statement block. You mark the boundaries of a statement block with the *BEGIN* and *END* keywords. For example, the following code shows how to run one type of process if it's the first day of the month, and another type of process if it isn't.

```
IF DAY(SYSDATETIME()) = 1
BEGIN
  PRINT 'Today is the first day of the month.';
  PRINT 'Starting first-of-month-day process.';
  /* ... process code goes here ... */
  PRINT 'Finished first-of-month-day database process.';
END
ELSE
BEGIN
  PRINT 'Today is not the first day of the month.';
  PRINT 'Starting non-first-of-month-day process.';
  /* ... process code goes here ... */
  PRINT 'Finished non-first-of-month-day process.';
END
```

## The *WHILE* Flow Element

T-SQL provides the *WHILE* element to enable you to execute code in a loop. The *WHILE* element executes a statement or statement block repeatedly while the predicate you specify after the *WHILE* keyword is *TRUE*. When the predicate is *FALSE* or *UNKNOWN*, the loop terminates.

T-SQL doesn't provide a built-in looping element that executes a predetermined number of times, but it's very easy to mimic such an element with a *WHILE* loop and a variable. For example, the following code demonstrates how to write a loop that iterates 10 times.

```
DECLARE @i AS INT = 1;
WHILE @i <= 10
BEGIN
  PRINT @i;
  SET @i = @i + 1;
END;
```

The code declares an integer variable called *@i* that serves as the loop counter and initializes it with the value 1. The code then enters a loop that iterates while the variable is smaller than or equal to 10. In each iteration, the code in the loop's body prints the current value of *@i* and then increments it by 1. This code returns the following output showing that the loop iterated 10 times.

```
1
2
3
4
5
6
7
8
9
10
```

If at some point in the loop's body you want to break out of the current loop and proceed to execute the statement that appears after the loop's body, use the *BREAK* command. For example, the following code breaks from the loop if the value of *@i* is equal to 6.

```
DECLARE @i AS INT = 1;
WHILE @i <= 10
BEGIN
  IF @i = 6 BREAK;
  PRINT @i;
  SET @i = @i + 1;
END;
```

This code produces the following output showing that the loop iterated five times and terminated at the beginning of the sixth iteration.

```
1
2
3
4
5
```

Of course, this code is not very sensible; if you want the loop to iterate only five times, you should simply specify the predicate @i <= 5. Here I just wanted to demonstrate the use of the *BREAK* command with a simple example.

If at some point in the loop's body you want to skip the rest of the activity in the current iteration and evaluate the loop's predicate again, use the *CONTINUE* command. For example, the following code demonstrates how to skip the activity of the sixth iteration of the loop from the point where the *IF* statement appears and until the end of the loop's body.

```
DECLARE @i AS INT = 0;
WHILE @i < 10
BEGIN
  SET @i = @i + 1;
  IF @i = 6 CONTINUE;
  PRINT @i;
END;
```

The output of this code shows that the value of @i was printed in all iterations but the sixth.

```
1
2
3
4
5
7
8
9
10
```

## An Example of Using *IF* and *WHILE*

The following example illustrates how you can combine the use of the *IF* and *WHILE* elements. The purpose of the code in this example is to create a table called *dbo.Numbers* and populate it with 1,000 rows with the values 1 through 1,000 in the column *n*.

```
SET NOCOUNT ON;
IF OBJECT_ID('dbo.Numbers', 'U') IS NOT NULL DROP TABLE dbo.Numbers;
CREATE TABLE dbo.Numbers(n INT NOT NULL PRIMARY KEY);
GO

DECLARE @i AS INT = 1;
WHILE @i <= 1000
BEGIN
  INSERT INTO dbo.Numbers(n) VALUES(@i);
  SET @i = @i + 1;
END
```

The code uses the *IF* statement to check whether the *Numbers* table already exists in the current database, and if it does, the code drops it. The code then uses a *WHILE* loop to iterate 1,000 times and populate the *Numbers* table with the values 1 through 1,000.

# Cursors

In Chapter 2, "Single-Table Queries," I explained that a query without an *ORDER BY* clause returns a set (or a multiset), whereas a query with an *ORDER BY* clause returns what standard SQL calls a *cursor*—a nonrelational result with order guaranteed among rows. In the context of the discussion in Chapter 2, the use of the term "cursor" was conceptual. T-SQL also supports an object called *cursor* that allows you to process rows from a result set of a query one at a time and in a requested order. This is in contrast to using set-based queries—normal queries without a cursor for which you manipulate the set or multiset as a whole and cannot rely on order.

I want to stress that your default choice should be to use set-based queries; only when you have a compelling reason to do otherwise should you consider using cursors. This recommendation is based on several factors, such as the following.

1. First and foremost, when you use cursors you pretty much go against the relational model, which is based on set theory.

2. The record-by-record manipulation done by the cursor has overhead. A certain extra cost is associated with each record manipulation by the cursor when compared to set-based manipulation. Given a set-based query and cursor code that do similar physical processing behind the scenes, the cursor code is usually many times slower than the set-based code.

3. With cursors, you spend a lot of code on the physical aspects of the solution—in other words, on how to process the data (declaring the cursor, opening it, looping through the cursor records, closing the cursor, and deallocating the cursor). With set-based solutions, you mainly focus on the logical aspects of the solution—in other words, on what to get instead of on how to get it. Therefore, cursor solutions tend to be longer, less readable, and harder to maintain compared to set-based solutions.

For most people, it is not simple to think in terms of sets immediately when they start learning SQL. In contrast to thinking in relational terms, it is more intuitive for most people to think in terms of cursors—processing one record at a time in a certain order. As a result, cursors are widely used, and in most cases they are misused; that is, they are used where much better set-based solutions exist. Make a conscious effort to adopt the set-based state of mind and to truly think in terms of sets. It can take time—in some cases years—but as long as you're working with a language that is based on the relational model, that's the right way to think.

Working with cursors is like fishing with a rod and catching one fish at a time. Working with sets, on the other hand, is like fishing with a net and catching a whole group of fish at one time. As another analogy, consider two kinds of orange-packing factories—an old-fashioned one and a modern one. The factories are supposed to arrange oranges in three different kinds of packages based on size—small, medium, and large. The old-fashioned factory works in cursor mode, which means that conveyor belts loaded with oranges come in, and a person at the end of each conveyor belt examines each orange and places it in the right kind of box based on its size. This type of processing is, of course, very slow. Also, order can matter here: If the oranges arrive on the conveyor belt already sorted by size, processing them is easier, so the conveyor belt can be set to a higher speed. The modern factory works in a set-based mode: All oranges are placed in a big container with a grid at the bottom with small holes. The machine shakes the container and only the small oranges go through the holes. The machine then moves the oranges to a container with medium holes and shakes the container, allowing the medium oranges to go through. The big oranges are left in the container.

Assuming you are convinced that set-based solutions should be your default choice, it is important to understand the exceptions—when you should consider cursors. One example is when you need to apply a certain task to each row from some table or view. For example, you might need to execute some administrative task for each index or table in your database. In such a case, it makes sense to use a cursor to iterate through the index or table names one at a time, and execute the relevant task for each of those.

Here's the output returned by this code, shown in abbreviated form.

```
custid      ordermonth qty          runqty
----------- ---------- ----------   -----------
1           2007-08    38           38
1           2007-10    41           79
1           2008-01    17           96
1           2008-03    18           114
1           2008-04    60           174
2           2006-09    6            6
2           2007-08    18           24
2           2007-11    10           34
2           2008-03    29           63
3           2006-11    24           24
3           2007-04    30           54
3           2007-05    80           134
3           2007-06    83           217
3           2007-09    102          319
3           2008-01    40           359
...
89          2006-07    80           80
89          2006-11    105          185
89          2007-03    142          327
89          2007-04    59           386
89          2007-07    59           445
89          2007-10    164          609
89          2007-11    94           703
89          2008-01    140          843
89          2008-02    50           893
89          2008-04    90           983
89          2008-05    80           1063
90          2007-07    5            5
90          2007-09    15           20
90          2007-10    34           54
90          2008-02    82           136
90          2008-04    12           148
91          2006-12    45           45
91          2007-07    31           76
91          2007-12    28           104
91          2008-02    20           124
91          2008-04    81           205

(636 row(s) affected)
```

As explained in Chapter 7, SQL Server 2012 supports enhanced window functions that allow you to provide elegant and highly efficient solutions to running aggregates, freeing you from needing to use cursors. Here's how you would address the same task with a window function.

```
SELECT custid, ordermonth, qty,
  SUM(qty) OVER(PARTITION BY custid
               ORDER BY ordermonth
               ROWS UNBOUNDED PRECEDING) AS runqty
FROM Sales.CustOrders
ORDER BY custid, ordermonth;
```

# Temporary Tables

When you need to temporarily store data in tables, in certain cases you might prefer not to work with permanent tables. Suppose you need the data to be visible only to the current session, or even only to the current batch. As an example, suppose that you need to store temporary data during data processing, as in the cursor example in the previous section.

SQL Server supports three kinds of temporary tables that you might find more convenient to work with than permanent tables in such cases: local temporary tables, global temporary tables, and table variables. The following sections describe the three kinds and demonstrate their use with code samples.

## Local Temporary Tables

You create a local temporary table by naming it with a single number sign as a prefix, such as *#T1*. All three kinds of temporary tables are created in the *tempdb* database.

A local temporary table is visible only to the session that created it, in the creating level and all inner levels in the call stack (inner procedures, functions, triggers, and dynamic batches). A local temporary table is destroyed automatically by SQL Server when the creating level in the call stack goes out of scope. For example, suppose that a stored procedure called *Proc1* calls a procedure called *Proc2*, which in turn calls a procedure called *Proc3*, which in turn calls a procedure called *Proc4*. *Proc2* creates a temporary table called *#T1* before calling *Proc3*. The table *#T1* is visible to *Proc2*, *Proc3*, and *Proc4* but not to *Proc1*, and is destroyed automatically by SQL Server when *Proc2* finishes. If the temporary table is created in an ad-hoc batch in the outermost nesting level of the session (in other words, when the value of the *@@NESTLEVEL* function is 0), it is visible to all subsequent batches as well and is destroyed by SQL Server automatically only when the creating session disconnects.

You might wonder how SQL Server prevents name conflicts when two sessions create local temporary tables with the same name. SQL Server internally adds a suffix to the table name that makes it unique in *tempdb*. As a developer, you shouldn't care—you refer to the table using the name you provided without the internal suffix, and only your session has access to your table.

One obvious scenario for which local temporary tables are useful is when you have a process that needs to store intermediate results temporarily—such as during a loop—and later query the data.

Another scenario is when you need to access the result of some expensive processing multiple times. For example, suppose that you need to join the *Sales.Orders* and *Sales.OrderDetails* tables, aggregate order quantities by order year, and join two instances of the aggregated data to compare each year's total quantity with the previous year. The *Orders* and *OrderDetails* tables in the sample database are very small, but in real-life situations such tables can have millions of rows. One option is to use table expressions, but remember that table expressions are virtual. The expensive work involving scanning all the data, joining the *Orders* and *OrderDetails* tables, and aggregating the data would have to happen twice with table expressions. Instead, it makes sense to do all the expensive work only once—storing the result in a local temporary table—and then join two instances of the temporary table, especially because the result of the expensive work is a very tiny set with only one row per each order year.

The following code illustrates this scenario using a local temporary table.

```
IF OBJECT_ID('tempdb.dbo.#MyOrderTotalsByYear') IS NOT NULL
  DROP TABLE dbo.#MyOrderTotalsByYear;
GO

CREATE TABLE #MyOrderTotalsByYear
(
  orderyear INT NOT NULL PRIMARY KEY,
  qty       INT NOT NULL
);

INSERT INTO #MyOrderTotalsByYear(orderyear, qty)
  SELECT
    YEAR(O.orderdate) AS orderyear,
    SUM(OD.qty) AS qty
  FROM Sales.Orders AS O
    JOIN Sales.OrderDetails AS OD
      ON OD.orderid = O.orderid
  GROUP BY YEAR(orderdate);

SELECT Cur.orderyear, Cur.qty AS curyearqty, Prv.qty AS prvyearqty
FROM dbo.#MyOrderTotalsByYear AS Cur
  LEFT OUTER JOIN dbo.#MyOrderTotalsByYear AS Prv
    ON Cur.orderyear = Prv.orderyear + 1;
```

This code produces the following output.

```
orderyear   curyearqty  prvyearqty
----------- ----------- -----------
2007        25489       9581
2008        16247       25489
2006        9581        NULL
```

To verify that the local temporary table is visible only to the creating session, try accessing it from another session.

```
SELECT orderyear, qty FROM dbo.#MyOrderTotalsByYear;
```

You get the following error.

```
Msg 208, Level 16, State 0, Line 1
Invalid object name '#MyOrderTotalsByYear'.
```

When you're done, go back to the original session and drop the temporary table.

```
IF OBJECT_ID('tempdb.dbo.#MyOrderTotalsByYear') IS NOT NULL
  DROP TABLE dbo.#MyOrderTotalsByYear;
```

It is generally recommended that you clean up resources as soon as you are done working with them.

# Global Temporary Tables

> **Note** At the date of this writing, global temporary tables are not supported by Windows Azure SQL Database, so if you want to run the code samples from this section, you will need to connect to an on-premises SQL Server instance.

When you create a global temporary table, it is visible to all other sessions. Global temporary tables are destroyed automatically by SQL Server when the creating session disconnects and there are no active references to the table. You create a global temporary table by naming it with two number signs as a prefix, such as *##T1*.

Global temporary tables are useful when you want to share temporary data with everyone. No special permissions are required, and everyone has full DDL and DML access. Of course, the fact that everyone has full access means that anyone can change or even drop the table, so consider the alternatives carefully.

For example, the following code creates a global temporary table called *##Globals* with columns called *id* and *val*.

```
CREATE TABLE dbo.##Globals
(
  id  sysname     NOT NULL PRIMARY KEY,
  val SQL_VARIANT NOT NULL
);
```

This table in this example is intended to mimic global variables, which are not supported by SQL Server. The *id* column is of a *sysname* data type (the type that SQL Server uses internally to represent identifiers), and the *val* column is of a *SQL_VARIANT* data type (a generic type that can store within it a value of almost any base type).

Anyone can insert rows into the table. For example, run the following code to insert a row representing a variable called *i* and initialize it with the integer value 10.

```
INSERT INTO dbo.##Globals(id, val) VALUES(N'i', CAST(10 AS INT));
```

Anyone can modify and retrieve data from the table. For example, run the following code from any session to query the current value of the variable *i*.

```
SELECT val FROM dbo.##Globals WHERE id = N'i';
```

This code returns the following output.

```
val
-----------
10
```

> **Note** Keep in mind that as soon as the session that created the global temporary table disconnects and there are no active references to the table, SQL Server automatically destroys the table.

If you want a global temporary table to be created every time SQL Server starts, and you don't want SQL Server to try to destroy it automatically, you need to create the table from a stored procedure that is marked as a startup procedure (for details, see "sp_procoption" in SQL Server Books Online at the following URL: *http://msdn.microsoft.com/en-us/library/ms181720.aspx*).

Run the following code from any session to explicitly destroy the global temporary table.

```
DROP TABLE dbo.##Globals;
```

## Table Variables

Table variables are similar to local temporary tables in some ways and different in others. You declare table variables much like you declare other variables, by using the *DECLARE* statement.

As with local temporary tables, table variables have a physical presence as a table in the *tempdb* database, contrary to the common misconception that they exist only in memory. Like local temporary tables, table variables are visible only to the creating session, but they have a more limited scope: only the current batch. Table variables are visible neither to inner batches in the call stack nor to subsequent batches in the session.

If an explicit transaction is rolled back, changes made to temporary tables in that transaction are rolled back as well; however, changes made to table variables by statements that completed in the transaction aren't rolled back. Only changes made by the active statement that failed or that was terminated before completion are undone.

Temporary tables and table variables also have optimization differences, but those are outside the scope of this book. For now, I'll just say that in terms of performance, usually it makes more sense to use table variables with very small volumes of data (only a few rows) and to use local temporary tables otherwise.

For example, the following code uses a table variable instead of a local temporary table to compare total order quantities of each order year with the year before.

```
DECLARE @MyOrderTotalsByYear TABLE
(
  orderyear INT NOT NULL PRIMARY KEY,
  qty       INT NOT NULL
);
```

```
INSERT INTO @MyOrderTotalsByYear(orderyear, qty)
  SELECT
    YEAR(O.orderdate) AS orderyear,
    SUM(OD.qty) AS qty
  FROM Sales.Orders AS O
    JOIN Sales.OrderDetails AS OD
      ON OD.orderid = O.orderid
  GROUP BY YEAR(orderdate);

SELECT Cur.orderyear, Cur.qty AS curyearqty, Prv.qty AS prvyearqty
FROM @MyOrderTotalsByYear AS Cur
  LEFT OUTER JOIN @MyOrderTotalsByYear AS Prv
    ON Cur.orderyear = Prv.orderyear + 1;
```

This code returns the following output.

```
orderyear    curyearqty   prvyearqty
-----------  -----------  -----------
2006         9581         NULL
2007         25489        9581
2008         16247        25489
```

Note that in SQL Server 2012, there is a more efficient way to achieve the same thing, by using the *LAG* function, like this.

```
DECLARE @MyOrderTotalsByYear TABLE
(
  orderyear INT NOT NULL PRIMARY KEY,
  qty       INT NOT NULL
);

INSERT INTO @MyOrderTotalsByYear(orderyear, qty)
  SELECT
    YEAR(O.orderdate) AS orderyear,
    SUM(OD.qty) AS qty
  FROM Sales.Orders AS O
    JOIN Sales.OrderDetails AS OD
      ON OD.orderid = O.orderid
  GROUP BY YEAR(orderdate);

SELECT orderyear, qty AS curyearqty,
  LAG(qty) OVER(ORDER BY orderyear) AS prvyearqty
FROM @MyOrderTotalsByYear;
```

# Table Types

SQL Server 2008 and SQL Server 2012 support table types. When you create a table type, you pre-serve a table definition in the database and can later reuse it as the table definition of table variables and input parameters of stored procedures and user-defined functions.

For example, the following code creates a table type called *dbo.OrderTotalsByYear* in the current database.

```
IF TYPE_ID('dbo.OrderTotalsByYear') IS NOT NULL
  DROP TYPE dbo.OrderTotalsByYear;

CREATE TYPE dbo.OrderTotalsByYear AS TABLE
(
  orderyear INT NOT NULL PRIMARY KEY,
  qty       INT NOT NULL
);
```

After the table type is created, whenever you need to declare a table variable based on the table type's definition, you won't need to repeat the code—instead you can simply specify *dbo.OrderTotalsByYear* as the variable's type, like this.

```
DECLARE @MyOrderTotalsByYear AS dbo.OrderTotalsByYear;
```

As a more complete example, the following code declares a variable called *@MyOrderTotalsByYear* of the new table type, queries the *Orders* and *OrderDetails* tables to calculate total order quantities by order year, stores the result of the query in the table variable, and queries the variable to present its contents.

```
DECLARE @MyOrderTotalsByYear AS dbo.OrderTotalsByYear;

INSERT INTO @MyOrderTotalsByYear(orderyear, qty)
  SELECT
    YEAR(O.orderdate) AS orderyear,
    SUM(OD.qty) AS qty
  FROM Sales.Orders AS O
    JOIN Sales.OrderDetails AS OD
      ON OD.orderid = O.orderid
  GROUP BY YEAR(orderdate);

SELECT orderyear, qty FROM @MyOrderTotalsByYear;
```

This code returns the following output.

```
orderyear   qty
----------- -----------
2006        9581
2007        25489
2008        16247
```

The benefit of the table type feature extends beyond just helping you shorten your code. As I mentioned, you can use it as the type of input parameters of stored procedures and functions, which is an extremely useful capability.

# Dynamic SQL

SQL Server allows you to construct a batch of T-SQL code as a character string and then execute that batch. This capability is called *dynamic SQL*. SQL Server provides two ways of executing dynamic SQL: using the *EXEC* (short for *EXECUTE*) command, and using the *sp_executesql* stored procedure. I will explain the difference between the two and provide examples for using each.

Dynamic SQL is useful for several purposes, including:

- **Automating administrative tasks**   For example, querying metadata and constructing and executing a *BACKUP DATABASE* statement for each database in an on-premises instance

- **Improving performance of certain tasks**   For example, constructing parameterized ad-hoc queries that can reuse previously cached execution plans (more on this later)

- **Constructing elements of the code based on querying the actual data**   For example, constructing a *PIVOT* query dynamically when you don't know ahead of time which elements should appear in the *IN* clause of the *PIVOT* operator

> **Note**  Be extremely careful when concatenating user input as part of your code. Hackers can attempt to inject code you did not intend to run. The best measure you can take against SQL injection is to avoid concatenating user input as part of your code (for example, by using parameters). If you do concatenate user input as part of your code, make sure you thoroughly inspect the input and look for SQL injection attempts. You can find an excellent article on the subject in SQL Server Books Online under "SQL Injection."

## The *EXEC* Command

The *EXEC* command is the original technique provided in T-SQL for executing dynamic SQL. *EXEC* accepts a character string in parentheses as input and executes the batch of code within the character string. *EXEC* supports both regular and Unicode character strings as input.

The following example stores a character string with a *PRINT* statement in the variable @sql and then uses the *EXEC* command to invoke the batch of code stored within the variable.

```
DECLARE @sql AS VARCHAR(100);
SET @sql = 'PRINT ''This message was printed by a dynamic SQL batch.'';';
EXEC(@sql);
```

Notice the use of two single quotes to represent one single quote in a string within a string. This code returns the following output.

```
This message was printed by a dynamic SQL batch.
```

# The *sp_executesql* Stored Procedure

The *sp_executesql* stored procedure was introduced after the *EXEC* command. It is more secure and more flexible in the sense that it has an interface; that is, it supports input and output parameters. Note that unlike *EXEC*, *sp_executesql* supports only Unicode character strings as the input batch of code.

The fact that you can use input and output parameters in your dynamic SQL code can help you write more secure and more efficient code. In terms of security, parameters that appear in the code cannot be considered part of the code—they can only be considered operands in expressions. So, by using parameters, you can eliminate your exposure to SQL injection.

The *sp_executesql* stored procedure can perform better than *EXEC* because its parameterization aids in reusing cached execution plans. An execution plan is the physical processing plan that SQL Server produces for a query, with the set of instructions regarding which objects to access, in what order, which indexes to use, how to access them, which join algorithms to use, and so on. To simplify things, one of the requirements for reusing a previously cached plan is that the query string be the same as the one for which the plan exists in cache. The best way to efficiently reuse query execution plans is to use stored procedures with parameters. This way, even when parameter values change, the query string remains the same. But if for your own reasons you decide to use ad-hoc code instead of stored procedures, at least you can still work with parameters if you use *sp_executesql* and therefore increase the chances for plan reuse.

The *sp_executesql* procedure has two input parameters and an assignments section. You specify the Unicode character string holding the batch of code you want to run in the first parameter, which is called *@stmt*. You provide a Unicode character string holding the declarations of input and output parameters in the second input parameter, which is called *@params*. Then you specify the assignments of input and output parameters separated by commas.

The following example constructs a batch of code with a query against the *Sales.Orders* table. The example uses an input parameter called *@orderid* in the query's filter.

```
DECLARE @sql AS NVARCHAR(100);

SET @sql = N'SELECT orderid, custid, empid, orderdate
FROM Sales.Orders
WHERE orderid = @orderid;';

EXEC sp_executesql
  @stmt = @sql,
  @params = N'@orderid AS INT',
  @orderid = 10248;
```

This code generates the following output.

```
orderid     custid      empid       orderdate
----------- ----------- ----------- -----------------------
10248       85          5           2006-07-04 00:00:00.000
```

This code assigns the value *10248* to the input parameter, but even if you run it again with a different value, the code string remains the same. This way, you increase the chances for reusing a previously cached plan.

## Using *PIVOT* with Dynamic SQL

This section is advanced and optional, and is intended for those readers who feel very comfortable with pivoting techniques and dynamic SQL. In Chapter 7, I explained how to use the *PIVOT* operator to pivot data. I mentioned that in a static query, you have to know ahead of time which values to specify in the *IN* clause of the *PIVOT* operator. Following is an example of a static query with the *PIVOT* operator.

```
SELECT *
FROM (SELECT shipperid, YEAR(orderdate) AS orderyear, freight
      FROM Sales.Orders) AS D
  PIVOT(SUM(freight) FOR orderyear IN([2006],[2007],[2008])) AS P;
```

This example queries the *Sales.Orders* table and pivots the data so that it returns shipper IDs in the rows, order years in the columns, and the total freight in the intersection of each shipper and order year. This code returns the following output.

```
shipperid   2006          2007           2008
---------   -----------   ------------   -------------
3           4233.78       11413.35       4865.38
1           2297.42       8681.38        5206.53
2           3748.67       12374.04       12122.14
```

With the static query, you have to know ahead of time which values (order years in this case) to specify in the *IN* clause of the *PIVOT* operator. This means that you need to revise the code every year. Instead, you can query the distinct order years from the data, construct a batch of dynamic SQL code based on the years that you queried, and execute the dynamic SQL batch like this.

```
DECLARE
    @sql      AS NVARCHAR(1000),
    @orderyear AS INT,
    @first    AS INT;

DECLARE C CURSOR FAST_FORWARD FOR
    SELECT DISTINCT(YEAR(orderdate)) AS orderyear
    FROM Sales.Orders
    ORDER BY orderyear;

SET @first = 1;

SET @sql = N'SELECT *
FROM (SELECT shipperid, YEAR(orderdate) AS orderyear, freight
      FROM Sales.Orders) AS D
  PIVOT(SUM(freight) FOR orderyear IN(';

OPEN C;
```

```
FETCH NEXT FROM C INTO @orderyear;

WHILE @@fetch_status = 0
BEGIN
  IF @first = 0
    SET @sql = @sql + N','
  ELSE
    SET @first = 0;

  SET @sql = @sql + QUOTENAME(@orderyear);

  FETCH NEXT FROM C INTO @orderyear;
END

CLOSE C;

DEALLOCATE C;

SET @sql = @sql + N')) AS P;';

EXEC sp_executesql @stmt = @sql;
```

> **Note** There are more efficient ways to concatenate strings than using a cursor, such as using Common Language Runtime (CLR) aggregates and the *FOR XML PATH* option, but they are more advanced and are beyond the scope of this book.

# Routines

Routines are programmable objects that encapsulate code to calculate a result or to execute activity. SQL Server supports three types of routines: user-defined functions, stored procedures, and triggers.

SQL Server allows you to choose whether to develop a routine with T-SQL or with Microsoft .NET code based on the CLR integration in the product. Because this book's focus is T-SQL, the examples here use T-SQL. Generally speaking, when the task at hand mainly involves data manipulation, T-SQL is usually a better choice. When the task is more about iterative logic, string manipulation, or computationally intensive operations, .NET code is usually a better choice.

## User-Defined Functions

The purpose of a user-defined function (UDF) is to encapsulate logic that calculates something, possibly based on input parameters, and return a result.

SQL Server supports scalar and table-valued UDFs. Scalar UDFs return a single value; table-valued UDFs return a table. One benefit of using UDFs is that you can incorporate them in queries. Scalar UDFs can appear anywhere in the query where an expression that returns a single value can appear (for example, in the *SELECT* list). Table UDFs can appear in the *FROM* clause of a query. The example in this section is a scalar UDF.

UDFs are not allowed to have any side effects. This obviously means that UDFs are not allowed to apply any schema or data changes in the database. But other ways of causing side effects are less obvious. For example, invoking the *RAND* function to return a random value or the *NEWID* function to return a globally unique identifier (GUID) has side effects. Whenever you invoke the *RAND* function without specifying a seed, SQL Server generates a random seed that is based on the previous invocation of *RAND*. For this reason, SQL Server needs to store information internally whenever you invoke the *RAND* function. Similarly, whenever you invoke the *NEWID* function, the system needs to set some information aside to be taken into consideration in the next invocation of *NEWID*. Because *RAND* and *NEWID* have side effects, you're not allowed to use them in your UDFs.

For example, the following code creates a UDF called *dbo.GetAge* that returns the age of a person with a specified birth date (*@birthdate argument*) at a specified event date (*@eventdate argument*).

```
IF OBJECT_ID('dbo.GetAge') IS NOT NULL DROP FUNCTION dbo.GetAge;
GO

CREATE FUNCTION dbo.GetAge
(
  @birthdate AS DATE,
  @eventdate AS DATE
)
RETURNS INT
AS
BEGIN
  RETURN
    DATEDIFF(year, @birthdate, @eventdate)
    - CASE WHEN 100 * MONTH(@eventdate) + DAY(@eventdate)
             < 100 * MONTH(@birthdate) + DAY(@birthdate)
         THEN 1 ELSE 0
      END;
END;
GO
```

The function calculates the age as the difference, in terms of years, between the birth year and the event year, minus 1 year in cases for which the year, the event month, and the day are smaller than the birth month and day. The expression *100 \* month + day* is simply a trick to concatenate the month and day. For example, for the twelfth day in the month of February, the expression yields the integer 212.

Note that a function can have more than just a *RETURN* clause in its body. It can have code with flow elements, calculations, and more. But the function must have a *RETURN* clause that returns a value.

To demonstrate using a UDF in a query, the following code queries the *HR.Employees* table and invokes the *GetAge* function in the *SELECT* list to calculate the age of each employee today.

```
SELECT
  empid, firstname, lastname, birthdate,
  dbo.GetAge(birthdate, SYSDATETIME()) AS age
FROM HR.Employees;
```

For example, if you were to run this query on February 12, 2012, you would get the following output.

```
empid        firstname  lastname              birthdate                 age
-----------  ---------- --------------------  ------------------------  ----
1            Sara       Davis                 1958-12-08 00:00:00.000   53
2            Don        Funk                  1962-02-19 00:00:00.000   49
3            Judy       Lew                   1973-08-30 00:00:00.000   38
4            Yael       Peled                 1947-09-19 00:00:00.000   64
5            Sven       Buck                  1965-03-04 00:00:00.000   46
6            Paul       Suurs                 1973-07-02 00:00:00.000   38
7            Russell    King                  1970-05-29 00:00:00.000   41
8            Maria      Cameron               1968-01-09 00:00:00.000   44
9            Zoya       Dolgopyatova          1976-01-27 00:00:00.000   36
```

(9 row(s) affected)

Note that if you run the query in your system, the values that you get in the age column depend on the date on which you run the query.

## Stored Procedures

Stored procedures are server-side routines that encapsulate T-SQL code. Stored procedures can have input and output parameters, they can return result sets of queries, and they are allowed to invoke code that has side effects. Not only can you modify data through stored procedures, you can also apply schema changes through them.

Compared to using ad-hoc code, the use of stored procedures gives you many benefits:

- **Stored procedures encapsulate logic.** If you need to change the implementation of a stored procedure, you can apply the change in one place in the database and the procedure will be altered for all users of the procedure.

- **Stored procedures give you better control of security.** You can grant a user permissions to execute the procedure without granting the user direct permissions to perform the underlying activities. For example, suppose that you want to allow certain users to delete a customer from the database, but you don't want to grant them direct permissions to delete rows from the *Customers* table. You want to ensure that requests to delete a customer are validated—for example, by checking whether the customer has open orders or open debts—and you may also want to audit the requests. By not granting direct permissions to delete rows from the *Customers* table but instead granting permissions to execute a procedure that handles the task, you ensure that all the required validations and auditing always take place. In addition, stored procedures can help prevent SQL injection, especially when they replace ad-hoc SQL from the client with parameters.

- **You can incorporate all error handling code within a procedure, silently taking corrective action where relevant.** I discuss error handling later in this chapter.

- **Stored procedures give you performance benefits.** Earlier I talked about reuse of previously cached execution plans. Stored procedures reuse execution plans by default, whereas SQL Server is more conservative with the reuse of ad-hoc plans. Also, the aging of procedure plans is less rapid than that of ad-hoc plans. Another performance benefit of using stored procedures is reduction of network traffic. The client application needs to submit only the procedure name and its arguments to SQL Server. The server processes all of the procedure's code and returns only the output back to the caller. No back-and-forth traffic is associated with intermediate steps of the procedure.

As a simple example, the following code creates a stored procedure called *Sales.GetCustomerOrders*. The procedure accepts a customer ID (*@custid*) and a date range (*@fromdate* and *@todate*) as inputs. The procedure returns rows from the *Sales.Orders* table representing orders placed by the requested customer in the requested date range as a result set, and the number of affected rows as an output parameter (*@numrows*).

```
IF OBJECT_ID('Sales.GetCustomerOrders', 'P') IS NOT NULL
  DROP PROC Sales.GetCustomerOrders;
GO

CREATE PROC Sales.GetCustomerOrders
  @custid   AS INT,
  @fromdate AS DATETIME = '19000101',
  @todate   AS DATETIME = '99991231',
  @numrows  AS INT OUTPUT
AS
SET NOCOUNT ON;

SELECT orderid, custid, empid, orderdate
FROM Sales.Orders
WHERE custid = @custid
  AND orderdate >= @fromdate
  AND orderdate < @todate;

SET @numrows = @@rowcount;
GO
```

When executing the procedure, if you don't specify a value in the *@fromdate* parameter, the procedure will use the default *19000101*, and if you don't specify a value in the *@todate* parameter, the procedure will use the default *99991231*. Notice the use of the keyword *OUTPUT* to indicate that the parameter *@numrows* is an output parameter. The *SET NOCOUNT ON* command is used to suppress messages indicating how many rows were affected by DML statements, such as the *SELECT* statement within the procedure.

Here's an example of executing the procedure, requesting information about orders placed by the customer with the ID of 1 in the year 2007. The code absorbs the value of the output parameter *@numrows* in the local variable *@rc* and returns it to show how many rows were affected by the query.

```
DECLARE @rc AS INT;

EXEC Sales.GetCustomerOrders
  @custid  = 1,
```

```
@fromdate = '20070101',
@todate   = '20080101',
@numrows  = @rc OUTPUT;

SELECT @rc AS numrows;
```

The code returns the following output showing three qualifying orders.

```
orderid      custid       empid        orderdate
-----------  -----------  -----------  -----------------------
10643        1            6            2007-08-25 00:00:00.000
10692        1            4            2007-10-03 00:00:00.000
10702        1            4            2007-10-13 00:00:00.000

numrows
-----------
3
```

Run the code again, providing a customer ID that doesn't exist in the *Orders* table (for example, customer ID 100). You get the following output indicating that there are zero qualifying orders.

```
orderid      custid       empid        orderdate
-----------  -----------  -----------  -----------------------

numrows
-----------
0
```

Of course, this is just a basic example. You can do much more with stored procedures.

# Triggers

A trigger is a special kind of stored procedure—one that cannot be executed explicitly. Instead, it is attached to an event. Whenever the event takes place, the trigger fires and the trigger's code runs. SQL Server supports the association of triggers with two kinds of events—data manipulation events (DML triggers) such as *INSERT*, and data definition events (DDL triggers) such as *CREATE TABLE*.

You can use triggers for many purposes, including auditing, enforcing integrity rules that cannot be enforced with constraints, and enforcing policies.

A trigger is considered part of the transaction that includes the event that caused the trigger to fire. Issuing a *ROLLBACK TRAN* command within the trigger's code causes a rollback of all changes that took place in the trigger, and also of all changes that took place in the transaction associated with the trigger.

Triggers in SQL Server fire per statement and not per modified row.

## DML Triggers

SQL Server supports two kinds of DML triggers—*after* and *instead of.* An *after* trigger fires after the event it is associated with finishes and can only be defined on permanent tables. An *instead of* trigger fires instead of the event it is associated with and can be defined on permanent tables and views.

In the trigger's code, you can access tables called *inserted* and *deleted* that contain the rows that were affected by the modification that caused the trigger to fire. The inserted table holds the new image of the affected rows in the case of *INSERT* and *UPDATE* actions. The deleted table holds the old image of the affected rows in the case of *DELETE* and *UPDATE* actions. Remember that *INSERT*, *UPDATE*, and *DELETE* actions can be invoked by the *INSERT*, *UPDATE*, and *DELETE* statements, as well as by the *MERGE* statement. In the case of *instead of* triggers, the inserted and deleted tables contain the rows that were supposed to be affected by the modification that caused the trigger to fire.

The following simple example of an *after* trigger audits inserts to a table. Run the following code to create a table called *dbo.T1* in the current database, and another table called *dbo.T1_Audit* that holds audit information for insertions to *T1*.

```
IF OBJECT_ID('dbo.T1_Audit', 'U') IS NOT NULL DROP TABLE dbo.T1_Audit;
IF OBJECT_ID('dbo.T1', 'U') IS NOT NULL DROP TABLE dbo.T1;

CREATE TABLE dbo.T1
(
  keycol  INT         NOT NULL PRIMARY KEY,
  datacol VARCHAR(10) NOT NULL
);

CREATE TABLE dbo.T1_Audit
(
  audit_lsn  INT         NOT NULL IDENTITY PRIMARY KEY,
  dt         DATETIME    NOT NULL DEFAULT(SYSDATETIME()),
  login_name sysname     NOT NULL DEFAULT(ORIGINAL_LOGIN()),
  keycol     INT         NOT NULL,
  datacol    VARCHAR(10) NOT NULL
);
```

In the audit table, the *audit_lsn* column has an identity property and represents an audit log serial number. The *dt* column represents the date and time of the insertion, using the default expression *SYSDATETIME()*. The *login_name* column represents the name of the logon that performed the insertion, using the default expression *ORIGINAL_LOGIN()*.

Next, run the following code to create the *AFTER INSERT* trigger *trg_T1_insert_audit* on the *T1* table to audit insertions.

```
CREATE TRIGGER trg_T1_insert_audit ON dbo.T1 AFTER INSERT
AS
SET NOCOUNT ON;

INSERT INTO dbo.T1_Audit(keycol, datacol)
  SELECT keycol, datacol FROM inserted;
GO
```

As you can see, the trigger simply inserts into the audit table the result of a query against the inserted table. The values of the columns in the audit table that are not listed explicitly in the *INSERT* statement are generated by the default expressions described earlier. To test the trigger, run the following code.

```
INSERT INTO dbo.T1(keycol, datacol) VALUES(10, 'a');
INSERT INTO dbo.T1(keycol, datacol) VALUES(30, 'x');
INSERT INTO dbo.T1(keycol, datacol) VALUES(20, 'g');
```

The trigger fires after each statement. Next, query the audit table.

```
SELECT audit_lsn, dt, login_name, keycol, datacol
FROM dbo.T1_Audit;
```

You get the following output, only with *dt* and *login_name* values that reflect the date and time when you ran the inserts, and the logon you used to connect to SQL Server.

```
audit_lsn   dt                        login_name        keycol        datacol
----------- ------------------------- ----------------- ----------- ----------
1           2012-02-12 09:04:27.713   K2\Gandalf        10            a
2           2012-02-12 09:04:27.733   K2\Gandalf        30            x
3           2012-02-12 09:04:27.733   K2\Gandalf        20            g
```

When you're done, run the following code for cleanup.

```
IF OBJECT_ID('dbo.T1_Audit', 'U') IS NOT NULL DROP TABLE dbo.T1_Audit;
IF OBJECT_ID('dbo.T1', 'U') IS NOT NULL DROP TABLE dbo.T1;
```

## DDL Triggers

SQL Server supports DDL triggers, which can be used for purposes such as auditing, policy enforcement, and change management. On-premises SQL Server supports the creation of DDL triggers at two scopes, the database scope and the server scope, depending on the scope of the event. SQL Database currently supports only database triggers.

You create a *database* trigger for events with a database scope, such as *CREATE TABLE*. You create an *all server* trigger for events with a server scope, such as *CREATE DATABASE*. SQL Server supports only *after* DDL triggers; it doesn't support *instead of* DDL triggers.

Within the trigger, you obtain information on the event that caused the trigger to fire by querying a function called *EVENTDATA* that returns the event information as an XML value. You can use XQuery expressions to extract event attributes such as post time, event type, and logon name from the XML value.

The following code creates the *dbo.AuditDDLEvents* table, which holds the audit information.

```
IF OBJECT_ID('dbo.AuditDDLEvents', 'U') IS NOT NULL
  DROP TABLE dbo.AuditDDLEvents;

CREATE TABLE dbo.AuditDDLEvents
(
  audit_lsn        INT      NOT NULL IDENTITY,
  posttime         DATETIME NOT NULL,
  eventtype        sysname  NOT NULL,
  loginname        sysname  NOT NULL,
  schemaname       sysname  NOT NULL,
  objectname       sysname  NOT NULL,
  targetobjectname sysname  NULL,
  eventdata        XML      NOT NULL,
  CONSTRAINT PK_AuditDDLEvents PRIMARY KEY(audit_lsn)
);
```

Notice that the table has a column called *eventdata* that has an XML data type. In addition to the individual attributes that the trigger extracts from the event information and stores in individual attributes, it also stores the full event information in the *eventdata* column.

Run the following code to create the *trg_audit_ddl_events* audit trigger on the database by using the event group *DDL_DATABASE_LEVEL_EVENTS*, which represents all DDL events at the database level.

```
CREATE TRIGGER trg_audit_ddl_events
  ON DATABASE FOR DDL_DATABASE_LEVEL_EVENTS
AS
SET NOCOUNT ON;

DECLARE @eventdata AS XML = eventdata();

INSERT INTO dbo.AuditDDLEvents(
  posttime, eventtype, loginname, schemaname,
  objectname, targetobjectname, eventdata)
  VALUES(
    @eventdata.value('(/EVENT_INSTANCE/PostTime)[1]',         'VARCHAR(23)'),
    @eventdata.value('(/EVENT_INSTANCE/EventType)[1]',        'sysname'),
    @eventdata.value('(/EVENT_INSTANCE/LoginName)[1]',        'sysname'),
    @eventdata.value('(/EVENT_INSTANCE/SchemaName)[1]',       'sysname'),
    @eventdata.value('(/EVENT_INSTANCE/ObjectName)[1]',       'sysname'),
    @eventdata.value('(/EVENT_INSTANCE/TargetObjectName)[1]', 'sysname'),
    @eventdata);
GO
```

The trigger's code first stores the event information obtained from the *EVENTDATA* function in the *@eventdata* variable. The code then inserts a row into the audit table with the attributes extracted by using XQuery expressions by the *.value* method from the event information, plus the XML value with the full event information.

To test the trigger, run the following code, which contains a few DDL statements.

```
CREATE TABLE dbo.T1(col1 INT NOT NULL PRIMARY KEY);
ALTER TABLE dbo.T1 ADD col2 INT NULL;
ALTER TABLE dbo.T1 ALTER COLUMN col2 INT NOT NULL;
CREATE NONCLUSTERED INDEX idx1 ON dbo.T1(col2);
```

Next, run the following code to query the audit table.

```
SELECT * FROM dbo.AuditDDLEvents;
```

You get the following output (split here into two sections for display purposes), but with values in the *posttime* and *loginname* attributes that reflect the post time and logon name in your environment.

| audit_lsn | posttime | eventtype | loginname |
|---|---|---|---|
| 1 | 2012-02-12 09:06:18.293 | CREATE_TABLE | K2\Gandalf |
| 2 | 2012-02-12 09:06:18.413 | ALTER_TABLE | K2\Gandalf |
| 3 | 2012-02-12 09:06:18.423 | ALTER_TABLE | K2\Gandalf |
| 4 | 2012-02-12 09:06:18.423 | CREATE_INDEX | K2\Gandalf |

| audit_lsn | schemaname | objectname | targetobjectname | eventdata |
|---|---|---|---|---|
| 1 | dbo | T1 | NULL | <EVENT_INSTANCE>... |
| 2 | dbo | T1 | NULL | <EVENT_INSTANCE>... |
| 3 | dbo | T1 | NULL | <EVENT_INSTANCE>... |
| 4 | dbo | idx1 | T1 | <EVENT_INSTANCE>... |

When you're done, run the following code for cleanup.

```
DROP TRIGGER trg_audit_ddl_events ON DATABASE;
DROP TABLE dbo.AuditDDLEvents;
```

# Error Handling

SQL Server provides you with tools to handle errors in your T-SQL code. The main tool used for error handling is a construct called *TRY...CATCH*. SQL Server also provides a set of functions that you can invoke to get information about the error. I'll start with a basic example demonstrating the use of *TRY...CATCH*, followed by a more detailed example demonstrating the use of the error functions.

You work with the *TRY…CATCH* construct by placing the usual T-SQL code in a *TRY* block (between the *BEGIN TRY* and *END TRY* keywords), and all the error-handling code in the adjacent *CATCH* block (between the *BEGIN CATCH* and *END CATCH* keywords). If the *TRY* block has no error, the *CATCH* block is simply skipped. If the *TRY* block has an error, control is passed to the corresponding *CATCH* block. Note that if a *TRY…CATCH* block captures and handles an error, as far as the caller is concerned, there was no error.

Run the following code to demonstrate a case with no error in the *TRY* block.

```
BEGIN TRY
  PRINT 10/2;
  PRINT 'No error';
END TRY
BEGIN CATCH
  PRINT 'Error';
END CATCH;
```

All code in the *TRY* block completed successfully; therefore, the *CATCH* block was skipped. This code generates the following output.

```
5
No error
```

Next, run similar code, but this time divide by zero. An error occurs.

```
BEGIN TRY
  PRINT 10/0;
  PRINT 'No error';
END TRY
BEGIN CATCH
  PRINT 'Error';
END CATCH;
```

When the *divide by zero* error happened in the first *PRINT* statement in the *TRY* block, control was passed to the corresponding *CATCH* block. The second *PRINT* statement in the *TRY* block was not executed. Therefore, this code generates the following output.

```
Error
```

Typically, error handling involves some work in the *CATCH* block investigating the cause of the error and taking a course of action. SQL Server gives you information about the error via a set of functions. The *ERROR_NUMBER* function returns an integer with the number of the error and is probably the most important of the error functions. The *CATCH* block usually includes flow code that inspects the error number to determine what course of action to take. The *ERROR_MESSAGE* function returns error message text. To get the list of error numbers and messages, query the *sys.messages* catalog view. The *ERROR_SEVERITY* and *ERROR_STATE* functions return the error severity and state. The *ERROR_LINE* function returns the line number where the error happened. Finally, the *ERROR_PROCEDURE* function returns the name of the procedure in which the error happened and returns *NULL* if the error did not happen within a procedure.

To demonstrate a more detailed error-handling example including the use of the error functions, first run the following code, which creates a table called *dbo.Employees* in the current database.

```
IF OBJECT_ID('dbo.Employees') IS NOT NULL DROP TABLE dbo.Employees;
CREATE TABLE dbo.Employees
(
  empid    INT          NOT NULL,
  empname  VARCHAR(25) NOT NULL,
  mgrid    INT          NULL,
  CONSTRAINT PK_Employees PRIMARY KEY(empid),
  CONSTRAINT CHK_Employees_empid CHECK(empid > 0),
  CONSTRAINT FK_Employees_Employees
    FOREIGN KEY(mgrid) REFERENCES dbo.Employees(empid)
);
```

The following code inserts a new row into the *Employees* table in a *TRY* block, and if an error occurs, shows how to identify the error by inspecting the *ERROR_NUMBER* function in the *CATCH* block. The code uses flow control to identify and handle errors you want to deal with in the *CATCH* block, and re-throws the error otherwise.

> **Note** The ability to re-throw an error by using the *THROW* command was added in SQL Server 2012.

The code also prints the values of the other error functions simply to show what information is available to you upon error.

```
BEGIN TRY

  INSERT INTO dbo.Employees(empid, empname, mgrid)
    VALUES(1, 'Emp1', NULL);
  -- Also try with empid = 0, 'A', NULL

END TRY
BEGIN CATCH

  IF ERROR_NUMBER() = 2627
  BEGIN
    PRINT '    Handling PK violation...';
  END
  ELSE IF ERROR_NUMBER() = 547
  BEGIN
    PRINT '    Handling CHECK/FK constraint violation...';
  END
  ELSE IF ERROR_NUMBER() = 515
  BEGIN
    PRINT '    Handling NULL violation...';
  END
  ELSE IF ERROR_NUMBER() = 245
  BEGIN
    PRINT '    Handling conversion error...';
  END
  ELSE
```

```
BEGIN
  PRINT 'Re-throwing error...';
  THROW; -- SQL Server 2012 only
END

PRINT '    Error Number  : ' + CAST(ERROR_NUMBER() AS VARCHAR(10));
PRINT '    Error Message : ' + ERROR_MESSAGE();
PRINT '    Error Severity: ' + CAST(ERROR_SEVERITY() AS VARCHAR(10));
PRINT '    Error State   : ' + CAST(ERROR_STATE() AS VARCHAR(10));
PRINT '    Error Line    : ' + CAST(ERROR_LINE() AS VARCHAR(10));
PRINT '    Error Proc    : ' + COALESCE(ERROR_PROCEDURE(), 'Not within proc');

END CATCH;
```

When you run this code for the first time, the new row is inserted into the *Employees* table successfully, and therefore the *CATCH* block is skipped. You get the following output.

```
(1 row(s) affected)
```

When you run the same code a second time, the *INSERT* statement fails, control is passed to the *CATCH* block, and a primary key violation error is identified. You get the following output.

```
Handling PK violation...
Error Number  : 2627
Error Message : Violation of PRIMARY KEY constraint 'PK_Employees'. Cannot insert duplicate key
in object 'dbo.Employees'.
Error Severity: 14
Error State   : 1
Error Line    : 3
Error Proc    : Not within proc
```

To see other errors, run the code with the values 0, 'A', and *NULL* as the employee ID.

Here, for demonstration purposes, I used *PRINT* statements as the actions when an error was identified. Of course, error handling usually involves more than just printing a message indicating that the error was identified.

Note that you can create a stored procedure that encapsulates reusable error-handling code like this.

```
IF OBJECT_ID('dbo.ErrInsertHandler', 'P') IS NOT NULL
  DROP PROC dbo.ErrInsertHandler;
GO

CREATE PROC dbo.ErrInsertHandler
AS
SET NOCOUNT ON;

IF ERROR_NUMBER() = 2627
BEGIN
  PRINT 'Handling PK violation...';
END
ELSE IF ERROR_NUMBER() = 547
```

```
BEGIN
  PRINT 'Handling CHECK/FK constraint violation...';
END
ELSE IF ERROR_NUMBER() = 515
BEGIN
  PRINT 'Handling NULL violation...';
END
ELSE IF ERROR_NUMBER() = 245
BEGIN
  PRINT 'Handling conversion error...';
END

PRINT 'Error Number  : ' + CAST(ERROR_NUMBER() AS VARCHAR(10));
PRINT 'Error Message : ' + ERROR_MESSAGE();
PRINT 'Error Severity: ' + CAST(ERROR_SEVERITY() AS VARCHAR(10));
PRINT 'Error State   : ' + CAST(ERROR_STATE() AS VARCHAR(10));
PRINT 'Error Line    : ' + CAST(ERROR_LINE() AS VARCHAR(10));
PRINT 'Error Proc    : ' + COALESCE(ERROR_PROCEDURE(), 'Not within proc');
GO
```

In your *CATCH* block, you check whether the error number is one of those you want to deal with locally, in which case you simply execute the stored procedure; otherwise, you re-throw the error.

```
BEGIN TRY

  INSERT INTO dbo.Employees(empid, empname, mgrid)
    VALUES(1, 'Emp1', NULL);

END TRY
BEGIN CATCH

  IF ERROR_NUMBER() IN (2627, 547, 515, 245)
    EXEC dbo.ErrInsertHandler;
  ELSE
    THROW;

END CATCH;
```

This way you can maintain the reusable error-handling code in one place.

# Conclusion

This chapter provided a high-level overview of programmable objects so that you can be aware of SQL Server's capabilities in this area and start building your vocabulary. This chapter covered variables, batches, flow elements, cursors, temporary tables, dynamic SQL, user-defined functions, stored procedures, triggers, and error handling—quite a few subjects. I hope that you focused on concepts and capabilities rather than getting sidetracked by every bit of code in the examples.

# Getting Started

The purpose of this appendix is to help you get started and set up your environment so that you have everything you need to get the most out of this book.

You can run all of the code samples in this book on an on-premises installation of Microsoft SQL Server—box flavor—and most of the examples on Windows Azure SQL Database (formerly called SQL Azure)—cloud flavor. For details about the differences between the flavors, see the section "The ABC Flavors of SQL Server" in Chapter 1, "Background to T-SQL Querying and Programming."

The first section, "Getting Started with SQL Database," provides a link to the website where you can find the information you need to get started with SQL Database.

The second section, "Installing an On-Premises Installation of SQL Server," assumes that you want to connect to an on-premises instance of SQL Server to run the code samples in this book, and that you don't have an instance to connect to already. This section walks you through the installation process for a SQL Server 2012 instance. If you already have an instance of SQL Server to connect to, feel free to skip the first section.

The third section, "Downloading Source Code and Installing the Sample Database," points you to the website where you can get the downloadable source code for the book and provides instructions for installing the book's sample database on both an on-premises SQL Server instance and SQL Database.

The fourth section, "Working with SQL Server Management Studio," explains how to develop and execute T-SQL code in SQL Server by using SQL Server Management Studio (SSMS).

The last section, "Working with SQL Server Books Online," describes SQL Server Books Online and explains its importance in helping you get information about T-SQL.

## Getting Started with SQL Database

If you want to run the code samples in this book on SQL Database, you will need access to a SQL Database server, with an account that has privileges to create a new database (or ask an administrator to create the sample database for you). If you don't already have access to SQL Database, you can find useful information on how to get started on the Windows Azure main page at *http://www.windowsazure.com*.

You will need a Windows Live ID so that you can set up a Windows Azure platform account. If you don't already have a Windows Live ID, you can create one at *https://signup.live.com*. When you have a Windows Azure subscription, you can connect to the Windows Azure Platform Management Portal, from which you can manage your SQL Database servers and databases.

The Windows Azure main page offers different options for getting started (by buying a subscription or getting a free trial) and provides access to various resources such as the management portal, community, and support.

When you have access to SQL Database, proceed to the instructions on how to download the source code and install the sample database later in this appendix.

# Installing an On-Premises Implementation of SQL Server

This section is relevant for those who want to run the code samples in this book and practice the exercises against an on-premises instance of SQL Server and don't already have access to one. You can use any edition of SQL Server 2012 except SQL Server Compact, which doesn't have full-fledged T-SQL support as the other editions do. Assuming that you don't already have an instance of SQL Server to connect to, the following sections describe where you can obtain SQL Server and how to install it.

## 1. Obtain SQL Server

As I mentioned, you can use any edition of SQL Server 2012 except SQL Server Compact to practice the materials in this book. If you have a subscription to the Microsoft Developer Network (MSDN), you can use the SQL Server 2012 Developer for learning purposes. You can download it from *http://msdn.microsoft.com/en-us/sqlserver/default.aspx*. Otherwise, you can use the free trial software of SQL Server 2012, which you can download from *http://www.microsoft.com/sqlserver/en/us/get-sql-server/try-it.aspx*. In this appendix, I demonstrate the installation of the SQL Server 2012 Enterprise evaluation edition.

## 2. Create a User Account

Prior to installing SQL Server, you need to create a user account that you will later use as the service account for SQL Server services.

### To create a user account

1. Right-click Computer and choose Manage to open the Computer Management snap-in.

2. Navigate to Computer Management (Local) | System Tools | Local Users and Groups | Users.

3. Right-click the Users folder and choose New User.

4. Fill in the details for the new user account in the New User dialog box, as shown in Figure A-1.

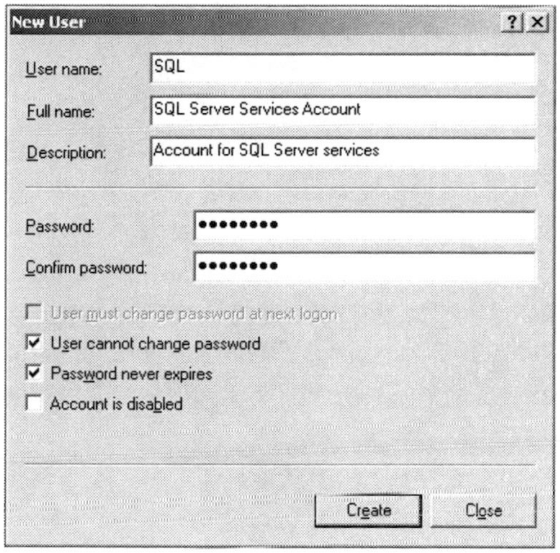

**FIGURE A-1** The New User dialog box.

**4-1.** Type a user name (for example, **SQL**), a full name if you want to (for example, **SQL Server Services Account**), a description if you want one (for example, **Account for SQL Server services**), and a secure password, and then confirm the password.

**4-2.** Clear the User Must Change Password At Next Logon check box.

**4-3.** Select the User Cannot Change Password and Password Never Expires check boxes.

**4-4.** Click Create to create the new user account.

## 3. Install Prerequisites

At this point, you can start the setup.exe program from the SQL Server installation folder. Before installing SQL Server, the setup program checks to determine whether all of the prerequisites are already installed. The prerequisites include the Microsoft .NET Framework 3.5 SP1 and the .NET Framework 4, and an updated Windows Installer. If .NET 3.5 doesn't exist on your computer, the setup program will generate an error and provide you with a link to the download center. The other prerequisites will be installed by the setup program if it doesn't find them. You may be required to restart the computer and rerun the setup program.

## 4. Install the Database Engine, Documentation, and Tools

When all prerequisites have been installed, you can move on to installing the actual product.

### To install the database engine, documentation, and tools

1. After all prerequisites have been installed, run the setup.exe program. You should see the SQL Server Installation Center dialog box shown in Figure A-2.

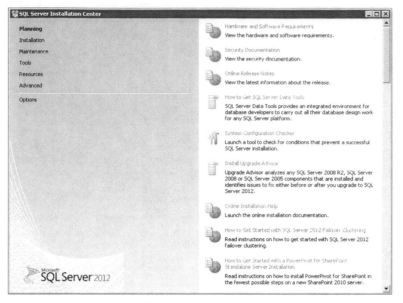

**FIGURE A-2** SQL Server Installation Center.

2. In the left pane, choose Installation. Note that the screen changes.

3. In the right pane, choose New SQL Server Stand-Alone Installation Or Add Features To An Existing Installation. The Setup Support Rules dialog box appears.

4. Click Show Details to view the status of the setup support rules, as shown in Figure A-3, and ensure that no problems are indicated.

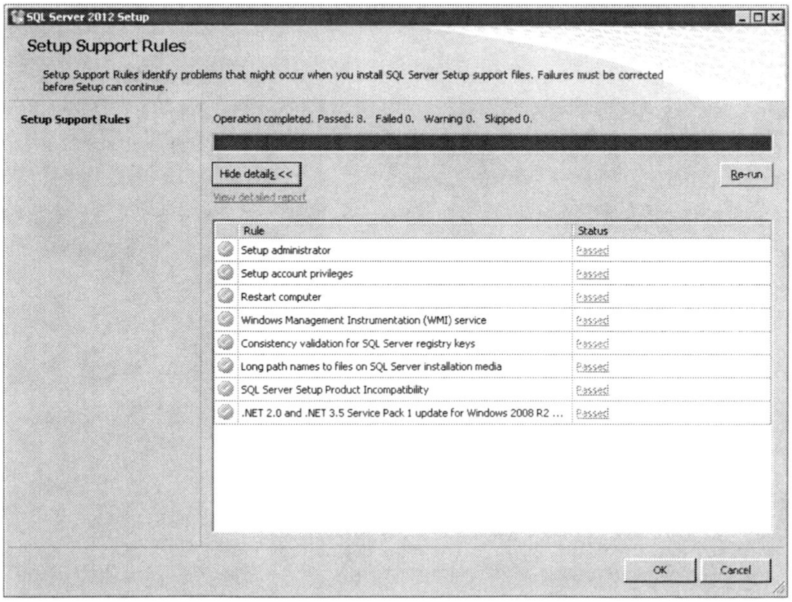

**FIGURE A-3** The Setup Support Rules dialog box.

5.  When you are done, click OK to continue. The Product Key dialog box appears, as shown in Figure A-4.

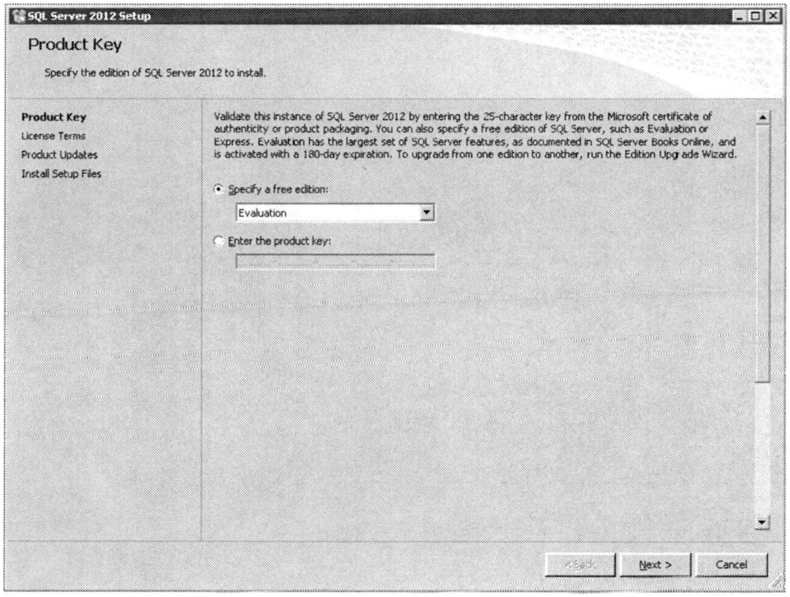

**FIGURE A-4** The Product Key dialog box.

Note that in certain circumstances, the Setup Support Files and Setup Support Rules dialog boxes described in steps 7–9 might appear before the Product Key dialog box. If they do, simply follow the instructions in steps 7–9 now instead of later.

6.  Make sure that Evaluation is chosen in the Specify A Free Edition list box, and click Next to continue. The License Terms dialog box appears.

7.  Confirm that you accept the license terms, and click Next to continue. The Setup Support Files dialog box appears.

8.  Click Install to continue. The Setup Support Rules dialog box appears again.

9.  Click Show Details to view the status of the setup support rules and ensure that no problems are indicated. Click Next to continue. The Setup Role dialog box appears. Leave the SQL Server Feature Installation option selected and click Next to continue. The Feature Selection dialog box appears. Select the features to install, as shown in Figure A-5.

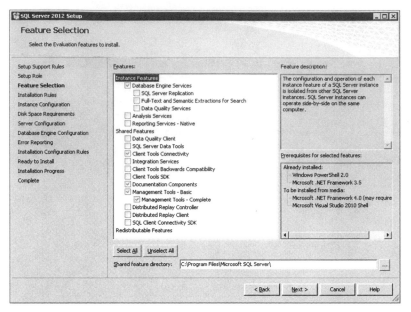

**FIGURE A-5** The Feature Selection dialog box.

Select the following features:

- Database Engine Services

- Client Tools Connectivity

- Documentation Components

- Management Tools - Complete

For the purposes of this book, you don't need any of the other features.

When you are done, click Next to continue. If the Installation Rules dialog box appears, click Next to continue. The Instance Configuration dialog box appears, as shown in Figure A-6.

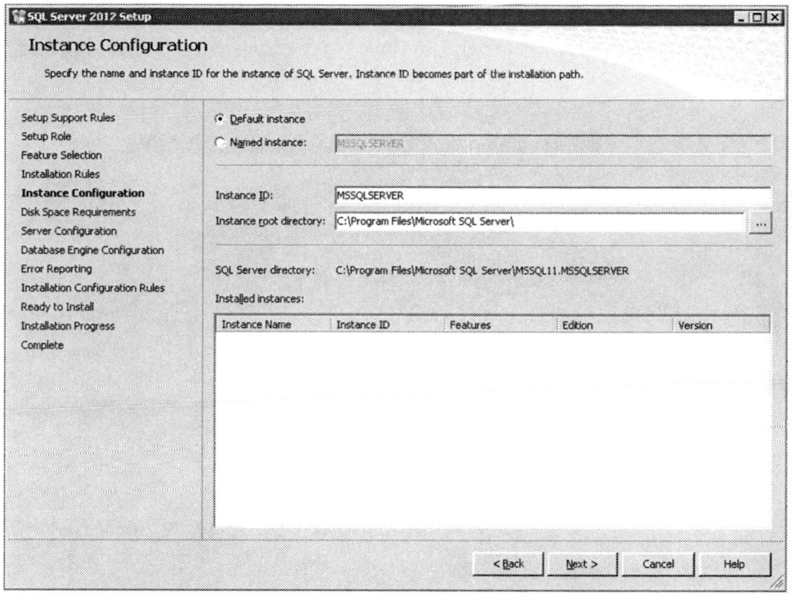

**FIGURE A-6** The Instance Configuration dialog box.

If you are not familiar with the concept of SQL Server instances, you can find details in Chapter 1, in the "SQL Server Architecture" section.

10. If a default instance of SQL Server is not installed on your computer and you would like to configure the new instance as the default, simply confirm that the Default Instance option is selected. If you want to configure the new instance as a named instance, make sure the Named Instance option is selected and that you specify a name for the new instance (for example, **SQL2012**). When you later connect to SQL Server, you will specify only the computer name for a default instance (for example, **DENALI**), and the computer name\instance name for a named instance (for example, **DENALI\SQL2012**).

11. When you're done, click Next to continue. The Disk Space Requirements dialog box appears. Make sure that you have enough disk space for the installation.

12. Click Next to continue. The Server Configuration dialog box appears.

**13.** As shown in Figure A-7, for the service account for the SQL Server Agent and SQL Server Database Engine services, specify the user name and password of the user account you created earlier.

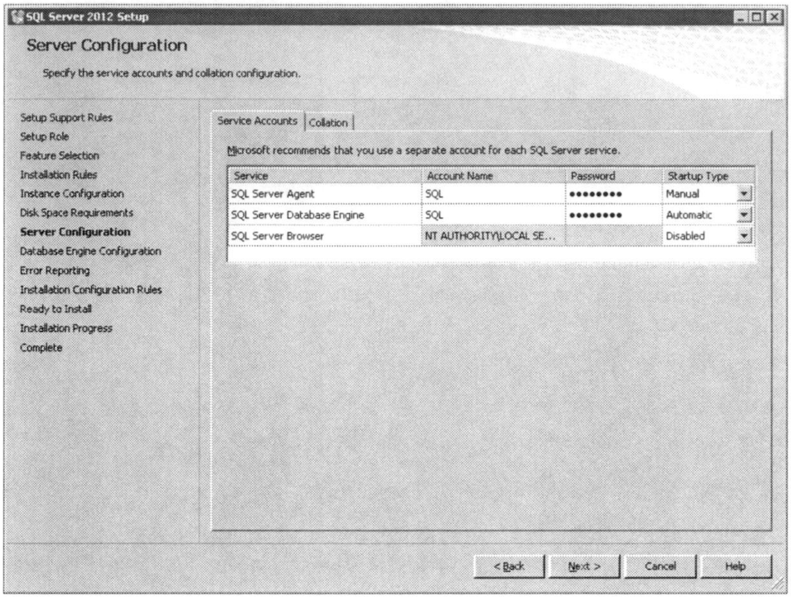

**FIGURE A-7** The Server Configuration dialog box.

Of course, if you named your user account something other than *SQL*, specify the name you assigned to the account.

For the purposes of this book, you do not need to change the default choices in the Collation dialog box, but if you want to know more about collation, you can find details in Chapter 2, "Single-Table Queries," in the "Working with Character Data" section.

**14.** Click Next to continue. The Database Engine Configuration dialog box appears.

**15.** On the Server Configuration tab, ensure that under Authentication Mode the Windows Authentication Mode option is selected. Under Specify SQL Server Administrators, click Add Current User to assign the current logged-on user with the System Administrator (sysadmin) server role, as shown in Figure A-8. SQL Server administrators have unrestricted access to the SQL Server database engine.

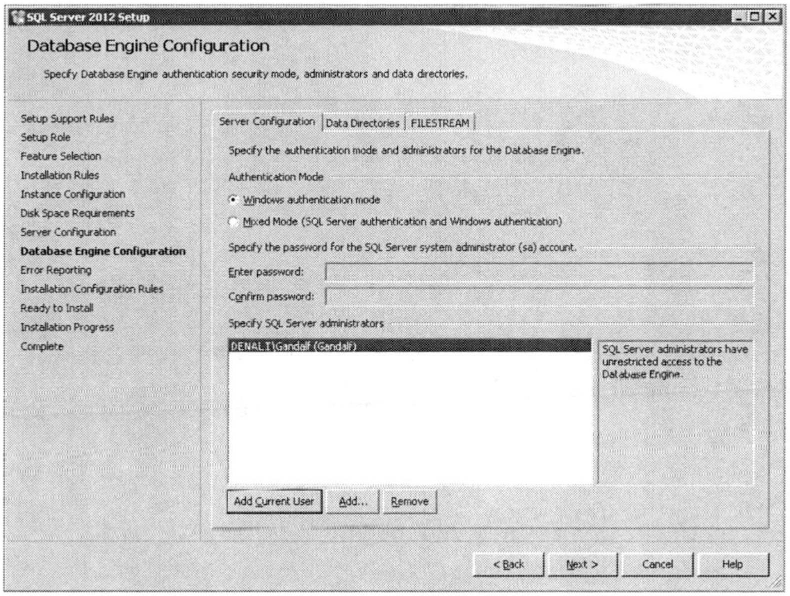

**FIGURE A-8** The Database Engine Configuration dialog box.

Of course, in your case, your current user name will appear instead of *DENALI\Gandalf*.

If you want to change the setup program's defaults in terms of data directories, you can do so on the Data Directories tab. For the purposes of the book, you don't need to configure anything on the FILESTREAM tab.

16. Click Next to continue. The Error And Usage Reporting dialog box appears. Make your choices based on your preferences, and click Next to continue. The Installation Configuration Rules dialog box appears.

17. Click Show Details to view the status of the installation rules and ensure that no problems are indicated. Click Next to continue. The Ready To Install dialog box appears with a summary of the installation choices.

18. Ensure that the summary indicates your choices correctly, and click Install to start the actual installation process. The Installation Progress dialog box appears and remains open throughout the remainder of the installation process. This dialog box provides a general progress bar as well as indicating the status of each feature that is being installed (see Figure A-9). When the installation is complete, a Setup Process Complete message appears above the general progress bar.

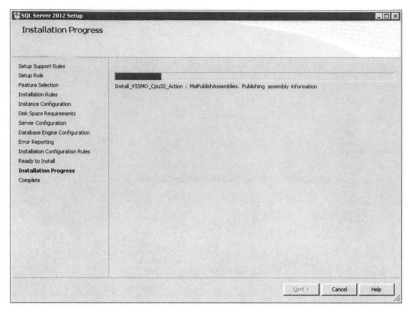

**FIGURE A-9** The Installation Progress dialog box.

**19.** Click Next to continue. The Complete dialog box appears, as shown in Figure A-10.

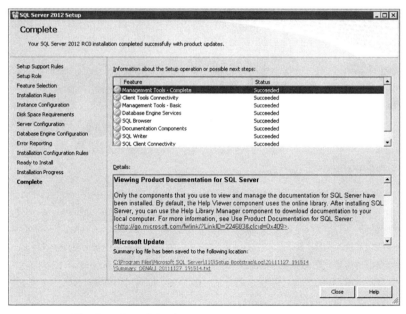

**FIGURE A-10** The Complete dialog box.

This dialog box should indicate the successful completion of the installation.

**20.** Click Close to finish.

# Downloading Source Code and Installing the Sample Database

You can find the instructions to download the source code here: *http://tsql.solidq.com*. In this website, go to the Books section, and select the main page for the book in question. This page has a link to download a single compressed file with the book's source code, as well as a script file called TSQL2012.sql that creates the sample database. Decompress the files to a local folder (for example, C:\TSQLFundamentals).

You will find up to three .sql script files associated with each chapter of the book. One file contains the source code for the corresponding chapter and is provided for your convenience, in case you don't want to type the code that appears in the book; this file name matches the title of the corresponding chapter. A second file contains the exercises for the chapter; this file name also matches the title of the corresponding chapter but includes the suffix "Exercises." A third file contains the solutions to the chapter's exercises; this file name matches the title of the corresponding chapter but includes the suffix "Solutions." You use SQL Server Management Studio (SSMS) to open the files and run their code. The next section explains how to work with SSMS.

You will also find a text file called orders.txt, for use when practicing the materials from Chapter 8, "Data Modification." Also included is a script file called TSQL2012.sql, which creates the book's sample database, *TSQL2012*.

To create the sample database in an on-premises SQL Server instance, you simply need to run this script file while you are connected to the target SQL Server instance. If you aren't familiar with running script files in SQL Server, you can follow these steps to complete the database creation.

### To create and populate the sample database in an on-premises SQL Server instance

1. Double-click the TSQL2012.sql file name in Windows Explorer to open the file in SSMS. The Connect To Database Engine dialog box appears.

2. In the Server Name box, ensure that the name of the instance you want to connect to appears. For example, you would type the name **DENALI** if your instance was installed as the default instance in a computer called **DENALI**, or **DENALI\SQL2012** if your instance was installed as a named instance called *SQL2012* in a computer called *DENALI*.

3. In the Authentication box, make sure Windows Authentication is chosen. Click Connect.

4. When you are connected to SQL Server, press F5 to run the script. When the execution is done, the Command(s) Completed Successfully message should appear in the Messages pane. You should see the *TSQL2012* database in the Available Databases box.

5. When you are done, you can close SSMS.

### To create and populate the sample database in SQL Database

1.  Double-click the file name in Windows Explorer to open the file in SSMS. The Connect To Database Engine dialog box appears.

2.  In the Server Name box, ensure that the name of the SQL Database server you want to connect to appears—for example, *myserver.database.windows.net*.

3.  In the Authentication box, make sure SQL Authentication is chosen and the correct logon name and password are entered. Click Options.

4.  On the Connection Properties tab, type **master** in the Connect To Database text box, and then click Connect.

5.  Skip the instructions under Section A in the script (for an on-premises SQL Server instance) and follow the instructions under Section B in the script (for SQL Database). The most important instruction is the one telling you to run the following command to create the *TSQL2012* database.

    CREATE DATABASE TSQL2012;

6.  Right-click any empty area in the query pane and choose Connection | Change Connection. The Connect To Database Engine dialog box appears. Specify *TSQL2012* as the database to connect to, and click Connect. You should see the *TSQL2012* database in the Available Databases box.

    As an alternative, you can simply select the *TSQL2012* database from the Available Databases box.

7.  Highlight the code in Section C (beginning with Create Schemas and all the way to the end of the script file). Press F5 to run the script. When the execution is done, the Command(s) Completed Successfully message should appear in the Messages pane. Note that on slow connections it might take the code a few minutes to complete.

8.  When you are done, you can close SSMS.

The data model of the *TSQL2012* database is provided in Figure A-11 for your convenience.

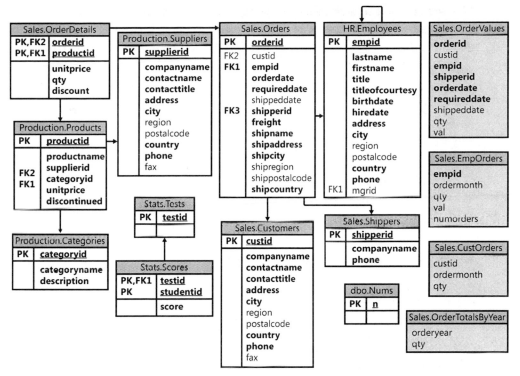

**FIGURE A-11** The data model of the *TSQL2012* database.

# Working with SQL Server Management Studio

SQL Server Management Studio (SSMS) is the client tool you use to develop and execute T-SQL code against SQL Server. The purpose of this section is not to provide a complete guide to working with SSMS, but rather just to help you get started.

### To start working with SSMS

1.   Start SSMS from the Microsoft SQL Server program group.

2.   If this is the first time you have run SSMS, I recommend setting up the startup options so that the environment is set up the way you want it.

3.   If a Connect To Server dialog box appears, click Cancel for now.

4. Choose the Tools | Options menu item to open the Options dialog box. Under Environment | Startup, set the At Startup option to Open Object Explorer And Query Window. This choice tells SSMS that whenever it starts, it should open the Object Explorer and a new query window.

The Object Explorer is the tool you use to manage SQL Server and graphically inspect object definitions, and a query window is where you develop and execute T-SQL code against SQL Server. Feel free to navigate the tree to explore the options that you can set, but few of them are likely to mean much at this point. After you gain some experience with SSMS, you will find many of the options more meaningful and will probably want to change some of them.

5. When you're done exploring the Options dialog box, click OK to confirm your choices.

6. Close SSMS and start it again to verify that it actually opens the Object Explorer and a new query window. You should see the Connect To Server dialog box, as shown in Figure A-12.

**FIGURE A-12** The Connect To Server dialog box.

7. In this dialog box, you specify the details of the SQL Server instance you want to connect to.

   **7-1.** Type the name of the server you want to connect to in the Server Name box.

   **7-2.** If you're connecting to an on-premises SQL Server instance, make sure Windows Authentication is chosen in the Authentication box; if you're connecting to SQL Database, make sure that SQL Server Authentication is selected. Specify the logon and password information; click Options, and specify *TSQL2012* in the Connect To Dataset box in the Connection Properties dialog box.

**7-3.** Click Connect. SSMS should start, as shown in Figure A-13.

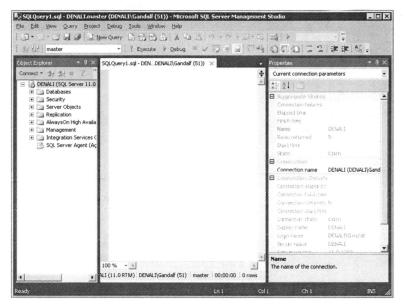

**FIGURE A-13** The opening screen of SSMS.

The Object Explorer window appears on the left, the query window appears to the right of Object Explorer, and the Properties window is to the right of the query window. You can hide the Properties window by clicking the Auto Hide button (in the upper-right corner of the window, to the left of the x). Although the focus of this book is on developing T-SQL code and not SQL Server management, I urge you to explore the Object Explorer by navigating the tree and by right-clicking the various nodes. You will find the Object Explorer a very convenient tool for graphically inspecting your databases and database objects, as shown in Figure A-14.

Note that you can drag items from the Object Explorer to the query window.

**Tip** If you drag the Columns folder of a table from the Object Explorer to the query window, SQL Server will list all table columns separated by commas.

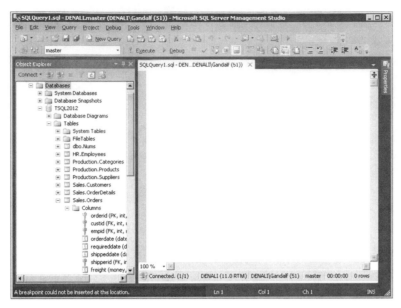

**FIGURE A-14** The Object Explorer.

In the query window, you develop and execute T-SQL code. The code you run is executed against the database you are connected to. If you're connected to an on-premises SQL Server instance, you can choose the database you want to connect to from the Available Databases combo box, as shown in Figure A-15. In SQL Database, you cannot switch between databases, so make sure you initially get connected to the right database.

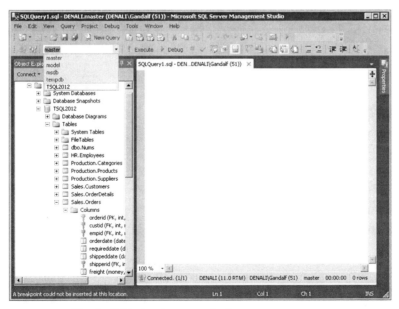

**FIGURE A-15** The Available Databases combo box.

8. Make sure you are currently connected to the *TSQL2012* sample database.

   Note that at any point, you can change the server and database you are connected to by right-clicking an empty area in the query window and then choosing Connection | Change Connection.

9. You are now ready to start developing T-SQL code. Type the following code into the query window.

   ```
   SELECT orderid, orderdate FROM Sales.Orders;
   ```

10. Press F5 to execute the code. Alternatively, you can click Execute (the icon with the red exclamation point—not the green arrow, which starts the debugger). You will get the output of the code in the Results pane, as shown in Figure A-16.

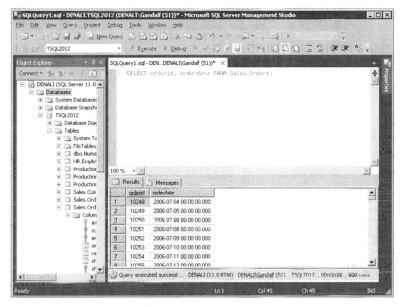

**FIGURE A-16** Executing the first query.

You can control the target of the results from the Query | Results To menu item or by clicking the corresponding icons in the SQL Editor toolbar. You have the following options: Results To Grid (default), Results To Text, and Results To File.

Note that if some of the code is highlighted, as shown in Figure A-17, when you execute the code, SQL Server executes only the selected part. SQL Server executes all code in the script only if no code is highlighted.

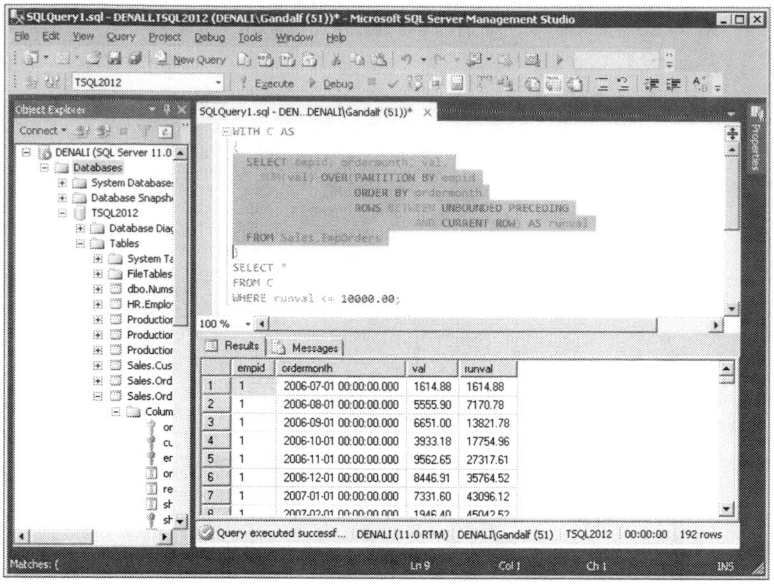

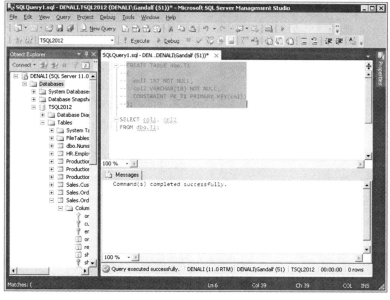

**FIGURE A-17** Executing only selected code.

> **Tip** If you press and hold the Alt button before you start highlighting code, you can highlight a rectangular block that doesn't necessarily start at the beginning of the lines of code, for purposes of copying or executing, as shown in Figure A-18.

**FIGURE A-18** Highlighting a rectangular block.

Finally, before I leave you to your own explorations, I'd like to remind you that all of the source code for the book is available for download from the book's website. The previous section in this appendix, "Downloading Source Code and Installing the Sample Database," provides the details. Assuming that you downloaded the source code and extracted the compressed files to a local folder, you can open the script file you want to work with from File | Open | File or by clicking the Open File icon on the standard toolbar. Alternatively, you can double-click the script file's name in Windows Explorer to open the script file within SSMS.

# Working with SQL Server Books Online

Microsoft SQL Server Books Online is the online documentation that Microsoft provides for SQL Server. It contains a huge amount of useful information. When you are developing T-SQL code, think of Books Online as your best friend—besides this T-SQL fundamentals book, of course.

You can access Books Online through the Microsoft SQL Server program group, by clicking Documentation & Community | SQL Server Documentation. If you're starting the product documentation for the first time, you will be asked to choose a default setting for Help—specifically, whether to get the Help content from the Internet or store it locally on your computer. Make a choice based on your preferences. You can always change your choices later from the Help Library Manager (accessible via the rightmost icon in the top toolbar). For example, in my environment, I chose local help and installed all topics under the SQL Server 2012 category locally.

Note that if you choose to store the Help content locally, you actually have to go to the help library manager and download it. Also, updates to Books Online aren't linked to service pack releases, so it's a good idea to check for updates from time to time in the Help Library Manager.

Books Online for SQL Server 2012 is also available directly on the Internet through the following link: *http://msdn.microsoft.com/en-us/library/ms130214(v=SQL.110).aspx*. The examples that I demonstrate are based on a local installation of Books Online on my machine.

Learning to use Books Online is not rocket science, and I don't want to insult anyone's intelligence by explaining the obvious. Dedicating a section to Books Online in the "Getting Started" appendix is more about making you aware of its existence and emphasizing its importance rather than explaining how to use it. Too often, people ask others for help about a topic related to SQL Server when they can easily find the answer if they only put a little effort into searching for it in Books Online.

I'll explain a few of the ways to get information from Books Online. One of the windows that I use most in Books Online to search for information is the Index tab, shown in Figure A-19.

Type what you are looking for in the Look For box. As you type the letters of the subject you are looking for (for example, **window function**), Books Online positions the cursor on the first qualifying item in the sorted list of subjects below. You can type T-SQL keywords for which you need syntax information, for example, or any other subject of interest.

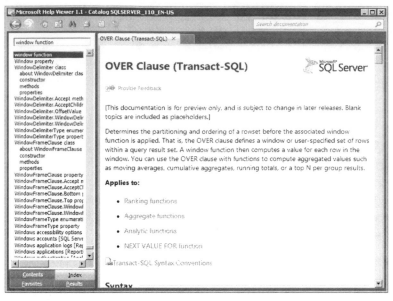

**FIGURE A-19** The Books Online Help Index window.

You can add the topic to the Help Favorites by clicking the Add To Favorites button from the toolbar, making it easy to get back to later. You can also sync the current help item with the respective topic on the Content tab by clicking the Sync ToC button.

When you are looking for a general item rather than a specific item, such as What's New In SQL Server 2012 or the T-SQL Programming Reference, you will probably find the Contents tab useful (see Figure A-20).

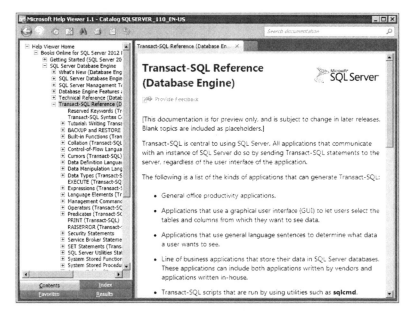

**FIGURE A-20** The Books Online Help Contents window.

Here you need to navigate the tree to get to the topic of interest.

Another very useful tool is the Search documentation option in the upper-right corner of the Help window, as shown in Figure A-21.

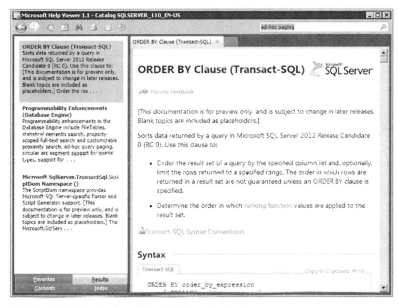

**FIGURE A-21** The Books Online Help Search window.

You use the search box when looking for articles that contain words you are looking for. This is a more abstract search than a search on the Index tab—somewhat similar to a search performed by an Internet search engine. Note that if you want to find a certain word in an open article, click the Find button on the toolbar or press Ctrl+F to activate the Find bar.

> **Tip** Finally, before I leave you to your own explorations, let me add a last tip. If you need help on a syntax element while writing code in SQL Server Management Studio, make sure your cursor is positioned somewhere in that code element and then press Shift+F1. This will load Books Online and open the syntax page for that element, assuming that such a Help item exists.

# Index

## Symbols

## A

## G

# About the Author

ITZIK BEN-GAN is a mentor with and co-founder of SolidQ. A SQL Server Microsoft MVP since 1999, Itzik has taught numerous training events around the world focused on T-SQL querying, query tuning, and programming. Itzik is the author of several books about T-SQL. He has written many articles for *SQL Server Pro* as well as articles and white papers for MSDN and *The SolidQ Journal*. Itzik's speaking engagements include Tech-Ed, SQL PASS, SQL Server Connections, presentations to various SQL Server user groups, and SolidQ events. Itzik is a subject-matter expert within SolidQ for its T-SQL related activities. He authored SolidQ's Advanced T-SQL and T-SQL Fundamentals courses and delivers them regularly worldwide.

# What do you think of this book?

We want to hear from you!
To participate in a brief online survey, please visit:

**microsoft.com/learning/booksurvey**

Tell us how well this book meets your needs—what works effectively, and what we can do better. Your feedback will help us continually improve our books and learning resources for you.

Thank you in advance for your input!